Joseph Butler's Moral and Religious Thought
TERCENTENARY ESSAYS

Edited by
Christopher Cunliffe

CLARENDON PRESS · OXFORD
1992

Oxford University Press, Walton Street, Oxford OX2 6DP
Oxford New York Toronto
Delhi Bombay Calcutta Madras Karachi
Petaling Jaya Singapore Hong Kong Tokyo
Nairobi Dar es Salaam Cape Town
Melbourne Auckland
and associated companies in
Berlin Ibadan

Oxford is a trade mark of Oxford University Press

Published in the United States
by Oxford University Press, New York

© Christopher Cunliffe 1992

All rights reserved. No part of this publication may be reproduced,
stored in a retrieval system, or transmitted, in any form or by any means,
electronic, mechanical, photocopying, recording, or otherwise, without
the prior permission of Oxford University Press

British Library Cataloguing in Publication Data
Data available

Library of Congress Cataloging in Publication Data
Joseph Butler's moral and religious thought: tercentenary essays
edited by Christopher Cunliffe.
Includes bibliographical references and index.
1. Butler, Joseph, 1692–1752. I. Cunliffe, Christopher.
B1363.Z7J67 1992 230'.3'092-dc20 92-4280
ISBN 0-19-826740-1

Typeset by Joshua Associates Ltd., Oxford
Printed in Great Britain by
Bookcraft (Bath) Ltd., Midsomer Norton

JOSEPH BUTLER
1692–1752

Philosopher, Theologian, and Pastor

Foreword

DAVID JENKINS, BISHOP OF DURHAM

Bishop Butler's untimely death shortly after his sixtieth birthday meant that he scarcely had time to make his mark as bishop of Durham. He appears in what is now the list of sixty-nine bishops (stretching over almost 1,000 years) for a mere two years—1750-2. Just over 200 years later another philosopher and theological thinker who was to become bishop of Durham published in 1957 a small book entitled *Religious Language*. In it, Professor Ian Ramsey set out: 'To show how the contemporary philosophical interest in language, far from being soul-destroying, can be so developed as to provide a novel inroad into the problems and controversies of theology, illuminating its claims and reforming its apologetic' (p. 11).

Theological thinking, Ramsey argued, could only benefit from facing the challenges posed by the then prevailing logical empiricism. These challenges were 'to state a case for religious language' and 'to try to elucidate the logic of some of its characteristic claims'. To face these challenges, he wrote, we need to ask 'at the outset, and as a leading question: to what kind of situation does religion appeal? What kind of empirical anchorage have theological words?' He goes on, 'to answer that question, let our memories first go back to Joseph Butler who in the eighteenth century and in his own way likewise attempted Christian apologetic in the face of contemporary empiricism' (p. 14).

Ramsey then proceeds to argue that in introducing the argument of his *Analogy* by a discussion on Immortality, Butler is developing a vital point about the basic characteristic about religious thinking, awareness, and attitudes. Ramsey points out that Butler, in summarizing his chapter Immortality when concluding part 1 of the *Analogy*, argues it is 'contrary to experience' to suppose that 'gross bodies' are ourselves. Ramsey then goes on:

Belief in immortality is thus founded in an awareness that as 'living agents' we are more than our public behaviour. Here, I suggest, is the discernment without which no distinctive theology would ever be possible; a 'self-awareness' that is more than 'body awareness' and not exhausted by spacio-temporal 'objects'. Such a discernment lies at the basis of religion, whose characteristic claim is that there are situations that are spacio-temporal and more. Without such 'depths'; without this which is 'unseen', no religion will be possible... Here it seems to me is the abiding significance of Butler's opening Part I of his *Analogy* with the discussion *Of a Future Life*. We cannot usefully begin theological apologetic without first making plain the distinctive kind of discernment in which theology is founded.

Ramsey, however, draws more from Butler about the logic of the characteristic claims of religious language. He goes on to consider Butler's famous 'probability is the very guide of life' in order to argue that Butler was drawing attention to, and basing important arguments on, a central feature of the moral and practical experience of human beings. This is that in what Butler calls 'questions of great consequence' we are regularly aware with something approaching certainty of what we ought to do, although the probability of ever being able to bring the action to a satisfactory conclusion is not very high. We know, for example, that if we see a child drowning in a river and there is any chance of our saving it we should *certainly* dive into the river for the saving of the life of a child is a 'question of great consequence'. Ramsey then continues:

> Now it is such a total commitment, appropriate to a 'question of great consequence', a commitment which is based upon but goes beyond rational considerations which are 'matters of speculation'; a commitment which sees in a situation all that the understanding can give us and more; a commitment which is exemplified by conscientious action building on 'probabilities', which Butler thinks to be characteristic of a religious attitude.

So, according to Ramsey, Butler suggests that religion claims (1) a fuller discernment, to which we respond with (2) a total commitment. Ramsey then comments: 'Such a commitment without any discernment whatever is bigotry and idolatry; to have the discernment without an appropriate commitment is the worst of all religious vices. It is insincerity and hypocrisy.'

I am not sure whether Butler's eighteenth-century mind

Foreword ix

working in the context of eighteenth-century arguments with the Deists does produce a structure of argument or a method of arguing which can be taken over and adapted by those of us who, in the circumstances of the late twentieth century, share his Christian faith in God. But the reflections of Ian Ramsey, one of Butler's successors and one of my predecessors as bishop of Durham, do suggest that Butler remains a possible quarry for ideas and suggestions to those who derive from Christian faith in God a continuing conviction that there must be ways of being reasonable which can make claims on the attending, the reflecting, and the deciding of all human beings wherever they are who are prepared to think about their thinking, feeling, and acting.

Thus it seemed to me not inappropriate that as Butler's contemporary successor in the See of Durham I should respond to an invitation to contribute a foreword to these *Tercentenary Essays* on Butler's moral and religous thought. By virtue of the wide range of subjects which are treated in these fourteen essays and of the detailed knowledge of the authors in their various subjects, we are provided with a comprehensive survey which can inform us of the sort of thinker Butler was and therefore of the possible resources he offers those of us who seek to continue, in our time, the various issues and tasks he addressed himself to in his.

It so happened that during the period when I was reading through the manuscripts of the pieces that make up this volume I was also catching up on some recent back numbers of *Concilium* including the 1990 Special Issue entitled *On the Threshold of the Third Milennium*. One of the Congress Lectures included is an essay by Hans Küng entitled *Rediscovering God*. In this he writes:

For human beings to 'discover' God is and remains a risk, a venture in which a human being must risk life and limb, heart and head.

—Or, in positive and very summary terms, the fact that God, though not detectable or deducible, nevertheless really exists is not a matter of rational demonstration, as many Catholic theologians believed in the Middle Ages.

—Nor, however, is it a matter of irrational experience or feeling, as many Protestant theologians assumed in the face of post-Enlightenment difficulties.

—But it is a matter of *reasoned trust*. What we Christians with Jews and Muslims, call 'faith'. It is a reasoned trust which can no more be proved by any sort of argument than love, but can be made intelligible by a whole range of reasoning. And why is this confidence in a totally different, 'invisible' reality reasonable and intelligible? Because—and for the moment this can only be stated as a thesis, but will be illustrated later—it is supported, rooted, in our everyday experience and so can be, at least indirectly, justified, tested, *verified*, in the context of our lived experience. (Special Issue of *Concilium*, (Feb. 1990), 88 ff.)

Butler did not share Küng's conclusion and assumption that God's existence 'is not a matter of rational demonstration'. But I think that Butler would, none the less, have been very sympathetic to the idea of 'reasoned trust' which 'can be made intelligible by a whole range of reasoning' and which, further, could be, 'at least indirectly, justified, tested, verified, in the context of our lived experience'. It may well be, therefore, that there are more than a few nuggets of argument, method, and convictions about both God and reasoning, which can be quarried from a tercentenary volume on Joseph Butler for the tasks of believers, thinkers, and decision-makers in the run up to the Second Christian Millennium.

David Dunelm

Contents

Contributors	xiii
References and Abbreviations	xiv
Introduction	1
CHRISTOPHER CUNLIFFE	
1. Butler and Deism	7
DAVID BROWN	
2. *Deus absconditus*: Some Notes on the Bearing of the Hiddenness of God upon Butler's and Pascal's Criticism of Deism	29
ALBINO BABOLIN	
3. The 'Spiritual Sovereign': Butler's Episcopate	37
CHRISTOPHER CUNLIFFE	
4. Bishop Butler and the *Zeitgeist*: Butler and the Development of Christian Moral Philosophy in Victorian Britain	63
JANE GARNETT	
5. Butler as a Christian Apologist	97
BASIL MITCHELL	
6. Butler and Human Ignorance	117
TERENCE PENELHUM	
7. A God most Particular: Aspects of Incarnation in Butler's Morality	141
GORDON KENDAL	
8. Butler and Immortality	169
T. A. ROBERTS	
9. Our Knowledge of Ourselves	189
ANDERS JEFFNER	
10. Butler on Conscience and Virtue	197
BRIAN HEBBLETHWAITE	
11. Conscience as Self-Authorizing in Butler's Ethics	209
STEPHEN DARWALL	

12. Butler on Self-Love and Benevolence R. G. FREY	243
13. Butler on Benevolence DAVID MCNAUGHTON	269
14. Butler on God and Human Nature ALAN MILLAR	293
Index	317

Contributors

ALBINO BABOLIN, Professor of the Philosophy of Religion, University of Perugia.

DAVID BROWN, Van Mildert Professor of Divinity, University of Durham.

CHRISTOPHER CUNLIFFE, Vocations Officer and Selection Secretary, Advisory Board of Ministry, Church House, Westminster.

STEPHEN DARWALL, Professor of Philosophy, University of Michigan.

R. G. FREY, Professor of Philosophy, Bowling Green State University, Ohio.

JANE GARNETT, Fellow of Wadham College, Oxford.

BRIAN HEBBLETHWAITE, Fellow of Queen's College, Cambridge.

ANDERS JEFFNER, Professor of Theological and Ideological Studies, Uppsala University.

GORDON KENDAL, Assistant Master, Manchester Grammar School.

DAVID MCNAUGHTON, Lecturer in Philosophy, University of Keele.

ALAN MILLAR, Senior Lecturer in Philosophy, University of Stirling.

BASIL MITCHELL, Emeritus Professor of the Philosophy of the Christian Religion, University of Oxford.

TERENCE PENELHUM, Emeritus Professor of Religious Studies, University of Calgary.

T. A. ROBERTS, Emeritus Professor of Philosophy, University of Wales.

References and Abbreviations

There is no modern standard edition of Butler's works. The edition used in this book is that edited by J. H. Bernard, *The Works of Bishop Butler* (London, 1900). Bernard's edition, unlike that of Gladstone in 1896, has the advantage of retaining Butler's original paragraphs, which Bernard numbered. The references in this book take the form of an abbreviated title followed by one or more arabic numerals, the last of which is the paragraph number in Bernard. So the reference *A.* 2. 6. 7 is to part 2, chapter 6, paragraph 7 of the *Analogy*; *S.* 5. 13 to paragraph 13 of Sermon 5; and DI 4 to paragraph 4 of the dissertation 'Of Personal Identity'. Readers using other editions of Butler should be able to locate the references with relative ease. The abbreviations used are as follows:

A.	*Analogy of Religion* (1736)
C.	*A Charge to the Clergy of the Diocese of Durham* (1751)
DI	Dissertation, 'Of Personal Identity' (1736)
DII	Dissertation, 'Of the Nature of Virtue' (1736)
S.	*Fifteen Sermons Preached at the Rolls Chapel* (1726)
SP	Preface to 1729 edition of *Fifteen Sermons*
SS	*Six Sermons Preached upon Public Occasions* (1749)

Introduction

CHRISTOPHER CUNLIFFE

When Queen Caroline, who claimed to be an avid reader of the *Analogy of Religion*, assumed in conversation that its author was dead her interlocutor, Archbishop Blackburne of York, replied, 'No, madam, he is not dead, but he is buried.' The knowledge of his continued physical existence stirred the queen to action on Butler's behalf, setting his career on a more public trajectory.

There is some evidence that, after a period of relative decline in his reputation, Butler's thought is now in the process of disinterment. The purpose of the essays in this book is to explore some of the facets of that thought and to suggest points of interest to modern philosophers and theologians. Butler is once more attracting critical attention and finding his way back on to university syllabuses, although there is—surprisingly—no modern critical edition of the *Analogy*. The essays here reflect the contribution of Butler to central concerns in moral philosophy and philosophical theology yet they also suggest other aspects of his thought and reputation which are worthy of consideration. The volume as a whole may stand by way of a small tribute to a profound thinker and churchman on the tercentenary of his birth.

Butler is known by theologians as the hammer of deism, or at least its manifestation in eighteenth-century Britain. In his essay David Brown places Butler's attack on deism in a broader historical context, suggesting that Butler's thought, in reacting against the extreme rationalism of his opponents, marks an early move away from reason towards experience and feeling, a foretaste of Romanticism. There are parallels with French and German thought, and Brown focuses on Voltaire and Lessing as representatives of continental deism before discussing Butler as a resource for the criticism of modern forms of deism. Albino Babolin, too, is interested in Butler's strategy against the deists and draws attention to the similarities between Butler and Pascal in their use of the notion of the hiddenness of God in the framing of a new form of apologetic to counter the deists' conception of divine revelation.

Butler's historical setting is emphasized by Christopher Cunliffe in his essay on Butler's episcopate, in which the theologian is shown applying his intellectual concerns to the conduct of a pastoral ministry to those in his care, commenting on the great social issues of his day, and endeavouring to make the Church's mission more effective. Jane Garnett, in her wide-ranging essay on the ways in which Butler was read during the second half of the nineteenth century, suggests a more complex story than the commonplace of the steady decline of Butler's influence during the period. Butler's integration of natural theology and moral philosophy was an important stimulus to many significant thinkers at the time.

The question of Butler's relevance to the modern world is raised by Basil Mitchell. Is his thought trapped irrecoverably in a world very different from ours in its understanding of reason and the possibility of discovering objective truth? Mitchell takes full account of those parts of Butler's system that are now only of historical interest, but argues that his refusal to accept a sharp contrast between faith and reason provides, in a suitably reconstructed form, powerful support to modern Christian apologetics in its dialogue with secular thought.

Terence Penelhum is also concerned with Butler's apologetic and particularly with his emphasis on the limits to human knowledge and understanding. Why, if God has chosen to reveal himself to us, is that revelation not unambiguously clear? Penelhum traces Butler's indebtedness to Locke in the development of the argument that, whatever the limits on our understanding the system of the world, we are capable of understanding the fact that it is indeed a created system. However, Penelhum also recognizes that Butler's suggestion that our awareness of the limitations of our knowledge should not lead us to dismiss Christianity because of obscurities in the evidence for it is inconsistent with his view of the morality of divine providence.

Introduction 3

Theological concerns are at the heart of Gordon Kendal's detailed survey of the evidence for Butler's views on the doctrine of the incarnation. Kendal argues that Butler's moral philosophy has an implicit theological centre, that the death of Jesus is the supreme and decisive paradigm of a moral action in history. His analysis of moral action gives rise to a view of God as intimately engaged with particular people at particular times and places. In his essay T. A. Roberts provides a careful analysis of Butler's arguments in favour of immortality and sees them as well balanced and effective in terms of the philosophical presuppositions of his day. The crux of Butler's discussion, for Roberts, is in the notion of incorporeal substances, such as the Self, which exist independently of matter. Butler's handling of this issue in relation to personal identity provides the foundation of his argument for a future life. Further exploration of Butler's theory of personal identity is undertaken by Anders Jeffner in his essay, which contrasts Butler's view with those of Hume and modern empiricist philosophy, and suggests that Butler's intuitionist arguments in the dissertation 'Of Personal Identity' may have relevance for contemporary debate.

Another aspect of the theological content of Butler's moral philosophy is explored by Brian Hebblethwaite, who argues, against Anscombe, that Butler's exaltation of conscience as a moral authority is accompanied by an error theory concerning self-deceit which allows him to refute the view that conscience may prompt a person to vicious actions, and, against Szabados, that this conscience free from corruption is not part of a purely naturalistic ethic but has an essentially religious foundation as a form of religious natural law theory.

Hebblethwaite's focus on conscience in Butler's moral philosophy is taken up by others, for it is central to his thought. Stephen Darwall's essay argues that, for Butler, the authority of conscience is a condition of the very possibility of an agent's having reasons to act at all. Only a being who has the capacity for maintaining a self-regulated constitutional order can have reasons to act, and this capacity depends on the view that conscience is authoritative. Darwall argues here against Sturgeon's view that the authority of conscience is superfluous in Butler's system.

Two essays are concerned with Butler's hierarchical ordering of the elements of the human mind, and the place of benevolence within this hierarchy. Is benevolence a superior principle, like self-love and conscience, or is it a mere affection, like the appetites and passions? R. G. Frey argues, against the common interpretation, that benevolence is a particular passion rather than a general principle of action. Frey suggests that for Butler human nature has two levels, with the particular passions and benevolence on one level and self-love and conscience as the governing principles on a superior level. Butler, on Frey's account, is more Hobbesian than previous commentators have allowed, taking full account of the strength of self-love within us. David McNaughton provides a thorough analysis of the relationship between benevolence and self-love and concludes that although benevolence is a *rational* general principle it is not a *superior* principle. McNaughton suggests that, if Butler had allowed sufficient flexibility to his classificatory system of superior and inferior principles, he could have allowed a distinction between rational and non-rational inferior principles. Benevolence on this understanding, is a rational inferior principle.

In the final essay in this collection Alan Millar returns to the broader issue of Butler's methodology in the *Sermons*. In his discussion of Butler's account of such topics as compassion, resentment, and love of neighbour, Millar draws out the teleological theology which he sees as central to Butler's thought—we are made for virtue because that is God's intention for us. He then goes on to raise the possibility of embedding some of Butler's key ideas about human nature in a non-theological view of the world. Millar uses a discussion of modern evolutionary theory to highlight the possibilities and difficulties in developing Butler's view that virtue is natural and vice unnatural in terms of modern concepts of human nature and its development.

So, despite being addressed to particular contemporary problems, Butler's thought is not a museum-piece. It still has the power to engage the interest of modern commentators in their clarification of the issues which concern them. Butler's influence as a philosopher and theologian is rooted in his conviction as a thinker and pastor that the careful and accurate presentation of the Christian religion could be a significant contribution to the uncertain times in which he lived. In the words of Basil Mitchell at the end of his essay, '[Butler] believes that faith should be both firm and critical, both rational and committed. In this he provides a model that is worthy of imitation.'

I
Butler and Deism

DAVID BROWN

Butler's *Analogy of Religion* of 1736 was intended as a response to deism and so successful was it that it can in many ways be seen as having dealt the mortal blow.[1] As Hume's attitude well illustrates,[2] Butler's reputation was quickly established, and the work was to remain a classic text for over a century. In determining the reasons for this success Butler's own account of his strategy[3] is somewhat misleading. He talks of the same sort of difficulties being found in nature to which the deists take exception in the case of Scripture. But one suspects that for most readers the argument was read in a much more positive light: that, so far from the God of revelation adding nothing significant to the God of nature (as the deists claimed), revelation could be seen as the natural next step to what had already been disclosed in nature. So, for instance, dramatic discontinuities in nature such as worms into flies (*A.* 1. 1. 2) established an already existing pattern of divine action upon which the scriptural hope of a *post mortem* existence could build, just as the suffering of the innocent on behalf of the guilty (*A.* 2. 5. 21) already points the way towards the scriptural doctrine of the atonement. Put that way, it also becomes much easier to comprehend why the popularity of the work plummeted in the second half of the nineteenth century.[4] The God of nature

[1] Here I follow the verdict of Norman Sykes in his *Church and State in England in the Eighteenth Century* (Cambridge, 1934), 346. Two years later E. C. Mossner in *Bishop Butler and the Age of Reason* (New York, 1936) contended that Butler's importance had been greatly exaggerated, with deism already very much on the wane in 1736.

[2] 'Dr Butler' is spoken of in laudatory terms in his *Treatise of Human Nature* (Oxford, 1888), p. xxi, and in fact Hume had sought Butler's opinion of the manuscript, deleting the section on miracles out of deference to him (restored only in 1748).

[3] J. Butler, *The Analogy of Religion*, ed. E. C. Mossner (New York, 1961), Introd., p. 4.

[4] Symbolized by Mark Pattison's success in 1860 in having the work eliminated from the Oxford Schools examinations: *Memoirs* (London, 1885), 324.

to whom the God of revelation was being compared was now in the light of evolution seen as 'red in tooth and claw' and in no way concerned providentially with the details of the natural order. In fact one might be inclined to say that deism had the last word. For it was its exclusive concentration on the God of nature which had forced Butler to make a detailed comparison between the God of revelation and the God of nature, and it was now a changing conception of the God of nature which undermined Butler's picture of both.

But if at one level the reason for Butler's success is to be explained by his demonstrating the essential reasonableness of Christianity (the congruity between the God of nature and the God of revelation), ironically that same success must in part also be explained by the way in which the *Analogy* endorses a declining confidence in the power of reason. Not only does Butler retreat from proof to probability, he also at several points expresses scepticism about how much can be known. So, despite the lack of meeting of minds in his encounter with Wesley,[5] it is arguable that his continued popularity can in part be seen as due to him representing an early anticipation of the move away from reason towards experience and feeling that characterized both Methodism and more generally the Romantic movement. In this he was by no means alone. Leslie Stephen in similar vein points to Watts and Law,[6] but strangely ignores the more intellectual preparation that Butler provided. Certainly it was the less rationalistic features in his thought which seem to have appealed to Newman[7] and led him to describe Butler as 'the greatest name in the Anglican Church'.

If the previous paragraph is a correct analysis, then Butler would represent part of a pattern which repeats itself in French

---

[5] For a brief account of the meeting, see W. A. Spooner, *Bishop Butler* (London, 1901), 25-6. As J. Downey remarks on the sermon in *The Eighteenth-Century Pulpit* (Oxford, 1969), 48: 'Having denied the sufficiency of reason, he was forced to assign to conscience intuitional as well as rational powers. In spite of himself, he had, in theory at least, opened the door to the religious enthusiasm of Methodism.'

[6] In his section on 'The Religious Reaction', he draws attention to 'the emotional current' in Watts and, at greater length, to the mystical piety of Law as both anticipating Wesley: *History of English Thought in the Eighteenth Century*, 2nd edn. (London, 1881), ii. 383 ff.

[7] J. H. Newman, *Apologia pro vita sua* (London, 1959), pt. III, p. 103: 'To Butler I trace these two principles of my teaching, which have led to a charge against me both of fancifulness and scepticism' (by 'fancifulness' he means the unreality of the world).

and German thought. For among both peoples what sounded the death-knell for Enlightenment deism was the rise of the Romantic movement with its suspicion of reason and identification of an alternative source of knowledge in intuition and feeling, and in both cases there are important precursors even while rationalism apparently remained in the ascendancy. Thus in France even before the Revolution, far less before it had gone wrong and thereby concretely demonstrated the bankruptcy of deifying reason, Rousseau was offering his unique combination of reason and emotion, while in Germany Kant (partly under Rousseau's influence) can be seen as already anticipating Schleiermacher's justification of religion experientially, and that despite the Enlightenment character of so much of what he writes about our knowledge of the world. Indeed it would be a fascinating historical exercise to compare these three thinkers (Butler, Rousseau, and Kant) and measure the comparative extent to which they anticipated future directions of thought. Butler is of course writing much earlier, but there is the same curtailment of the powers of reason that we find in Rousseau and in Kant and, though not explicitly the same stress on the epistemological role of experience, one could argue that it is there implicitly in the key role he gives to the formation of the moral virtues.

It would be naïve of course to suppose that purely intellectual factors could be used to explain either the rise or the demise of deism. History (and the human beings who help to make the history) is more complicated than that. For instance, in explaining the rise of deism Basil Willey points to such varied influences as the way in which doubt was engendered by the existence of sects with alternative perspectives on religion, a decline in the tragic sense of life, and the importance of the discovery of the phenomenon of the civilized savage,[8] while it is the main argument of John Redwood's book that it was ridicule rather than reason which endangered the Church the most.[9] However, Redwood also suggests that the replies themselves did much to foster its growth,[10] a judgement endorsed by Peter Gay: 'Anthony Collins's well-known witticism against the learned Dr.

---

[8] B. Willey, *The Eighteenth Century Background* (London, 1974), 6, 10, 12.
[9] J. Redwood, *Reason, Ridicule and Religion* (London, 1976), esp. 196.
[10] Ibid. 29.

Samuel Clarke—that no one had doubted the existence of God until Dr. Clarke tried to prove it—may well be extended: no one had thought that Christianity might give way to rationalism until Christians tried to prove that Christianity was reasonable.'[11]

But even with such caveats it is still worth attempting an assessment of the arguments. Not only did they play some role, but they are also of interest in themselves. In what follows therefore I shall take two of the principal representatives of English deism, Toland and Tindal, and examine how successful Butler was in his response, drawing parallels, where appropriate, with two major representatives of deism on the continent, Voltaire in France and Lessing in Germany. Butler was anticipated in his reply to Tindal by Waterland and Law.[12] Two less well-known responses also came from Balguy and Atkey; I shall use these to illustrate the extent to which Butler had also been anticipated in the form of his arguments. As my primary purpose is assessment rather than historical context, I shall end by noting how in the twentieth century the nature of the deist challenge has changed, and consider whether Butler might offer us any guide-lines in answering deism in its contemporary presentation.

With deism in its original form two main types of challenge may be discerned: one stemming from the universality of reason and the other from the assumption of its primacy. As the latter is more complicated, I shall begin with arguments based on the alleged universality of reason.

The recurring point made here is that for God to show favour or judge people on any basis other than their use of this universal faculty would be essentially unfair and arbitrary. So for instance Matthew Tindal heads the opening chapter of what was to become known as 'the Deists' Bible', *Christianity as Old as the Creation* (1730), as follows: 'That God, at all times, has given mankind sufficient means, of knowing whatever he requires of them; and what these means are.' Such means he quickly

---

[11] P. Gay, *The Enlightenment: An Interpretation* (London, 1966), i. 326. The point is well argued at greater length in M. J. Buckley, *At the Origins of Modern Atheism* (New Haven, Conn., 1987).

[12] D. Waterland, *Scripture Vindicated: In Answer to a Book Intituled, Christianity as Old as the Creation* (1730); W. Law, *The Case of Reason, or of Natural Religion, Fairly and Fully Stated* (1731).

identifies as our rational faculties: 'If God will judge mankind as they are accountable, that is, as they are rational; the judgement must hold in exact proportion to the use they make of their reason.'[13] This is because it is the only faculty equally available to all, whereas the Bible is necessarily particular and by no means of universal access. 'Can it be supposed an infinitely good and gracious Being, which gives men notice, by their senses, what does good or hurt to their bodies, has had less regard for their immortal parts, and has not given them at all times, by the light of their understanding, sufficient means to discover what makes for the good of their souls?'[14] Indeed, even if the revelation were to be universally available, that would still not suffice since 'faith considered in itself can neither be a virtue, or a vice; because men can no otherwise believe than as things appear to them'.[15] In other words, to add specific biblical injunctions must result in an essentially arbitrary God: 'To suppose some men who, though they exactly obey the law of Nature, may yet be punished, even eternally, for not obeying another law besides, would be to make God deal infinitely less mercifully with them, than with those that have no other law.'[16] Yet 'in this miserable case are all Christians involved' unless they take Tindal's advice and retreat to a Christianity based exclusively on the creation, that is, on the universal faculty of reason which God has given us. For 'I cannot help thinking, but that (such is the divine goodness) God's will is so clearly and fully manifested in the Book of Nature, that he who runs may read it.'[17]

It is this same concern which explains the degree of vitriol in Voltaire's writing about the Augustinian scheme of original sin and grace. Under the entry on Original Sin in his *Dictionnaire philosophique*, after noting that there is no evidence for the doctrine in Scripture, he goes on to observe that it is to Augustine that one must trace 'this strange idea worthy of the heated and romantic brain of a debauched and repentant African ...

---

[13] M. Tindal, *Christianity as Old as the Creation* (London, 1730), 7. In the case of this and other 18th-century works, I have taken the liberty of modernizing the punctuation and capitalization.
[14] Ibid. 10.
[15] Ibid. 44.
[16] Ibid. 109.
[17] Ibid. 23.

who spent his life contradicting himself'.[18] But, if one objection was the lateness of the doctrine, undoubtedly most deeply felt was the reason which he gives in his final paragraph: 'How awful it is to slander the author of nature to the extent of imputing to him continual miracles so as to damn for ever men whom he brings to birth for so short a time.' It is an objection which recurs in his entry on 'Grace': 'You can do nothing to deserve it; my master has drawn up the list for all time; he has consulted his own whim: he is constantly engaged in making an infinite number of chamber-pots and a few dozen vessels of gold. If you are chamber-pots, so much the worse for you.'

But it is not just the arbitrary and unfair character of the Augustinian system to which he takes exception; he seems also to think that there is no way of making grace fair except by confining it to acts of general providence. God must act by 'general laws, eternal like himself'; otherwise he will seem like 'an insane master who gives wages to one slave and refuses nourishment to another'. All the various technical terms for types of grace are ridiculed: for instance, he speaks of 'efficacious grace which is sometimes without effect' and of 'sufficient which sometimes does not suffice'—statements which are of course literally true in terms of the Augustinian tradition. But the underlying objection remains the essential arbitrariness of such a picture of divine action. Indeed, Voltaire appears to want to say not only that it is unfair but that it is demeaning to God to suggest that any such corrective actions should have been necessary on his part. 'Raise your eyes to heaven', he tells us, 'behold the eternal Demiurge creating millions of worlds ... amid this general obedience of all of nature, dare to believe, if you can, that God concerns himself with giving one type of grace (*versatile*) to sister Theresa and another (*concomitante*) to sister Agnes.'

J. H. Brumfitt in his book on *The French Enlightenment* has commented that:

to examine this debate in the terms in which it was actually conducted is perhaps to miss the point. The *philosophes*' real objection to original

---

[18] Voltaire, *Dictionnaire philosophique* (Paris, 1964), 215-17, for 'Grâce'; 310-11 for 'Péché originel'. All the translations which follow are my own, with the exception of the first on the theme of grace, which is that of A. J. Ayer (using a different edition of the Dictionary) in *Voltaire* (London, 1986), 135.

sin, and indeed to most forms of Christian orthodoxy, was that they inhibited progress by insisting that, in purely human terms at any rate, it was impossible. Human nature was corrupt... Such an assumption, which seemed to deny the possibility of any successful human initiative, appeared to condemn mankind to stagnation... To deny man's natural goodness seemed to the *philosophes* the best way of ensuring that he would never become better.[19]

But, while that is no doubt true at one level, it should not be used to undermine the sincerity of Voltaire's concern. Though orthodox Christian he was not, his deism was sincere, as is well illustrated by the fact that when atheism became a real threat, he turned with equal force against it, as in his late work *Histoire de Jenni* of 1775.

Butler's response to the challenge of arbitrariness follows his usual pattern of analogy.

Those who think the objection against revelation, from its light not being universal, to be of weight, should observe, that the author of Nature, in numberless instances, bestows that upon some which he does not upon others, who seem equally to stand in need of it. Indeed, he appears to bestow all his gifts with the most promiscuous variety among creatures of the same species: health and strength, capacities of prudence and of knowledge, means of improvement, riches and all external advantages. (*A.* 2. 6. 3)

In giving such an answer he had been anticipated by earlier responses to Tindal. For instance, John Balguy, writing in 1731, comments: 'Is it not undoubted fact, that the blessings of Heaven are conferred in quite a different manner? For has not God made some of his creatures angels; some, men; and some, insects? Even in the same species, what diversity of talents, and variety of conditions?'[20]

Nor is Butler the first to offer a particular kind of answer to the question of how God's justice is compatible with such variety. He writes: 'Nor is there anything shocking in all this... All shadow of injustice... would be lost, if we would keep in mind... that every man shall be "accepted according to what he had, not according to what he had not".'[21] Butler's language is

---

[19] J. H. Brumfitt, *The French Enlightenment* (London, 1972), 89.
[20] J. Balguy, *A Second Letter to a Deist Concerning a Late Book Entitled 'Christianity as Old as the Creation'* (London, 1731), 54.
[21] *A.* 2. 6. 5. The quotation is from 2 Cor. 8: 12.

more biblical, but the form of the argument is already to be found in Anthony Atkey's response to Tindal of 1733: 'Sincerity will, I think, in all cases be sufficient to make men acceptable to God... By virtue of this principle it may charitably be presumed, that many among the heathen will be accepted at last, even though they have lived in the breach of what we justly suppose parts of the Law of Nature.'[22] Accordingly Atkey concludes: 'If sincerity is that which renders men acceptable to God, it unavoidably follows that every equal degree of sincerity will entitle men to an equal degree of divine favour.'[23]

Whatever the nature of Butler's indebtedness to others, it cannot be doubted that the only viable approach for the Christian theologian today continues to be along similar lines. Indeed, Karl Rahner's notion of 'anonymous Christians' can be interpreted as doing just that, though he carefully avoids the rather Pelagian way in which Atkey expresses himself. On Rahner's view the initiative always lies with God; his offer of grace is present to all humanity, and its rejection only becomes culpable when it constitutes a deliberate rebellion against the divine call present in conscience. The result is that the situation of sincere atheists or believers in other religions is described in the following terms: 'The transcendental experience of God is present of necessity, and is also freely accepted in a positive decision to be faithful to conscience, but it is incorrectly objectified and interpreted.'[24]

But even so that cannot be the whole answer. For it leaves unexplained why God allows such variety of opportunities to be present. Butler himself opens his response with a declaration of scepticism: 'What, in particular, is the account or reason of these things, we must be greatly in the dark, were it only that we know so very little even of our own case.'[25] Initially we are offered a brief comment on the implications of system: 'A system, or constitution, in its notion, implies variety; and so complicated a one as this world, very great variety.' Here, once more, he has been anticipated by Balguy, though Balguy puts it in more

---

[22] A. Atkey, *The Main Argument of a Late Book Intitled Christianity as Old as the Creation Fairly Stated and Examined* (London, 1733), 21.

[23] Ibid. 23.

[24] Rahner's remarks on 'anonymous Christianity' are most easily consulted in *A Rahner Reader*, ed. G. A. McCool (London, 1975), 211-24, the quotation being from p. 223.

[25] This and the following quotation both from *A.* 2. 6. 7.

obviously aesthetic terms: 'That variety, distribution, subordination, which are visible everywhere, and prevail over all the creation ... are sure to promote the beauty of nature, and the perfection of the universe.'[26] But for Butler it had constituted a mere passing reference, and the next few pages are in fact devoted to arguing that such variety adds to the effectiveness of this world as a place of moral trial.

As an answer it would seem more effective in dealing with differences in the natural order than differences in exposure to divine revelation. For the former are a matter of God setting the initial conditions under which the world would operate, whereas the latter on the surface at least appear to be a case of adding to that initial variety, as though it were not enough, and that surely requires further explanation. As we shall see, explanations were already being attempted in the eighteenth century, but to set them in their proper context we need first to turn to the other principal argument of deism which I earlier distinguished, that from the primacy of reason.

Though this takes a variety of forms, essentially it involves the claim that revelation could contribute nothing wholly new since reason is our sole guide and so, whatever is putatively new in revelation, has still in the end to win favour at the bar of reason. One version of this thesis is to be found in John Toland's influential work of 1695 *Christianity not Mysterious*. The subtitle well illustrates his intent: 'or a Treatise shewing that there is nothing in the Gospel contrary to Reason, nor above it: And that no Christian doctrine can properly be called a Mystery.' Though Aquinas remains unmentioned, there is no doubt that Toland's intention is to refute the classic Thomist distinction between truths contrary to reason and those above reason, with only the latter having a claim to be part of the Christian dispensation.

Toland doubts even this much. Yet the argument he offers us is no arbitrary dismissal, but a model of carefully reasoned debate. He begins with the premiss that 'reason is the only foundation of all certitude', a premiss which he is able to support on his title-page with words from Tillotson, the recently deceased archbishop of Canterbury: 'We need not desire a better evidence that any man is in the wrong, than to hear him declare

---

[26] Balguy, *Second Letter*, 56.

against reason, and thereby acknowledge that reason is against him.' In other words, once the possibility of contradiction is permitted, there ceases to be any means of distinguishing truth and falsehood: 'every contradiction, which is a synonym for impossibility, is a pure nothing.'[27] So one is not surprised to find him declaring that 'the first thing I shall insist upon is that if any doctrine of the New Testament be contrary to reason, we have no manner of idea of it. To say for instance that a ball is white and black is to say just nothing ... So to say, as the Papists, that children dying before baptism are damned without pain, signifies nothing at all.'[28]

This is perhaps sufficient to explain why he rejects the possibility of truths contrary to reason in revelation. But why is he equally emphatic in rejecting what is above reason? He writes: 'Nothing can be said to be mystery, because we have not an adequate idea of it, or a distinct view of all its properties at once; for then everything would be a mystery.'[29] What in fact he wants to claim is that we can only rightly assent to a proposition in so far as we can understand it, and in so far as it is not comprehended, no meaningful assent is possible, irrespective of whether we are dealing with the natural world or the world of revelation. Thus, following Locke, 'an excellent modern philosopher',[30] he insists that only the 'nominal', not the 'real, essences' of things in the world can be known and so, in excluding knowledge of what is above reason in the case of the supernatural, he is doing no more than applying a pattern of knowledge with which we are already acquainted from within the natural order.

As a claim it is surely not without its plausibility, especially once this parallel with the natural order is drawn. Just as there are many things in the natural world of which we can say that we know that they are the case without knowing how they are the case, so also with the divine attributes; for instance, from revelation we may know in respect of his actions towards us that God is loving, but we cannot claim to know what it 'feels like' for such an incorporeal being to be loving. So it would be entirely misleading to say that anything mysterious has been revealed; it is

---

[27] J. Toland, *Christianity not Mysterious*, 2nd edn. (London, 1696), 40.
[28] Ibid. 28–9.
[29] Ibid. 74.
[30] Ibid. 82.

only the non-mysterious aspect of which we can claim to have gained any knowledge.

Even if one takes something as apparently mysterious as the doctrine of the Trinity, it is not clear that Toland's case is undermined. Inevitably of course much in the Trinity must remain inexplicable to the human mind, but that cannot alter the fact that all we can assent to is those aspects which are explicable to us and without obvious contradiction. Despite the popularity among theologians of talking about the ineffability of God, there is no shortage of philosophers today who point to the radical incoherence of any such claim.[31] We can only assent to a doctrine in so far as it makes some sort of sense to us.

Fortunately, Butler is a wiser man. He does not challenge the view that reason must be our final court of appeal.[32] His strategy is rather to question whether that precludes anything new being disclosed by revelation. Tindal, the immediate object of Butler's attack, had excluded such a possibility. As the subtitle of his work indicates ('or the Gospel, a Republication of the Religion of Nature'), there could be nothing in the gospel which was not independently ascertainable by reason, and it must be easily ascertainable; otherwise his objection on grounds of fairness would once again be made. What is surprising in such a position is not merely the fact that Tindal fails to take note of the actual fallible use to which human beings put their reason, but that he totally ignores Toland's earlier introduction of just such a distinction. Though he insists that the faculty itself is perfect, 'if by reason be understood a constant right use of these faculties ... then I confess that it is extremely corrupt'.[33] The gospel thus becomes, according to Toland, extremely useful in disclosing what 'vicious habits' have clouded our reason from seeing.

It was an avenue of reply which earlier respondents to Tindal were also to utilize. For instance, Atkey writes: 'It is one thing to see the advantage of a discovery (when it is once made) and quite another thing to have discovered it. It is one thing to see the reasons of a proposition, and quite another one to be led

---

[31] To give two recent examples at random: K. E. Yandell, *Hume's 'Inexplicable Mystery'* (Philadelphia, 1990), 144-57; D. A. Pailin, *The Anthropological Character of Theology* (Cambridge, 1990), 40-1.

[32] Unequivocally expressed in several places, e.g. *A* 2. 1. 28.

[33] Toland, *Christianity not Mysterious*, 57. The reference to 'vicious habits' is on the following page.

antecedently by the first principles to the discovery of the proposition.'[34] Butler proceeds rather differently. His principle of analogy provides him with a two-pronged strategy. He argues first in general terms that the incompleteness of the natural order as a system of moral probation requires its completion in some other form[35]—which gives an obvious place for what is disclosed in revelation—and, second, in a chapter specifically devoted to consideration 'Of our incapacity of judging what were to be expected in a revelation' (*A.* 2. 3), that just as prior to the actual world we could not have predicted its actual pattern, so we have no more sound rational basis upon which to predict the likely pattern of revelation.

In arguing thus Butler seems very much to have hit his target, and indeed to have anticipated future lines of discussion. The form of his first argument, despite differences of detail, neatly anticipates Kant's argument from practical reason for the immortality of the soul: that the pursuit of virtue would be unsatisfyingly incomplete unless there is some further life in which a reconciliation is effected between realization of the moral end and happiness. Again, the second argument, like so much of what Butler writes, attempts to undermine the deists' confidence in the certainties of reason, and move us instead towards a more probabilistic account of human reasoning, as in his famous phrase: 'probability is the very guide of life.' It was a notion of which Newman was to make much in his *Grammar of Assent*; philosophers of religion have in general been slow to follow suit, but the recent work of Mitchell and Swinburne shows that the tide is turning.

Yet theologians have been equally slow to respond. Nowhere is this more marked than in their reaction to the deist challenge to the traditional external proofs of revelation, namely those of prophecy and miracles. At this point Butler fails us, since he uses these two proofs in a very conventional way. But that is perhaps not altogether surprising, since he writes before the appearance of Lessing's essay 'On the Proof of the Spirit and of Power'. The odd title is an allusion to Origen's description of the two proofs, with 'Spirit' referring to fulfilled prophecies and 'Power' to miracles. What Lessing does is raise the historical question: that

---

[34] Atkey, *Main Argument*, 34.
[35] He helpfully summarizes his argument in *A.* 1. 3. 28.

it is one thing to have experienced them at the time; quite another to believe them on the basis of others' testimony, from which he draws his famous conclusion: 'Accidental truths of history can never become the proof of necessary truths of reason.'[36] Nor is it, he argues, any help to appeal to biblical infallibility since the justification for that is itself historical. So he concludes, 'that, then, is the ugly, broad, ditch which I cannot get across, however often and however earnestly I have tried to make the leap'.

Seldom has so short an essay been so influential. One can trace to its influence numerous theological attempts to discover an incontrovertible core to Christianity which can remain immune to historical criticism. Let us take three twentieth-century theologians, almost at random. For Bultmann the Bible's mythology encapsulates eternal existential truths about the human condition, and so one is not surprised to learn that on his view the Resurrection is merely a mythological way of expressing the existential significance of the Cross. Likewise Tillich concedes so much to historical doubt that he is even willing to admit the possibility that Jesus never lived; none the less he insists that 'while faith cannot even guarantee the name "Jesus" in respect of him who was the Christ ... it does guarantee the factual transformation of reality in that personal life which the New Testament expresses in its picture of Jesus as the Christ'.[37] Again, we find Schubert Ogden equally insistent that 'faith is by no means completely contingent on a particular historical event'. Instead, the significance of the New Testament writings lies in the fact that something has 'become manifest' which had always been 'possible' for everyone.[38]

But instead of accepting the deist challenge for certainty on its own terms, it is possible to follow Butler's lead elsewhere, and ask why in this case too probability will not suffice. The fact that the New Testament admits of a number of possible interpretations does not mean that they are all equally likely, even if none is absolutely certain. For a Christian to concede that Jesus may not have risen from the dead is not to concede that anything other

---

[36] G. Lessing, *Theological Writings*, ed. H. Chadwick (London, 1956), 53.
[37] P. Tillich, *Systematic Theology* (Chicago, 1951), ii. 107.
[38] Quoted in G. E. Michalson, *Lessing's 'Ugly Ditch': A Study of Theology and History* (London, 1985), 113. Michalson provides a very helpful discussion of the issues.

than this remains for him the most plausible reading of the available evidence. Of course, were religion unique in having to rely on probability in this way, this might be a legitimate source of worry. But, as Butler observes, the truth is quite otherwise. To the objection that religious evidence not only leaves room for doubt but could even be called 'weak', he responds: 'the observation that, from the natural constitution and course of things, we must in our temporal concerns, almost continually, and in matters of great consequence, act upon evidence of a like kind and degree to the evidence of religion, is an answer to this argument' (*A.* 2. 8. 7).

Indeed, it is. One need only consider questions of life and death. Only a very unreflective person would deny that the arguments for and against the legitimacy of abortion are finely balanced, but yet what may be at stake is the life of a human being. Again, even where the case for a just war can be strongly argued, rights are seldom wholly on one side; yet once again what is at stake is the lives of human beings. Religious faith is thus by no means unique in involving the serious risk of being wrong. But that does not lessen the worth of the risk, nor mean that there are no helps towards coming to a decision.

To all such talk of probabilities it may still be objected, in the manner of Matthew Arnold, that it stands in irreconcilable contradiction to the Bible: 'After reading the *Analogy* one goes instinctively to bathe one's spirit in the Bible again, to be refreshed by its boundless certitude and exhilaration.'[39] But this is to confuse two very different things, the theoretical weighing of probabilities and the practical decision which results. Indeed, even Arnold himself goes on to speak of 'an experiential sense of the truth of Christianity of the strongest possible kind'.[40]

But with biblical criticism having undermined the evidences from prophecy and miracles, it is no longer possible for us to construct an argument from probability in the same way as Butler does. It also means that far more stress must now be laid on finding an adequate answer to deism's attack on the internal marks of revelation's divine origins. It is particularly at this point that Tindal is relentless in his critique, though he begins by

[39] M. Arnold, 'Bishop Butler and the Zeit-Geist', in *Last Essays on Church and Religion* (London, 1877), 139.
[40] Ibid. 147.

remarking that internal marks are really more decisive than external: 'Would not Christians themselves think it sufficient proof of a religion not coming from God if it wanted any of these internal marks by which the truth of all religion is to be tryed, without inquiring into its miracles or any other external proofs? and consequently, whenever these internal marks are found, are not external marks needless?'[41] Here he seems right, that it is only in proportion as internal marks such as heightened moral perceptivity engage our interest that we are likely to take external marks such as miracles seriously.

That of course makes it all the more important to answer Tindal's critique, strange mixture though it is. At times it is extraordinarily wooden, as for instance when he objects to the metaphorical use by Jesus and Paul of the image of the seed dying: 'there's scarce a countryman so ignorant as not to know that, if the seed thrown into the earth is killed by drought or dies by any other accident, it never rises.'[42] At other times he is remarkably modern in his comments; for example he uses Romans 16 to argue that 'there was in the days of the apostles an order of women who had something more to do in the Church than sweep it'.[43] But in general his illustrations of falsehood, inconsistency, and immorality in Scripture are of the sort which might have been expected, though his account has none of the humour that characterizes so much of Voltaire's critique.

To contemporary eyes Butler's response is surprisingly ineffective, mainly because of his determination to continue to defend the infallibility of the Bible. For the result is that his main line of defence is to argue from the unpredictability of nature to the incapacity of reason to judge what might reasonably be expected of a revelation. Even his belief in the natural springs of morality is made subservient to this aim. So instead of rejecting the savage divine injunctions which occasionally characterize the Old Testament, he argues that 'none of these precepts are contrary to immutable morality', the justification given being that 'men have no right to either life or property, but what arises solely from the grant of God' (*A.* 2. 3. 13). Gladstone goes to elaborate pains to defend Butler at this point,[44] but his carefully

---

[41] Tindal, *Christianity*, 170.
[42] Ibid. 185. [43] Ibid. 290.
[44] W. E. Gladstone, *Studies Subsidiary to the Works of Bishop Butler* (Oxford, 1896), 36–40.

reasoned elaboration only serves to emphasize all the more the need for an alternative solution.

Ironically the makings of the most plausible solution are to be found in one of the deists themselves, in the writings of Lessing. Even Voltaire, despite his considerable output as an historian, failed to take the historical character of the Bible seriously, whereas Lessing's *Education of the Human Race* of 1780 at least opened up the possibility of reinterpreting revelation as something not static, but in continual process of development.

In the previous year his best-known play *Nathan the Wise* had appeared, with its famous parable of the rings. Adapted from Boccaccio, it tells the story of how a sultan, instead of giving the ring of succession to his eldest son, has two identical copies made, and so all three sons are given a ring with the injunction that only the virtue of their lives will reveal which of the three is his true heir. The point of the parable was a plea for religious toleration: for the present we should not attempt to distinguish between Christianity, Judaism, and Islam; only at the end of time will God reveal which was most in accord with his purposes. The *Education* of the following year, since it only discusses Christianity and places it alone at the end of a process of divine education, might seem now to be giving the palm exclusively to Christianity, but that is not, I think, the point. Rather, the intention is simply to take Christianity as a prime example of how revelation might provide an alternative means of access to the truth, which in theory at least could still have been directly deduced by reason. The application to all religions is in fact mentioned in the Preface: 'This is what I have in mind. Why are we not more willing to seek in all positive religions simply the process by which alone human understanding in every place can develop and still further will develop?'[45]

The Jews are, then, taken as an example, a people, 'the most rude and the most ferocious', 'so raw, so incapable of abstract thoughts, and so entirely in their childhood'.[46] Yet, though 'the child of education ... is late in overtaking many a more happily placed child of nature',[47] the Jews did finally achieve this according to Lessing in the reign of Cyrus, when they discovered their

---

[45] G. Lessing, *Education of the Human Race* (London, 1858), 82.
[46] Ibid. 83, s. 8; 84, s. 16.
[47] Ibid. 85, s. 21.

ideas confirmed in what the Persians already knew by reason.[48] At the last 'a better instructor must come and tear their exhausted primer from the child's hands—Christ came!'[49] But even in the case of Christ his educative role will eventually also become redundant: 'As we by this time can dispense with the Old Testament for the doctrine of the unity of God, and as we are gradually beginning also to be less dependent on the New Testament for the doctrine of the immortality of the soul: might there not be mirrored in this book also other truths of the same kind, which we are to gaze at in awe as revelations, just until reason learns to deduce them from its other demonstrated truths, and to connect them with them?'[50]

Even from this brief summary it must be obvious that Lessing's concessions to revelation are of a strictly limited kind. Its role is essentially to disclose to primitive peoples truths which their as yet unformed reason has been unable to discover for itself. None the less there is no reason why we should not allow his proposal to point the way forward. For, if God really does take seriously the historical situatedness of human beings, what else could he do than reveal his character and purposes gradually, according to the degree to which the recipient was able to make sense of them? So for instance there could be no point in revealing his trinitarian character until monotheism had been firmly established; otherwise tritheism would have been the inevitable result. Likewise the demand for forgiveness of enemies is more readily intelligible against a framework of retributive justice than it would have been in the context of what preceded it, the lust for revenge where the objective is normally to secure even more harm to one's opponent than what was inflicted.

Of course, it could be objected that, had God wished, he could easily have overridden the forces of historical circumstance to make the truth known. One form of response to this would be to reply that God valued something more, that human beings of their own free will accept what he had to say to them, since for this to be possible there must not be too radical a discontinuity between their present assumptions and what was proposed. But

---

[48] Ibid. 89, s. 39.
[49] Ibid. 91, s. 53.
[50] Ibid. 94, s. 72.

there is also a more fundamental conceptual objection. It is not clear that even God could successfully communicate what was radically at variance with what was already believed. For the only means of assessing a proposed new belief is our existing canons of judgement, and so any new belief to be intelligible has to be such as to be capable of being accommodated within those canons. That is to suggest that changes in belief occur gradually,[51] with existing patterns of thought exercising a considerable restraining influence; but this seems confirmed by the history of thought. As philosophers are increasingly recognizing, even reason itself is not immune from the fact of historical conditioning. Models of rationality vary from century to century, and are often affected by hidden influences of which even outstanding intellects may be only partially aware.[52]

But now, it may be objected, I have proved my point too well. For, if all thought, including the canons of reason, is historically conditioned, what grounds could there be for identifying an additional causal factor in the form of divine revelation? Such indeed is the line of attack which contemporary deism takes. Whereas in the eighteenth century the appeal was to canons of reason which transcended particular historical circumstance, in the twentieth the very fact of historical conditioning is used to undermine any claim that the means of access to knowledge could be fundamentally different from one generation to another. The result is that not only is miracle excluded but the insights of Scripture become merely a powerful expression of what was potentially available to us all.

In replacing the rationalist critique with an historicizing one Ernst Troeltsch played a leading role. His claim[53] is that there are three main criteria with which the historical method operates, and that all three must inevitably rule out of court any theology which appeals to miracle or assigns a specific causal role to the supernatural. The three are: criticism (by which he means that historical judgements are always subject to revision

---

[51] This seems true even of paradigm shifts of the sort discussed in T. S. Kuhn, *The Structure of Scientific Revolutions*, 2nd edn. (Chicago, 1970).

[52] For an excellent treatment of the way in which contemporary concepts of God exercised a largely hidden influence on philosophical models of reason, cf. E. Craig, *The Mind of God and the Works of Man* (Oxford, 1987).

[53] E. Troeltsch, 'Über historische und dogmatische Methode in der Theologie', in *Gesammelte Schriften* (Tübingen, 1913), ii. 729–53.

and so never get beyond the status of assessments of probability); analogy (the need to assess such probability by comparison with our own experience and what we know to have happened elsewhere); and correlation (the assumption that events are intelligible only in so far as they can be shown to be part of an already existing causal pattern).

Earlier in this essay in effect I accepted Troeltsch's first criterion, when, following Butler, I argued that certainty was unnecessary to religious belief. His other two criteria, analogy and correlation, may conveniently be taken together. At this juncture it is interesting to observe analogy as a form of argumentation once again being employed, but used this time to argue in precisely the opposite direction from that which Butler would have approved; still more intriguing to observe that the most obvious avenue of reply is to develop an alternative analogy.

Troeltsch closes off a specific causal role for the supernatural on the grounds that the world we now encounter leaves no room for such a role, and so by analogy other cultures must have been similarly placed, however differently they may have expressed themselves. But it is arguable that he has misread the character of our world and that by taking seriously an alternative analogy a very different picture emerges, one in which a divine causal role once again becomes a serious possibility. This is the analogy between our own personal action and divine action.

However tight causal laws are at the inanimate level, most of us continue to believe in the fact of human freedom: that, though much may incline us to act in a particular way, under normal circumstances nothing forces us to do so. One way of making sense of this belief is to think that once a certain level of complexity is reached such as the human brain, the causal processes cease to operate entirely in one direction, from below to above, but that initiative becomes possible, with causal processes operating from above to below, and that is what we mean by the relative independence of the mind: without a brain the human mind cannot operate, but this does not preclude the mind controlling the operations of that brain. If that is so, it also becomes possible to understand how free human communication takes place. At one level it is all a matter of normal causal processes, the reception of sound and so forth, but at another it involves free human decision. Address and response are results of the human will, even though the means of communication are entirely determined by causal laws and indeed even the decision to communicate or respond may be heavily conditioned by the individual's historical circumstances. (To 'condition', however extreme, is not of course to 'determine'. There remains some room for manœuvre on the part of the individual, however small.)

So, then, with God. To assert that God is personal must be to claim that there is at least as much room for manœuvre for him in his dialogue with us as there is in normal human intercourse. Just as we can initiate an address to another human being without that address being caused, so similarly can God. Again, for that address to be heard various causal processes must operate, but once more there is no reason to think the situation any different with respect to God. For he too may be envisaged as normally operating through the usual causal processes. Occasionally, no doubt, visions and similar phenomena occur, but there is no reason to think this the normal pattern of divine interchange with human beings. Instead we may think of ideas apparently spontaneously occurring in our subconscious that really have their origin in divine action.[54] Nor is that to speak of miracle, any more than is the appearance of such thoughts when they are produced by our own mind acting upon our brain. Then, what we make of these divinely given 'thoughts' will be partly up to us and our free decision, and partly a matter of the particular historical circumstances in which we find ourselves and the degree of cultural conditioning which these have exercised upon us.

With that as our model of the way in which grace can operate in our own lives, of the way in which God can interact with human beings in the present, it then becomes much easier to answer Troeltsch. For applying this analogy between human and divine communication to biblical revelation, we may say that the latter differs only in degree and not in kind from what we experience in our own lives. His objections on grounds of analogy and correlation are thus misplaced. The problem of

---

[54] I have tried to develop this way of understanding revelation in 'God and Symbolic Action', in B. Hebblethwaite and E. Henderson (eds.), *Divine Action*, (Edinburgh, 1990), 103–22.

correlation is answered because divine action is to be placed in the wider context of other kinds of personal action, not simply the unbroken system of cause and effect which pertains at the sub-personal level. Similarly the problem of analogy is answered because the activity of the biblical God is directly paralleled to the activity of God today, which in turn is paralleled by our own activity as personal agents. To object that what I have said thus far ignores the question of miracle would be to miss my point; for it is precisely my contention that to make the notion of revelation credible there is no need to resort to miracle. That is a distinct issue.

Of course to demonstrate the feasibility of revelation is not to show that it has actually occurred. But analogy does take us an important step if it allows the activity of revelation to have taken place in a historical world not fundamentally different from our own. The next step would then be to ask whether the way in which the moral insights of the Bible carry us further than we seem able to achieve by ourselves does not point to a distinctive divine contribution. The more readily we are prepared to answer in the affirmative, the more likely are we also to take seriously its other insights as having a divine origin, and perhaps too in due course the possibility of miracle.

There in outline is the structure of a possible response to modern versions of deism. Mossner in his book on Butler delivered a generally negative judgement, describing him as largely unoriginal and 'distinctly a man of his age'.[55] Yet, if the argument of this essay is correct, despite the passage of time he still offers the best strategy of response to deism. The details of his specific arguments lost their relevance once evolution established a much more remote relation between God and the natural order. But his general strategy for dealing with the two main challenges of eighteenth-century deism must also be ours.

Thus, though the question of the universality *of reason* is no longer ours, universality does continue to be a problem for Christianity, and we noted that Rahner's plausible notion of 'anonymous Christians' continues the same line of response as that once adopted by Butler. Again, though historicity has replaced the primacy of reason as the other challenge to revelation, we still

---

[55] Mossner, *Bishop Butler and the Age of Reason*, 79, 13.

found ourselves developing similar avenues of reply: that probability is enough, and that an analogy is not wanting which could make the notion of revelation credible. So it is far from clear that *The Analogy of Religion* is without relevance to theological problems of our own day.

2
Deus absconditus: Some Notes on the Bearing of the Hiddenness of God upon Butler's and Pascal's Criticism of Deism

ALBINO BABOLIN

Some scholars have recently called attention to certain structural similarities between Butler and Pascal. One of the most interesting aspects of this relationship is the role that the topic of *Deus absconditus* plays in their critical attitude to deism (Pascal was a severe critic of early deism; *déisme* is a word that occurs, in a quite definite sense, in his *Lettres provinciales*, letter XVI, and three times in a crucial fragment of his Christian apologetic[1]). For John Barker, Butler's view about probability as 'the very guide of life' is reminiscent of Pascal's Wager, and Butler's familiarity with Pascal 'makes it likely he was conversant with Pascal's reasoning in a more than general way'.[2] There may also be echoes of the *Pensées* in Butler's sermons upon human nature. Nevertheless, for Barker, beyond these broad impressions, a profound dissimilarity separates the *Pensées* from the *Analogy*, making the *Analogy*, for all its aims, point more in the direction of mid-eighteenth-century rationalism than to the balance between faith and reason represented by Pascal.[3] Terence Penelhum lays stress on the prudential argument. Butler's arguments are intended as an antidote to the frivolity with which he thought his contemporaries chose to approach the claims of

[1] B. Pascal, *Pensées*, fragment 449, in Pascal, *Œuvres complètes*, ed. and notes by Louis Lafuma (Paris, 1963), 557–8.
[2] J. Barker, *Strange Contrarieties: Pascal in England during the Age of Reason* (Montreal, 1975), 137.
[3] Ibid. 138. On the comparison between Butler and Pascal, see the literature quoted in A. Babolin, *Joseph Butler* (Padua, 1973), 49, 61, 62, 88, 338, 344, 354, 490; and M. Micheletti, *Il problema religioso del senso della vita: Da Pascal a Wittgenstein e alla filosofia analitica* (Perugia, 1988), 82.

Christianity. 'He intends to attack it by showing it to be unreasonable and *imprudent* ... His procedure, though not his language, is strongly reminiscent of that of Pascal, and justifies comparison between them.'[4] Penelhum sees indeed another likeness, in that the theme of God's hiddenness is fundamental both in Butler and in Pascal. For Butler, God makes his intentions known to us, but only in limited ways. He both reveals and hides himself, in nature as well as in the Scriptures. 'The metaphysical and epistemological model which Butler uses is that of a God whose laws, both within and beyond observed nature, are through and through intelligible, but only partially known to *us*.'[5] Nevertheless, Butler thinks of God's hiddenness in a less radical way than Pascal does, even though he partially shares Pascal's view that it is a test God imposes in the face of human corruption.[6]

Another scholar has noticed a singular continuity, as regards the theme of *Deus absconditus*, from Pascal to Barrow and Butler. Mario Micheletti points out that, like Pascal, and employing the same biblical text, Isaiah 45: 15, and like Butler later on, Isaac Barrow admits that, though Providence may be obscure and intricate, the ultimate reason available to man for trusting to the divine scheme of salvation may still be alive and well grounded.[7] Such obscurity also is to be included in the designs of divine will. 'Also divers notions' says Barrow, 'not simply passing our capacity to know, we are not yet in condition to ken, by reason of our circumstances here, in this dark corner of things, to which we are confined, and wherein we lie under many disadvantages of attaining knowledge ... Our ratiocination consequently from such principles must be very short and defective.'[8] In particular, it is not perspicuous why God framed man, 'the prince of visible creatures', so fallible and frail, so prone to sin, so liable to misery. Barrow comes to this conclusion:

---

[4] T. Penelhum, *Butler* (London, 1985), 90.
[5] Ibid. 95.
[6] Ibid.
[7] Micheletti, *Il problema religioso del senso della vita*, 72.
[8] *The Theological Works of Isaac Barrow*, ed. A. Napier (Cambridge, 1859), iii. 461. See Pascal, *Pensées*, fragment 198, where Pascal talks of man 'sans lumière abandonné à lui-même, et comme égaré dans ce recoin de l'univers'. See Barker, *Strange Contrarieties*, 57: 'On Barrow's death in 1677, Newton compiled a catalogue of his books, in which both the *Pensées* and the *Lettres provinciales* were listed.'

That Providence sometimes is obscure and intricate, may be attributed to the will of God, upon divers good accounts designing it to be such: *Verily*, saith the Prophet, *thou art a God that hidest thyself, O God of Israel*, the *Saviour* ... He will not glare forth in discoveries so bright as to dazzle, to confound our weak sight; therefore he veileth his face with a cloud, and wrappeth his power in some obscurity.[9]

Micheletti, who lays stress on these passages of Barrow, points out that, on the theme of the 'necessary obscurity of religion', the comparison between Butler and Pascal is legitimate, too. He calls attention not only to various passages of Butler's works but also to a conversation that took place in 1737 and was reported in *The Private Journal and Literary Remains of John Byrom* (the conversation, in which Butler took a part, was about Newton, Pascal, prophecy, as well as on reason and authority).[10]

The theme of the hiddenness of God is not a minor one in Butler's works, as it has not merely the character of a moral exhortation to humility and to the proper acknowledgement in man of his own limits. It is indeed a fundamental aspect of Butlerian anti-deistic strategy, an aspect of that *moderate* rationalism, in which Butler's response to the absolute rationalism vindicated by deists has its roots.

Butler's likeness to Pascal becomes more significant if the rejection of deism, of early forms of it, can be shown to be a fundamental tendency also in Pascal's apology for the Christian religion. In his essay on Pascal, Micheletti has recently argued that the criticism of deism was already a major theme in Pascal's apologetic, in so far as the *déisme* censured by Pascal was not an ideal category, but a historical reality.[11] In the sixteenth letter of the *Provinciales* Pascal means by 'deism' the rejection of the gospel and of Jesus Christ; the effort towards deism is seen as a consequence of the rejection of the mystery of Incarnation, and of the gospel as 'apocryphal history'.[12] In fragment 449 of the *Pensées*, speaking of *déisme*, Pascal connects it with the pride of

---

[9] *The Theological Works of Isaac Barrow*, iii. 479. Barrow refers to Isa. 45: 15 and Ps. 89: 47. See also p. 481: 'It is needful that the present course of Providence should not be transparently clear and satisfactory, that we may be well assured concerning a future account.'

[10] *The Private Journal and Literary Remains of John Byrom*, ed. R. Parkinson (Manchester, 1856), vol. ii, pt. I, pp. 96–7. See Micheletti, *Il problema religioso del senso della vita*, 82.

[11] Micheletti, *Il problema religioso del senso della vita*, 95 ff.

[12] Pascal, *Œuvres complètes*, 452.

the philosophers who have known God and not their misery, with a way of knowing and serving God without a mediator, that is with what Pascal most frequently ascribes to Stoicism as he characterizes it both in the *Entretien avec M. de Saci* and in the *Pensées*. Therefore, the rejection of Stoic features in contemporary deistic tendencies is linked to the basic drift of Pascalian apologetic. The relation between the criticism of deism and the theme of God's hiddenness is made evident by fragment 446:

S'il n'y avait point d'obscurité, l'homme ne sentirait point sa corruption; s'il n'y avait point de lumière, l'homme n'espérerait point de remède. Ainsi, il est non seulement juste, mais utile pour nous que Dieu soit caché en partie, et découvert en partie, puisqu'il est également dangereux à l'homme de connaître Dieu sans connaître sa misère, et de connaître sa misère sans connaître Dieu.[13]

As is well known, the hiddenness, for Pascal, does not prevent God from affecting the human heart, from making himself present to the heart of the believer. Butler does not deny that, though he also stresses that our reason can convince us of the presence of God. It is important to realize that the hiddenness of God, for Butler, is not merely a theme epistemologically grounded on the ignorance of man or on the bounds of human knowledge, but it is also a doctrine ontologically grounded on the biblical God's willingness to conceal himself, as the following passage makes clear:

There is no manner of absurdity in supposing a veil on purpose drawn over some scenes of infinite power, wisdom, and goodness, the sight of which might some way or other strike us too strongly; or that better ends are designed and served by their being concealed, than could be by their being exposed to our knowledge. The Almighty may cast 'clouds and darkness round about Him', for reasons and purposes of which we have not the least glimpse or conception.[14]

I believe that this assumption plays a greater role in Butler's thought than is generally recognized in framing such a conception of God as can be opposed to the fully rationalized deistic conception of divine reality. The mysteriousness of *this* God does not mean his indifference to the world or to men, or his remoteness, as occurs in a deistic perspective. The 'Author and

---

[13] Ibid. 557.
[14] *S.* 15. 8. See Ps. 97: 2.

Cause of all things' is for Butler 'more intimately present to us than anything else can be'; with him 'we have a nearer and more constant intercourse, than we have with any creature' (SP 44). God is not indeed to be discerned by any of our senses. 'But is He then afar off? does He not fill heaven and earth with His presence?' (*S.* 13. 11) Butler quotes Job 23: 8–9, 3: 'I go forward, but He is not there; and backward, but I cannot perceive Him: He hideth Himself on the right hand, that I cannot see Him. O that I knew where I might find Him! that I might come even to His seat!' (*S.* 13. 11) For Butler, it is not only reasonable, but also natural, to be affected with a presence, though it be not the object of our senses. We can consider God as present through our rational certainty that he is near us. 'Must He, Who is so much more intimately with us, that "in Him we live and move and have our being", be thought too distant to be the object of our affections?' (*S.* 13. 11) 'Our Reason convinces us that God is present with us, and we see and feel the effects of His goodness' (*S.* 14. 2).

The hiddenness of God affects, of course, the theme of the evidential grounds of a supposed revelation. The *importance* of religion, and particularly of the Christian faith, along with the degree of evidence and probability of its truth, is sufficient to put man under strict obligations. For Pascal, likewise, negligence in the search for truth is unacceptable, in so far as this search is something that profoundly concerns ourselves, as it regards that which is for us of the greatest consequence.[15] For Butler it is 'unspeakable irreverence', 'the most presumptuous rashness', to treat Christianity 'as a light matter', or to disregard the vital question concerning a future life (*A.* 2. 1. 19; *A.* 1. 2. 1). As to the evidences of revealed religion, Butler argues that, upon supposition of a divine revelation, the analogy of nature makes it a priori highly credible, or rather probable, that 'many things in it must appear liable to great objections; and that we must be incompetent judges of it, to a great degree' (*A.* Con. 2), and 'admitting the fact, that God has afforded to some no more than doubtful evidence of religion; the same account may be given of it, as of difficulties and temptations with regard to practice' (*A.* Con. 2).

---

[15] Pascal, *Pensées*, fragment 427 (*Œuvres complètes*, 552).

Where Butler's and Pascal's views about God chiefly differ is with reference to the relationship between the God of faith and the God of natural religion and the evidential value of final causes. For Butler, final causes are 'proofs of wisdom and design in the Author of nature', and along with them we must grant the natural government of God and, consequently, a moral scheme of government (*S.* 6. 1; *A.* 1. 2. 6; *A.* 1. 3. 1–10), which, of course, has its proper analogies in the Christian scheme. On the contrary, Pascal does not rely at all upon teleological considerations.[16] Moreover, though they both make a case against deism (Pascal against a very early stage of it; Butler against a mature or maybe a declining one), Butler's defence of Christian religion is grounded on the notoriously complex and perplexing notion of analogy. This implies a continuity of a sort with natural religion, though Butlerian analogy has chiefly negative shades, whereas Pascal relies upon proofs of Christian religion which are worked out to stand by themselves. Pascal's God conceals himself in Scripture, as well as in nature and history, and those proofs can also be understood as a cumulative case for Christian theism. The 'analogy of religion natural and revealed to the constitution and course of nature' plays a role in Butler that has only a feeble correspondence in Pascal's conviction, which is addressed to the *libertins*, that both in the world and in Scripture we have to interpret signs; that we are, as it were, in the realm of hermeneutics. 'In Pascal', says P. Force, 'hermeneutics and apologetic are intimately linked: when Pascal puts the question of the foundations of religion, it is the problem of hermeneutics that arises.'[17] On the other hand, the method of Pascal aims at a demonstration of Christianity that is founded upon a proof of the credibility of the Bible. Wetsel lays stress on Pascal's assertion that God has built convincing proofs of the truth of revelation into the fabric of sacred history.[18] It was for Butler to elaborate the 'analogy of religion' in great detail, stressing chiefly the negative aspects, but also the positive ones. And again and again similarities to Pascal arise, along with differences, from the view that it is unavoidable that there are obscurities in a revela-

---

[16] See Pascal, *Pensées*, fragment 3.
[17] P. Force, *Le Problème herméneutique chez Pascal* (Paris, 1989), 9.
[18] D. Wetsel, *L'Écriture et le reste: The Pensées of Pascal in the Exegetical Tradition of Port-Royal* (Columbus, Oh., 1981), p. xxi.   [19] See *A.* 2. 3. 1.

tion[19] to the positive thesis about the role of prophecy, including the conviction that the 'apparent completions of prophecy must be allowed to be explanatory of its meaning'.[20]

Thus, the hiddenness of God, God's revealing himself through his concealing himself, is a central theme both in Butler and in Pascal, that is in that new form of apologetic which was contrived to face deists and freethinkers, in successive stages of the development of deism and libertinism. The main assumption is that it is quite absurd to claim that if God is known, then he is wholly evident to our minds, his reality wholly unambiguous. It is of considerable importance that in Pascal's thought that theme chiefly pointed to a sort of hermeneutics, while in Butler's it pointed to a rational form of argument grounded on the notions (not, however, quite unknown to Pascal) of analogy and probability.

[20] *A.* 2. 7. 25. See Pascal, *Pensées*, fragment 936 (*Œuvres complètes*, 624).

3
The 'Spiritual Sovereign': Butler's Episcopate

CHRISTOPHER CUNLIFFE

I

By the time he became a bishop Joseph Butler had completed the work which has engaged the attention of philosophers and theologians. The Rolls Chapel *Sermons* and the *Analogy of Religion* were the fruit of the years between 1719 and 1736, the work of a man in the prime of life. Though retiring by nature Butler had not dropped entirely from public view during these years, despite Queen Caroline's tenuous awareness of his fate. After his resignation of the Rolls preachership in 1726 he spent the greater part of his time in the rectory at Stanhope, until the prompting of his old friend Thomas Secker and the reliable patronage of the Talbot family drew him back to London, as chaplain to Lord Chancellor Talbot in 1733 and as a member of the circle of clerical intellectuals around Queen Caroline, to whom he became clerk of the closet in 1736, the year in which the *Analogy* was published.[1] His regular, indeed daily, attendance upon the queen and his service to the king after her death in November 1737 encouraged the confident prediction that Butler, following the other members of the Talbot circle, would soon receive preferment to the episcopal bench; it is believed that Queen Caroline entrusted this matter to Archbishop Potter on her death-bed.[2] On Sir Thomas Gooch's translation from

[1] Thomas Bartlett, *Memoirs of the Life, Character, and Writings of Joseph Butler D.C.L., Late Lord Bishop of Durham* (London, 1839), 37-42. I am grateful to Jane Garnett for her comments on an earlier draft of this essay. Dates before 1 Jan. 1752, when the Gregorian calendar came into effect, are given in the old style, with the year taken as beginning on 1 Jan.

[2] Historical Manuscripts Commission, Egmont Diary, ii. 476 (6 Apr. 1738); E. C. Mossner, *Bishop Butler and the Age of Reason* (New York, 1936), 5, citing John, Baron Hervey, *Memoirs of the Reign of George the Second, from His Accession to the Death of Queen Caroline*, ed. J. W. Croker (London, 1848).

Bristol to Norwich in 1738 a suitable opportunity arose and Butler was duly nominated to the poorest see in England, where he was to remain for twelve years until his translation to Durham, where a brief episcopate ended with his death in 1752. During these fourteen years he wrote nothing which has survived of the power and originality of the *Fifteen Sermons* or *Analogy*. His *Six Sermons on Public Occasions* date from these years, however, as does his notable primary (and only) visitation charge to the diocese of Durham in 1751. In these works and in the details of his episcopal duties it is possible to detect something of the way in which one of the most interesting figures in the intellectual history of eighteenth-century Britain gave practical effect to his philosophical and theological concerns.

II

Lastly, 'tis my positive and express will that all my sermons and letters and papers whatever which are in a deal box lock'd directed to Dr Forster and now standing in the little Room within my Library at Hampstead, be burnt without being read by anyone, as soon as may be after my decease.[3]

It is one of the frustrations of Butler scholarship that so much evidence is missing. Very little appears to have survived the general destruction stipulated in Butler's will, or the similar instructions of his nephew, to whom any papers would have passed. No personal letters have survived, only a few of an official nature. It was reported in 1862 that five manuscript sermons remained in the possession of the Butler family, two of which might have provided evidence of Butler's reaction to the Jacobite rising of 1745, one of which was a copy of a sermon by Isaac Barrow.[4] There are other fragmentary manuscript remains, including an extract from a visitation charge at Bristol. We still have the touching letters written to Archbishop Secker by Butler's close friend Martin Benson, bishop of Gloucester, and his domestic chaplain Nathaniel Forster, at the time of Butler's

---

[3] University of Durham, Department of Palaeography and Diplomatic, SGD 35/14, copy of Butler's will.
[4] *The Sermons and Remains of... Joseph Butler*, ed. E. Steere (London, 1862), pp. xxxiv–xxxv.

last illness and death. Episcopal records of a formal and routine nature survive, giving some insight into Butler's management of his dioceses, but even here ill fortune dogs the historian, for many of the Bristol diocesan records were destroyed by the fire which swept the bishop's palace during the Reform Bill riots in 1831.[5]

However assiduously he might seek to cover his tracks it is very difficult for a person with important political and social responsibilities—and these an eighteenth-century bishop had in abundance—to disappear entirely. And Butler was no more successful in this respect than other self-effacing prelates have been. We can trace his attendance in the House of Lords and on official committees; we can read what his contemporaries thought of him. By placing the various pieces of evidence in their historical context and by recognizing the constraints under which someone in Butler's position was placed—the expectation of the appropriate behaviour and way of life of a bishop—an impression of Butler the bishop emerges which adds substance to the shadowy and elusive author of the *Sermons* and the *Analogy*.

III

Butler was nominated to the see of Bristol on 19 October 1738. He was consecrated in the chapel of Lambeth Palace on 3 December by the archbishop of Canterbury (Potter) and the bishops of Rochester (Wilcocks), St Davids (Claggett), and Ely (Butts).[6] It is unlikely that he took up residence in Bristol, apart from the occasional brief visit, until after the parliamentary session of 1739, which ended on 14 June.

Not only was Bristol the poorest diocese in England, yielding an annual income of between £300 and £450 for much of the eighteenth century, it was also the oddest geographically.[7] The diocese consisted of the deanery of Bristol, roughly conterminous with the city, and the county of Dorset. The larger part of the diocese was thus detached from the cathedral city. This

---

[5] I. M. Kirby, *Diocese of Bristol: A Catalogue of the Records of the Bishop and Archdeacons and of the Dean and Chapter* (Bristol, 1970), pp. x–xi.
[6] Lambeth Palace Library (subsequently LPL), VB1/8, Act Book 1734–50, fo. 120ʳ.
[7] N. Sykes, *Church and State in England in the Eighteenth Century* (Cambridge, 1934), 61.

peculiar arrangement lasted from the foundation of the see in 1542 until it was united (briefly) with Gloucester in 1836, when Dorset returned to the diocese of Salisbury, its natural ecclesiastical home. Moreover the bishops of Bristol did not have the assistance of an archdeacon in Bristol itself, which came under the direct administration of the bishop. Dorset formed an archdeaconry, of which the archdeacon throughout Butler's episcopate was Edward Hammond. To the inconvenience of geography was thus added inconsistency of administration. In addition the bishop's powers of clerical patronage were severely limited: of some 240 parishes in the diocese only about thirty were in the bishop's direct patronage, a figure exceeded by the forty parishes in Dorset which were peculiars of the dean of Salisbury.[8]

Although Bristol was a diocese from which many bishops in the eighteenth century sought to escape as soon as possible— Gooch and Bagot after one year, Cecill, Secker, Hume, and Madan after two—it was not an insignificant preferment. Bristol itself was the second city and second port in the kingdom, with a population which rose from around 20,000 at the beginning of the century to 64,000 by 1801. Its port dominated the Irish and the West Indian trade and was the principal centre for the slave-trade. The mercantile life of the city was particularly susceptible to the fortunes of war, which dealt severe blows to Bristol trade during the eighteenth century. There was a marked decline in the volume of trade, for example, between 1744 and 1747, during Butler's episcopate. There were about 200 merchants of substance in the city and an active civic and social life. Ecclesiastically the deanery of Bristol consisted of thirty-five parishes, many of them surrounding the medieval parish churches which crowded the city centre. The growing working population on the margins of the city were less well provided for, and provided a willing congregation for Whitefield and Wesley from 1739 onwards.[9]

Butler began his episcopate as he was to end it: worrying. In a

---

[8] G. Hill, *English Dioceses: A History of Their Limits from the Earliest Times to the Present Day* (London, 1900), 389, 398; Bristol Record Office (subsequently Bristol RO), EP/A/2/1, Diocese Book, c.1735.

[9] G. Shelton, *Dean Tucker and 18th Century Economic and Political Thought* (London, 1981), 23.

letter to Walpole on receiving the news that he was to be appointed to Bristol he bemoaned his fate:

Indeed, the bishoprick of Bristol is not very suitable either to the condition of my fortune, or the circumstances of my preferment; nor, as I should have thought, answerable to the recommendation with which I was honoured.[10]

Fuelling Butler's prickly self-doubt was the financial and pastoral predicament in which his preferment placed him. The income of the see was insufficient to provide for him and necessitated the holding of other posts in plurality, the common practice of the time. Butler therefore retained his incumbency at Stanhope, which provided an income almost twice that of Bristol (£700)[11] but was hardly conveniently placed, and his prebendal stall at Rochester, to which he had been appointed, through Talbot's patronage, in 1736. In addition to Bristol and Stanhope, however, he had to maintain a household in London during parliamentary sessions, which he did by hiring lodgings, so it seemed likely that the three-way pull would prove insupportable. It was nearly two years before a convenient solution presented itself and Butler was appointed to the deanery of St Paul's Cathedral, providing him with a realistic income and a house in London. He was then able to resign from his posts at Stanhope and Rochester.

Once settled into his new position Butler conformed to contemporary practice and resided in his diocese during the summer months and on other special occasions, moving to London in the autumn for the parliamentary session.[12] After the first two or three years of his episcopate, when he did not have a permanent London home and had to repair the dilapidated palace in Bristol, his normal custom was to come to London in mid-October and stay there until the end of June, moving back to his diocese for three months or so in the summer. Incumbents who wished to be instituted to their livings had, therefore, in many cases to travel to London to go through the formalities

---

[10] Butler to Walpole, Stanhope (28 Aug. 1738), cited in Bartlett, *Memoirs*, 73-4.
[11] J. C. Shuler, 'The Pastoral and Ecclesiastical Administration of the Diocese of Durham 1721-1771; with Particular Reference to the Archdeaconry of Northumberland', Ph.D. thesis (Durham, 1975), 110.
[12] Sykes, *Church and State in England*, 93-4.

with their bishop, until 1740 in St James's Westminster and latterly in the deanery of St Paul's. On occasion such duties were carried out in Bristol by the bishop's commissary.[13]

In his supervision of the diocese Butler had the great advantage of access to Thomas Secker's diocesan survey of 1735-7, a typically meticulous account of every parish in the diocese. Not only did Secker provide a short description of each parish—the number of houses, whether there was a school, the number of Dissenters and papists—but he also wrote his, often forthright, opinions of the clergy, not neglecting their political allegiance. So his successors were able to read of one incumbent, 'warm whig, imprudent, vain', of another that he 'values himself rather too much', and of a third, 'I have admonished and threatened him severely'.[14] There are, no doubt, disadvantages in knowing one's predecessor's opinions of one's flock but the document is a fascinating record of the personnel of an English diocese. Perhaps it was because Secker's work was so thorough that Butler added very little to the book beyond a simple record of institutions to benefices.

There were 142 institutions during Butler's episcopate at Bristol, forty-seven performed by commissaries.[15] Of the regularity of ordinations, visitations, and confirmations little evidence has survived, though it is likely that Butler, along with his colleagues Benson and Secker, was among the more diligent of eighteenth-century bishops in this respect. The surviving fragment of a visitation charge, on ministry to the sick, is said to be from Butler's fourth charge and dated 1749.[16] We know also that Butler conducted a visitation in 1746 and that he confirmed in the Bristol deanery in August and September 1743.[17] It was usual in the eighteenth century for visitations and confirmations to happen concurrently. The remaining evidence of Butler's incursions into his Dorset archdeaconry tends to confirm the pattern of a visitation every three years, which was the stipulation of canon law. He was in Dorchester in July 1740, in Sherborne in July 1743, in Cerne Abbas in July 1746, and in Bridport and

[13] Bristol RO, EP/A/5/1/2, Institution Book 1739-61, fos. 1ʳ-24ʳ.
[14] Bristol RO, EP/A/2/2, Secker's Diocesan Survey 1735-7, fos. 35, 41, 47.
[15] Bristol RO, EP/A/5/1/2, Institution Book 1739-61.
[16] Bernard, i. 302-4.
[17] Bristol RO, EP/V/1, 1746 Visitation Process; EP/A/21/1, confirmation schedule.

Dorchester in July 1749,[18] in each case for an institution, though this is almost certainly the surviving evidence of the broader pastoral activity of visitation and confirmation at important centres in the county. This, together with other evidence, would suggest a primary visitation of the diocese in 1739 or 1740, and further visitations in 1743, 1746, and 1749.

When an eighteenth-century bishop resided on his see he was expected to provide hospitality, both to his clergy and to the leading citizens of the diocese. Butler's later practice in Durham was to keep open house three days a week,[19] and it is probable that he instituted a similar regime in Bristol, particularly when he was able to use his income from the deanery of St Paul's to refurbish his palace. His relations with the mercantile community were good and he received a gift of cedar wood from the merchants of Bristol, some of which he used in the renovation of his chapel, and the rest he took to Durham, where it was later used by Bishop Barrington for furniture.[20] An important intermediary in Butler's relations with the city of Bristol was the young Josiah Tucker.[21] Tucker had arrived in Bristol in 1737 as a curate of St Stephen's church and a minor canon in the cathedral. When Butler came to Bristol he made Tucker his domestic chaplain, securing for him the living of All Saints and a prebendal stall in the cathedral; later, in 1749, Tucker became rector of St Stephen's, Bristol, and, in 1758, dean of Gloucester. Tucker was Butler's frequent companion, not least during nocturnal walks in the palace garden, with Butler musing on the possibility that communities and public bodies, as well as individuals, might become insane.[22] It was a sermon by Tucker which triggered the notorious confrontation between Butler and John Wesley in August 1739,[23] and it was Tucker who, at Butler's prompting, wrote *A Brief History of the Principles of Methodism*. This pamphlet was one of the most balanced and perceptive of

---

[18] Bristol RO, EP/A/5/1/2, Institution Book 1739-61, fos. 4ᵛ-5ʳ, 8ᵛ, 14ᵛ-15ʳ, 20ʳ.
[19] *Sermons and Remains*, ed. Steere, p. xxxi.
[20] Bartlett, *Memoirs*, 90.
[21] For Tucker see Shelton, *Dean Tucker*; J. G. A. Pocock, 'Josiah Tucker on Burke, Locke, and Price', in *Virtue, Commerce, and History* (Cambridge, 1985), 157-91.
[22] Bartlett, *Memoirs*, 92-3.
[23] Norman Sargent, 'John Wesley's Meetings with Bishop Butler 1739', *Report of the Friends of Bristol Cathedral* (1981), 23-7. A reading of the entire conversation does far more justice to Butler's position than the excerpts normally cited.

the many attacks on Methodism which appeared at the time, outlining the context of the development of Methodist theology and drawing attention to its inconsistencies. Wesley considered Tucker to be an opponent worthy of reply, in *Principles of a Methodist*.[24] Tucker, like his bishop, was closely involved in the development of the new Bristol Infirmary. He was a member of the weekly committee for a while in the mid-1740s and preached the annual infirmary sermon in 1745, suggesting that the hospital should be equally concerned for the moral and spiritual welfare of its patients. Butler preached the infirmary sermon in 1747 but it has not survived, though it was probably along similar lines to the one he preached for the London Infirmary in the following year.[25]

Tucker also published a pamphlet on the Jacobite rebellion in 1745 and *Two Dissertations*, against Thomas Chubb, in 1749. The economic writings for which he is best known date from after his close association with Butler, although it is likely that Butler discussed with Tucker the content of his 1740 sermon on wealth and luxury.[26] Tucker's avowed debt to Butler was in the field of moral philosophy and theology. Recommending Butler to young readers he wrote:

As to Bishop Butler himself, he certainly pursues a method, the fittest in the world to put to silence the superficial, licentious extravagances of modern times; were his manner of writing a little more pleasing and alluring. For by demonstrating, that there is a system actually carrying on by the Author of the Universe, both in the natural and moral world, he confutes the sceptics on one extreme; and by proving how imperfectly this system is yet comprehended by us, he checks that arrogance, and self-sufficiency on the other, which are too natural to young minds just tinctured with a smattering of knowledge.[27]

Butler's attempts to respond to the increasing activity of the Methodists in Bristol were not confined to words. The arrival of first Whitefield and then Wesley in the city early in 1739, and

[24] Shelton, *Dean Tucker*, 31.
[25] Bristol RO, MS 35893(1)a, Bristol Infirmary Minute Book 1736-72, entries for 15 Mar. 1742, 6 Sept. 1743, and 14 July 1747.
[26] Pocock, 'Josiah Tucker', 179-85, for a discussion of Tucker's view of the historical development of economic life.
[27] Shelton, *Dean Tucker*, 107. The original is in *Instructions for Travellers* (London, 1757), 6.

their popularity in the mining area of Kingswood Chase, convinced Butler that something should be done for the unchurched working people on the margins of Bristol society. He therefore spent time and money, buying the land himself for £400, to secure the necessary financial and parliamentary support for the establishment of the new parish and church of St George in that part of Bristol. The church, started after Butler left Bristol, was consecrated in 1756. It has been called his 'most lasting gift to the diocese'.[28]

IV

As a bishop of the established Church Butler had a seat in the House of Lords. Throughout the eighteenth century the episcopal presence in the upper house was significant, numbering twenty-six out of over 200 members, with a regular attendance rarely exceeding 120 to 145.[29] It is not surprising, therefore, that the king's ministers sought the appointment to the bench of those who would provide political support for the government of the day. On the whole the bishops were compliant with ministerial pressure of this kind and were usually to be relied upon in the lobby. Butler was among the more compliant. Steere, writing in 1862 and using Secker's parliamentary journal as his guide, stated that Butler attended Parliament very regularly and voted with the government, though there is no evidence that he spoke in debate. Steere went on to say that Butler seems always to have attended and voted with his friends Secker and Benson.[30]

Evidence from other sources suggests a more complex account. Butler sat in fourteen parliamentary sessions, from February 1739 to March 1752. His attendance record was not notably regular or frequent. In his first session, in 1739, he attended the House on sixty-eight occasions and was absent on eleven. In every other session, with the exception of 1742–3, he was absent more often than he was present. His attendance tailed off during the second half of his episcopate. In 1744–5 he

---

[28] *Sermons and Remains*, ed. Steere, p. xxvii; B. Little, *The City and County of Bristol: A Study in Atlantic Civilization* (London, 1954), 192.
[29] Sykes, *Church and State in England*, 49.
[30] *Sermons and Remains*, ed. Steere, p. xxviii.

attended on thirteen out of a possible seventy occasions, in 1748-9 on nineteen out of eighty-eight, in 1749-50 on eight out of a possible sixty-seven, and the same in 1751-2.[31] In this last session illness limited his attendance, as it might have done in previous years. However, his attendance was by no means exemplary.

Butler's voting record in the House did not please Secker, who obviously expected that his newly consecrated friend would take an active and critical view of his new political role. A month after Butler took his seat in the Lords, Secker, Benson, and the bishops of Lincoln and Lichfield voted against the government after a debate on the Convention of the Pardo, which settled trade disputes with Spain. Butler was present on that occasion and, presumably, voted with the government.[32] Again, on 28 January 1741 Secker and Benson voted with the 'formed opposition' against Walpole and in favour of a Secret Committee to enquire into the conduct of the war. Benson's political opposition lapsed at this point but there was sufficient concern in court circles about Secker for the king to object in 1750 to his appointment to the deanery of St Paul's.[33]

That Butler's consistent support for the government was part of a carefully considered political stance is probable; his sermons display a sophisticated and nuanced support for the *status quo* and a characteristic horror of political disorder. Yet many junior bishops in the eighteenth century recognized the spur of ministerial pressure as an incentive to preferment. Loyal political service might bring rapid rewards—the case of Hoadly being the most startling example—while opposition might leave a bishop languishing in an impecunious diocese, like Secker's sixteen years in Bristol and Oxford. Thomas Herring's staunch support for the government during the Jacobite rising in 1745, when he rallied the gentlemen of Yorkshire behind the crown, did no harm to his chances of preferment to Canterbury two years later. In the same way Butler knew that political quiescence might serve a certain purpose. As Clerk of the Closet after 1746 he was, once again, a member of the royal household, an additional constraint on political manoeuvring. He was, apparently, promised

---

[31] *Journals of the House of Lords* (subsequently *LJ*), vols. xxv-xxvii, *passim*.
[32] Sykes, *Church and State in England*, 64; *LJ* xxv. 306-9.
[33] Sykes, *Church and State in England*, 64.

Durham at the next vacancy, and there is a story that he was (among others) offered Canterbury in 1747, but declined, claiming that 'it was too late for him to try to support a falling Church'.[34]

Secker did not take as understanding a view of his contemporary's attitude. In his *Autobiography*, not intended for publication, Secker wrote of this period:

As my Favour with the Court & Ministry declined, his [Butler's] friendship did. He said to me, at the End of the first Session, in which he sat in the House of Lords, that the ministers were both wicked Men & wicked Ministers. Yet he not only always voted with them, but expressed Contempt & Dislike of me for doing otherwise: & never, that I could hear, spoke a Word by way of Apology for me to any other Person.[35]

The frostiness in Secker's relationship with Butler seems to have dated from the mid-1730s, when Secker thought Butler insufficiently grateful for the time and effort Secker had expended both in providing further patronage for Butler from the Talbot family and in helping him to make the language and argument of the *Analogy of Religion* more accessible to its potential readers.[36]

As it is, the only recorded occasion on which Butler supported Secker's opposition to a measure was on 25 February 1743, when Butler and nine other bishops—including Secker and Benson—protested against the Spirituous Liquors Bill.[37] Otherwise his life in the upper house was uneventful; a certain amount of committee work, sermons before the Lords in Westminster Abbey in 1741 and 1747, and attendance on noteworthy occasions such as the trial of Lord Lovat for treason in 1747.[38]

Another body which Butler attended while in London was the Society for the Propagation of the Gospel in Foreign Parts. His attendance at the monthly meetings of the SPG was erratic. He first attended in November 1738, as bishop elect of Bristol, and his last meeting was in September 1750, as bishop elect of

---

[34] Bartlett, *Memoirs*, 95-6, 98. For the offer of the see of London to Butler in 1748 if the bishop of Salisbury (Sherlock) refused it see Mossner, *Bishop Butler*, 181.
[35] *The Autobiography of Thomas Secker, Archbishop of Canterbury*, J. S. Macauley and R. W. Greaves (Lawrence, 1988), 22.
[36] Ibid. 15-16.
[37] *LJ* xxvi. 218.
[38] *LJ* xxv-xxvii, *passim*.

Durham. He was sworn a vice-president of the society on 20 March 1740 and chaired the meeting in August of that year. In 1739 he preached before the Society.[39] Butler was to leave the SPG £500 in his will and took a close interest in its affairs. He was among several bishops at the time who put forward plans for the introduction of the episcopate in the American colonies.[40] His scheme, devised in 1750, was very cautious, and would have given bishops jurisdiction only over their clergy and not over the large Dissenting population. However, like the similar schemes put forward in the middle of the century, it fell victim to colonial alarm at the prospect of the kind of ecclesiastical regulation from which their forebears had escaped.

V

An important aspect of Butler's public ministry as bishop was the preaching of sermons before public bodies. Many institutions and organizations in the eighteenth century, from Parliament to local hospitals, had an annual sermon or sermons, at which a distinguished divine was expected to remind his congregation of the principles underlying its particular enterprise. Sermons, many of which were published, still formed an important part of the literary culture of the time and Butler's preaching developed during the period of the greatest vogue for ethical preaching.[41] His *Fifteen Sermons* in the Rolls Chapel were an ornament of that movement but the *Six Sermons on Public Occasions*, published in a collected edition in 1749, were equally significant in their discussion of the place of religion in society. The sermons were preached in London churches between 1739 and 1748, while Butler was bishop of Bristol, and form a small fraction of his preaching output as bishop. They display the same characteristics as his other writing, a cautious approach to

---

[39] LPL, SPG Papers, vol. iii, fo. 203; vol. iv, fos. 9, 29; vol. v, fo. 293.

[40] N. Sykes, *From Sheldon to Secker: Aspects of English Church History, 1660–1760* (Cambridge, 1959), 205–10, for the background to this debate and esp. p. 210 for the contributions of Butler and Sherlock, with their rebuttal by Horace Walpole on the ministry's behalf; Bartlett, *Memoirs*, 122–7.

[41] J. Downey, *The Eighteenth-Century Pulpit* (Oxford, 1969), 9. Chapter 2 (pp. 30–57) of Downey's book is a study of Butler's sermons.

the complexity of the issues, an awareness of the other side of the argument, and the careful attention to specific criticisms that had been raised. Yet the tone is invariably constructive; there is a clear message which is preached with conviction, even if that conviction is markedly unpolemical.

Of the six sermons three are concerned with the responsibility for charitable giving, two—preached before the House of Lords in 1741 and 1747—raise questions about political society, while the first sermon addresses itself to the mission of the Church. In the sermons, as in the Durham *Charge* of 1751, Butler sees his teaching function as a bishop as strengthening the religious cement which holds a civilized society together and provides it with shared assumptions and a common moral discourse. This is not the spiritually arid but politically useful civic religion of Gibbon's *Decline and Fall* or Rousseau's *Social Contract* but the articulation of human values within a providentially ordered universe. Butler is aware of the need to steer a middle course; that of true religion, rather than atheism on the one hand or superstition on the other; of civil liberty (that 'severe and ... restrained thing' (*SS* 3. 17)), rather than tyranny or licentiousness. And he is acutely aware of the danger of disorder whenever we stray from the middle way, both religiously and socially. The danger of excess is a constant theme of his preaching as of his writing, 'the excess of anything being always to its hurt, and tending to its destruction' (*SS* 3. 17). So excessive liberty becomes licentiousness, in the same way that excessive liberality becomes extravagance, and an excess of misplaced religious zeal becomes superstition. Liberty only makes sense for Butler in the context of obedience to authority: 'the love of liberty, which is not a real principle of dutiful behaviour towards authority, is as hypocritical as the religion which is not productive of a good life' (*SS* 3. 17). This leads, for him, to the need to inculcate the sense of authority as God's ordinance and of social ranks as providential:

Since men cannot live out of society, nor in it without government, government is plainly a Divine appointment; and consequently submission to it, a most evident duty of the law of nature ... Nor can this obligation be denied formally upon any principles, but such as subvert all other obligations. Yet many amongst us seem not to consider it as any obligation at all. (*SS* 3. 20)

Reverence for authority and the growth of true religion are inseparable. They also entail an obligation towards the disadvantaged in society. 'Every one of ability then is to be persuaded to do somewhat towards this, keeping up a sense of virtue and religion among the poor, and relieving their wants' (*SS* 2. 10). This obligation is laid upon the wealthier members of society and Butler is anxious to stress the important function of the trading and commercial classes in this respect, 'by natural providence, as much as by revealed appointment' (*SS* 2. 10). This notion of stewardship of the disadvantaged extends to the obligation to support missionary work in the colonies. Although 'all knowledge from reason is as really from God as revelation is' (*SS* 1. 7), revelation is a 'distinguished favour to us' through our membership of the Christian Church and therefore puts us under an obligation to communicate it, an obligation to 'assist in keeping up the profession of Christianity ... in our factories abroad; and in the colonies, to which we are related', whose inhabitants are 'subjects ... to the same government with ourselves' (*SS* 1. 7)—once again civic and religious duties cohere. Butler, whose cathedral city was at the centre of the slave-trade, had very clear views about the status of slaves and of the indigenous populations of the colonies. Slaves are to be considered as 'inferior members' of colonies, 'and therefore are to be treated as members of them; and not merely as cattle or goods, the property of their masters ... Despicable as they may appear in our eyes, they are the creatures of God, and of the race of mankind, for whom Christ died.' If we oppress them in this world we ought to put them in as good a position as possible with regard to the next (*SS* 1. 8). Similarly with the natives. 'These poor uninformed creatures' are 'of one family with ourselves', and therefore we must 'instruct them in our common salvation' (*SS* 1. 9). Butler was equally aware of the harsh labour practices existing in parts of England. Preaching before the House of Lords on the anniversary of the king's accession in 1747 he praised the passing of legislation to ease the lot of the mining population in the north:

For we have at length, to the distinguished honour of those who began, and have more particularly laboured in it, emancipated our northern provinces from most of their *legal* remains of slavery: for *voluntary* slavery cannot be abolished, at least not directly by law. I take leave to speak of this long desired work as done; since it wants only his concurrence, who, as we have found by many years' experience, considers the good of his people as his own. (*SS* 5. 5)

Obligations towards the poor are the major theme of Butler's charity sermons in support of the growing charity-school and hospital movements. His unstinting support for the movements in his dioceses was an important practical achievement of his episcopate and his sermons provide some of the theoretical underpinning. He stresses that such charitable activity is a practical outworking of the Christian religion, and he was severely critical of a religious life which bore no such fruit. Preaching at the annual meeting of the London and Westminster charity-school children in 1745 he informed his congregation of the children's right to a proper education and, 'when this is not given them by their parents, the care of it devolves upon all persons, it becomes the duty of all, who are capable of contributing to it, and whose help is wanted' (*SS* 4. 2). Such education is not to be bare instruction but '*training them up*' and forming 'truths into practical principles in the mind so as to render them of habitual good influence upon the temper and actions, in all the various occurrences of life'. There are compelling social reasons for this, as 'upon the whole incapacity and ignorance must be favourable to error and vice' (*SS* 4. 4), while 'knowledge and improvement contribute, in due course, to the destruction of impiety as well as superstition, and to the general prevalence of true religion' (*SS* 4. 10). Theological, moral, and pragmatic arguments come together at this point; the case is a cumulative one.

In his two surviving hospital sermons, preached in 1740 and 1748, Butler develops the theme of charitable giving. The earlier sermon includes a long introductory passage on the origins and progress of wealth creation and the dangers of luxury, designed to point to the important role of the 'middle rank of people', who are free, many of them, from the 'vices of the highest and lowest part of mankind' (*SS* 2. 4). But although charity may have the effect of making amends for past misdemeanours it should not, for Butler, be unthinking. In the 1748 sermon he defines charity as: 'Such hearty love to our fellow-creatures, as produceth a settled endeavour to promote, *according to the best of our judgment, their real lasting good, both present and future*' (*SS* 3. 3). An obvious way of promoting this kind of charity is through the establishment of public infirmaries, which are the most effective way of extending the medical relief which God has made available to us and the only possible means by which 'the poor of London can be provided with several kinds of assistance'. As was common in such sermons the opportunities provided in hospitals for moral and spiritual instruction were seen as distinct advantages. The onset of illness or affliction was an obvious opportunity for the clergy to direct their charges' attention to serious matters. Hence hospitals were seen as part of a general scheme of 'improvement' in society, to which all members of that society were obliged to contribute in recognition of their mutual responsibility to each other and their status as members of the same human family, 'under the direction of one righteous Governor' (*SS* 1. 1).

For such is the overriding theme of these occasional sermons, that as the external religion of communities and churches is a republication of the revealed Christian gospel, so 'civil government has been, in all ages, a standing publication of the law of nature, and an enforcement of it ... part of God's government over the world' (*SS* 5. 2. 3). It is precisely because Butler saw, in his day, the gradual erosion of religious belief and practice that he was so concerned about the political and social consequences of such decay, fearing the manipulation of the resultant moral confusion by cynical, or simply unthinking, people. It was in this sombre mood that he prepared to move to Durham and exercise his authority in a new sphere.

VI

Edward Chandler, bishop of Durham since 1730, died on 20 July 1750. Speculation in Durham about Chandler's successor, which had started long before his death, was allowed little further scope, as Butler was nominated to the vacant see at the end of the month.[42] The appointment was duly confirmed in October

---

[42] Shuler, 'Pastoral and Ecclesiastical Administration', 115. For Butler's warm letter of thanks to the king see British Library, Additional MS 32722, fo. 58, Butler to George II (5 Aug. 1750), cited in Mossner, *Bishop Butler and the Age of Reason*, 9.

and Butler did homage and was enthroned by proxy at Durham on 9 November.[43] However, he did not take possession of his see until the following June and died less than a year later, so his stay in one of the most important preferments in the Church was not as long as he, and many others, had hoped.

Butler's characteristic scrupulousness had threatened to delay the appointment. By long custom the bishops of Durham were also Lords Lieutenant of the County Palatine. The duke of Newcastle, George II's chief minister, wished to detach the lord lieutenancy from the bishopric and give it to Lord Barnard. Butler objected to the peremptory ending of the ancient privilege of the see, claiming that he was quite happy where he was and that he would not accept Durham without the lord lieutenancy. Newcastle relented on this point as he did with regard to the appointment of Thomas Chapman to the prebendal stall at Durham vacated by Secker, who succeeded Butler as dean of St Paul's. Butler was anxious that Chapman's appointment should not be seen as a condition of his own preferment.[44] His apprehension was expressed in a letter to a friend shortly after his nomination to Durham:

It would be a melancholy thing in the close of life, to have no reflections to entertain oneself with, but that one had spent the revenues of the bishoprick of Durham, in a sumptuous course of living, and enriched one's friends with the promotions of it, instead of having really set one's self to do good, and promote worthy men.[45]

Butler's anxiety about returning to the diocese where he had spent several contented years as an incumbent was not shared by his expectant flock. When his appointment was announced it was thought that Butler was 'a man of unexceptionable character in private life', who would 'be much loved in the County'.[46] His arrival in Durham on 28 June 1751 was a happy occasion.

Dr Butler, bishop of Durham, was met at Fairwellhall on his first coming into the country, by many of the gentry and clergy in about 18 or 19 coaches. He came out of his coach and was complimented in

---

[43] Shuler, 'Pastoral and Ecclesiastical Administration', 117; Bartlett, *Memoirs*, 117.
[44] Bartlett, *Memoirs*, 113-14.
[45] Ibid. 116.
[46] Shuler, 'Pastoral and Ecclesiastical Administration', 116, quoting Henry Thomas Carr.

very few words by Dr Eden on the behalfe of the Chapter, and in about four or five minnits he got into his coach and drove to the church, went into the Galilee and there put on his robes, and at the pillar facing the north door of the Abbey, Sir John Dolben, then sub-dean, complimented the bishop in the name of the body, to which he returned an answer: then went up into the quire and proceeded to the communion table where he made a short prayer, and from thence went up into the throne and heard evening service and an anthem; and from the church he went to the castle, and several gentlemen and clergy waited on him there and drank a glass of wine.[47]

After his arrival in Durham, with its attendant official dinners and social functions, Butler began the primary visitation of his new diocese. The visitation involved a gruelling schedule of travelling over the counties of Durham and Northumberland with occasional periods of rest. Starting in Newcastle on 17 July he travelled as far north as Berwick, visiting the deaneries of Corbridge, Bamburgh, Alnwick, and Morpeth, before returning to Durham on 27 July for a rest.[48] His visitation of the Durham archdeaconry was more leisurely, based on just two centres. The deaneries of Easington and Chester-le-Street were summoned to Durham on 30 July, and the visitation of the deaneries of Stockton and Darlington was held at Stockton on 27 August. Butler then returned to Auckland Castle but was back in Newcastle on 5 September to lay the foundation stone of the new infirmary.[49]

Butler had moved to Durham hoping to be able to appoint men of quality to the positions in his gift. As bishop he had the patronage of forty-two livings, twelve coveted prebendal stalls, and the two archdeaconries of Durham and Northumberland. His brief tenure of the see, however, prevented him from acting as patron in more than four of these. In addition Butler appointed as his domestic chaplain Nathaniel Forster, an agreeably scholarly companion who soon became devoted to the bishop.[50]

---

[47] Diary of Thomas Gyll, in *Six North Country Diaries*, Surtees Society Publications 118 (Durham, 1910), 187-8.

[48] Shuler, 'Pastoral and Ecclesiastical Administration', 118; University of Durham, Department of Palaeography and Diplomatic, Durham Diocesan Records (DDR), vol. clxvii, esp. fo. 18^r.   [49] Shuler, 'Pastoral and Ecclesiastical Administration', 118.

[50] Forster (1718-57), Fellow of Corpus Christi College, Oxford, was a classical and biblical scholar. After Butler's death he was taken up by Archbishop Herring and became

One of the prebendaries of Durham was Butler's old friend Martin Benson, the bishop of Gloucester, who kept his residence regularly and was able to act as episcopal surrogate for both Butler and his predecessor Chandler. In this capacity Benson officiated at the necessary ordinations before Butler's arrival in Durham.[51] Butler himself conducted the ordination of two deacons and seven priests in September 1751, as well as confirming throughout the diocese.[52]

The middle of the eighteenth century saw the Church in the diocese of Durham under severe pressure. Decaying buildings, especially in Northumberland, and significant population changes demanded a level of flexibility of response which it proved very difficult to provide.[53] Wesley's activity in Durham and Northumberland between 1742 and 1753 increased the pressure on the established Church and its leaders; pressures which led the long-serving and exemplary archdeacon of Northumberland, Thomas Sharp, to report on the 'visible decay of religion' in his archdeaconry by 1752.[54] It was this sense of decay and a growth in scepticism about the claims of the Christian religion which had fuelled much of Butler's preaching over the previous decade and was the context for his primary visitation charge of 1751, one of the most significant pastoral documents written by a member of the eighteenth-century episcopate.

The Durham *Charge*, on which Butler worked during the weeks before his journey north, is often read as a homily on the importance of external forms of religion. It was a too literal reading of this kind which gave Butler's opponents the opportunity of accusing him of papist leanings.[55] While Butler speaks a good

an unsuccessful vicar of Rochdale. A few months before his own death he was appointed to Butler's former post as preacher at the Rolls Chapel. Forster's mother was the niece of Matthew Tindal, Butler's deist protagonist. *DNB*, art. 'Nathaniel Forster', by Thompson Cooper.

[51] Shuler, 'Pastoral and Ecclesiastical Administration', 421; for Butler and Benson in Durham see *Letters of Spencer Cowper, Dean of Durham 1746-74* (London, 1956), 142, Cowper to Earl Cowper, Durham (13 Sept. 1751).
[52] Shuler, 'Pastoral and Ecclesiastical Administration', 421; DDR, subscription book, fo. 259.
[53] Shuler, 'Pastoral and Ecclesiastical Administration', 464, 470.
[54] Ibid. 204.
[55] The attack on Butler started in 1752 with the anonymous publication of *A Serious Inquiry into the Use and Importance of External Religion* by Francis Blackburne, archdeacon of

deal about the external structure of religion, from the maintenance of church buildings to the importance of family prayers and grace at meals, it is, for him, impossible to draw a clear distinction between external and internal religious devotion and practice. He clearly warns his clergy about the dangers of an intrusive piety: 'Indeed all *affectation* of talking piously is quite nauseous and though there be nothing of this, yet men will easily be disgusted at the too great frequency or length of these occasional admonitions' (*C.* 20).

The Butler of the 1751 *Charge* is the Butler of the confrontation with Wesley, wary of religious enthusiasm, reticent in his own articulation of the Christian faith, which is not a matter for common conversation,[56] aware of the part played by external forms in generating a settled and confident faith. It is not that he doubts the truth of what he preaches but that he is acutely aware of the risks involved in communicating a religion, the evidence for which 'is complex and various' (*C.* 5), to an audience with the alarming ability to misinterpret the message, to get the wrong end of the stick. This concern lies behind his practical suggestions about handling religious subjects when they arise in general conversation and his conviction that sermons are inappropriate vehicles for open theological speculation: it is 'improper ... at a time of devotion' for people 'to hear religion treated of as what many deny and which has much to be said against it as well as for it' (*C.* 7).

Butler's task in the *Charge* is to encourage his clergy to make constructive use of the opportunities available to them to press the claims of the Christian religion on a sceptical, or simply apathetic, society. He is aware of the difficulty of the task, as he states at the beginning of the *Charge*:

It is impossible for me, my brethren, upon our first meeting of this kind, to forbear lamenting with you the general decay of religion in this nation; which is now observed by every one, and has been for some time the complaint of all serious persons. (*C.* 1)

Cleveland and a leading campaigner for the abolition of subscription to the Thirty-Nine Articles. Blackburne's attack was published under his name in 1767 and, together with another criticism of Butler in the same year, prompted Secker to write in his former colleague's defence. There is a detailed discussion of the controversy in Bartlett, *Memoirs*, 143 ff.

[56] *C.* 5; cf. *A.* 2. 7. 44.

This is not, however, a situation in which to despair. Butler stresses the absurdity of taking 'the supposed doubtfulness of religion for the same thing as proof of its falsehood' (*C.* 4). The author of the *Analogy* is well equipped to expose the slipshod thinking of those who demand knock-down proofs of religious truth. It is in conscientious pastoral practice, using external forms as a way of making people aware of the power of religion in their lives, that the clergy should be engaged. This will be difficult. Some parishes are very large, many people will resist the kind of serious conversation in which Butler wishes his clergy to engage them, many parents will not be interested in their children's welfare (*C.* 22). The task is sufficiently important, though, to be persevered with:

If others deal uncharitably with us, we must deal impartially with ourselves, as in a matter of conscience, in determining what good is in our power to do: and not let indolence keep us from setting about what really is in our power; nor any heat of temper create obstacles in the prosecution of it, or render insuperable such as we find, when perhaps gentleness and patience would prevent or overcome them ... By being faithful in the discharge of this our trust ... we shall do our part towards reviving a practical sense of religion amongst the people committed to our care. (*C.* 22, 24)

As in Bristol Butler was concerned with the social and charitable aspects of Christian witness. His interest in charity schools stood out among eighteenth-century bishops of Durham and he maintained his support of the hospital movement.[57] On 5 September 1751 he laid the foundation stone of the new infirmary in Newcastle. His involvement with the infirmary was not merely nominal and he took a particular interest in its establishment, although the initial moves had been made before he became bishop of Durham. The sermon which he had preached before the governors of the London Hospital in 1748 was reprinted in Newcastle together with a covering letter from Butler to Archdeacon Sharp, as a way of raising interest and money for the infirmary. In his prefatory letter Butler stressed the civil as well as the moral and religious advantages of the

---

[57] For Butler and charity schools see J. C. Tyson, 'The Church and School Education', in W. S. F. Pickering (ed.), *A Social History of the Diocese of Newcastle* (Stocksfield, 1981), 271.

establishment of an infirmary. More good could be done by such associations than by individuals, the practice of medicine and surgery was improved to the general benefit, and the establishment of centres of excellence and authority, open to all, would 'prevent all Counterfeits'.[58]

Nor was Butler's concern for the Newcastle Infirmary simply hortatory. In the initial list of subscribers his was the most generous gift, £100 a year for five years and then £20 a year for life.[59] His death in the following year did not substantially diminish his generosity as the infirmary was left £500 in his will. It would be no exaggeration to say that his concern for the Newcastle Infirmary, of which he was Grand Visitor, was the most lasting practical legacy to his new diocese.[60]

Butler continued the tradition of episcopal hospitality and generosity which he had established at Bristol. He kept open house at Durham or Auckland Castle for three days a week. He was always happy to retire to Auckland Castle, where the extensive park gave him some escape from the rigours of his work, 'my Park being a favourite article with me as, before I had one, my garden was'.[61] His time there saw the addition of the South Park and the rebuilding of the garden wall; 'Butler's Steps' still survive in the Castle. There is a charming tradition, too, that Butler, when tired, sat in the chapel at Auckland Castle, listening to the organ being played by his secretary.[62] His generosity to those in need became legendary also, with much of his greatly increased income—Durham was the second wealthiest see in the Church of England—being spent on worthy causes. It was not in his nature to be profligate, however, and generosity with his own income went hand in hand with a firm and shrewd oversight of diocesan property.

---

[58] Joseph Butler, *A Sermon Preached before His Grace, Charles Duke of Richmond . . . and the Governors of the London Infirmary . . .* (Newcastle upon Tyne, 1751), p. iv.
[59] Ibid. 12.
[60] W. E. Hume, *The Infirmary, Newcastle upon Tyne 1751-1951: A Brief Sketch* (Newcastle upon Tyne, 1951), 5, 14; Butler's will. Butler was also a generous subscriber to the County Hospital in Durham; see Bartlett, *Memoirs*, 194.
[61] Shuler, 'Pastoral and Ecclesiastical Administration', 119, Butler to Gregory Bowes, early 1752.
[62] H. C. G. Moule, *Auckland Castle: A Popular History and Description* (London, 1918), 28-9.

VII

I am much obliged to you for yr kind disposal of this see in yr own mind, but I believe, without flattering our new Spiritual Sovereign, one has it, who will in all likelyhood do great good if he continues in it any time.[63]

The dean of Durham's satisfaction at Butler's appointment as bishop was shared by many clergy and laity in the diocese. These hopes were not to be fulfilled. Only four months after his arrival in Durham Butler returned to London, to his house in Hampstead, for the new session of Parliament, which began on 14 November 1751.[64] There is no evidence that he ever returned to Durham. He sat in the Lords on only eight occasions during the session, which ended on 26 March 1752—an indication of his declining health.[65] On 25 April he wrote a codicil to his will and by the end of May his health was causing sufficient concern to his doctors for a visit to Bath to be recommended. He arrived there on 3 June, staying two nights at Cuddesdon with Secker on the way.[66] Although Secker's impression was that Butler was not alarmed by his condition, he deteriorated rapidly. Benson reported to Secker on 12 June that Butler's case was hopeless.[67] He died on 16 June, attended by his chaplain, Nathaniel Forster.

Butler's last days were a harrowing time for his friends. Benson interrupted his diocesan duties to visit Butler at least once, and he and the fretful and exhausted Forster kept Secker in constant touch with Butler's progress, detailing the treatment prescribed, agonizing over the adequacy of the medical attention, coping with those of Butler's relatives who were present, and making tentative arrangements for the funeral.[68] Benson found his leave-taking exceptionally painful and it was left to Forster to announce tersely to Secker, 'This morning about eleven o'clock my best of Friends exchang'd this life for a far better.'[69]

---

[63] *Letters of Spencer Cowper*, 130, Cowper to Earl Cowper, Durham (21 Sept. 1750).
[64] *LJ* xxvii. 606.
[65] *LJ* xxvii. 689, for Butler's last appearance, 17 Mar. 1752.
[66] Secker, *Autobiography*, 30.
[67] LPL, MS 1373, fos. 5-7, Benson to Secker, Bath (12 June 1752).
[68] LPL, MS 1373, fos. 10-25, Forster to Secker, Bath (4-21 June 1752).
[69] LPL, MS 1373, fos. 18-19, Forster to Secker, Bath (16 June 1752).

Butler's body was taken to Bristol, where, as arranged by Benson and Forster, it was buried with simple but solemn ceremony in the chancel of the cathedral on the afternoon of 20 June. The hearse was followed by only two coaches and six, preceded by servants in livery on horseback. The pall bearers were senior Bristol clergy with whom Butler had worked, followed by Forster and the rest of Butler's household in the same order in which they used to attend him to the cathedral at Durham.[70]

The news of Butler's death did not reach Durham until three days after the funeral, although it had been known that he was beyond recovery. At 'about 6 the great bell in the Abbey tolled a short space on account of the bishop's death'.[71]

Butler's nephew Joseph, who was ordained by his uncle in St Paul's Cathedral in 1741, was once moved to expostulate, 'I think, my lord, it is a misfortune to be related to you.'[72] Butler's correctness and incorruptibility in the frenetic market-place of clerical appointments set him apart from many of his colleagues, although it was sufficiently common to be appreciated by the many people who took their religion seriously. Like many reticent people, Butler went through life on his own terms, refusing to compromise in his intellectual work, his style of life, or his public role with the rigorous standards which he had set himself and which had been nurtured in the company of Benson, Secker, and other members of the Talbot circle in the 1720s. Seriousness of purpose was by no means absent in the English Church of the mid-eighteenth century and Butler exemplified it to a degree. Spooner was to write of him that he was apart from his own time in his life and modes of thinking and was therefore misunderstood by his contemporaries.[73] Misunderstanding there certainly was. Butler was a subtle writer, not given to the propagation of simple slogans or maxims; he was a complex person, unwilling to reveal himself to others. The rumour that he had died a papist is a striking example of malice combining with genuine misunderstanding to create a ludicrous assertion,

---

[70] LPL, MS 1373, fo. 24ʳ, Forster to Secker, Bath (21 June 1752).
[71] Gyll, 'Diary', 191.
[72] C. J. Abbey, *The English Church and Its Bishops 1700–1800* (London, 1887), i. 60.
[73] W. A. Spooner, *Bishop Butler* (London, 1901), 48.

but one which needed authoritative crushing. Indeed, one wonders whether any of his contemporaries ever fully had the measure of Butler. Some years later Secker, who had known him as well as most, confided to his autobiography:

He was a serious, & in Matters of Money a generous Man: but in other respects too selfish; expecting every one to befriend & serve Him; but seldom thinking himself qualified or obliged to serve others. And that selfish Disregard increased in him greatly from his time of frequenting the Court. This Coldness of his produced a considerable Degree of it in me also towards Him.[74]

It was this refusal to do what was expected that makes Butler interesting for us today—he was *sui generis*. Yet it may also add weight to Spooner's judgement, that Butler died as he had lived, 'very much alone, alone with his own thoughts and God'.[75]

---

[74] Secker, *Autobiography*, 22.
[75] Spooner, *Bishop Butler*, 49.

4
Bishop Butler and the *Zeitgeist*: Butler and the Development of Christian Moral Philosophy in Victorian Britain

JANE GARNETT

In the introduction to a new edition of Butler's *Analogy and Two Dissertations* published in 1851, the Revd Albert Barnes asserted that 'Butler's *Analogy* stands complete ... a collection of *principles* to be carried into every region of morals and theology, as a standard of all other views of truth.'[1] The *Guardian* in December 1853 produced a similarly absolute statement: 'It is impossible to overrate either the value of his writings, or the interest of his character, standing as he does, like Melchizedec, without progenitor or descendants, in the midst of an infidel age.'[2] Yet in 1873, in a letter to James Knowles, Gladstone could exclaim, 'And oh! that this age knew the treasure it possesses in him, and neglects!'[3] How much of a change in Butler's status did Gladstone's comment in fact represent, and what sort of transition was it? This essay addresses the pattern of Butler's reputation over the second half of the nineteenth century, the changing context in which his works were read, and the implications which this had for his continuing influence. It suggests that to focus too much on the rhetoric of praise and dispraise which attached itself to Butler in the mid-century is to neglect significant ways in which his works continued to form a central pivot of debate. Within the context of intellectual developments

---

I am grateful to Christopher Cunliffe, Colin Matthew, and Gervase Rosser for their helpful comments on an earlier draft of this essay.

[1] *Butler's Analogy and Two Dissertations: A New Edition with an Introductory Essay*, ed. A. Barnes (London, 1851), 2.
[2] *Guardian*, 8 (7 Dec. 1853), 831.
[3] Gladstone to James Knowles (9 Nov. 1873), printed in *Spectator* (13 Dec. 1873), cited by R. W. Church, 'Bishop Butler', in *Pascal and Other Sermons* (London, 1895), 25.

in the latter part of the century, many perceived a continuing and even enhanced relevance in Butler's mode of integration of natural and moral philosophy. Butler's positive recognition, in all spheres of philosophical enquiry, of the fragmentary nature of human perception, and his emphasis on the value of reasoning from probability, were seen at this time to have fresh and creative significance.

The context of Gladstone's comment in 1873 was a very specific one: the mid-century debate on reform of the syllabus in Oxford. This debate had resulted—to Gladstone's distress—in the demotion of Butler's works from the privileged status which they had enjoyed since the early 1830s of being set as the central modern authority alongside the classical authors for the Greats course.[4] For participants in this debate, the rise and fall of the status of Butler's works as *the* modern textbooks in Oxford seemed symbolic. Symbolic the shift of emphasis had certainly become, but a misleadingly representative colouring can too easily be given to this. The Oxford debate itself cut across wider intellectual issues, and the particular view of Butler held by the 'liberal' reformers in Oxford should not be taken as normative. The fact that those recent works which have taken sustained account of Butler in the nineteenth century have focused primarily on the pre-1860s period has tended to reinforce the implication that Butler's fall out of fashion at that point was both general and lasting, and indeed was the natural result of new intellectual challenges. E. C. Mossner's general account of

---

[4] From 1831, the *Oxford University Calendar* specified that answers for Literae Humaniores 'should be illustrated, if need be, from modern authors', although it seems that this may have been codifying pre-existing practice. See *Oxford University Statutes*, 2 vols. (Oxford, 1851), ii. 166, Statute of 1830, which defined humane literature as including the science of morals and politics, '*still* allowing them occasionally, as may seem expedient, to be illustrated by the writings of the moderns' (my emphasis). R. D. Hampden was examiner in Greats from 1829 to 1832, and claimed to have been 'mainly instrumental in introducing the works of Bishop Butler into the course of reading for Academical Honours'. See R. D. Hampden, *The Scholastic Philosophy Considered in its Relation to Christian Theology in a Course of Lectures*, 3rd edn. (London, 1848), p. liii n. Certainly at this period Butler's works increasingly became the authoritative modern texts. Mark Pattison claimed that when he was an examiner (which he was from Easter Term 1848 to Michaelmas 1849; from Michaelmas 1853 to Easter 1854; and again in Michaelmas 1870 and Trinity 1871), he removed Butler from the list of books to be taken up. M. Pattison, *Memoirs* (London, 1885), 135. Montagu Burrows's statement that he was the last to take up Butler in the Schools is implausible (he matriculated in 1853), although it reflects a perception of Butler's declining popularity at that point. *Autobiography of Montagu Burrows*, ed. S. M. Burrows (London, 1908), 200–1.

Butler, written in 1936, did give a broad bibliographical survey of the second half of the century, but put forward little detailed analysis. The thrust of his argument was that the demotion of Butler's works in Oxford in the 1860s had the practical effect of discouraging their study thereafter, and he assumed that Butler's arguments were prima facie insufficient to meet 'the devastating implications of recent science'.[5] Hamish Swanston's analysis of Anglican theological renewal in the mid-nineteenth century, which focuses in detail on the differing interpretations of Butler by Hampden, Mansel, Maurice, and Jowett, goes no further chronologically than Jowett's rejection of Butler, only remarking in passing on Westcott's and Lightfoot's continued devotion to him.[6] Ieuan Ellis's study of *Essays and Reviews* (1860) is naturally confined to the immediate context of that debate. In projecting forward, however, he refers to 'alternatives to Butler' having been provided by Coleridge and the Mauricean school; this formulation implicitly reflects the one-sided view of Butler shaped by the Essayists. It neglects the very different but important emphasis which Coleridge and Maurice themselves placed on Butler, and the degree to which this affinity was picked up by those who acknowledged their debt to all three thinkers. This was especially true in Cambridge, where the revival of Butler in the 1830s was very much in the Coleridgean tradition, but also in Oxford at the same time, where R. W. Church read Butler seriously for his fellowship exam, alongside Coleridge and Maurice.[7] Boyd Hilton's recent discussion of Butler *inter alia* equally focuses on the early to middle part of the century, and relates the demise of Butler to the intellectual challenges of positivism, agnosticism, and evolutionism; the sweeping away of Butler and the increased emphasis on Plato are held to have contributed to the renewal of incarnationalism in Oxford. Hilton carries his account of Butler forward to address Gladstone's

[5] E. C. Mossner, *Bishop Butler and the Age of Reason* (New York, 1936), 205, 219.

[6] H. Swanston, *Ideas of Order: Anglicans and the Renewal of Theological Method in the Middle Years of the Nineteenth Century* (Assen, 1974), 215.

[7] I. Ellis, *Seven against Christ: A Study of 'Essays and Reviews'* (Leiden, 1980), 276. On Coleridge and Butler see E. C. Mossner, 'Coleridge and Bishop Butler', *Philosophical Review*, 45 (1936), 206-8. For Maurice, see below, pp. 72-3. For Church, see M. C. Church (ed.), *Life and Letters of Dean Church* (London, 1895), 17. See also S. Prickett, *Romanticism and Religion: The Tradition of Coleridge and Wordsworth in the Victorian Church* (Cambridge, 1976), for discussion of the influence of Coleridge and Butler on Maurice and the Tractarians.

edition of Butler's *Works* and the *Studies Subsidiary* to them (1896). Since his focus here is predominantly on Gladstone rather than on Butler, he portrays Gladstone's continuing preoccupation with Butler as an almost unique eccentricity. There was no place to distinguish between Gladstone's particular approach (parts of which were by then dated and did no service to Butler) and other interpretations of Butler in the 1890s.[8] J. D. Yule's observation—drawn on by Hilton—that by the 1880s Butler was merely regarded as a Christian 'classic' rather than as a philosopher of contemporary significance, is misleading.[9] There continued to be studies of Butler which simply accorded him the status of a classic,[10] but in general he was discussed increasingly critically both as a moral philosopher and as a defender of the intrinsic credibility of Christianity. Butler's role in the revival of moral philosophy from the 1870s in Oxford and elsewhere was complemented by a shift in the emphasis of Christian apologetic, and the demand for a firmer basis in moral theology, which his works could supply. J. B. Schneewind's study of Sidgwick has stressed Butler's importance in the development of Victorian moral philosophy, but is not concerned with the ways in which this related to the renewal of a philosophical basis for Christian apologetic in the later part of the century.[11] The development of Butler's role in this context is the chief focus of this essay.

It had been avowedly as a move towards establishing a more sophisticated and critical relationship between moral philosophy and Anglican apologetic that Hampden (the second holder of the Chair in Moral Philosophy which had only been revived in 1829) had originally promoted Butler's works to a place alongside Aristotle's *Ethics* in Oxford. Butler was explicitly com-

---

[8] B. Hilton, *The Age of Atonement: The Influence of Evangelicalism on Social and Economic Thought 1795–1865* (Oxford, 1988), 340 ff.

[9] Ibid. 171. The reference is to J. D. Yule, 'The Impact of Science on British Religious Thought in the Second Quarter of the Nineteenth Century', Ph.D. thesis (Cambridge, 1976), 165. Yule's emphasis is in fact slightly—but importantly—different. He argues specifically that by this period the *Analogy* was no longer seen as a work of contemporary significance for the *theological* student. However he cites no evidence for this statement.

[10] e.g. *Butler's Analogy of Religion, with a Life, Introduction, Epitome and Notes*, ed. F. A. Malleson (London, 1878), as part of Ward and Lock's Christian Knowledge Series; an edition of the *Analogy* published with an introduction by Henry Morley as the twelfth in Morley's Universal Library (London, 1884).

[11] J. B. Schneewind, *Sidgwick's Ethics and Victorian Moral Philosophy* (Oxford, 1977).

mended as a Christian moral philosopher, in contradistinction to Paley, who, Hampden argued, had been approved simply because of his fundamental piety, rather than because of his merits as an ethical theorist.[12] But by the 1840s, when Stanley and Jowett first concertedly campaigned to demote Butler's works, their place in the syllabus had become identified by reforming opinion with Tractarianism, and specifically with the increasing intransigence of the Tractarian rump with regard to academic study at Oxford. Jowett, Stanley, and Pattison came to identify the whole of Butler's approach with the particular aspects of his evidential argument and the particular uses of it to which they objected. Mark Pattison polemically singled out Frederick Oakeley's Tractarian reading of Butler into Aristotle as a prime example of the uncritical approach to moral philosophy in Oxford.[13] Butler was equated by Jowett with Paley—ironically, in view of Hampden's reasons for promoting Butler, and of the fact that Butler's renewed popularity in general had much to do with a reaction against Paley's utilitarianism.[14] The form in which Butler's works had been prescribed had tended increasingly to give him precisely the ahistorical apologetic role characterized approvingly by the *Guardian* and the Revd Albert Barnes. Frank Turner has discussed the degree to which Aristotle suffered during the period in which the *Ethics* were studied uncritically in the light of Butler.[15] In some ways Butler suffered comparably. He became implicitly associated with a particular intellectual and political approach in Oxford, and when this

[12] R. D. Hampden, *A Course of Lectures Introductory to the Study of Moral Philosophy, Delivered in the University of Oxford in Lent Term, 1835* (London, 1835), 15. Compare W. Mills, *Lecture on the Theory of Moral Obligation; being the First of a Course of Lectures Delivered before the University of Oxford, Lent Term MDCCCXXX* (Oxford, 1830). Mills was the first holder of the revived professorship. He too was critical of Paley's conception of moral philosophy (p. 11). It is perhaps significant that he regarded Butler's Discourses on Human Nature as too well known to need mentioning, and discussed Butler in relation to Plato and the Cambridge Platonists as well as to Aristotle (p. 37).
[13] M. Pattison, 'Oxford Studies', in *Oxford Essays* (Oxford, 1855), 288; F. Oakeley, *Remarks upon Aristotelian and Platonic Ethics as a Branch of the Studies Pursued in the University of Oxford* (Oxford, 1837); F. M. Turner, *The Greek Heritage in Victorian Britain* (New Haven, Conn., 1981), 332-5, for discussion of this.
[14] C. D. Cashdollar, *The Transformation of Theology 1830-1890; Positivism and Protestant Thought in Britain and America* (Princeton, NJ, 1989), 379; for Cambridge, see M. M. Garland, *Cambridge before Darwin: The Ideal of a Liberal Education 1800-1860* (Cambridge, 1980), 57-63.
[15] Turner, *The Greek Heritage in Victorian Britain*, 326-40.

approach came under sustained attack, the status of his works was in turn assailed. Butler was seen by the liberals as the most obvious manifestation of an outmoded refuge of authority, and was condemned accordingly.[16] This identification represented the hardening of a polemic which obscured the variety and subtlety of the ways in which Butler's works had been read in the first half of the century, both within and outside Oxford, in evangelical and liberal as well as Tractarian circles.[17] The nature of analogical reasoning was itself controversial. Even amongst Tractarians, Newman and Keble notoriously developed very different interpretations of Butler's famous dictum 'Probability is the guide of life.'[18] Butler's argument on probability incorporated a fundamental debate about the nature of religious and moral understanding, and his works were thus open to continuing discussion at the centre of the development of this discourse.

Mansel's controversial Bampton Lectures of 1858 on 'The Limits of Religious Thought' raised this discourse to the forefront of debate, and catalysed conflicting approaches to Butler. The question whether Mansel had legitimately drawn on Butler, and, if so, to what effect, was widely seen as central.[19] Mansel's own standpoint reinforced the attack on Butler within Oxford,

---

[16] See also Ellis, *Seven against Christ*, 274; *Dear Miss Nightingale: A Selection of Benjamin Jowett's Letters to Florence Nightingale 1860–1893*, ed. V. Quinn and J. Prest (Oxford, 1987), 70, for Jowett's comment (Aug. 1865) on the widening of studies from the very narrow basis of authority (Butler and Aristotle's *Ethics*) prevalent when he was an undergraduate.

[17] By Evangelicals, Butler was commonly used to support a moderate Calvinism. See *The Autobiography of the Rev. William Jay*, ed. G. Redford and J. A. James, 2nd edn. (London, 1855), 166–8. I am grateful to John Walsh for drawing my attention to this. In a lecture to the YMCA in 1863, A. S. Farrar stressed the particular importance of Butler for Evangelicals in reinforcing the philosophical evidences for Christianity: 'In the present day, among evangelical Christians, there is no lack of the preaching of the doctrines, but there is a special need, in the midst of a great deal of very active and dangerous speculation, that Christian congregations should be also educated in the evidences of the faith, and especially in the philosophical as distinct from the historical evidences—the proof that Christianity is credible, as well as true.' A. S. Farrar, 'Bishop Butler and the Religious Features of His Times', *Lectures Delivered before the Y.M.C.A. in Exeter Hall* (London, 1863), 325–62, at 354–5.

[18] *The Letters and Diaries of John Henry Newman*, ed. C. S. Dessain *et al.* (London, 1964–), xv. 456; Newman to Edward Healy Thompson (7 Oct. 1853); xxi. 129; Newman to Henry Coleridge (24 June 1854).

[19] As much as, if not more than, Mansel's use of Kant, which has attracted more recent attention. See B. Lightman, *The Origins of Agnosticism: Victorian Unbelief and the Limits of Knowledge* (Baltimore, 1987), esp. ch. 2.

and provided some of the momentum behind *Essays and Reviews* (1860). At the same time the lectures provoked a fierce reaction, most notably from F. D. Maurice, which was to underpin the renewal of a positive interpretation of Butler. Mansel drew on his own reading of Butler and of Kant, mediated through Sir William Hamilton, to argue for the limitation of the human mind receiving revelation, and for the proposition that God was wholly transcendent and wholly other. His argument for the unknowability of God led him to assert that 'in Religion also, [God] has given us truths which are designed to be regulative, rather than speculative; intended, not to satisfy our reason, but to guide our practice'.[20] His intention was to provide a counterblast both to positivism and to rationalist empiricism (especially to Mill's *Logic*, which was gaining a dominant position at Oxford), and also to biblical criticism; in forging it he represented one aspect of the growing High Church suspicion of rationalistic reasoning.[21] In fact his approach went contrary to the central preoccupations of both Butler and Kant, who had been attempting not to sunder reason and faith, but to draw the two closer together.[22] Just as Mansel drew on the negative aspects of Kant, he stressed the negative aspects of Butler.[23] To Mansel as to Pusey the circumstances in which Anglicanism seemed under threat made any critical approach to Scripture appear dangerous, and the reassertion of the authority of scriptural revelation to be the only safe course. Hence Pusey's resistance to the development of modern subjects within the Oxford syllabus; hence Mansel's protection of revelation from reason, with the alleged support of Butler; and hence the continued identification for some of Butler with the forces of reaction. Leslie Stephen was later able to identify Butler, Newman, and Mansel as equally

---

[20] H. L. Mansel, *The Limits of Religious Thought Examined in Eight Lectures* (Oxford, 1858), 143.
[21] For discussion of this see Lightman, *The Origins of Agnosticism* 61-4, and ch. 2, *passim*.
[22] Even Rowland Williams felt that Mansel's argument was 'surely a strange parody of Butler'. R. Williams, 'Bunsen's Biblical Researches', *Essays and Reviews* (1860), 50-93, at 67.
[23] Cf. René Wellek's comment that it was very characteristic of early 19th-cent. English Kantians to stress the negative side of Kant, that is, his role in combating rationalistic metaphysics. R. Wellek, *Immanuel Kant in England 1793-1838* (Princeton, NJ, 1931), 51.

inclined to denounce the role of reason in matters of religion.[24] Newman, however, whilst recognizing Mansel's apparent debt to his own Anglican writings, was none the less very concerned to distinguish his approach from Mansel's, in order to vindicate his fundamental conviction of the possibility of knowing God: 'To assert, with the School of Sir W.H. [Hamilton] and Mansel, that nothing is known because nothing is known luminously and exactly, seems to me saying that we do not see the stars because we cannot tell the number, size, or distance from each other.'[25] Newman's reading of Butler to argue that religious belief does not in fact present different epistemological problems from those posed by the rest of human experience was to find parallels. But in Oxford in the 1860s in some quarters Butler continued to suffer by association with Mansel, and to many Mill's influence 'swept all before it'. Edward Talbot recalled his undergraduate days in Oxford in the 1860s, and commented that Mansel's 'cold paradoxes' and his partisan Toryism made him unattractive. Yet there were undergraduates like himself who were disturbed at not being able to reconcile Mill's account of conscience with their Christian beliefs, and could find at that point no alternative philosophical position which could underpin and reinforce their religion.[26]

Mansel's lectures provided for the crystallization of a range of at times contradictory criticisms of Butler. The criticisms mostly focused on the *Analogy*, and few of them were unqualified. The

[24] L. Stephen, 'An Agnostic's Apology' (first pub. *Fortnightly Review*, OS 25, NS 19 (1876), 840–60), in *An Agnostic's Apology and Other Essays* (London, 1893), 1–41, esp. 8–9, 10–13, 33–5.
[25] Newman, *Letters and Diaries*, xix. 335: letter from Newman to Charles Meynell (9 May 1860); cf. ibid. xix. 256: letter from Newman to Meynell (20 Dec. 1859).
[26] E. Talbot, *Memories of Early Life* (London, 1924), 42–5. Compare, however, W. Hayter, *Spooner: A Biography* (London, 1977), 43. Spooner read for Greats between 1864 and 1866. For Ethics he read Butler's *Fifteen Sermons*, 'which we knew well, Mackintosh, Mill's *Utilitarianism*, and a few of the earlier English moralists'. Mr C. Appleton's evidence given before the House of Lords Select Committee on University Tests in 1870–1 stressed the role of Mill's *Logic*, although also stated that he was read in a much more critical spirit than had formerly been the case. *Parliamentary Papers* (1871), ix, Q. 516, 517. Jowett commented that philosophy as a whole was beginning to be studied more historically, and contrasted this development favourably with the practice prevalent in his youth of examining books narrowly as textbooks (Q. 3167–9). It was in the role of textbooks that Butler's works (in particular the *Analogy*) were deemed less fashionable. Compare *Christian Observer*, 71 (1871), 681, in which the hope was expressed that the evidence given by the Oxford witnesses to the Select Committee was not the sign of a general change of feeling towards Butler. See also below, n. 77.

Unitarian James Martineau (himself a great admirer of Butler's ethics) introduced his review of Mansel by expatiating on the flaws of Butler's argument in the *Analogy*, seeing that Mansel's use of Butler could help to unsettle the very bases of belief which his lectures were written to support, and regarding the role of Butler in this as fundamental. On the one hand Martineau felt that theologians greatly overrated the power of 'mere critical refutation' directed against doubt, and that the problem with Butler's approach was that he failed to produce more than a soulless, uninspirational intellectual argument; on the other he questioned the soundness of the argument itself, especially its *tu quoque* logic.[27] Sara Hennell, whose essay on *The Scepticism of Butler's Analogy* was in part derived from Martineau, also dwelt on the lack of provision in Butler 'for ever kindling up again the genial warmth of cordial faith'. On the other hand she formulated what was to become a common line of attack: that the nature of Butler's argument was *ad homines* (i.e. against eighteenth-century deists), which by definition rendered it inadequate in the mid-nineteenth century. She also, as Martineau and Walter Bagehot had done, felt that Butler's argument by analogy was unsatisfactory, in that it assumed that the same difficulties were presented by revelation as occurred in nature.[28] As a reviewer argued, this particular criticism could be held to rest on a misinterpretation of analogy to mean identity.[29] More importantly the criticism of Butler rested on what was hardly an uncontroversial view of the proper function of revelation. For Newman, who had drawn on Butler in finding the primary authentication of revelation in the conscience, 'Revelation was not given us to satisfy doubt but to make us better men; and it is as we become better men, that it becomes light and peace to our souls; even though to the end of our lives we shall find difficulties both in it and in the world around us.'[30] Hennell's

[27] [J. Martineau], review of Mansel's Bampton Lectures, *National Review*, 8 (1859), 209–16, at 210–12.
[28] S. Hennell, *Essay on the Sceptical Tendency of Butler's 'Analogy'* (London, 1859), 5, 20; [W. Bagehot] in *Prospective Review*, 10 (1854), 559. Hennell drew on Martineau's earlier critique of Butler in his *Inconsistency of the Scheme of Vicarious Redemption* (London, 1839). See also G. Smith, *Rational Religion, and the Rationalistic Objections of the Bampton Lectures for 1858* (London, 1861), 76.
[29] *British Quarterly Review*, 38 (1863), 116.
[30] J. H. Newman, *Parochial Sermons*, 2 vols. (London, 1834), i. 264 (Sermon 18), cited by R. W. Church, 'The "Pensées" of Blaise Pascal', in *Pascal and Other Sermons*, 22; W. E.

negative interpretation of Butler's argument on probability was echoed in Baden Powell's essay in *Essays and Reviews*, in which he criticized 'orthodox writings' for making distinctions between what was and what was not open to critical scrutiny.[31] The same arguments were rehearsed by Goldwin Smith in a rather confused series of interventions into debate with Mansel. Smith oscillated between criticizing Mansel's use of Butler (and by extension criticizing Butler's status at Oxford), and attacking Butler's arguments themselves, ending up by doing scant justice to either. One of his particular concerns was with the relationship between an understanding of human and divine morality, and the failure of Mansel to provide for sufficient connection between the two to maintain a basis for religion or morality at all.[32] This was a key argument which was pressed from different perspectives, and most forcefully in fact by those who tried to rescue Butler from Mansel's interpretation.

It was F. D. Maurice's attack on Mansel which helped to reinvigorate a more rounded and affirmative approach to Butler. Maurice's *What is Revelation?* (1859) was powered by the passionate conviction which supported all his teaching—that men have a capacity to perceive the spiritual and the real. His understanding of revelation was not as a series of propositions, but as an unveiling of God to the conscience and the heart. He stressed that, far from being content with lack of knowledge, Butler was seeking for the fixed and certain. It followed for Maurice that Oxford could not cultivate the true spirit of Butler if Mansel's interpretation of him was allowed to stand. The development of Maurice's argument was confused, but his fundamental revulsion from Mansel's position was widely compelling.[33] This was particularly important in relation to the moral

---

Gladstone, *Studies Subsidiary to the Works of Bishop Butler* (Oxford, 1896), 26–7; *The Works of Bishop Butler*, ed. J. H. Bernard, 2 vols. (London, 1900), vol. i, p. xxiii; H. S. Holland, *The Optimism of Butler's 'Analogy'* (London, 1908), 34–6.

[31] B. Powell, 'On the Study of the Evidences of Christianity', *Essays and Reviews*, 94–144, at 98. Cf. Powell's earlier debts to Butler; see P. Corsi, *Science and Religion; Baden Powell and the Anglican Debate, 1800–1860* (Cambridge, 1988), 76–7.

[32] Smith, *Rational Religion*, esp. 'Defence of the Remarks contained in the "Postscript" against Mr Mansel's letter to Mr Goldwin Smith', 24, 43–4, 73–6.

[33] F. D. Maurice, *What is Revelation? A Series of Sermons on the Epiphany; to which are Added Letters to a Student of Theology on the Bampton Lectures of Mr Mansel* (London, 1859), 168. Neither Maurice nor Mansel understood the other's position, and thus they argued

aspects of Butler's apologetic, of which Mansel made so little. Maurice developed his view of Butler in his treatise on the history of moral philosophy, published in 1862, in which he argued for the importance of seeing Butler's works *en bloc*, and not taking proof texts on which to build elaborate theories which ran against the essential spirit of the whole. He especially argued that Butler's letters to Clarke should be read before the *Analogy*, since this would make clearer the ground of Butler's preference for probable over demonstrative evidence.[34] He pointed sharply to the irony that Butler had been claimed as the champion of probabilities, in the sense 'which supposes that in physics every step is sure, and leads to knowledge, that in morals we are left to guesses'. In fact, 'To save us from guesses—to make our steps as sure and as firm in the one region as the other . . . was Butler's evident design.' Maurice had rested his whole commitment to Christian life on Butler's injunction to 'take up and rest satisfied with any evidence whatever, which is real'. As Newman had, Maurice drew a certitude out of Butler.[35] James Martineau wrote that Mansel's lectures had been justified if only for the fact that they had stimulated Maurice's riposte. He reiterated that what men know in this world may be relative, but is direct, and 'carries with it a certainty that depths will only deepen the knowledge at which we have arrived'.[36] We may walk now by twilight, but the light thrown is not intrinsically of a different kind from the full light of day.[37] A review of the whole

at cross purposes, employing different meanings of 'knowledge' and 'revelation'. See K. D. Freeman, *The Role of Reason in Religion: A Study of Henry Mansel* (The Hague, 1969), esp. 109-10.

[34] F. D. Maurice, *Moral Philosophy; or, A Treatise of Moral and Metaphysical Philosophy from the Fourteenth Century to the French Revolution, with a Glimpse into the Nineteenth Century* (London, 1862), 459-60, 463-4. Cf. J. H. Bernard, 'Butler', in *Encyclopaedia of Religion and Ethics*, ed. J. Hastings, 12 vols. and index vol. (Edinburgh, 1908-26), iii. 49, where Bernard discusses this correspondence and Butler's pondering therein on the abstract and metaphysical arguments for the Being of God with which he is not directly concerned in the *Analogy*.

[35] Maurice, *Moral Philosophy*, 465; *S.* 15. 12.

[36] [J. Martineau], 'Revelation: What it is not and what it is', *National Review*, 9 (1859), 200-29, at 202, 211-12. Martineau was to develop this line of argument in his refutation of Spencer's claim that we can only know *that* the Absolute exists, but cannot know *what* it is. J. Martineau, *A Study of Religion, Its Sources and Contents*, 2 vols. (Oxford, 1888), i. 131-2.

[37] Cf. Duke of Argyll, 'On the Limits of Human Knowledge Considered with Reference to the Unity of Nature', *Contemporary Review*, 38 (1880), 878-83.

debate in *Fraser's Magazine* in 1859[38] glossed Butler when drawing attention to the dangerous moral implications of Mansel's argument: 'The Love of Truth must be deadened by hearing the announcement that the *real truth* is unattainable.'[39] R. W. Dale in 1875 also drew on Butler's second sermon to counteract what he felt to be the corrosive effect of Mansel's approach on the very foundations of religious faith.[40] 'A Lancashire Manufacturer' was even moved to publish in 1876 a defence of Butler's *Analogy* which dissociated Butler from Mansel, and cited both J. S. Mill's critique of Mansel and Coleridge's *Aids to Reflection* in his support.[41] It was this broad strand of interpretation of Butler which was to maintain itself and indeed develop greater intellectual and practical force by the 1880s and 1890s.

Gladstone's edition of Butler's *Works*, and his *Studies Subsidiary to the Works of Bishop Butler* (1896), were the fruit of a lifetime's gestation, and his reading of Butler needs to be understood in this context. His defence of Butler from his principal critics, which was first published in 1895 and reprinted in a slightly amended form in his *Studies Subsidiary* in 1896, focused mainly on Bagehot, Hennell, Leslie Stephen, and Matthew Arnold, the critics of the 1850s-1870s.[42] Gladstone's contribution was thus largely shaped by a debate which was by the 1890s somewhat *passé*: his comments, deriving from work done half a century before, were not surprisingly somewhat removed from

---

[38] Signed FG: possibly Francis Garden, a theologian who greatly admired Maurice. See *The Wellesley Index to Victorian Periodicals 1824-1900*, ed. W. E. Houghton, 5 vols. (Toronto, 1966-89), ii. 446 (item 3909).

[39] *Fraser's Magazine*, 60 (1859), 574. Compare Sidgwick on Kant: 'Nor can I fall back on the Kantian resource of thinking myself under a moral necessity to regard all my duties *as if they were* commandments of God, although not entitled to hold speculatively that any such Supreme Being exists "as real".' *The Methods of Ethics* (London, 1874), 471, discussed in D. G. James, *Henry Sidgwick: Science and Faith in Victorian England* (Oxford, 1970), 38. See also Lightman, *The Origins of Agnosticism*, 51, 66, on Kant's understanding of reason.

[40] R. W. Dale, *The Atonement* (London, 1875), 365-6, citing Butler's second sermon.

[41] [H. Bleekley], *Butler's 'Analogy': A Lay Argument by a Lancashire Manufacturer* (London, 1876), 27.

[42] Gladstone, *Studies Subsidiary*, 21-76. Gladstone had written the essay on probability in 1845 and first published it in the *Nineteenth Century* in Mar. 1879. Earlier versions of other chapters had appeared in *Good Words*. In a letter to W. S. Jevons on 10 May 1874, Gladstone compared Jevons's epistemology to Butler's, and to convictions of his own, and mentioned his hope of 'doing something, before I die, to sustain and illustrate' them. *Correspondence on Church and Religion of W. E. Gladstone*, ed. D. Lathbury, 2 vols. (London, 1910), ii. 100-1.

the concerns of those several intellectual generations younger. He failed significantly to draw on more recent developments in philosophy, theology, or scientific thinking to illuminate the ways in which the range of possible responses to the mid-century critique had been extended. The more serious reviewers of Gladstone were at one in feeling that, despite the obvious depth of his commitment to Butler (the *London Quarterly Review* commented that there was 'even a sort of "revivalistic" intensity' about parts of Gladstone's writing[43]), Gladstone was not in fact doing Butler justice. It was an irony that, although Gladstone's concern was to stress the continued pertinence of Butler's mode of argument, his own defensive stance served somewhat to undercut this. The most excoriating review was by Richard Armstrong—author of the article on Butler in the 1876 edition of the *Encyclopaedia Britannica*—who argued how limited Gladstone's theological thinking was, how suspicious he showed himself of new approaches, how ignorant he seemed of biblical criticism and comparative theology, and how reluctant to engage with contemporary science. Armstrong further felt that even Gladstone's ethical standpoint was unfavourably affected by the 'ecclesiasticism in which he is immured'—that he conjoined the doctrinal and moral elements in Christianity, thus overthrowing the whole intuitive evidence of morals. Armstrong also criticized Gladstone's edition on the ground that he had failed to distinguish the elements of Butler which were still relevant from those which had necessarily been superseded.[44] Although he was more hard-hitting than other reviewers, the main points which Armstrong made were to be found elsewhere. The reviewer in *Mind* felt that Gladstone's 'way of looking at things often belongs to the past rather than to the present'.[45] In a generally more favourable account in the *London Quarterly Review*, the reviewer felt that Gladstone should have engaged with the critical aspects of Armstrong's *Encyclopaedia* article (especially his references to Kant and Hegel), and that his notes should have discussed Butler in the context of late nineteenth-century developments in philosophy, psychology, and natural

---

[43] Anon., 'Mr Gladstone's "Butler"', *London Quarterly Review*, 27 (1897), 248.
[44] R. A. Armstrong, 'Mr Gladstone and Bishop Butler', *New World*, 5 (1896), 692-705; cf. *Guardian*, 51 (1896), 176.
[45] *Mind*, NS 23 (1897), 423-4.

science. The reviewer noted that evolution had its place, but commented, reasonably enough, that in places Gladstone referred to the Bridgewater Treatises[46] without any hint that they might not vindicate his case in the light of subsequent developments in natural science.[47] It was true, as J. Hyslop Bell commented, that in places Gladstone's determination to defend Butler in almost all aspects involved him in curiously strained argument. In a discussion of Sara Hennell's critique, for example, Gladstone addressed the oft-quoted remark of Pitt's that the *Analogy* raised more difficulties than it solved—and he made extraordinarily heavy weather of disposing of it.[48] Lord Acton too picked up Gladstone on this point.[49] In many of these particular respects Gladstone's edition and *Studies* were marginal to debate in the 1890s, but not because Butler's works were no longer of interest: the reviews indicate a critical context of engagement with Butler. Nor was Gladstone's approach entirely out of the mainstream: some elements of his discussion, especially on the practical force of Butler's conception of the relationship between belief and action, concurred with important strands of the debate on Butler in the last two decades of the century.

Aspects of Butler's method of argument were felt by many to be given renewed force by developments in modern thought since the 1860s. Butler himself had been responsive to new fields of discovery, and, as Gladstone stressed, his Sermon upon the Ignorance of Man was far from acting as an encouragement to the limitation of investigation.[50] Instead Butler was building on the important observation that every extension of our knowlege

[46] The Bridgewater Treatises were eight treatises on natural theology published between 1833 and 1836 in fulfilment of a bequest of the earl of Bridgewater.

[47] *London Quarterly Review*, 27 (1897), 253-5. Cf. *Athenaeum*, 818 (1896), 142, on Gladstone's curious footnote to Butler's point about 6,000 years of biblical chronology (*The Works of Joseph Butler, D.C.L.*, ed. W. E. Gladstone, 2 vols. (Oxford, 1896), i. 333). The *Athenaeum* reviewer also commented (p. 141) that Gladstone was in many ways more scholastic than Butler. See also *Works*, i. 331. n. 1 on primitive religion, and compare Max Muller, 'The Dawn of Reason in Religion', in J. Samuelson (ed.), *The Civilization of Our Day* (London, 1896), 357-8, on Gladstone's citation of Butler in this context.

[48] J. Hyslop Bell, 'Gladstone on Butler', *Primitive Methodist Quarterly Review*, 19 (1897), 21-32, at 25, 28.

[49] Gladstone, *Studies Subsidiary*, 29-32; *Selections from the Correspondence of the First Lord Acton*, ed. J. N. Figgis and R. V. Laurence (London, 1917), 226-7: letter to Gladstone (12 Apr. 1896); cf. Bernard, 'Butler', 50; Church, 'Butler', 32.

[50] Gladstone, *Studies Subsidiary*, 104-5.

is an extension of our ignorance. Developments in scientific understanding had indeed reinforced this emphasis, and had served to undermine positivistic confidence. Where earlier commentators had made the analogy between Butler and Bacon,[51] later nineteenth-century interpreters tended to emphasize Butler's awareness of the limitations of strict induction. In his discussion of Butler published in 1893, Alexander Eagar commented: 'Many ... of the most important scientific questions cannot easily be inductively treated, since causes are not under our control; or cannot be treated inductively at all, since the causes are always present and are unvarying.' Hence the use of hypotheses, of which examples in physical science included the 'force of gravitation, the luminous ether, the wave-theory of light, the existence of atoms, the belief that heat is a mode of motion, the nebular theory, the doctrine of Evolution'.[52] Ironically, whilst many scientific agnostics had been influenced by Mansel's arguments about the knowledge of God, they failed to follow through the epistemological implications for scientific knowledge. They remained confident in a particular view of science, from which they tried to disengage theology (whilst retaining a form of religious impulse). The development of different methodological approaches to the physical and biological sciences presented challenges firstly to their scientific assumptions and hence to their particular arguments for agnosticism.[53] The assurance which Huxley expressed in a letter to Kingsley in 1860 did not rest on a ground which could easily be sustained. Responding to Kingsley's condolence on his son's death, Huxley exclaimed: 'It is no use to talk to me of analogies and probabilities. I know what I mean when I say I believe in the

[51] For discussion of such an analogy, see Yule, 'The Impact of Science', 29. This of course rested on a one-sided view of Bacon, which predominated in the early and mid-century. See R. Yeo, 'An Idol of the Market Place: Baconianism in Nineteenth Century Britain', *History of Science*, 23 (1985), 251-98; esp. his citation (p. 281) of Jevons's *Principles of Science* (London, 1872), which stated that great scientific discoveries had been achieved by the opposite method to Bacon's. Compare James Stephen's impatience with the commonplace comparison of Butler and Bacon, with its implied black and white contrast between a priori and inductive reasoning. J. Stephen, *Horae sabbaticae*, 2nd ser. (London, 1892), 283-4. T. Case, *Realism in Morals: An Essay* (Oxford, 1877), represented a late flowering of such a simplistic understanding of Bacon and identification of Butler with him.
[52] A. Eagar, *Butler's 'Analogy' and Modern Thought* (London, 1893), 42-3.
[53] See Lightman, *The Origins of Agnosticism*, 62 and ch. 6, *passim*.

law of inverse squares, and I will not rest my hopes upon weaker convictions. I dare not if I would.'[54]

Huxley's desire for certainty notwithstanding, science itself was to become increasingly obviously reliant on probable argument. As David Knight has recently commented, Butler's illustration of the cumulative nature of argument by probability is pertinent to Darwin's method, where the weight of numerous individual cases carries conviction even though no single one would.[55] This was an analogy of method which scientists and philosophers were to draw on in the 1880s and 1890s. Robert Flint, successively Professor of Moral Philosophy at St Andrew's and of Divinity at Edinburgh, was strongly influenced by Butler's method and his stress on the cumulative force of arguments, in his pursuit of a secure apologetic which would refute positivism.[56] His colleague Henry Calderwood also recognized the degree to which developments in scientific method were bringing the logic respectively of science and religion closer together on the common basis of probability and belief.[57] Whilst specific arguments of Butler's for immortality or the chronology of the Old Testament could seem to be untenable, it became less possible to attack his overall approach and his practical methodology for dealing with conditions of uncertain knowledge. When John Tyndall took Butler as the foil for Lucretius in his *Belfast Address* (1874), he was in fact taking issue with the most discardable aspects of Butler. His treatment of Butler is not unambiguous: he distinguishes nuances in Butler's position to which he is sympathetic (but his discussion of which led his critics to accuse him of patronizing religion).[58] The *Address* is certainly not a vindication of a simple materialist position. As

---

[54] L. Huxley (ed.), *Life and Letters of Thomas Henry Huxley*, 2 vols. (London, 1900), i. 217–18.

[55] D. Knight, *The Age of Science* (Oxford, 1986), 38.

[56] R. Flint was Professor of Moral Philosophy from 1864 to 1876 (having defeated T. H. Green in competition for the post); Professor of Divinity from 1876 to 1903. His *Theism* (1876) reached its 11th edition by 1905, and 13th by 1929. See A. P. F. Sell, *The Philosophy of Religion 1875–1980* (London, 1988), 8.

[57] For discussion of Flint and Calderwood, see Cashdollar, *The Transformation of Theology*, 342–5. In 1861 Calderwood had produced a 2nd edition of his *The Philosophy of the Infinite* (1st edn., London, 1854), which responded to Mansel's Bampton Lectures by reiterating his conviction that man can and does have a positive notion of the Infinite.

[58] J. Tyndall, *Address Delivered before the British Association Assembled at Belfast* (London, 1874), 27–35, p. vi.

Tyndall had earlier affirmed: 'The problem of the connection of the body and soul is as insoluble in its modern form as it was in the pre-scientific ages.'[59] Yet Tyndall continued to make a distinction between the status of religious understanding and of scientific knowledge,[60] apparently denying that a priori assumptions and intuitions formed a basis of the latter as much as of the former. This sort of inconsistency amongst scientific naturalists was addressed by George Romanes, who in the last years of his life read very attentively a number of books on Christian evidences, including Butler's *Analogy*.[61] He came to feel that modern agnosticism was performing the great service to Christian faith of silencing a priori rational scepticism. The pure agnostic, by Romanes's definition, must increasingly recognize, in logic, that all antecedent objections to Christianity founded on reason (in the sense of strict scientific ratiocination) are *ipso facto* nugatory. 'Now all the strongest objections to Christianity have ever been those of the antecedent kind, hence the effect of modern thinking is that of more and more diminishing the purely speculative difficulties, such as that of the incarnation etc. In other words, the force of Butler's argument about our being incompetent judges, is being more and more increased.'[62] Romanes argued that the reasonable response of the pure agnostic should be to try the experiment of faith, and if Christianity were true, verification would come through spiritual intuition. He developed this line of argument to aver that Butler's analysis would have been much reinforced if he had known about the theory of evolution: 'Gradual evolution is in analogy with God's other work ... [and] gives ample scope for persevering research at all times.' It provided a moral test and not merely an intellectual assent to some one (*ex hypothesi*) unequivocally attested event in history.[63] Although this was inadequate to give force to the particularity of Christian apologetic, it was a significant line of thinking which exposed some of the limitations of scientific agnosticism. The teleological questions still posed and unanswered by the evolutionary process

[59] J. Tyndall, 'Presidential Address to the British Association 1868', reported in *Athenaeum*, 2131 (29 Aug. 1868), 273–5, at 275. Cf. Eagar, *Butler's 'Analogy'*, 102–26.
[60] Tyndall, *Belfast Address*, 61.
[61] G. J. Romanes, *Thoughts on Religion*, ed. C. Gore (London, 1890), 95.
[62] Ibid. 166–7. Here he referred to *A.* 1. 7; *A.* 2. 3, 4, etc.
[63] Romanes, *Thoughts on Religion*, 168–71.

were indeed recognized by Huxley in his *Evolution and Ethics* (1893). The problem of explaining moral self-consciousness and assurance about values, and of building a rigorous philosophy of life upon these, yet remained.

It was in the context of this broadening definition of human experience that the late 1870s and 1880s saw a revival of moral philosophy, and the development of a greater pluralism of approach in reaction to the predominant utilitarian ethics. In part this took the form of a greater appreciation of the subtleties and the developing historical context of that tradition itself, as it became clear that there had been too black and white a view of it and its intuitionist counterpart. The question of the role of religion in the setting of moral limits to the principle of utility was central, and Butler's philosophy was seen to be fundamental to this debate. J. S. Mill himself in his posthumous essay 'Theism' (written between 1868 and 1870) had moved beyond a straightforward utilitarian ground to focus on the possibility of religious truth, a belief in which could have the beneficial effect of enlarging 'the general scale of feelings'. In this context he raised the question of the role of the workings of the imagination in rational argument.[64] Imagination once introduced in this way, questions could be posed about the perception of morality. What was the significance of the fact that men did not merely evaluate the content of moral conduct, but imagined themselves bound by moral obligations?[65] This was a distinction which Mill did not integrate systematically into his philosophy, but which was obviously critical to any discussion of the viability of utilitarian or naturalistic ethics. It was to form the crux of debate between Sidgwick, in his attempt to validate a modified utilitarianism, and James Martineau. Both men were disciples of Butler in different ways: both, as Hastings Rashdall said of Sidgwick, refused to treat 'the Science of Morals as a branch of Natural History'.[66] Yet despite his recognition that the definition of the good was ultimately an intuitive assumption without which no ethical system could operate, Sidgwick was never able philo-

[64] J. S. Mill, 'Theism', *Collected Works of J. S. Mill*, ed. F. E. L. Priestley *et al.* (Toronto, 1963-), x. 483-6.
[65] See O. Pfleiderer, *The Development of Theology in Germany since Kant and Its Progress in Great Britain since 1825* (London, 1890), 321-3.
[66] H. Rashdall, 'Professor Sidgwick's Utilitarianism', *Mind*, 10 (1885), 200-26, at 214; H. Rashdall, *The Theory of Good and Evil* (1907; 2nd edn., London, 1924), 53.

sophically to affirm any transcendental sanction for this.[67] Martineau started from the different premiss of an assumed divine order,[68] which meant that their arguments at one level glanced off each other. Martineau's approach is open to critical attack by twentieth-century philosophers, but Sidgwick took Martineau's position very seriously, as did many contemporaries.[69] Martineau's ideas were in many ways reinforced by the development of idealist philosophy, which in its nineteenth-century origins in Britain was a religious impulse, a reaction against narrow empiricism and evolutionism.

In 1886 the *Guardian* reviewed Martineau's *Types of Ethical Theory* and discussed his work alongside that of T. H. Green.[70] The reviewer observed that a growing interest in moral philosophy was one of the signs of the times, and that 'those who are content with a superficial explanation of new phenomena might plausibly argue that it is due to the fact that the age of supernaturalism has passed away. A people, it may be said which has outgrown metaphysics and theology is driven to seek aid from the natural and the human.'[71] But he pointed out that those who were really influencing thought and life were 'more and more fearlessly connecting their ethics with the belief in God'. The reviewer felt regret at their respective conceptions of that God, but asserted that 'the present generation will owe it to Professor Green and Dr Martineau, that moral philosophy has been raised to a position, in which it awaits its transformation, and, at the same time, its true development, in the light of the incarnation'.[72]

Moral philosophy was reviving, inside and outside universities, in ways which were to become increasingly important for the strengthening of confidence in Christian doctrine and social purpose. This was a matter not simply of a new openness to

[67] Sidgwick, *The Methods of Ethics* 470–3.
[68] See J. Martineau, *Types of Ethical Theory*, 2 vols. (London, 1885), i. xvi–xvii, for Martineau's defence of this.
[69] Schneewind, *Sidgwick's Ethics*, 237 ff.
[70] *Guardian*, 41 (13 Jan. 1886), 57–8.
[71] Cf. T. H. Green, *Prolegomena to Ethics*, ed. A. C. Bradley (Oxford, 1885), introd. Compare Frederic Harrison's argument for the power of Humanity, which 'is simply a matter for social science, not for analogies or probabilities', *Fortnightly Review*, 50 (1888), 679–80, cited by Cashdollar, *The Transformation of Theology*, 214; J. C. Shairp, 'The Moral Dynamic' in *Studies in Poetry and Philosophy* (Edinburgh, 1868), 348–51.
[72] *Guardian*, 41 (13 Jan. 1886), 57–8.

German thought—particularly that of Kant and Hegel—but of looking at the British philosophical tradition in different ways. For many, for example, the foundation of an interpretation of Kant was laid in the prior study of Butler, and for some a critical comparison of Kant and Butler suggested ways in which Butler's arguments and modes of arguing continued to seem productive. Acton, who himself argued that Kant took his theory of conscience and of probability from Butler,[73] commented that in Newman 'the Butler of early life coalesced with Kant, whom he only got to know very late'.[74] This order of reading and influence seems to have continued more generally. In Cambridge in 1874 students reading for the Moral Sciences tripos were urged to begin their course with Butler and proceed through Stewart, Mackintosh, Whewell, Bentham, Mill, Plato, and Aristotle to culminate with Kant: a significant indication of the lens through which Kant might be viewed.[75] In Trinity College, Dublin, which was to become famous for the study of Kant, Butler's works continued to be fundamental through the 1880s and 1890s, and examination questions were asked which related Butler to Kant and to Green. J. H. Bernard, the scholar of Butler and Kant, read Butler seriously for a prize examination at Trinity in 1880, before he read Kant and the Neo-Platonists, and his perspective on Kant was shaped by a continuing sympathy for, and study of, Butler.[76] In Oxford, Butler continued to be read alongside Locke, Hume, and Kant.[77] Moreover, in the new philosophical climate,

---

[73] Acton, *Selections from the Correspondence*, 225, 226: letters to Gladstone (23 Sept. 1892, 3 Oct. 1892). I am grateful to David Nicholls for this reference.
[74] Ibid. 226.
[75] *The Student's Guide to the University of Cambridge*, 3rd edn. (Cambridge, 1874), 186-8.
[76] *Dublin University Examination Papers 1895* (Dublin, 1895), esp. 369-71; R. H. Murray, *Archbishop Bernard: Professor, Prelate and Provost* (London, 1931), 36, 45.
[77] It is clear that, despite the loss of textbook status, Butler continued to be read for Greats in the 1860s. In 1874 the specifications were changed to admit modern philosophers, but not to *require* knowledge of them. No specific authors were at this stage nominated. The *Analogy* was set for the new Theology school. In the 1870s there were special subjects on Locke, Hume, and Butler, and on Kant (although it is not clear how many undergraduates offered these). From 1874 to 1883 the paper on Moral and Political Philosophy contained questions worded in very general terms, for which Butler could have been useful. In 1883 Moral Philosophy became a paper on its own, and initially included much more specific questions on Plato and Aristotle, and increasingly on other named authors (especially Kant); from 1891 to 1894 there was one specific question each year on Butler. In 1895 Moral and Political Philosophy were again combined, and in Trinity Term of that year there was one question focused directly on

Butler was more appreciated for his qualities as a generative thinker than deprecated for his failings as a systematic one.[78] This was an aspect of the practical power of his writing: in certain respects, for example in his understanding of the very close relationship between thought and action, sensation and thought, Butler approached a subtlety which was only now beginning to be appreciated. This was something which Jowett and Pattison had too prejudiced a view of Butler to grasp. Jowett's reservation about German philosophy as being too metaphysical, not practical, and not offering a principle of action,[79] was shared by others in Oxford, who in fact found in Butler a philosophically sophisticated supplement. Hastings Rashdall's critical comments on Kant's attempts to break up knowledge into sensation and thought were later developed by A. E. Taylor, and Taylor's own philosophical approach, shaped in Oxford in the 1880s, embodied Butler's scrupulous recognition of the range of types of reasoning and judgement which we use in everyday life.[80]

Although his emphasis was particularly resonant in the context of his own theology, F. D. Maurice's conception of the right relationship between moral philosophy and moral theology was to be endorsed by Martineau, by idealist philosophers like

---

Butler, as well as general questions for which study of him would be relevant. In Trinity Term 1898 a special paper on English Moralists (Hobbes, Clarke, Butler, and Hume) was set. See *Oxford University Calendar*; *Oxford University Literae Humaniores Second Public Examination Papers* (Trinity Term 1888 to Trinity Term 1899).

[78] See e.g. Maurice, *Moral Philosophy*, 460; A. Whyte, *Bishop Butler: An Appreciation* (Edinburgh, 1903), 44–5; *Christian Observer*, 71 (1871), 684.

[79] P. Hinchliff, *Benjamin Jowett and the Christian Religion* (Oxford, 1987), 87; *Dear Miss Nightingale*, 241 (25 June 1873); Ellis, *Seven against Christ*, 286. Compare Eagar, *Butler's 'Analogy'*, 118; *Guardian*, 51 (1896), 176.

[80] H. Rashdall, Bodleian Library, Ripon MSS, Box 105, 'Kant and after Kant', 10, 14. A. E. Taylor, 'Some Features of Butler's Ethics' (1926), in his *Philosophical Studies* (London, 1934), 298–300, 319: Taylor argued that Butler's reference to 'sentiment of the understanding', 'perception of the heart', in the *Dissertation on Virtue* was intended deliberately to express the subtlety of the relationship between intellect and feeling; hence Taylor criticized Whewell's earlier attempt to tidy Butler up by altering the phrases to 'perception of the understanding', 'sentiment of the heart'. Cf. Taylor's comment that, in ascribing to conscience authority rather than infallibility, Butler made more sense than Kant. Compare *British Quarterly Review*, 38 (1863), 122. Mossner's comment that *in fact* the affinities between Butler's and Kant's thought were not so close is not germane to a discussion of the ways in which 19th-century perceptions were shaped. Mossner, *Bishop Butler and the Age of Reason*, 235.

Hastings Rashdall and A. E. Taylor, and by incarnationalist theologians like Scott Holland and Gore. In his inaugural lecture as Professor of Casuistry, Moral Philosophy, and Moral Theology in Cambridge in 1858, Maurice was concerned to redefine casuistry in anti-scholastic terms, as investigation rather than systematization. He took Butler as both the model and the starting-point for such a pursuit. Butler's recognition of the centrality of the conscience and his method of explicating its meaning were exemplary in the most valuable sense of not being absolute or confining. The role of theology was not to silence philosophical enquiry, but in fact to prevent its being controlled by narrow systems.[81] In his *Types of Ethical Theory* (1883), Martineau stressed that 'the return to the essential foundation at once of the Christian religion and ethical philosophy is due in this country to Bishop Butler', although 'unfortunately it has been but scantily imitated and accepted'. To Martineau, Butler had restored psychological ethics and the necessary basis of self-reflection which was the foundation of moral action. Butler's conception of the active role of man in interpreting his experience was important in drawing Martineau away from his earlier attachment to associationism. At the conclusion to his work he explained why he had given a place neither to Butler nor to Kant amongst his 'types'. His plea was one of 'essential accordance' in both cases. Of Butler he said that 'he occupies, more nearly, perhaps, than any other writer, the position of a discoverer in moral theory; nor can its problem ever be adequately discussed without some reference to his thought'. He stressed also that since his sermons by definition could not constitute a system, their importance lay in stimulating further developments and elaborations of particular insights.[82] Green, on the other hand, made only passing references to Butler's moral philosophy, although late nineteenth-century commentators clearly saw the affinities between the two. J. B. Schneewind has argued convincingly that, although in his study of Hume Green repeated the familiar criticism that Butler's account of the moral good was circular, ultimately he came to the conclusion that any definition of the

---

[81] F. D. Maurice, *Casuistry, Moral Philosophy, and Moral Theology: An Inaugural Lecture* (London, 1866), esp. 21, 25, 28–9, 48.
[82] Martineau, *Types of Ethical Theory*, i. 19; ii. 522.

moral ideal which came close to the truth was bound to be open to this charge. Green's definition of practical reason was in fact very close to Butler's voice of God speaking within us.[83]

Partly because of the particular position which Butler's works had held in Oxford, his role there in the development of new philosophical and theological emphases tended to be underplayed by some at the time, and by many more in retrospect. In a review of the Hegel scholar W. L. Courtney's *Constructive Ethics* in 1886, Hastings Rashdall criticized Courtney for his superficial reading of Butler, and argued that one might as well say that Kant had an 'old-world air' as that Butler did; 'in another sense Kant and Butler have formulated in different, but not, I believe, fundamentally antagonistic ways the first principles of all ethical systems which apply any real basis for moral obligation.' He maintained that Courtney's critique was deeply unhistorical and hence concentrated on the limitations of Butler's thought rather than its abiding legacy and stimulus. In fact, Rashdall argued, in some respects (e.g. in discussion of motive and desires) Butler was closer to the modern Hegelians than was Kant, and his writings were fundamental in making possible the answers to the ethical problems attempted not only by Sidgwick but also by Green in his *Prolegomena to Ethics*.[84] However, in relation specifically to the power of a final cause, Rashdall recognized that the most fashionable type of idealism, which he saw represented by Hegel and Green, followed a line which to his mind was as mechanistic as the materialism which it set out to refute, and was unhelpful in validating religion or morality. On the less fashionable but more constructive side of idealism Rashdall put Lotze (who was known to have admired Butler),[85] Pfleiderer, James Ward, G. F. Stout, and James Martineau (although he was not strictly an idealist).[86] Rashdall himself was concerned to forge a form of idealism which was yet practical as a guide to living. He eschewed the absolute idealism represented by Bradley, but drew on Butler in refuting the counter-arguments

---

[83] Schneewind, *Sidgwick's Ethics*, 408-9.

[84] H. Rashdall, 'Mr W. L. Courtney on Bishop Butler', *Mind*, NS 44 (Oct. 1886), 555-62. See Bodleian Library, MS Eng. Lett. c. 342 (1885-8), fos. 73, 79: G. Croom Robertson commending Rashdall's criticism of Courtney.

[85] Cf. Gladstone, *Studies Subsidiary*, 131; *Guardian*, 51 (1896), 175; W. A. Spooner, *Bishop Butler* (London, 1901), 244.

[86] Bodleian Library, Ripon MSS, Box 105, 'Kant and after Kant', typescript, 18-19.

put forward by pragmatists such as William James and Schiller.[87] He argued that the pragmatists were quite right to complain about the faulty psychology in some idealists' treatment of ethical and speculative problems, and recognized that the 'scheme of substituting a series of working assumptions for the attempt to unlock the riddle of the Universe has obvious attractions for an age which has witnessed the break-up of many traditional systems of Theology, and yet feels the necessity of a creed to live by'. But he rejected totally such a scheme, and affirmed that whilst there might be no absolute moral truth any more than any other kind of truth, this was not a reason to abandon the search for truth: 'However exact and far-reaching may be the correspondence between objective truth and practical utility, that will not remove our inexpugnable conviction of an irreducible difference between truth and utility.'[88]

Rashdall taught Philosophy, Divinity, and History in Oxford from 1888 to 1917, from 1895 as Fellow of New College. He lectured in 'Moral Philosophy from Hobbes to Kant', and held open sessions in his rooms on questions affecting the relationship between religion and philosophy. At the same time he was a prominent member of the Christian Social Union, and edited the *Economic Review* from 1892 to 1910.[89] His pupil, friend, and long-standing correspondent A. E. Taylor remarked in 1926 how much more independent in thought and how much more interested in the English philosophical tradition Rashdall had been than most of 'the men about Green', 'as was even more manifest in the admirable lectures which he used to deliver in Oxford some thirty years ago than in his writings'.[90] Rashdall recommended Butler's *Fifteen Sermons* alongside Mill's *Utilitarianism* as

---

[87] Bodleian Library, Ripon MSS, Box 105, 'Pragmatism', 3. Cf. A. E. Taylor's criticism of the absolute idealists. See Sell, *The Philosophy of Religion 1875–1980*, 19.

[88] Rashdall, 'Pragmatism', 9, 14.

[89] See P. E. Matheson, *The Life of Hastings Rashdall* (Oxford, 1928), 83–4; Oxford University Programme of Special Studies for 1906–7, appended to *Student's Guide to the University of Oxford*, 17th edn. (Oxford, 1906). See also Bodleian Library, MS Eng. Lett. c. 344 (1896–7), fos. 190^v–191^r: Grant Robertson to Rashdall (22 Aug. 1897), reporting a conversation with Methuen on whether Rashdall should edit a Broad Church *Lux mundi*.

[90] Taylor, 'Some Features of Butler's Ethics', 292. See also Bodleian Library, MS Eng. Lett. d. 360 (1905–6), fo. 4: A. E. Taylor to Rashdall (30 Jan. 1905), in which Taylor commented that Rashdall's lectures on Ethics were the first philosophical lectures which he had attended in Oxford, and that he always remembered them with pleasure.

the starting-point of the study of moral philosophy.[91] Rashdall's interest in Butler was not uncritical (not in fact as whole-hearted as Taylor's own), but Butler was central to his philosophical preoccupations and also provided a ready point of reference for his social theory. Around 1895-6 he was preparing a book on Butler, which might have been published in the series in which Spooner's book on Butler was eventually published in 1901.[92] An article on Butler was posthumously published in 1927 in the *Modern Churchman*, in which Rashdall distinguished the aspects of Butler which he had long felt to be of continuing importance, and not simply of historical interest.[93] In discussing the tendency of modern philosophy towards pantheism rather than deism in religious thought, Rashdall urged that, although parts of the *Analogy* were clearly outdated (especially the second part), others were yet valuable. Rashdall emphasized that the strongest obstacle for those disposed to believe in a loving God was still that of the existence of evil: 'If Theism cannot account for the existence of evil, either modern man will reject arguments which would otherwise incline him to a theistic view and fall back on Agnosticism, or . . . will feel driven to believe in an Absolute—a universal Being who is thought of in some sense as spiritual, but not as personal or moral.' Rashdall urged Butler's continued relevance in this context. He laid great stress on Butler's insistence that God governs the world through general laws, and that one must therefore not judge each particular piece of divine action as if it had no relation to other acts; Butler, to him, saw the world as an organic whole, and defended the existence of evil on the ground of the necessity of free will to virtue (an interpretation of free will which, as Rashdall admitted,

---

[91] H. Rashdall, *Ethics*, (London, 1913), 95. In Edinburgh, Butler's *Sermons on Human Nature* and Mill's *Utilitarianism* were prescribed in 1895 as foundations for the study of Moral Philosophy. C. Douglas (ed.), *Guide to the Study of Philosophy in the University of Edinburgh* (Edinburgh, 1895), 19.

[92] See Bodleian Library, MS Eng. Lett. c. 344 (1896-7), fos. 14-15: A. Robertson to Rashdall (24 Feb. 1896): 'I was talking to Methuen and Co. the other day, and he suggested that a book you are preparing on Butler might very well come in amongst his "Handbooks of Theology". Do you approve of this idea, and if so, will you let me know what you think?' It is not clear why negotiations proceeded no further, nor at what stage Spooner was approached.

[93] H. Rashdall, 'Bishop Butler', repr. from *Modern Churchman*, 16 (Mar. 1927), 678-94, in H. D. A. Major and F. L. Cross (eds.), *God and Man* (Oxford, 1930), 231-50, at 231.

Butler pushed much further than most modern philosophers).[94] Rashdall regarded the parts of the *Analogy* on life as a state of discipline to be the most fundamental to any current discussion which recognized evil as evil, and felt that in this respect Butler qualified Sidgwick's attempt to reconcile a hedonistic conception of the 'good' with a rationalistic theory of duty.[95] One of the key lessons which Rashdall felt was to be learnt from Butler was that an appeal to the authority of conscience must be at the forefront of Christian apologetic. 'The chief ground for our belief in Christ, and the exceptional and unique Incarnation of God in Christ, must lie in the appeal which His teaching makes to reason, conscience and heart.' This was fundamental to his own idea of the relationship between philosophy and theology, to which the personality of God was central. When discussing the argument that, historically, religious motives had always been the most powerful motives of the highest morality, Rashdall emphasized that this was not a function of the hope of reward or fear of punishment so much as of an understanding of the personal relationship between God and man.[96] This underpinned his refutation of the ethical humanism which maintained that Christian moral ideals could be sustained without the Christian theology which gave them force. 'Those phrases so popular in the philosophical cant of our day ... self-development, self-realisation, self-culture' could be interpreted in Christian terms, 'but implied no necessary conception of self-sacrifice which was crucial to Christian faith and to Christian morality'. Rashdall here reaffirmed the consistency and power of Butler against what he saw as the murkiness of thought of some modern Aristotelians.[97]

[94] Ibid. 236–41. See, however, J. H. Bernard's comment on this point in his 'Butler', 48–9.
[95] Rashdall, *The Theory of Good and Evil*, 62–3. See also review in *Times Literary Supplement*, 298 (26 Sept. 1907), 290.
[96] Bodleian Library, Ripon MSS, Box 111, Rashdall's draft on 'The Relation of Moral Philosophy to Other Sciences'. Cf. Spooner, *Bishop Butler*, 227–9, on Butler's vindication of the independence and authority of the conscience and, from this, the reinforcement of a deep sense of direct obligation to a moral and personal God; A. Fairbairn, *The Philosophy of the Christian Religion* (London, 1902), 89–93; A. E. Taylor's later dismissal of the imputation that Butler's argument for the obligation to obey conscience depends on a self-interested calculation on the likelihood of the existence of Hell. Taylor stressed that Butler's concern throughout is rather to show the intrinsic authoritativeness of the moral law. Taylor, 'Some Features of Butler's Ethics', 328.
[97] Bodleian Library, Ripon MSS, Box 106, Rashdall, sermon on 1 Cor. 12: 14, typescript, fos. 2–4.

Rashdall's emphasis here provided a point of affinity with his fellow promoters of the Christian Social Union. Scott Holland, Gore, Westcott, and Rashdall did not share a church party nor a philosophical system but they shared an interest in, and debt to, Butler, in the development of their incarnationalist social philosophy. The influence of Butler provided a common thread in their ideas of reason and of personality. In Oxford, the deeper cause of the division between the *Lux mundi*[98] writers and the particular Tractarian line represented by Liddon was held in retrospect to have been the Mansel–Maurice debate. Liddon had continued to maintain the Manselian view of reason, whilst Scott Holland and Gore acquired a broader view of divine reason in man, which they defined as 'the ordering and harmonising element in a perpetually growing experience'.[99] Their sympathy with Maurice's position is clear, but the immediate line of influence was only indirectly from Maurice in the first instance, and may more directly have been from Butler and from Newman's interpretation of Butler. Whilst the impact of Green in pointing the way to a philosophical alternative to individualism and materialism was crucial, the influence of Butler was in many ways deeper and more sustained both in providing continuity with one emphasis of the Tractarian heritage and in offering a more rigorous Christian philosophy of human personality.[100]

Gore extolled Butler's inductive method as against the tendencies to a priori dogmatism said to be inherent in Hegelianism, although in fact the real influence of Butler may have been to make this less of a black and white contrast of method in Gore's own thought.[101] Gore's *Lux mundi* essay began with an appeal to experience, coupled with an emphasis that this was the appeal of the Church Fathers (who, as he said, knew that Christianity was not a past event, but present life). His conception of experience was a broad one, which he felt was justified by the critical methods of the physical and historical sciences.

---

[98] A 'Series of Studies in the Religion of the Incarnation', published by a group of Oxford Anglican teachers in 1889. The volume was edited by Charles Gore, and other contributors included H. S. Holland and E. S. Talbot.
[99] W. Richmond (ed.), *The Philosophy of Faith and the Fourth Gospel* (London, 1920), 6.
[100] Cf. D. Mackinnon, 'Scott Holland and Contemporary Needs', in his *Borderlands of Theology* (London, 1968), 113.
[101] Compare J. Carpenter, *Gore: A Study in Liberal Catholic Thought* (Leighton Buzzard, 1960), 66.

There were also related echoes both of Coleridge and of Newman's distrust of eighteenth-century rationalism, which had underestimated the extent of man's power of spiritual perceptions: in order to explore the truth 'we must trust the whole of our faculties—not our powers of abstract reasoning only, or only our powers of scientific discovery higher and lower, but also the more emotional and active powers of our nature—its capacities for intuition, feeling and willing'.[102] Modern psychology reinforced this emphasis. As Scott Holland was to observe, Butler would have entered with zest into the novel psychology of the early twentieth century, and 'would have revelled in exhibiting the selective fertility with which our experience created its own values out of the qualities of its moral character and purpose'.[103] For Gore, as for Butler and Newman, faith was not opposed to reason, but was an intellectual act done in a certain moral disposition. His emphasis on moral consciousness and experience was central, and made it all the more important to make the figure and personality of Christ an immediate and familiar guide to moral behaviour.[104] It is this emphasis which marks the distinctiveness of his position in relation to Green's idealism and to naturalism. Although Gore acknowledged the influence of Green's ideas of self-conscious personality, he was concerned about the potential implications of Green's linking of God's mind and the individual's, and of the theory of divine immanence. He was aware of the dangers of pantheism which could result, and always maintained the necessary particularity in the tension between God's immanence and transcendence. Gore also argued against the development of naturalist ideas of man's constant adaptation to environment, which could be used to undermine an individual's sense of moral freedom.[105]

[102] C. Gore, 'The Holy Spirit and Inspiration', *Lux mundi* (London, 1889), 315-62, esp. 315-18; C. Gore, *Belief in God* (London, 1922), 39, cited by Carpenter, *Gore*, 68.
[103] Holland, *The Optimism of Butler's 'Analogy'*, 45; cf. H. S. Holland, 'Consciousness, Sub-consciousness and Super-consciousness' (1907), in Richmond (ed.), *The Philosophy of Faith and the Fourth Gospel*, 97-101, in which Scott Holland develops a very Butlerian argument; cf. A. Lefevre, 'Conscience and Obligation in Butler's Ethical System', *Philosophical Review*, 9 (1900), 395-410, on the distinction between the working of the whole moral consciousness and a particular kind of reasoning.
[104] Cf. P. Avis, *Gore: Construction and Conflict* (Worthing, 1988), 28, on Gore's stress on Christ's principle of reserve; Mackinnon, *Borderlands*, 113, on Butler's distinction between power and authority in the working of the conscience.
[105] Avis, *Gore*, 55-6, 67-8.

Scott Holland similarly drew profoundly on Butler's approach. The idea for his 1905 Romanes lecture on Butler had been germinating from at least the 1890s: in 1897 he had written to Gladstone's daughter, after reading some proofs of Gladstone's edition of Butler: 'I am so very anxious that the constructive side of the *Analogy* should be brought out into prominence over the negative arguments, which are apt to stick in men's minds.'[106] This comment was perhaps to be the more keenly felt given his own early difficulty in reading Butler.[107] The force and subtlety of Butler evidently grew on him, and was instrumental in forging his Christian philosophy. Out of Butler he drew a very positive impulse. As he said in his Romanes lecture, Butler would never have made such a profound and continuing impact if he had simply engaged in the defensive enterprise of pointing out that the deists had as difficult a cause to justify as any Christian.[108] In writing of Gladstone's attraction to Butler, Scott Holland wrote of Gladstone's perception in Butler of 'the central fire of love and adoration for a God incarnate'.[109] Scott Holland implicitly argued against Matthew Arnold's one-sided account of Butler in his lectures on 'Bishop Butler and the Zeit-Geist' (1876), and against Leslie Stephen's emphasis on Butler's melancholy and pessimism.[110] Scott Holland emphasized the constructive and organic character of Butler's thought, its combination of 'Hellenic width of outlook' with 'the practical securities of the concrete Hebraistic mind'. He drew out Butler's affinity with Origen, who was 'optimistic to a fault', who laboured 'to expand the scope of our speculation over the widest horizons ... [trusting] to attain this magnificent consummation by confident use of the inspired and imaginative reason, which could, by mystical synthesis, transform and transcend the limitations of a narrow logic. And this is Butler's master.'[111] He drew attention to the practicality of Butler's religion, his treatment of it as a 'problem

[106] H. S. Holland, *Memoirs and Letters*, ed. S. Paget (London, 1921), 234; cf. J. Stephen on the need to put aside the controversial aspect of the *Analogy* and to look at it afresh alongside the *Fifteen Sermons*. Stephen, *Horae sabbaticae*, 307-8.
[107] Holland, *Memoirs and Letters*, 49.
[108] Holland, *The Optimism of Butler's 'Analogy'*, 7.
[109] H. S. Holland, 'Mr Gladstone's Religion', in his *Personal Studies* (London, 1905), 53.
[110] See M. Arnold, 'Bishop Butler and the Zeit-Geist', *Contemporary Review*, 27 (1876), 377-95, 571-92; L. Stephen, *History of English Thought in the Eighteenth Century*, 2 vols. (London, 1876), ii. 46.
[111] Holland, *The Optimism of Butler's 'Analogy'*, 8, 13.

of action', and in this context reiterated that by giving to *effective* certitude the name of probability, Butler did not mean to imply that he had no intellectual ground to offer.[112] Scott Holland provided an eloquent account of the soundness of Butler's position *vis-à-vis* both agnosticism and positivism:

> For him, the limitations of our faculties are drawn from their knowledge, not from their ignorance; from their exercise, not from their impotence. It is not because the scheme presented to them baffles their power, that they own it to be beyond them. On the contrary, it is because they understand it, and in understanding it, recognise how much lies beyond what they now cover.[113]

Thus Butler's arguments could repudiate the agnostic challenge. To the positivist claim that one can attain complete knowledge of what lies within the limitation of our faculties, Butler's analysis also posed a challenge: 'For that which is inside is bound up with that which is outside.'[114] Scott Holland recognized Butler's respect for the mystery of faith which he incorporated into his account of its intimate touching of everyday experience, and reaffirmed that 'It is not mystery which Reason objects to, but only mystery brought in to silence legitimate inquiry.'[115]

The influence of Origen was strong on both Westcott and Gore, and Westcott explicitly related what he saw as most impressive in Origen to the central thrust of Butler's *Analogy*. Concluding his discussion of Origen's *On First Principles* in his important article for the *Dictionary of Christian Biography*, Westcott said: 'The intellectual value of the work may best be characterised by one fact. A single sentence taken from it was quoted by Butler as containing the germ of his *Analogy*.'[116] The features of Origen which Westcott singled out were suggestive of links with Butler: the stress on 'the unity of all Creation, as answering

[112] Ibid. 18, 16.
[113] Ibid. 22–3; cf. H. S. Holland, 'Change', in *Christ or Ecclesiastes* (London, 1888), 53, on the real meaning of miracles: 'not in impertinent curiosity, not in unsteady ignorance, do we look for a miracle. But in the sober, solemn passion of self-humiliation.'
[114] Holland, *The Optimism of Butler's 'Analogy'*, 23.
[115] H. S. Holland, introd. to W. J. Carey, *The Reasonableness of Christianity* (London, 1904), p. xiii; cf. J. H. Bernard, 'The Knowledge of God', in his *From Faith to Faith* (London, 1895), 21. Contrast Matthew Arnold's comment: 'Religion must be built on ideas about which there is no puzzle.' Arnold, 'Bishop Butler and the Zeit-Geist', 585.
[116] *Dictionary of Christian Biography*, ed. W. Smith and H. Wace, 4 vols. (London, 1877–87), iv. 96–142, at 121. The article was written in 1882.

to the thought of a Creator infinitely good, and infinitely just, and the power of moral determination in rational beings', 'the treatment and the apprehension of these two truths' being 'modified for man by the actual facts of sin'. Underpinning this was his moral dynamic: 'For him ethics were a life, and not only a theory. The four cardinal virtues of Plato, practical wisdom, self-control, righteousness, courage seemed to him to require for their maturing careful and diligent introspection and culture.'[117] The Platonic strain in Westcott has been discussed by David Newsome.[118] But the influence of Butler on Westcott, who had been an undergraduate at Trinity College, Cambridge, in the 1840s in the heyday of Whewell's promotion of Butler, and who had previously been introduced to Butler by James Prince Lee at King Edward's School, Birmingham,[119] has not been developed and related to the broader current of incarnationalist theology and social thought in the 1880s and 1890s.

The Irish philosopher and liberal churchman J. H. Bernard, whose edition of Butler's *Works* in 1900 was to become standard, preached in Oxford in 1895 on 'The Knowledge of God', a sermon in which Butler's thought was central. Contrasting Butler favourably to the mainstream of eighteenth-century apologetic literature, Bernard identified the chief element of his superiority as his 'reverence in the presence of mystery' which is the root of religion. Bernard drew from Butler the culmination of his sermon, which was an argument about personality, and the transcendental quality at the core of friendship: Butler's apologetic incorporated the fundamental truth that ultimately knowledge of God, like knowledge of human friends, is transcendental: 'love is a condition of knowledge in that sphere also.'[120] For Bernard, as for the Oxford incarnationalists, this emphasis and reference to Butler's writings on the love of God provided the Christian response to the challenges of a purely ethical humanism, and a renewed vindication of the fundamental basis of Butler's apologetic. Bernard's work on Butler was significant in

---

[117] Ibid. 134, 101.
[118] D. Newsome, *Bishop Westcott and the Platonic Tradition* (Cambridge, 1969).
[119] A. Westcott, *Life and Letters of Brooke Foss Westcott*, 2 vols. (London, 1903), i. 25–6, cited by Swanston, *Ideas of Order*, 215.
[120] 'The Knowledge of God', 24–8. See also Robert Flint, cited by Cashdollar, *The Transformation of Theology*, 343–5.

that he put Butler back into his historical context (as Acton had urged Gladstone to do), whilst by extension giving his argument more force in the present. In dicussing the point that an argument based on man's ignorance could be pressed so far as to deprive men of any confidence as to their knowledge of the spiritual world, Bernard drew attention to Bishop Peter Browne of Cork, who in 1733 published *Things Divine and Supernatural Conceived by Analogy with Things Natural and Human*. Browne had argued that the divine attributes and essence were beyond us. Bernard stressed, however, that this view had been attacked by Berkeley in *Alciphron* 'as leading to what is now called Agnosticism; but it has always found supporters, and in our own time was advocated in Dean Mansel's Bampton Lectures.'[121] Bernard argued convincingly that Butler must have been aware of the controversy, and that it was in this context that one must understand the subtlety of Butler's own approach and the care which he took in delimiting the argument from human ignorance, 'lest it should be made the plea for arrest of judgement as to the entire spiritual order' (*A*. 1. 7). For Bernard, the focus on the historical context of the eighteenth-century debate was crucial in reinforcing the stimulus which could be gained from Butler's arguments in the early twentieth century. In arguing that his works continued to offer such stimulus, he separated Butler clearly from other strands of eighteenth-century apologetic.[122]

An article on the philosophy of Butler published in 1919 in the *Transactions of the Victoria Institute, or the Philosophical Society of Great Britain* (an explicitly Christian philosophical institute) was confident in pointing to the fact that the *Analogy* was still on the list of theological books for most bishops' ordination reading, and had a place in the philosophical syllabuses of the universities.[123] The author, the Revd H. J. R. Marston, stressed the appeal of Butler's discussion of human nature to a generation for whom psychology had assumed far greater importance, and the pertinence of Butler's ideas in the development of the humanitarian strain of modern thought.[124] In the same year, A. E.

[121] *The Works of Bishop Butler*, ed. Bernard, i, p. xxvii. Compare L. Stephen on Browne: *History of English Thought in the Eighteenth Century*, i. 113–14.
[122] Bernard, 'Butler', 50.
[123] H. J. R. Marston, 'The Philosophy of Bishop Butler', *Journal of the Transactions of the Victoria Institute, or the Philosophical Society of Great Britain*, 51 (1919), 56.
[124] Ibid. 58; cf. Spooner, *Bishop Butler*, 246 ff.

Taylor, writing as a Christian moral philosopher, looked back over the previous forty years of philosophical developments, and pointed to a contrast between the 1870s and the 1900s. Arguing that the traditionalization of systems was the deadliest enemy of the true spirit of philosophy, he was optimistic that this tendency posed less of a problem by the early twentieth century. In his estimation, there had been more concern in the 1870s to damage theology than to build up philosophy, and this had led to the substitution of crude philosophical and scientific dogmatisms for perceived theological dogmatism. Taylor saw developments in both philosophical and scientific method as having challenged such crudenesses, although he argued that philosophers still needed to take theology more seriously. Taylor urged that 'the doctrine which accounts for what is by what ought to be is the *only* philosophical theory on which it ceases to be an unintelligible mystery that we should have—as I maintain we certainly have—the same kind of assurance about values as we have about facts'. In this context he expressed the criticism of Bertrand Russell that in his 'zeal for the unification of science' he seemed inclined 'to assume that the larger problem of the co-ordination of Science with Life does not exist, or, at any rate, need not occupy our minds'.[125]

It was certainly true that in the years between the 1870s and 1914 the development of moral philosophy at the universities had served to expand the range of debate, and the application of comparative and historical methods had led to the more flexible study of different traditions. The same was true in theology, and the relationship between the two had in many ways become more fruitful, although philosophers like Russell posed fresh challenges to this. The place of those Christian moral philosophers who saw the development of this relationship as critical and who looked to Butler for inspiration in this context, has been obscured by the subsequent wave of positivism and the intensity of the reaction against idealism. Equally the force of Butler's own influence in this period has been understated, due to the continued emphasis on the independent role of continental philosophy. It is striking that the *DNB* article on Bernard (who died in 1927) stressed his Kantian scholarship, but did not

[125] A. E. Taylor, 'Philosophy' (delivered 1919), in F. S. Marvin (ed.), *Recent Developments in European Thought* (Oxford, 1920), 49-56, 47, 45-6.

even mention his work on Butler and the influence of Butler which he himself so clearly acknowledged.[126] Yet an increasingly subtle appreciation of Butler's place in the development of a Christian moral philosophy had clearly developed. He was discussed in a critical context, in relation both to his eighteenth-century contemporaries and to nineteenth-century philosophical trends. Demoted from textbook status at Oxford, his works continued to be discussed, as they were elsewhere, and they were taken up as part of a burgeoning debate on social ethics. Mark Pattison wrote in 1885 of his attack on Butler's *Analogy* that it was not a book adapted for an educational instrument.[127] This was a rather partial account of his approach to the *Analogy* in the 1850s, but it made a point which was increasingly understood in a different sense: that Butler's works were difficult, that this was indeed part of their importance, and that they needed to be set in a context if their force was to be understood. Butler's works were seen as significant precisely because they did not pretend to constitute an absolute system, and indeed because they argued against excessive confidence in systems. As the *Guardian* put it in 1896:

Butler's greatness does not consist in the supply of portable arguments with which he provides controversialists ... It lies in the combined reality and breadth of his view of life and the world; and in the intensity, 'the deep, steadily burning fire' of his faith in that purpose of righteousness and moral discipline which affords an answer, though, as he confesses, 'but a partial answer, a very partial one indeed,' to the perplexities of existence.[128]

---

[126] *Dictionary of National Biography 1922–1930*, ed. J. R. H. Weaver (Oxford, 1937), 78–81. Entry by E. J. Gwynn.

[127] Pattison, *Memoirs*, 135. Compare Rashdall's comments on not requiring ordination students to read Butler's *Analogy* before they had read anything else. 'Bishop Butler', 231. This remark is quoted out of context by Mossner, who cites it to imply that Rashdall thought that Butler was completely out of date. Mossner, *Bishop Butler and the Age of Reason*, 227–8.

[128] *Guardian*, 51 (1896), 176.

5
Butler as a Christian Apologist

BASIL MITCHELL

On the occasion of the tercentenary of his birth it is natural to concentrate on Butler's relevance today. Of what value is his thought *now* to Christian apologetics?

To ask the question is to assume that some useful answer might be forthcoming. But this assumption is open to two major objections, one more radical than the other. The first, more radical, objection is that any attempt to answer the question overlooks the enormous chasm that lies between his thought-world and our own, brought about in the first instance by the Romantic movement and then by that complex of attitudes which we may call modernity. The eighteenth century, it may be said, was the last period in European history when educated men could seriously believe that the truth about things could be arrived at by a process of reason or, indeed, that there could in any objective sense be a truth about things. Butler was a child of his time, a time which is now from us infinitely remote. Between him and us there has developed, not least among Christian theologians, a suspicion of all large-scale explanations, except perhaps in the realm of natural science, and a reluctance to claim knowledge of the transcendent. Hence the distinction which Butler received from Locke and, further back, from Aquinas between natural and revealed religion has little appeal either to those who attack Christianity or to those who defend it.

The second objection follows from this. Butler's carefully constructed argument in *The Analogy of Religion* is directed against a position which is rarely held today. It is an *ad hominem* argument, whose dialectical force depends upon the assumption that the reader will grant as non-controversial what few modern readers will grant, that God can be known through reason and experience to be the creator of the world and to exercise providential government over it. That granted, Butler goes on to argue that there is as good reason to believe that the same God is a moral governor and has revealed himself to mankind in the pages of Scripture; and that he deals with mankind according to similar principles whether in creation or redemption:

> As God governs the world, and instructs his creatures, according to certain laws or rules, in the known course of nature, known by reason together with experience: so the scripture informs us of a scheme of divine Providence, additional to this. It relates that God has, by revelation, instructed men in things concerning his government, which they could not otherwise have known; and reminded them of things which they might otherwise know: and attested the truth of the whole by miracles. (*A.* 2. 3. 5)

The deists, whom Butler opposed, took the existence of God for granted as vouched for by reason and experience, but rejected orthodox Christianity as a tissue of mysteries unsupported by evidence. For them the existence of God is required to explain the fact that there is a universe and that it exhibits intelligible order. So much was taken to be plain and luminous, and evident to all persons of sense and goodwill. By contrast the revealed doctrines of the Church, together with the Church itself, were products of superstition and obscurantism.

The modern reader, however, Christian as well as atheist, requires to be persuaded equally of both the elements in Butler's case: that there is a God who creates and sustains us and is knowable to us through the world of nature; and that through his son Jesus Christ he has redeemed us, as we can learn through the Scriptures.

It follows that, if Butler's apologetic is to be employed at all today, his argument will have to be reconstructed, using the materials he provides and following the principles he acknowledges, but assembling them and applying them differently. And we shall need to bear in mind each of the two objections that may be raised to the whole project. That is to say, we shall need to ask whether he affords the resources to combat the irrationalism and the relativism that are characteristic of so much modern thought and if so, whether he can do anything to justify the distinction between natural and revealed theology and to vindicate their claims.

REASONING IN RELIGION

Without doubt the most important feature of Butler's thought for either purpose is the account he gives of the sort of reasoning which is required if the case is to be made and of the degree of proof which is needed. His deistic opponents maintained that deism admitted of strong proofs comparable to those available in science or mathematics, whereas Christianity rested on weak and disputable grounds. Butler replies in effect that in this respect deism is no better placed than Christianity; both rest on weak and disputable grounds. But this does not settle the matter, for human life is such that most of the beliefs upon which we rely, and cannot but rely, in the ordinary conduct of our lives, are similarly insecure, if viewed from a purely theoretical standpoint. He complains that his opponents constantly set standards of proof for revelation which are not satisfied by the deistic beliefs which they maintain so confidently or by a host of other common-sense beliefs which they never think of questioning. The evidence of Christianity is, he claims:

> the kind of evidence upon which most questions of difficulty in common practice are determined: evidence arising from various coincidences, which support and confirm each other, and in this manner prove, with more or less certainty, the point under consideration. ... And ... though each of these direct and circumstantial things is indeed to be considered separately, yet they are afterwards to be joined together; for that the proper force of the evidence consists in the result of these several things, considered in their respects to each other, and united into one view. (*A.* 2. 7. 30)

The reference here to 'common practice' is central to Butler's argument. He constantly directs attention to the way we ordinarily think and insists that we cannot and should not proceed differently in matters of religion. In religion as in ordinary life what is needed for reasonable belief is not certainty but enough probability to warrant action:

> It ought to be forced upon the reflection of these persons, that our nature and condition necessarily require us, in the daily course of life, to act upon evidence much lower than what is commonly called probable; to guard, not only against what we fully believe will, but also against what we think it supposable may, happen; and to engage in

pursuits when the probability is greatly against success, if it be credible, that possibly we may succeed in them. (*A* 2. 6. 24)

The deists had complained (like Bertrand Russell in a celebrated remark) that, in respect of Christianity, we are not given enough evidence. Butler replies that we have enough evidence to make up our minds upon and as much as we habitually deem sufficient in the ordinary business of life. These arguments about the need to rely on probabilities and the necessity of deciding in practice between alternatives which can none of them be proved beyond doubt are found embedded in Butler's main analogical scheme as he elaborates it against the deists; but they are entirely general and were later to be developed in other contexts by John Henry Newman and William James.

The fact, however, that Butler advances his thesis in the course of his dispute with the deists leads him, if anything, to exaggerate the unsatisfactoriness of the human predicament in respect of knowledge by way of challenging their unjustified optimism. For it was a characteristic move of theirs to reject the claims of the Christian revelation on the ground that, if God was going to reveal himself to mankind otherwise than through the natural order, he would do so more clearly. He would make it much more evident than it is when and where a given revelation had occurred and how it was to be understood. The sacred story, they complained, as set forth in the Bible, is full of inconsistencies and improbabilities; it takes an unconscionable time to reach its climax; and, when it does, it is tied, implausibly, to particular times and places. The God in whom there is reason to believe, omnipotent, omniscient, benevolent, would not choose to communicate with his creatures in so circuitous and ambiguous a manner.

Butler for his part does not wish to deny that we have reason to believe that God ordains things for the best. There is, for example, enough evidence in experience to suggest that virtue tends in the end to be rewarded. There are indications, that is to say, of God's moral government of the universe; but they are little more than 'hints and guesses' and fall far short of the luminous certainty that the deists claim to possess. The unsatisfactory way in which, so the deists complain, God deals with us in revelation is not significantly different from his treatment of us in the ordinary course of our natural lives:

> Nor are we informed by nature, in future contingencies and accidents, so as to render it all certain, what is the best method of managing our affairs. What will be the success of our temporal pursuits, in the common sense of the word success, is highly doubtful. And what will be the success of them, in the proper sense of the word; i.e. what happiness or enjoyment we shall obtain by them, is doubtful in a much higher degree. Indeed the unsatisfactory nature of the evidence, with which we are obliged to take up, in the daily course of life, is scarce to be expressed. (*A.* 2. 8. 17)

Whatever the force of this argument against the deists, it makes things more difficult for the modern reader, for whom Butler has only moved the problem one stage back. If we are asked to believe that there is a God who seeks our good and guides our lives providentially and who, moreover, has revealed himself in and through the biblical story, unclear and ambiguous though it often is, it is no help to us to be assured that the same unsatisfactoriness we discern in the Christian revelation is to be found also in our everyday experience of life. We are bound to ask whether, taken together, they provide enough evidence to go on.

Butler is not insensitive to this complaint. His response is twofold. It comes partly in the form of a general intellectual stance to be adopted in relation to the claims of any world-view whatever; and partly as an element in his defence of Christianity as such. There is, in the first instance, a strong dose of agnosticism in his intellectual make-up. The world, as he represents it to us, does not afford us much in the way of certainty, so that 'probability is the guide of life'. Moreover, we rarely encounter very strong probabilities. In most matters, especially most matters of importance, we must make do with a good deal of ignorance and insecurity. The mistake made by the deists is to demand a higher degree of certainty and clarity in the case for Christianity than is in fact to be had; and to suppose that deism itself is more strongly supported than in fact it is. In all this Butler is protesting that the critics of Christianity (and this would apply to Russell as well as to the deists) set standards of proof for the truth of Christianity which are unrealistically high and which take no account of the inevitable incompleteness and fallibility of all human knowledge. Here then is an *ad hominem* argument of wider scope than at first appears, for it challenges not only the deistic opponents Butler himself had in mind but any opponents at all whose opposition to Christianity is based upon some alternative world-view for which the evidence is alleged to be better.

But, in the second place, in advancing this consideration, Butler is also claiming that Christianity is able to explain (better than deism and, by implication, any other rival scheme of thought) why it is that human beings are left in ignorance to the extent that they are. Without any such explanation it would be open to the critic to retort that, even if Butler is right and Christianity is no worse off then deism or any other world-view so far as the strength and intelligibility of its evidence is concerned, within its own terms of reference it *ought* to be better off. For, if there is a God and he is as Christians believe him to be, he could and should have made things plainer. That ours is, as Butler insists, a world in which comparatively little is made plain to us and we are given very little to go on, even in respect of what matters most to us, is in itself a convincing argument against Christianity.

Butler's explanation of this human predicament is that we are in all respects in a state of probation. Just as in childhood we have to learn through appropriate discipline to make the sort of decisions that are needed in maturity, so in our present life we are meant to cultivate those virtues which alone will fit us to enjoy life with God in the Communion of Saints: 'In these respects, and probably in many more, of which we have no particular notion, mankind is left by nature an unformed, unfinished creature; utterly deficient and unqualified, before the acquirements of knowledge, experience, and habits, for that mature state of life which was the end of his creation, considering him as related only to this world' (*A.* 1. 5. 15). And so 'Our being placed in a state of discipline throughout this life for another world is a providential disposition of things exactly of the same kind as our being placed in a state of discipline during childhood for mature age' (*A.* 1. 5. 17).

We are given, then, by Butler an account of the sort of reasoning by which the truth of Christianity or deism or, by implication, any rival world-view would need to be established, together with an indication of the degree of probability that is required for its acceptance, bearing in mind that what is demanded is sufficient probability to warrant action. That degree of probability is less than the deists claimed for natural religion and less than we, as human beings, would like to have for the ordering of our lives. That we find ourselves in this precarious position is among the circumstances which any world-view is required to explain, and Butler argues that it is more congruent with Christianity than with deism or, by implication, any available alternative.

A MODERN TEST-CASE

Today's philosophical critic of Christianity is unlikely to be a deist. He is more likely to be a metaphysical materialist, and one is bound to ask how Butler's argument would fare against such an opponent. As it happens an apposite illustration is to be found in J. L. Mackie's *The Miracle of Theism*, which provides a careful and sympathetic critique of Christian theism on the part of an avowed materialist. Mackie agrees that a cumulative argument of the sort Butler proposes could in principle be developed in support of belief in God:

But there is at least one interesting and important possibility of consilience, namely that which would bring together (1) reported miracles, (2) inductive versions of the design and consciousness arguments, picking out as marks of design both the fact that there are causal regularities at all and the fact that the fundamental physical laws and physical constants are such as to make possible the development of life and consciousness, (3) an inductive version of the cosmological argument, seeking an answer to the question 'Why is there any world at all?' (4) the suggestion that there are objective moral values whose occurrence likewise calls for further explanation, and (5) the suggestion that some kinds of religious experience can be best understood as direct awareness of something supernatural. These various considerations might be held jointly to support the hypothesis that there is a personal or quasi-personal God.[1]

Here is a case of a recognizably Butlerian sort although some of the elements in it, notably the appeal to religious experience,

[1] J. L. Mackie, *The Miracle of Theism* (Harmondsworth, 1977), 251–2.

are not to be found in Butler. It is evident that Mackie regards this as the strongest case that can be made for theism.

Moreover, elsewhere in his book, Mackie considers and commends William James's insistence on the role of the emotions and the will in determining our beliefs in matters of importance where the evidence is inconclusive and choices are, in James's words, 'living, forced, and momentous'. The ultimate question, then, for Mackie is whether the cumulative case for theism is strong enough to make it, in James's sense, a 'living option'. Mackie thinks not, but he is prepared to admit that, in principle, it might be. In framing the question in this way he is following not only James but also Butler, who anticipated him in developing this line of argument. James, writes Mackie: 'rejects the agnostic rules for truth seeking, saying that "*a rule of thinking which would absolutely prevent one from acknowledging certain kinds of truth if those kinds of truth were really there, would be an irrational rule*" ... Not only is it a fact that "our passional nature" influences our opinions, it is also legitimate that it should do so.'[2] Butler maintains, in a manner later to be elaborated by Newman, that the attitude with which we approach the evidence may decisively affect our capacity to evaluate it properly. If we do not *want* to reach a certain conclusion, we shall be liable to overlook or to misinterpret evidence which tends to support it:

If there are any persons, who never set themselves heartily and in earnest to be informed in religion: if there are any, who secretly wish it may not prove true; and are less attentive to evidence than to difficulties, and more to objections than to what is said in answer to them: these persons will scarce be thought in a likely way of seeing the evidence of religion, though it were most certainly true, and capable of being ever so fully proved. (*A* 2. 6. 19)

All this Mackie can and does accept as affecting the strength of the case for theism. It involves extending to the Christian apologist the attentiveness which is due to all proponents of a serious position. We must be prepared to take account of the human propensity to neglect or distort evidence through passion or laziness. So Butler writes:

And in general levity, carelessness, passion, and prejudice, *do* hinder us from being rightly informed, with respect to common things: and they

[2] Ibid. 207.

may in like manner, and perhaps in some further providential manner, with respect to moral and religious subjects: may hinder evidence from being laid before us, and from being seen when it is. (*A* 2. 6. 19)

'And perhaps in some further providential manner' hints at Butler's belief in the probationary character of the human predicament. To what extent does this thesis enable Butler to turn the flank of Mackie's basic contention that, when all allowance has been made for the obstacles that often lie in the way of estimating properly the force of the religious case, that case is still not strong enough to warrant even a Jamesian experimental faith?

In developing his doctrine of probation Butler is endeavouring to meet a charge of incoherence in the Christian case which Mackie does not actually make (though he might well have agreed with it), namely that a benevolent God has denied his creatures the plain and intelligible marks of his existence and purposes which are due to them. Nevertheless, if Butler's argument succeeds, it not only relieves Christianity of this incoherence but strengthens its intellectual and spiritual resources. For it is a common human predicament to be compelled to make up our minds upon evidence that is less clear than we should like, and this is a feature of the human condition which we naturally rebel against and would wish to have explained, if explanation there is. The probation which all men have to undergo takes, in some persons, the form of being tempted to abandon their Christian faith because of intellectual difficulties, which are real enough but which ought not to prevail with them:

Thus in the great variety of religious situations in which men are placed, what constitutes, what chiefly and peculiarly constitutes, the probation, in all senses, of some persons, may be the difficulties in which the evidence of religion is involved: and their principal and distinguished trial may be how they will behave under and with respect to these difficulties. (*A* 2. 6. 18)

THE LIMITS OF AGNOSTICISM

Butler remains throughout a rationalist. He agrees that it is incumbent upon the Christian apologist to show reasons why the Christian revelation should be accepted; and this must set limits to his agnosticism:

And now what is the just consequence from all these things? Not that reason is no judge of what is offered to us as being of divine revelation. For, this would be to infer, that we are unable to judge of anything, because we are unable to judge of all things. Reason can, and it ought to judge, not only of the meaning but also of the morality and the evidence of revelation. (*A.* 2. 3. 26)

The problem with this for the modern reader, as much as for the deist to whom Butler's argument is addressed, is whether the degree of agnosticism which he allows, and which he provides Christian reasons for accepting, is not, nevertheless, so great as to weaken his entire case beyond the point at which it remains a 'living option'. For consider, again, the outline of Butler's apologetic. The deist has complained that, while we have firm proof of the existence of an omnipotent, omniscient, and benevolent God (i.e. we have good reason to embrace deism), the evidence we are offered for the revealed doctrines of Christianity, or for supposing there to have been a revelation at all, is far too weak. It is, that is to say, too weak to convince an impartial judge, and falls far short of what we should expect a loving God to provide if he were to communicate with his creatures in the way Christians believe he has. A large part of Butler's reply to this criticism consists in rejecting the critic's underlying assumption that we are in a position to know what God would do in this circumstance or that. It is a mistake in principle to criticize God for failing to match our expectations: 'It amounts to no more in conclusion than this, that a divine appointment cannot be necessary or expedient, because the objector cannot discern it to be so: though he must own that the nature of the case is such as renders him incapable of judging whether it be so or not; or of seeing it to be necessary, though it were so' (*A.* 2. 5. 23). Yet, surely, unless we are warranted in forming *some* judgement as to what a good God would or would not do, we are in no position to employ the arguments of natural theology at all—we cannot say, as Butler wants to say, 'the world is such as to suggest that it was created and is sustained by God'. The point is well put by Stewart Sutherland in criticizing the attempts of some modern writers to mitigate the problems of theodicy by an appeal to mystery:

The nub of the disagreement is this: if we are to invoke the ideas of mystery and incomprehensibility at all, by what criteria do we decide when to appeal to them? There is something unacceptable about the tendency to invoke them in response to the questions raised by evil and suffering, while apparently finding less difficulty in the *intellectually* equally problematic questions of the nature of God.[3]

Butler is aware of this problem and has a reply to it:

Though total ignorance in any matter does indeed equally destroy, or rather preclude, all proof concerning it; and objections against it; yet partial ignorance does not. For we may in any degree be convinced, that a person is of such a character, and consequently will pursue such ends; though we are greatly ignorant, what is the proper way of acting, in order the most effectually to obtain these ends: and in this case objections against his manner of acting, as seemingly not conducive to obtain them, might be answered by our ignorance; though the proof that such ends were intended might not be at all invalidated by it. Thus the proof of religion is a proof of the moral character of God, and consequently that his government is moral, and that everyone upon the whole shall receive according to their deserts; a proof that this is the designed end of his government. But we are not competent judges, what is the proper way of acting, in order the most effectually to accomplish this end. (*A.* 1. 7. 20)

This reply does not, however, do all that is required of it. It is true that, if we know the character of God, we can continue to trust him, even if it must remain mysterious to us how he achieves his purposes; but if, as Butler believes, we have to rely on our experiences in this life for our natural knowledge of God and these experiences are ambiguous, then, unless we have some further authority for our beliefs about the nature of God, we ought to consider modifying those beliefs. This is Sutherland's point and is also one of the main arguments of Hume's *Dialogues of Natural Religion*.

Butler does, of course, believe himself to have such further authority in the revealed doctrines of Christianity, and the question now arises to what extent he is entitled to draw on these to strengthen his case. I think that he is so entitled and that his overall strategy relies on the claim that Christianity, *taken as a whole*, can best explain our human predicament. But this is a stage at which once again Butler's argument is obscured by the

[3] Stewart Sutherland, *God, Jesus and Belief* (Oxford, 1984), 28.

tactics of his dispute with the deists. In seeking to vindicate the claims of revelation against the deists he tends to follow in essentials the pattern of Locke's argument in book IV of the *Essay*. According to Locke there are truths according to reason, which establish the existence and character of a God, and truths above reason, which tell us more than we could otherwise know about him and which come to us by way of revelation. Locke assumes, and Butler follows him in supposing, that there are two distinct stages in the argument. The first establishes the existence of God and the second shows that God has revealed himself. Once the latter has been proved, what remains is only to discover the true meaning of what has been revealed. It is assumed that any unprejudiced mind will admit the force of the evidence from miracle and prophecy; and throughout the eighteenth century and well into the nineteenth it was customary to appeal without further explanation to 'the evidences of Christianity'.

Too much, however, has happened since that time in the way of historical research in general and biblical criticism in particular for the Lockian pattern to be at all plausible to the modern reader. And even apart from that the argument from miracle and prophecy does not have the compelling quality that Locke and Butler ascribe to it, when considered in isolation from the rest of the Christian scheme. A critic of Christianity, even if persuaded that miraculous events might occur, will argue with Hume that it is more reasonable to ascribe them to some natural cause as yet unknown than to the intervention of a deity. Hence Mackie concludes: 'This entails that it is pretty well impossible that reported miracles should provide a worthwhile argument for theism addressed to those who are initially inclined to atheism or even to agnosticism.'[4]

Prophecy fares no better, if it is understood as it must be for the purposes of the argument, as miraculous foretelling of the future. Hence if miracles and prophecy are to form any part of Christian apologetic, it can only be as contributing to the explanatory power of the Christian story taken as a whole. It is not that the Resurrection of Christ, as we find it narrated in the Gospels, provides the warrant for interpreting Scripture as

---

[4] Mackie, *The Miracle of Theism*, 27.

God's revelation of himself, but rather that, given independent (though not coercive) grounds for belief in God, it makes better sense of all the evidence to accept the inspiration of the Bible and the genuineness of the Resurrection than to deny both and adopt an entirely naturalistic account of all the matters in dispute. In so far as the Bible, when carefully considered, lends itself to this interpretation, the antecedent assumptions about the existence and activity of God are themselves strengthened. This is how Butler's argument ought to go if it is to conform to his dominant teaching about the nature of rational belief.

BUTLER AND MODERN THEOLOGY

Yet it has to be admitted that, even in this revised form, Butler's apologetic would find comparatively few supporters among contemporary theologians. One is bound to ask why this is so, and whether in the circumstances it is at all worthwhile to try to reinstate his arguments.

The most striking change that has taken place since Butler wrote is the domination of Western culture by natural science. This is why the natural theology of the deists no longer convinces. It is not only that, as Butler constantly insisted, it is far less easy than they thought to discern the working out of God's purposes in the created order, but also that there is now available to us, as an alternative, an array of scientific explanations of phenomena which are impressively coherent and intelligible and which enable us to control our lives to a far greater extent than was possible in Butler's day. Not only the deists' confident appeal to design but also Butler's cautious agnosticism have given way to the ready assumption that everything can be explained and controlled scientifically and that, if anthing cannot be so explained, it is altogether beyond explanation. There is now, as there was not in Butler's day, a massive apparatus of scientific knowledge which can be made the basis of an entirely secular world-view of the sort Mackie adopts.

The effects of this development upon theology have been momentous. There are two in particular:

1. Theologians have been confronted not only by an alternative account of the world and man's place in it, but also by an alternative pattern of rationality, which many claim to be the

only legitimate one. This has cast doubts upon the possibility of theology as a rational enterprise. Theologians themselves, particularly upon the continent of Europe, have often abandoned the attempt to construct a reasoned Christian apologetic, the need for which Butler took for granted. Deeply influenced by Kant's call 'to deny reason to make room for faith', continental theologians in the nineteenth century began increasingly to interpret the doctrines of Christianity as expressions of emotion, imagination, or will which made no claim to describe or explain the way things are, this being the domain of science. Schleiermacher was characteristic of this trend in his assertion that 'religion ... resigns all claims on anything that belongs either to science or morality'.[5] When the reaction against liberal theology came with Karl Barth the new orthodoxy shared with its liberal opponents their repudiation of the claims of natural reason to adjudicate in matters of religion.

2. Together with the dominance of scientific method and the increased authority of the natural sciences came the application of 'scientific methods' to the study of the Bible, a development which Butler only just begins to anticipate. It would be a mistake to regard 'scientific history' as being simply the application of the methods of the natural sciences to the study of historical documents. Indeed history as a plainly rational enterprise is one of the most striking counter-examples to the thesis that scientific explanation (as practised in the natural sciences) is the only valid pattern of reasoning. Nevertheless in practice the critical study of the Bible tended to share with natural science the assumption that all events were to be explained naturalistically. The critic would approach the biblical writings with the same assumptions about causes and influences as those of an entirely secular scholar. Not only was it difficult from the resulting *disjecta membra* to assemble the body of traditional Christian doctrine, but the very idea of Scripture as the vehicle of revealed truth was increasingly hard to sustain. Given this state of affairs there seemed to be only two options left to the theologian. One was to scale down the fabric of Christian doctrine to what it was felt the remaining historical foundations would sustain; the other was to cut doctrine off altogether from the biblical record

---

[5] F. Schleiermacher, *On Religion* (New York, 1958), 35.

as established by scholarship and to substitute the Christ of Faith for the historical Jesus.

If these alternatives are indeed the only ones now open to theology, a large part of the *Analogy* is effectively obsolete. Of what use is it to draw analogies between natural and revealed theology if both are equally discredited as rational enterprises? To be sure, even if this conclusion is drawn, Butler's views on the nature of rationality remain of interest, but nothing could be made of his careful reflections upon the authority of Scripture.

BUTLER ON THE AUTHORITY OF SCRIPTURE

Before accepting this conclusion it is worth examining the issue more closely with Butler's arguments in mind. We may start with the thought that when modern theologians reject the traditional concept of revelation what they have in mind is often a rather crude doctrine of inspiration. It is, they feel, a mistake to suppose that God would or could communicate in propositional form certain truths about himself and his purposes which we could not otherwise learn. It makes too little allowance for individual creativity and cultural development. Human beings are thought of as passive recipients of a timeless message in a way that fails to take creation and the historical process seriously. Moreover the Bible does not read at all as if it were the medium of such a message.

The method of reasoning is clear. Revelation, if it were to occur, would have to take this or that form; it does not take such a form; therefore it does not occur. But this is just the approach that Butler objects to in his deistic opponents. They also claim to know what a revelation would have to be like and to know also that it could not possibly be like that. Butler replies:

As we are in no sort judges beforehand, by what laws or rules, in what degree, or by what means, it were to have been expected, that God would naturally instruct us: so upon the supposition of his affording us light and instruction by revelation, additional to what he has afforded us by reason and experience, we are in no sort judges, by what methods, and in what proportion, it were to be expected, that this supernatural light and instruction would be afforded us. (*A.* 2. 3. 7)

Butler did not, of course, realize the variety of methods that would be employed in the critical study of the Bible, but it is remarkable how far he anticipated their general character:

> We are equally ignorant, whether the evidence of it would be certain or highly probable, or doubtful: or whether all who should have any degree of instruction from it, and any degree of evidence of its truth, would have the same: or whether the scheme would be revealed at once, or unfolded gradually. Nay we are not in any sort able to judge, whether it were to have been expected, that the revelation should have been committed to writing; or left to be handed down, and consequently corrupted, by verbal tradition. (*A.* 2. 3. 7)

Lacking secure criteria of the genuineness of revelation, we are in no position to deny the genuineness of a purported revelation on the ground that it does not satisfy the criteria we have laid down: 'And therefore, neither obscurity, nor seeming inaccuracy of style, nor various readings, nor early disputes about the authors of particular parts; nor any other things of the like kind, though they had been much more considerable in degree than they are, could overthrow the authority of the scripture' (*A.* 2. 3. 9).

Butler's agnosticism is apparent again here and raises the same problem as we encountered earlier. Has he not so stressed our inability to provide criteria for the genuineness of revelation as to deprive us of any reason for believing in revelation at all? To adapt the analogy he himself uses of a master delivering a message by a servant, must not the context of the message and the circumstances of its delivery be such as to warrant the hearers in believing it to be genuine? Indeed Butler has already seen the need for caution in this matter: 'I express myself with caution, lest I should be mistaken to vilify reason; which is indeed the only faculty we have wherewith to judge concerning anything, even revelation itself' (*A.* 2. 3. 3). Thus he comes very close to inconsistency. To relieve him of the inconsistency the first move is to stress 'beforehand' in 'As we are in no sort judges beforehand ...' (*A.* 2. 3. 7). The deists were very clear on the basis of their natural theology how God would proceed if he were to reveal himself to mankind otherwise than through the workings of nature. Just as the truths of natural religion were bestowed universally and were capable of being formulated in abstract propositions, so should the truths of revelation be—if there were any. They were creatures of the Enlightenment, dedicated to 'clear and distinct ideas', and orthodox Christianity seemed to them to be, by contrast, obscure, ambiguous, mysterious, and, above all, unduly particular. Butler is not content simply to object to the actual criteria the deists employed, but calls in question their antecedent assumption that to judge of a revelation one must possess secure criteria of assessment in advance. It is this broader critique which remains relevant today. The problem as it confronts the contemporary theologian is clearly stated by Austin Farrer. Speaking of the Incarnation he says: 'The Incarnation must be acknowledged. How can it be? There is no special difficulty in seeing how a number of persons should come round to the belief that one of their number is divine ... we must agree that it has happened more than once. The difficulty is to see what would make any one such belief or acknowledgement valid.'[6] We need, then, criteria of validity:

But what are they? In most fields of enquiry it is possible to set up models of argument and canons of proof. The usefulness of such aids varies greatly from one field to another. In the matter of revelation it must surely reach a vanishing point. If there is no *a priori* model for the form of God's self-disclosure, how can there be *a priori* canons for the marks of its authenticity ... There existed in the minds of Christ's contemporaries certain premises about the supreme human instrument of divine intervention. The Gospels devote a surprising amount of time to the demolition of them.[7]

Butler seeks to meet the requirement for criteria which Farrer acknowledges not by listing in general terms criteria of the genuineness of revelation other than those provided by the deists, which would be to endorse their general method of argument, but by going over the entire Christian story in relation to the available evidence, and meeting objections to it as they arise, in such a way as to make the story as coherent and convincing as possible, making allowance at every stage for the inevitable limitations of human knowledge. It is as if one were to vindicate

---

[6] Austin Farrer, 'Revelation', in *Faith and Logic*, ed. Basil Mitchell (London, 1957), 100–1.
[7] Ibid.

the authenticity of the message the servant claims to have received from the master, not by showing how it satisfies certain criteria applicable to all such messages, but by displaying it as congruous with the character of the master and the situation of the servant in the light of all the evidence available in the particular case. This is an exercise of reason of the informal and cumulative kind that Butler has all along recommended.

But Butler has another, more particular, suggestion for reconciling the critical study of the Bible with a strong doctrine of revelation. As it happens, the inspiration of Scripture is an issue which has evoked a strain of deism in much contemporary theology. It is not only that it is difficult to find criteria for the validity of claims to revelation: it is also that, once a naïve concept of divine dictation is abandoned, it is hard to see how God can be supposed to have spoken through a miscellany of writings of varying genres, produced by different authors in a wide variety of historical contexts, which can for the most part be satisfactorily explained in terms of the immediate context in which they first appeared. If, then, God 'spoke by the prophets' it can only be in a purely metaphorical sense, namely that they arrived at certain conclusions about the purposes of God which were in fact true, being more sensitive than others to his creative and sustaining presence. The process by which this happened could in principle be interpreted in terms of personal experiences and cultural influences which are wholly explicable in terms available to the secular historian.

Butler is prepared to admit that the biblical writings can be treated in this way, which involves interpreting them in terms of the intentions of the original authors in so far as these can be determined, but denies that divine inspiration in a fuller sense is thereby ruled out. If a prophetic utterance is found in fact to illuminate a much later development which the author did not himself anticipate, this could be the outcome of divine inspiration:

> if one knew a person to have compiled a book out of memoirs, which he received from another, of vastly superior knowledge in the subject of it, especially if it were a book full of great intricacies and difficulties; it would in no wise follow that one knew the whole meaning of the book from knowing the whole meaning of the compiler: for the original memoirs, i.e. the author of them, might have, and there would

be no degree of presumption, in many cases, against supposing him to have, some further meaning than the compiler saw. (*A* 2. 7. 26)

Butler's argument here has some affinity with what modern writers have called 'canonical interpretation'. If a body of literature can be legitimately interpreted as presenting a coherent message, in spite of variations of style and content and inconsistencies between its several parts, so that it can properly be treated as a whole, it can also be seen as inspired by God. Whether and to what extent it should be so seen is a question, as Butler insisted, that can be answered only by looking carefully and patiently at all the facts of the case. It will not do to pre-empt the decision by laying down in advance requirements which must be satisfied by any body of literature with a claim to be inspired. An illustration of how such an argument may proceed is afforded by David Brown's discussion in *The Divine Trinity* of revelation as a divine dialogue.[8]

CONCLUSION

It has to be admitted, however, that Butler's detailed suggestions for dealing with the hermeneutic problem, although remarkable for their time, are now for the most part of merely historical interest. What is of permanent value is the solution he offers to the characteristic predicament of the modern theologian. The sharp contrast between faith and reason which has dominated modern theology is the legacy of Hume and Kant and derives, philosophically, from an inadequate conception of reason, based upon what was thought to be the procedure of the natural sciences. It is this legacy which prompts the objections, mentioned at the beginning of this essay, to our taking Butler seriously today as a Christian apologist. Since Christianity could not be established or even rendered probable by any such procedure, it was concluded that there was no place for reason at all in defence of Christian faith. Faith could preach to unbelief; it could not argue with it. Hence Christian apologetics was gravely weakened in its encounter with secular thought. Butler's power as a Christian apologist in his own day flowed from his refusal to accept uncritically certain assumptions which were widely

---

[8] David Brown, *The Divine Trinity* (London, 1985), 52–98.

current at the time, not dismissing them out of hand but submitting them to careful and painstaking examination. He believed that Christianity possessed the spiritual and intellectual resources to respond to the criticisms that were directed against it, so long as it was interpreted sensitively and, where necessary, with a salutary agnosticism. He believed that faith should be both firm and critical, both rational and committed. In this he provides a model that is worthy of imitation.

6

Butler and Human Ignorance

TERENCE PENELHUM

A fundamental feature of Butler's apologetic is his persistence in reminding us of the limits of our knowledge and understanding. He thinks, for example, that the deists who are his main targets in the *Analogy of Religion* do not show enough awareness of these limits, and are accordingly too ready to say that God would not choose to reveal himself to us in the ways Christians say he has. A similar form of argument appears in his ethics: his case against the equation of morality with benevolence is that we are not able to foresee the consequences of those choices that the exigencies of daily life continually force us to make. My purpose in this essay is that of clarifying and evaluating the nature and range of those arguments in which Butler stresses our epistemic limitations, as we find them in his defence of Christianity.

I

Butler has left us no writings on epistemology, and confines himself to incidental statements from which we have to infer what he thought on the subject. Even the famous fifteenth sermon 'Upon the Ignorance of Man' is addressed to problems of theodicy to which he applies such epistemological views as he has developed. But it is still helpful, I think, to begin by trying to state some important general facts about these views, as we can glean them from that sermon and from the *Analogy*. It is not to be expected that a thinker with such an overriding concern with practice would have an epistemological *system* in the way in which Descartes or Locke can be said to have; but the arguments he mounts require him to make commitments on quite a wide range of fundamental epistemological questions.

The first and most striking feature of Butler's epistemology is that his emphasis on our ignorance is not one that owes anything to classical or Cartesian scepticism, at least in any direct way. Where Pascal, whose apologetic his most resembles, explicitly ascribes correctness to some part of the Pyrrhonist stance in order to dissociate himself from philosophical attempts to attain knowledge of God,[1] Butler does not say or imply that all our aspirations to knowledge are vain ones. On the contrary, he continually urges us to seek that knowledge of our situation and our duties that we *can* achieve, through conscience and through Scripture, for example. The most picturesque passage in the fifteenth sermon (in paragraph 14) is the one where he likens us to persons walking in twilight, or taking a journey by night and heeding whatever illumination we are lucky enough to receive. He reminds us that 'darkness, ignorance, and blindness are no manner of security' (*S.* 15. 14), thus casting aside any attempt to represent scepticism as a potential way of life in itself, and then proceeds to tell us that 'we should acquiesce in, and rest satisfied with, our ignorance, turn our thoughts from that which is above and beyond us, and apply ourselves to that which is level to our capacities, and which is our real business and concern' (*S.* 15. 16).

The key disjunction, then, is that between what we can appropriately enquire into and what not. Let us first see how this disjunction is developed in the fifteenth sermon. In his first extrapolation of the text from Ecclesiastes on which the sermon is preached, Butler tells us that 'creation is absolutely and entirely out of our depth, and beyond the extent of our utmost reach' (*S.* 15. 5) and that 'the scheme of Providence, the ways and works of God, are too vast, of too large an extent for our capacities' (*S.* 15. 7). The former he has explained by saying that it is 'in general no more than effects, that the most knowing are acquainted with', and that we do not know causes; and we are 'altogether ignorant' of the 'real nature and essence of beings'. He explains the latter by saying that since the 'monarchy of the universe is a dominion unlimited in extent... the general system of it must necessarily be quite beyond our comprehension' (*S.* 15. 6). We find here the direct comparison between the sort

---

[1] Blaise Pascal, *Pensées*, ed. Louis Lafuma, (Paris, 1962), fragment 691. English translation by A. J. Krailsheimer (Harmondsworth, 1966).

of knowledge of the natural world available to us (with its limitations) and the sort of knowledge Butler thinks we can have of the whole providential order, natural and supernatural together (which has similar limitations), that is central to the later argument of the *Analogy*. Since our limited knowledge of the providential order is nevertheless enough to show it to be 'one administration or government', it follows that 'we cannot have a thorough knowledge of any part, without knowing the whole' (*S.* 15. 6).

Before drawing the morals he considers to follow, Butler introduces another consideration, which also foreshadows later and fuller argument in the *Analogy* (*S.* 15. 8). The ignorance which we must take so seriously may not always be due to our incapacity, although the fact of finitude obviously implies that much of our ignorance is due to this. Given that the universe is indeed the work of God, we cannot rule out the possibility that God may have chosen to hide some facts from us that we are quite capable of understanding, but which he thinks it better we should not know. God may hide himself.

Butler draws three morals. First, when reflecting on religion we should expect to find mysteries, but we should also be glad to accept 'any evidence whatever, which is real' (*S.* 15. 14). Second, our ignorance, though it does not *explain* any of the puzzling matters, such as evils, that are raised as objections to religion, is nevertheless 'the proper answer' to them. For what seems inconsistent with what we might expect from divine government may be due to causes we do not know about, but which full understanding would show to be instances of it. Third, we should recognize that 'knowledge is not our proper happiness', and that 'the only knowledge, which is of any avail to us, is that which teaches us our duty, or assists us in the discharge of it'; we should confine our enquiries to this, since the economy of the universe is a subject 'out of our reach' (*S.* 15. 16). While this is probably the only place where Butler's practical emphasis takes an overtly philistine expression, it serves as a reminder that his own arguments are directed always and only towards the removal of barriers to the practice of that mode of life we should be following, and never towards the satisfaction of mere curiosity.

II

Throughout Sermon 15 the influence of Locke is very apparent. The 'twilight' passage in paragraph 14, for example, is highly reminiscent of the second paragraph of chapter 14 of book IV of Locke's *Essay Concerning Human Understanding*:

Therefore, as God has set some things in broad daylight; as he has given us some certain knowledge, though limited to a few things in comparison, probably as a taste of what intellectual creatures are capable of to excite in us a desire and endeavour after a better state: so, in the greatest part of our concernments, he has afforded us only the twilight, as I may so say, of probability; suitable, I presume, to that state of mediocrity and probationership he has been pleased to place us in here; wherein, to check our over-confidence and presumption, we might, by every day's experience, be made sensible of our short-sightedness and liableness to error.[2]

The notion of probability does not make an explicit appearance in the sermon, though it is central in the *Analogy*; but the presentation of Butler's argument in the sermon makes obvious use of Locke's contrast between probability and certainty. When Butler tells us that we are ignorant of the real nature and essence of things, and of their causal powers, he echoes what Locke says to us in chapter 3 of book IV:

I doubt not but if we could discover the figure, size, texture, and motion of the minute constituent parts of any two bodies, we should know without trial several of their operations one upon another; as we do now the properties of a square or a triangle. Did we know the mechanical affections of the particles of rhubarb, hemlock, opium, and a man ... we should be able to tell beforehand that rhubarb will purge, hemlock kill, and opium make a man sleep.[3]

And therefore I am apt to doubt that, how far soever human industry may advance useful and experimental philosophy in physical things, *scientifical* will still be out of our reach: because we want perfect and adequate ideas of those very bodies which are nearest to us, and most under our command ... By the colour, figure, taste, and smell, and other sensible qualities, we have as clear and distinct ideas of sage and hemlock, as we have of a circle and a triangle: but having no ideas of

---

[2] John Locke, *Essay Concerning Human Understanding*, ed. Alexander Campbell Fraser (New York, 1959).

[3] Ibid. bk. IV, ch. 3, para. 25.

the particular primary qualities of the minute parts of either of these plants, nor of other bodies which we would apply them to, we cannot tell what effects they will produce; nor when we see those effects can we so much as guess, much less know, their manner of production.[4]

In these passages Locke suggests that genuine knowledge of the physical world would be knowledge of the interrelationships of the primary qualities of things, and would consist of necessary, and therefore a priori, truths. The actual world of 'experimental philosophy' is one in which we are denied this certainty, and are confined to probabilities. This conflates the contrast between the known and the probable with that between the macroscopic and the microscopic—one of the less fortunate side-effects of the distinction between primary and secondary qualities. It makes Locke suppose that better understanding of the microscopic structure of matter would yield, not merely a more accurate understanding of probabilities, but demonstrative mathematical certainty. In addition, Locke holds that this deeper understanding of the physical world would be fully systematic in a way that the knowledge now available to us is not; such systematic knowledge would view things not as discrete entities, but as part of the whole of creation:

We are then quite out of the way, when we think that things contain *within themselves* the qualities that appear to us in them . . . perhaps, to understand them aright, we ought to look not only beyond this our earth and atmosphere, but even beyond the sun or remotest star our eyes have yet discovered. For how much the being and operation of particular substances in this our globe depends on causes utterly beyond our view, is impossible for us to determine.[5]

So it seems clear that in the fifteenth sermon Butler is, for the most part, appropriating for his own purposes epistemological claims he inherits from Locke. He appropriates the view that our knowledge of the physical world around us is restricted to the observable qualities of things, which gives us the sort of information we need for practice and prediction, but that we are barred from certainty about their real natures. If such knowledge were available to us, it would be a knowledge of necessary truths, and would show how the superficial regularities and appearances

[4] Ibid. para. 26.
[5] Ibid. bk. IV, ch. 6, para. 11.

that we can learn about are manifestations of a wider and deeper systematic unity. This uneasy combination of rationalist and empiricist elements, when applied by Butler to apologetic purposes, yields the claim that the workings of Providence may, for all we can possibly know to the contrary, be systematic in a parallel way: that evils we encounter as puzzling brute facts will be the consequences of a system that would fully explain them, were we to understand it. Our inability so to understand it is not one that Butler ascribes wholly to our intellectual limitations; in some instances our ignorance may be due, for all we know to the contrary, to God's having deliberately withheld from us facts we could grasp well enough if he had made them available. This uncertainty about how far our ignorance is due to finitude in our faculties and how far to finitude in our opportunities is not surprising. For Butler follows Locke in another key respect that is quite fundamental to all his apologetic thinking: whatever the limits on our understanding the system of the world, we are capable of understanding the fact that it is indeed a created system—that God exists and governs it. Unlike Locke, who offers his own demonstrations of this,[6] Butler does not himself ever prove God's existence; but he clearly thinks it can be done, and that others have done it. It is self-evident that he does not ascribe our knowledge of God's existence to revelation, since he explicitly presupposes it in his apologetic attempts to establish revelation's credibility. So this knowledge is, prima facie, an exception to the limitations on our understanding that he emphasizes in Sermon 15. I shall return to this below. For the present, I turn to the *Analogy*, where all of these matters are elaborated.

III

While the Lockian provenance of Butler's position is easy enough to see from Sermon 15 taken alone, two notions are central in the *Analogy* itself that do not receive explicit treatment in the earlier work, though they too have Lockian ancestry. The first is that of probability; the second is that of analogy itself. In each case Butler appropriates a distinction Locke has

[6] Ibid. bk. IV, ch. 10. In *A.* 1. 6. 3 Butler appears merely to be rehearsing an argument from Clarke (see Bernard's note).

made in the *Essay*; but in each case we find him developing and using it in a distinctive manner.

Probability is one of the two themes of book IV of Locke's *Essay*. It is dealt with for itself in chapter 15. Locke tells us there that probability 'is likeliness to be true, the very notation of the word signifying such a proposition, for which there be arguments of proofs to make it pass, or be received for true'.[7] The mind's 'entertainment' of this sort of proposition is called 'belief, assent, or opinion', which Locke contrasts with 'certainty, faith, and knowledge' on the dual ground that the latter are characterized by intuition and the former are due to 'something extraneous to the thing I believe'. That which is probable I believe because of extraneous grounds, or evidence.

Locke introduces analogy in chapter 16 ('Of the Degrees of Assent'), paragraph 12. This paragraph deals with matters of fact that 'falling not under the reach of our senses... are not capable of testimony'.[8] He divides these into two. The first group are 'finite immaterial things without us', such as spirits, and materials things that are beyond our sensory powers, such as extraterrestrial life-forms; the second group are facts about 'the manner of operation in most parts of the works of nature', by which Locke means, once again, the inner workings of natural phenomena like animal nourishment or magnetism (his examples). In these latter cases we can discern superficial regularities of sequence, but can only 'guess and probably conjecture' their ultimate causes. In these matters '*analogy* is the only help we have, and it is from that alone we draw all our grounds of probability'. His two examples are interesting ones. The first is the observed connection between the violent rubbing of two bodies and the onset of heat or fire; the second is the observed connection between the arrangements and refraction of various bodies and materials, some of them 'pellucid', and the visual perception of colour. In both these cases, varied but analogous connections lead us to infer that the perceived (secondary) quality 'consists in' ('is nothing but') the agitation or arrangement of unperceived (primary) parts. Arguing by analogy, therefore, is not merely a matter of arguing inductively from one observed sort of natural sequence to another, although Locke's

[7] Locke, *Essay*, bk. IV, ch. 15, para. 3.
[8] Ibid. bk. IV, ch. 16, para. 12.

examples seem clearly to include this. It is a matter of taking a perceived regularity to be a sign of deeper and less varied connections that are unknown to us. Locke even continues, in this same paragraph, to sanction cautious inference from the presence of some qualities in humans and creatures beneath them, to their presence in higher beings, including God himself. It is not at all clear, of course, that this sort of analogical reasoning is parallel in all respects to that used in the cases of secondary and primary qualities.

If we turn from Locke's treatment to what Butler says about these notions in the Introduction to the *Analogy*, we find a treatment that is both derivative and distinctive. He follows Locke in telling us at the outset that probable evidence, in contrast to demonstration, 'admits of degrees', all the way from the lowest presumption to moral certainty. He also, in paragraph 3, says that the imperfection of probable evidence shows it to be 'relative only to beings of limited capacities', so that nothing can be probable to God. For God, everything 'cannot but be discerned absolutely as it is in itself, certainly true, or certainly false'. Here again we encounter the less-than-clear notion of the *extraneousness* of probability, which Locke detailed as knowledge of secondary rather than primary qualities, and of perceptually apparent features rather than systematic connections. For all of this, Butler tells us, here again echoing Locke's views on the practical importance of the probable, 'to us, probability is the very guide of life'. He develops this, however, in a way that owes more to Pascal than to Locke.[9]

Butler's total concern with the practical makes him introduce an important extension of the idea of probability. When he tells us that probability is the guide of life, he does not only mean that we have to make do with likelihood rather than certainty when we make our decisions. It is clear from the whole mode of apologetic in the *Analogy* that he also wants us to recognize that prudence will frequently require us to act on the supposed truth of some proposition that has only a very limited likelihood—provided it has *some*. The minimal case that he presents to his readers on behalf of the claims of the Christian revelation is the one he expresses in the Advertisement:

[9] See Terence Penelhum, *Butler* (London, 1985), ch. 4.

Thus much, at least, will be here found, not taken for granted, but proved, that any reasonable man, who will thoroughly consider the matter, may be as much assured, as he is of his own being, that it is not ... so clear a case, that there is nothing in it. There is, I think, strong evidence of its truth; but it is certain no one can, upon principles of reason, be satisfied of the contrary. And the practical consequence to be drawn from this is not attended to by every one who is concerned in it.

This makes it very clear that Butler's argument for Christianity is that although there is strong evidence for its truth, in his view, he can prove that those who think its falsity to be obvious are mistaken; and that when a rational person recognizes this, that person will give the evidences in its favour the most serious consideration, *and* lead a life that embodies the morality that the Christian revelation enjoins. In arguing this way, Butler is leaning on the fact that we frequently have to make practical decisions on a comparably insecure basis, where prudence requires us to act upon low, though real, probabilities.

This argument is reminiscent of Pascal's Wager,[10] but differs from it in important respects. In the first place, Pascal's argument is expressed in terms of a decision about the very existence of God; Butler assumes that his readers never question this, and is arguing for their careful consideration of the particular revelatory claims of Christianity.[11] Secondly, Pascal's case explicitly depends on the acceptance of the Pyrrhonist thesis that reason cannot tell us whether it is more likely that God exists or that he does not.[12] Pascal's particular appeal to prudence requires that there are no theoretical grounds for belief that are not counterbalanced by equally strong (though presumably not *stronger*) grounds for disbelief. Strictly speaking, this would mean that, for the purposes of this argument, Pascal estimates the probabilities of theism and atheism as exactly equivalent. Butler makes it

---

[10] *Pensées*, fragment 418. For discussion, see A. J. Krailsheimer, *Pascal* (Oxford, 1980), ch. 5; Terence Penelhum, *God and Skepticism* (Dordrecht, 1983), chs. 4, 5.

[11] Notoriously, Pascal does not stay with this elemental choice, but appears to assume that a choice for God is a choice for Catholic Christianity. This need not concern us here, however.

[12] 'Let us examine this point, and let us say: "Either God is, or he is not." But to which view shall we be inclined? Reason cannot decide this question. Infinite chaos separates us. At the far end of this infinite distance a coin is being spun which will come down heads or tails. How will you wager? Reason cannot make you choose either, reason cannot prove either wrong.' *Pensées*, trans. Krailsheimer, 150.

clear that he thinks the actual odds favour Christianity; but he also makes it clear that his case for Christianity, or rather his case for the serious consideration of its evidence and the practical adoption of the Christian ethic, is one that requires only that 'it is not so clear a case' that the probability of Christianity's being false is 1. He only needs the reader's agreement that its truth is a non-negligible possibility. Although he never says this explicitly, the merits of his case ought to stand even if the odds for atheism were markedly greater than those for theism—as long as the latter did not reduce to zero. Hence the great emphasis he lays, here again following Pascal, on the importance of Christianity's claims, especially in chapter 1 of part 2. When it would be a matter of such supreme importance not to choose mistakenly, it might be wiser to act as though Christianity were true, even if the odds in its favour were theoretically quite small.

This leads us to a third difference. Pascal is very clear that what is at issue between him and his sceptical interlocutor in the Wager argument is what it is best to *believe*. Notoriously, the argument ends with recommendations to be followed if one sees that it is prudentially best to believe in God, but is prevented by the evenness of the evidence from having this belief: they are recommendations for inducing it. I have myself argued that Butler's case finally depends on this also, but I am now inclined to doubt it.[13] He certainly refrains from saying it explicitly. He repeatedly urges that in his view, the evidences are strong; he suggests more than once that the barriers to accepting this are moral and not theoretical; but he does not say that, if one cannot so weigh the probabilities, one should induce belief by non-rational means. I quote here again from his *Charge to the Clergy of Durham*, of 1751:

Were the evidence of religion no more than doubtful, then it ought not to be concluded false any more than true, nor denied any more than affirmed; for suspense would be the reasonable state of mind with regard to it. And then it ought in all reason, considering its infinite importance, to have nearly the same influence upon practice, as if it were thoroughly believed. For would it not be madness for a man to forsake a safe road, and prefer it to one in which he acknowledges there is an even chance he should lose his life, though there were an even chance likewise of his getting safe through it? (*C* 4)

[13] See Penelhum, *Butler*, ch. 8.

This suggests a conscious likeness to Pascal, and a conscious difference. If the evidence is doubtful, suspense is to be preferred over negation; but intellectual suspense ought to lead to the same practice as affirmation. Butler also holds that the same is true even when the evidence is less than 50 per cent in favour, as long as there is *some* weight in it.[14] But the suggestion that one ought to try to induce belief, as distinct from practice, in such a situation, is conspicuous by its absence.

So much for probability. I turn now to analogy. Butler uses this notion repeatedly, but says very little to make clear what he means by it. We have seen that Locke seems to use it to include both ordinary inductive reasoning, and the special sort of reasoning from inductively recognized natural sequences to the postulation of hidden connections of primary qualities. Butler's main concern with the notion is to use it to ground inferences from the way he thinks we have come, inductively, to observe how the natural world is, to conclusions about the providential economy of the whole creation, natural and supernatural together:

It must be allowed just, to join abstract reasonings with the observation of facts, and argue from such facts as are known, to others that are like them; from that part of the Divine government over intelligent creatures which comes under our view, to that larger and more general government over them which is beyond it; and from that which is present, to collect what is likely, credible, or not incredible, will be hereafter. (*A.* Introd. 7)

In previous writing I have suggested that we can distinguish helpfully between *natural analogy*, or induction, which is the run-of-the-mill terrestrial reasoning from likenesses of sequence that Butler regards as the standard ground for judgements of probability, but whose theoretical basis he declines to examine (*A.* Introd. 5), and *religious analogy*. The latter is reasoning based on supposed likenesses between the world of nature (whose features we have learned of by natural analogy) and the whole creation, which comprises both the natural and the supernatural order. The full title of the book indicates that both natural religion and revealed religion (that is to say both the body of religious doctrine that can be acquired through reason and the

---

[14] The key passage here is *A.* Introd. 4.

body of doctrine that has to be acquired, if at all, from revelation) are to be compared with, and justified by the comparison with, truths known about nature that are not religious—presumably scientific and common-sense truths. Butler's main thrust is the claim that the extent and type of the knowledge the Christian claims to have regarding religion, and the extent and type of the ignorance the Christian must endure in it, are strictly comparable to that enjoyed and tolerated by all of us in relation to the natural world. This is his version of what I have elsewhere called the Parity Argument: the claim, roughly speaking, that it is not reasonable to demand higher standards of proof and evidence in matters of religion than in matters of science and common sense. And if the reader is tempted to retort that the claims of religion are more grandiose and ambitious than those of science, and can therefore be expected to require more rigorous examination, Butler's position is that the immense practical importance of the claims of religion for the life of each one of us is a reason for examining them with more patience and care, but not more rigour; and it is also a reason for acting upon the supposition of their truth, even if the evidences for them are less impressive than he personally believes that they are.

IV

Our ignorance, then, is very great but not total. At the natural level it is mitigated by our probable knowledge, which permits us to choose prudently and not walk completely in the dark. But it is a requirement of prudence to be aware at all times of the limitations of the knowledge we do have, and take steps to ensure that we protect ourselves against calamities that have even the most modest degree of real probability. At the natural level, our ignorance is simply a fact that prudence requires we recognize. When we turn to considerations of religious import, however, Butler sees our ignorance not only as a fact, but as a defence against Christianity's critics. Many of the evils that beset us seem to some to put God's goodness or love into question, and some features of the Christian revelation, such as the restrictedness of its earliest audience, have made some doubtful of its authenticity. Our ignorance of the system of Providence of which these phenomena are a part is a good reason to refrain from drawing negative conclusions from them, even though it is indeed not a proof that they conform to the Christian scheme. It is a good reason to place all the weight one can on the evidences in favour of the Christian scheme, and to continue to adhere to its ethical demands.

Butler is too astute, however, not to see that our ignorance can itself be viewed as a problem. Even though it is reasonable enough to tell over-confident critics to remember their finitude, thus turning apparent counter-evidences into mere mysteries, it is troubling that there is as much mystery as there is. Not all of those who doubt do so through unwillingness to recognize their own mental limits (or so it seems). Some are sincerely distressed at their lack of assurance of revealed truth. So Butler has to argue, not only that ignorance is a fact that it behoves us to recognize, but also that it may itself have a purpose in the providential scheme. He even stretches his use of religious analogy to suggest a purpose it might have. Before commenting on what he says on this, however, I must return to a fundamental matter on which I have touched only briefly, and which deeply affects any estimate of Butler's success in using our ignorance as an apologetic defence: our knowledge that God exists.

V

When Butler uses religious analogy, he sees his conclusions as probable ones. Indeed it is one of his main arguments against the deists of his day that they are inconsistent to hold views like his own on natural religion, and then to be so confident of the falsity of revealed religion, when the status of the doctrines of the former is merely probable and full of unanswered difficulties. This prompts the question of whether Butler thought the very existence of God was itself merely probable, rather than certain. It is clear that he did not think this.

Once more, the key text is the Introduction to the *Analogy*.[15] In paragraph 8 Butler tells us that he will introduce analogical reasoning into religious matters, 'taking it for proved, that there is an intelligent Author of Nature, and natural governor of the world'. On the surface this merely refers to the consensus

---

[15] See also *A*. 2. 8. esp. 5.

between himself and the deists, and is consistent with the possibility that if he had offered a proof of God's existence himself, it would be merely probable in its force. But he goes on to say it has often been proved 'from this argument of analogy and final causes' and from 'abstract reasonings', tradition, testimony, and general consent. This implies there are successful a priori proofs, as well as analogical ones. (From paragraph 3 of chapter 6, as Bernard tells us, it is clear that the abstract reasoning he has in mind is the version of the Cosmological Proof given by Samuel Clarke.[16])

If we take for granted that there is divine governance, in the way in which an a priori proof would entitle us to do, then facts which would otherwise appear as counter-evidence to that governance can only be apparent, and not real, exceptions to it, showing merely that the nature of God's rule is inadequately understood by us. What would otherwise make divine governance unlikely can then only be a mystery. And when faced with puzzling facts about the Christian religion, critics who have already accepted divine governance as proven can be softened by being reminded that they have already accepted parallel puzzles. (The point is less obviously inevitable in theory, but is as true in practice, if the critic is someone who has only satisfied himself of God's existence by probable inference, provided he has decided, as the deists had, that the probability is overwhelming.)

But this argument is gravely weakened if there is no a priori proof of God's being and governance to be had. For then, as Hume made so clear through Philo's arguments in the *Dialogues Concerning Natural Religion*, the case for God's existence itself is no longer to be taken for granted, but is itself a piece of religious analogy, one in which we are asked to infer intelligent creation of the whole universe from the very limited cases of those human artefacts that are a small part of it. Even if an argument of this form posed no problem in itself, it is merely question-begging to treat randomness, confusion, and evil (or the appearances of them) as mysteries rather than as straightforward counter-evidence. But if such phenomena are recognized as counter-evidence, then if we seriously try to follow the standards

---

[16] Samuel Clarke, *A Demonstration of the Being and Attributes of God* (1705).

of inductive reasoning that we claim to adhere to in religious analogy, we must conclude, at best, that the universe is the work of a less-than-infinite intelligence, or of a plurality of these, and that its maker or makers are, as likely as not, possessed of 'neither goodness nor malice'.[17] Hume, of course, concedes that we could save traditional theism by resorting to special hypotheses that explain away the awkward phenomena in ways that reconcile them to God's infinite power and goodness, but makes it clear that such saving moves only merit credence if we have independent grounds to accept these as realities before we start.

It is for reasons like this that scholars have for years dismissed the argument of the *Analogy* as a hopelessly dated one, that presupposes a consensus that no longer exists, since, it is said, there are no deists now. There is no doubt that Butler's case, as he presents it, does date in this way, and that the key appeal to ignorance is much damaged by this. But I wish now to suggest that it is not clearly damaged beyond repair as an apologetic device, when the prudential aspects of his argument are kept in view. These have, I think, a continuing value, and the appeal to ignorance retains some of its force even when religious doubts take atheistic, rather than deistic, forms.

VI

I have argued that although Butler takes over Locke's distinction between probable and certain knowledge without change, including the view that probable knowledge is suitable for creatures in a state of 'probationership', he offers us in the *Analogy* a distinctive view about its role in practice: that it is the mark of the prudent person to act not only in terms of the likelihood of some theoretical possibility being true, but also to take account of its importance; so that in matters of supreme moment, the prudent person will act as though that doctrine or hypothesis is true that it would be most disastrous to reject, should it indeed *be* true—provided it is not clear that there is 'nothing in it'. It is clear that on the question of the origin and purpose of the whole universe, the chances of error in our estimates of likelihood are very great. In these circumstances, Butler

---

[17] See Hume's *Dialogues Concerning Natural Religion*, esp. pts. x, xi. See also Terence Penelhum, 'Butler and Hume', *Hume Studies*, 14 (1988), 251–76.

tells us, we should act as though the Christian religion is true, even though we do not judge the arguments in its favour to be strong ones. I have also argued that Butler's prudential case differs from Pascal's in that Pascal's assumes the classical sceptic's intellectual equipoise between theism and atheism, whereas Butler's can proceed on the basis of any non-negligible degree of probability on the religious side.

We would look in vain for a specification of this. Its not being clear that there is nothing in the Christian case might be reducible to that case merely having logical possibility; but the text seems to require more than this. I shall assume in what follows that Butler's case requires (1) that, in general, the Christian scheme is consistent with the nature of our world as we find it; (2) that it can generate reasonable explanatory hypotheses, such as that of probationary trial, for those phenomena which seem to its critics to be difficulties for it, even though it may not have much in the way of internal warrant for all of them; and (3) that the previous two conditions, which amount to showing that the world is just about the sort of place it would be if Christianity were true, can still allow for *some* mysterious phenomena, though not too many—that these conditions serve to confine, though not necessarily to eliminate, the element of inexplicable mystery in the world. But (1), (2), and (3) together still do not provide any degree of probability for the Christian case, since the number of actual, let alone possible, world-views that would satisfy them is probably very large, and certainly includes atheistic ones. I shall therefore add another condition, (4): that the Christian world-view has some significant evidence in its favour—evidence, that is, for which some of its claims are natural explanations, not merely logically possible ones. In our day many Christian writers would be inclined to offer some of the facts of religious experience here; Butler himself offers, in part 1, facts that he says show the creator is a judge who 'declares for virtue' (*A.* 1. 3, 4), and in part 2 he offers the historical evidences associated with the beginnings of Christianity (*A.* 2. 7). We may or may not follow him in thinking these are enough to make Christianity more likely than any given one of its competitors; but I shall assume that Butler's prudential case does require some non-negligible degree of positive support that would have to be explained away by anyone who judged it to be false, and that this support is available. This would mean that the person Butler addresses is someone who is to some extent torn by conflicting evidence, whatever the relative weightings of that evidence might be.

I must turn now to the other difference between Butler and Pascal: the fact that Butler does not appear to advise us to induce belief in ourselves by non-intellectual means. He only stresses that we should consider such evidence as we have with the greatest care, and ensure, over and over, that our wilfulness does not make us underestimate the Christian case. Meanwhile, we should exercise prudence by acting, in spite of all the intellectual difficulties, as though Christianity were true.

The puzzle is to interpret what this acting-as-if amounts to. I confine myself in the first place to purely practical considerations. Butler believes, as everyone knows, that we do not need revelation, or even belief in God, to know what is right or wrong in the matter of secular duties. Our conscience tells us these. He also holds that, to a large extent, the Christian revelation enjoins us to do the same things that our unassisted consciences would dictate. But of course it adds others. These specifically religious obligations fall into two groups: there are those that conscience can clearly see to be obligations once one accepts the truth of the Christian revelation regarding the Trinity and the saving work of Christ (such as giving thanks to the Son as well as to the Father), and those which believers judge to be duties just because they conclude that God has commanded them (such as participation in the sacraments). While Butler is most anxious to stress the greater importance of those duties that conscience can itself discern over those we can only learn of through revelation (of moral over positive precepts, as he puts it in chapter 1 of part 2), it seems as though the prudent person would perform some at least of the latter as well as the former—as Pascal also recommended.

This prompts an immediate objection. Following Christian practice is not a mere matter of externals, but requires inner submission to God's will.[18] To submit requires acknowledgement that what one does is the will of God, and hence requires

---

[18] In *S.* 15. 9 he says, 'Religion consists in submission and resignation to the Divine will.'

the very belief that the person who needs the prudential argument does not have yet. (He or she merely has some inclination to believe.) I think that Butler is insufficiently sensitive to the gravity of this difficulty. He does address a problem that resembles it in chapter 5 of part 1. He has argued here that it is highly probable that we live in a state of divinely ordained moral discipline, and are subject to rewards and punishments designed to motivate us towards virtue. He imagines an objector saying that concern for rewards and punishments cannot generate virtue, only the appearance of it—what he calls materially virtuous behaviour. He responds as follows:

> But doing what God commands, because He commands it, is obedience, though it proceeds from hope or fear. And a course of such obedience will form habits of it. And a constant regard to veracity, justice, and charity, may form distinct habits of these particular virtues; and will certainly form habits of self-government. Nor is there any foundation for this great nicety, with which some affect to distinguish in this case, in order to depreciate all Religion proceeding from hope or fear. For, veracity, justice, and charity, regard to God's authority, and to our own chief interest, are not only all three coincident; but each of them is, in itself, a just and natural motive or principle of action. And he who begins a good life from any one of them, and perseveres in it ... cannot fail of becoming more and more, of that character, which is correspondent to the constitution of Nature as moral. (*A* 1. 5. 19)

This seems to tell us that habitual performance of duties, even when motivated by self-love, will lead in time to real virtue. But this does not fully meet the case expressed in our objection: that without the belief in God and his commands, it does not seem possible to perform *all* Christian religious duties, since acknowledgement of them as being commanded by God is of the essence of the duties themselves, in many cases. The quoted passage seems indeed to concede this. So it is only possible for the serious enquirer who does not have belief yet to discharge some religious duties, rather than all. Even if Butler's recommended course would eventually lead to the fullest religious life, the difference between where the seeker begins and where he ends is far greater than Butler seems to think it is.

Nevertheless, Butler's prudential argument still has considerable weight. I will attempt to judge it once more in a way that takes account of difficulties. In doing this I shall, once again, assume two things. The first is that the argument is used by Butler as a believer who thinks, himself, that the evidential case for Christianity is a strong one, but wishes to convince a serious but doubtful enquirer who merely concedes that there is some reason to believe it. The second is that Butler does not wish to undermine the intellectual integrity of his hearer, or to persuade him into a course of thought and action that involves him in self-conscious deadening of his intellectual scruples. (Pascal, it will be remembered, does the latter quite explicitly in the Wager argument.[19]) He merely hopes (and as a Christian no doubt expects) that habitual performance of Christian duties will result in the hearer coming to form a different estimate of the relative likelihoods of Christianity and the alternatives to it.

Butler's case is coherent. How strong is it? I think it is a strong one when its difference from Pascal is recognized, provided the ethical continuity between the prior deliverances of the hearer's conscience and the moral commands of Christianity is a fact— provided, that is, the hearer's ethic is a Christian one already, aside from specific religious duties.

The stress on our ignorance is an important component in this argument. The fact that the detailed understanding of human intellectual finitude that Butler inherits from Locke has unacceptable defects is unimportant here. The phenomenal growth of physical science since Locke's time may make us reject the suggestion that our probable knowledge is confined to the surface qualities of things, and that their inner natures are inaccessible to us; but if this has any relevance at all to the assessment of Butler's prudential argument, it seems to me that it strengthens it. For the history of physical science shows us that a recognition of the extent of our ignorance at any one time is a necessary spur to further enquiry, as Butler says it should be; and Butler's prudential case is surely enhanced by the realization that time and again, when our ignorance of physical nature has

[19] 'Vous voulez aller à la foi et vous n'en savez pas le chemin. Vous voulez vous guérir de l'infidélité et vous en demandez les remèdes, apprenez de ceux, etc. qui ont été liés comme vous et qui parient maintenant tout leur bien. Ce sont gens qui savent ce chemin que vous voudriez suivre et guéris d'un mal dont vous voulez guérir; suivez la manière par où ils ont commencé. C'est en faisant tout comme s'ils croyaient, en prenant de l'eau bénite, en faisant dire des messes, etc. Naturellement même cela vous fera croire, *et vous abêtira*' (my italics). *Pensées*, 178.

been replaced by greater knowledge, that knowledge has involved the understanding of facts that were problematic or even anomalous when judged in the light of the earlier state of science.

But however this may be, our ignorance of God's nature and purposes has a dark, as well as a bright, aspect when we consider Butler's case for the troubled enquirer's tentative adoption of the Christian way. While the fact of our ignorance may make it prudent to continue to take Christian doctrine seriously on the chance that it might, after all, be true, is it not a theological problem for the Christian tradition itself that it is so great? We cannot reasonably expect to understand all of God's ways, if he exists, but why is our understanding so limited that we are faced with facts that make it reasonable to doubt whether he does? It is hard enough to live out the commands of the Christian life when one is convinced of the truth of the Christian faith. Surely it is inconsistent with the justice and goodness of God that we should be in a position where its truth can reasonably be doubted? Does this fact not count against Butler's own insistence that we have enough light to do our duty by? Human ignorance may be something that adds strength to Butler's prudential case; but is it not also an additional item of counter-evidence to the very scheme of things he is trying to persuade us to adopt? Butler is keenly aware of this difficulty, and I shall conclude this examination of his apologetic by seeing what he has to say in response to it. It need hardly be said that it is a greater difficulty in the post-deist era than it was before.[20]

VII

Butler makes important contributions to the discussion of the problem of evil. These are found for the most part in his use of the idea of moral probation. He argues in part 1 of the *Analogy*, especially chapters 4 and 5, that there is strong reason to suppose that God places us in this life in settings that enable us, if we use them rightly, to fit ourselves for another and better one, by developing moral character, and that this requires the protracted exercise of virtue—which can only be a real option for us

---

[20] See, however, Penelhum, *Butler*, 187-93.

in a world where we can elect to behave viciously as well. Probation, therefore, requires temptation and trial. This special version of the free-will defence anticipates in many respects the 'soul-making' theodicy of John Hick in our own day.[21] Butler extends this notion of probationary trial to suggest an explanation of the fact that God's revelation is not more obvious, or more nearly indubitable, than it is. It is stated in Sermon 15, but developed much more fully and clearly in chapter 6 of part 2 of the *Analogy*. In the sermon, Butler says that God may deliberately hide himself from us, even if his workings are not beyond our intellectual capacities to understand, for purposes that we cannot now grasp, but which relate to our probationary state: 'difficulties in speculation as much come into the notion of a state of discipline, as difficulties in practice: and so the same reason or account is to be given of both.' In the *Analogy* he tries to indicate a possible reason why God may have hidden himself in this way. The difficulties that stand in the way of accepting Christian claims are difficulties that give us scope for frivolous disregard of those claims, and inattention to our obligation to examine the evidence. This is a special form of probationary test. In case we wonder why there is this apparently superfluous opportunity for sin, Butler points out that there are some people who do not experience the common forms of temptation to neglect duties that are clear to them, because they 'not only see, but have a general practical feeling, that what is to come will be present, and that things are not less real for their not being the objects of sense' (*A.* 2. 6. 13). For such serious-minded persons life would flow dangerously easily, and for them speculative difficulties may be the 'principal part' of the trial Providence arranges for them.

This theory of what I have called intellectual probation is not the same as the view found in Pascal, John Hick, and others that God hides himself from those who do not sincerely seek him, so that his hiddenness is the divine response to the corruption of their minds. It is rather the theory that those disposed to seek the truth with full seriousness might have to be presented with obstacles to test their moral determination.[22] It is a weak

---

[21] John Hick, *Evil and the God of Love* (London, 1966).
[22] I owe the recognition of this difference to John Schellenberg, who discusses both forms of response to the problem of divine hiddenness in *Divine Hiddenness and Human*

argument, partly, as John Schellenberg has made clear, because these seem a particularly inappropriate group of persons to present with *this* hurdle to surmount, and partly because any unsuspected reluctance or frivolity could as well be brought to the surface by strong evidences as by weak and obscure ones. Few tasks are as appealing to frivolous intellectuals as the demolition of apparently compelling arguments in favour of orthodox truths. In general, the sins that attend the evaluation of evidence are sins it is easier to commit when the evidence favours conclusions one does not want to accept; and the hesitation a thinker has in the face of weak evidence is a sign of the very care and attention that Butler keeps urging upon us.

So the specific form his theory of intellectual probation takes is a very unpersuasive one. It is possible to suggest a slightly more persuasive form it might have taken, however, using the sentiments he expresses in paragraph 14 of the fifteenth sermon: 'Due sense of the general ignorance of man would also beget in us a disposition to take up and rest satisfied with any evidence whatever, which is real. I mention this as the contrary to a disposition, of which there are not wanting instances, to find fault with and reject evidence, because it is not such as was desired.' This could yield the following argument: God may reveal himself in obscure or difficult ways because those who are inclined to give low priority to the deepest questions of human life can more easily defer considering them if the evidences for God are weak than if they are strong. This net would certainly catch a larger number of people than the ones referred to in the actual argument Butler uses. For we are all subject to the temptation to ignore the importance of ultimate questions, and the weakness of this evidence gives us an excuse to yield to it.

The problem is that one can overcome this temptation by giving careful and unbiased consideration to this evidence and then rejecting it. The only reason for not rejecting weak evidence for Christianity is its importance. But it is surely possible to recognize its importance, give it all the serious consideration Butler urges, and still reject it, however reluctantly. Butler may think that anyone who genuinely met his criteria

Reason (Ithaca, forthcoming). This is an important work which carries forward the understanding of this fundamental but neglected issue in a major way. The discussion of Butler is in ch. 7.

would be saved from such rejection by divine grace. But this cannot be persuasive to someone who is held back by the weakness of the evidence from being sure there *is* divine grace; and in any case, the existence of widespread conscientious unbelief counts against its being true. It is a necessary truth that the stronger the evidence is, the less it can be rejected conscientiously; and the weaker it is, the more it can. Butler is inevitably in difficulty if he wants to argue that weak evidence is a deliberate divine test of our doxastic conscientiousness, for it is generally a sign of such conscientiousness that weak evidence is rejected.

So although Butler is wholly right to argue that we should be aware of our limitations and not dismiss Christianity because of obscurities in the evidences for it, his suggested explanation of those limitations and those obscurities does not seem consistent with his view of the morality of divine Providence. This failure does not blunt the force of his prudential apologetic, but it does leave an important difficulty unanswered: if Christianity is true, why is this not unambiguously clear? Someone heeding this difficulty, but seeking also to follow his prudential advice, has no choice but to question anew the received post-Humean wisdom that tells us natural theology must fail. For if it can succeed, even the difficulty of divine hiddenness, like other forms of counter-evidence, must have a solution, even if we have to live in ignorance of what it is.

7
A God most Particular: Aspects of Incarnation in Butler's Morality

GORDON KENDAL

Butler's moral philosophy is a blend of English common sense and pastoral sensitivity, interleaved with elements from the long natural law tradition and (even more significantly, though not so overtly) with a conviction that the death of Jesus was a redemptive action by an omnipresent God. This theological determinant of his thought is rarely placed in the centre, either by Butler himself or by his expositors and critics, but it is crucial. For Butler the supreme and decisive instance of a moral action ('instance' is too weak, as we shall see), the volitional event that ought to condition and shape the whole of our moral analysis, already exists in history; in (paradoxically) the death of a man, a man with divine ramifications. This is why morality and moral philosophy are so important. What we might call the 'moral relationship to reality' is, if not fundamental in human life, at least very nearly so, and at any rate inescapable: in engaging in it we are, humanly speaking, being conducted as far as we might ever conceive ourselves being conducted into the unfathomed mysteries of existence. Out of the Christian theism developed above all in the Fourth Gospel and in the Epistle to the Hebrews (his favourite texts) Butler has furnished himself with a standpoint for examining and describing moral experience. This gives him his motive (all his writing is a practical response to people's needs and problems) and it also gives him a set of categories, even pre-categories, to apply to the data. It is in the light of his own faith and Christian understanding that he takes it to be straightforward empirical common ground with his adversaries, if they will only be ingenuous, that our nature is 'the voice of God within us' (*S.* 6. 7), or that '[a]n Author of Nature being supposed, it is not so much a deduction of reason, as a matter of experience, that we are thus under his government' (*A.* 1. 2. 6). Butler is never embarrassed by an urge to find a 'rigorously neutral, theology-free' description of moral phenomena. His natural law is in this way more Augustinian than Thomist. In a blended universe the only accurate moral philosophy is itself blended. So in trying to recover to a distinctively Christian understanding of the world those of his readers who have strayed into natural religion, or in trying to reinforce the grasp on practical Christian truths and obligations of those of his readers who have been weakened either by the prevailing godlessness or by their own frailty, Butler in effect wants them to begin by being more realistic: to see things more clearly. He wants to share a perception with them. And the genesis and firmament of the perception are theological.

Now if this process of modification were entirely in the one direction (from theology to moral analysis) we might feel that it lessened the interest, and indeed the legitimacy, of Butler's project. Having failed to rewrite him in convincingly non-theological terms, we might find ourselves casting his prejudiced books aside. But the same intimacy between moral analysis and Christian theism that has disappointed critics and admirers alike, when they were resolutely intent upon treating Butler simply as a philosopher, works also in reverse. His perception of morality (theologically determined as it is) affects in turn the way in which he envisages central Christian doctrines. This feature is naturally less evident in his published writings than the former: he is not writing as a systematic theologian. But the link is there, and in the remainder of this article I want to examine one set of implications. The question is this: the character of morality, and specifically of moral action, being what it is, what light does this shed on the nature and significance of that supreme and decisive action of God that Christian faith finds embodied in the redemptive life and death of Jesus of Nazareth?

Clearly there are dangers in trying to answer a question that Butler neither tackled nor formulated; dangers of reading too much into his moral analysis, and of reading too much out of it when we try to align it with his doctrine of the Incarnation (a phrase, incidentally, which he never uses: the word 'incarnation' appears theologically only once in the entire *Analogy*, and then quite unimportantly). To say that a philosopher's ideas lend themselves to a certain application may mean only that we intend to borrow them. But I believe it is worth risking. Butler has a characteristic way of portraying the moral relationship that exists for us within a world belonging to, and sustained by, a God who himself has a fundamental moral concern; and in the process he inevitably (whether he means to or not) sharpens the theological notion of what God has made himself to be. The result is a contribution to the traditional understanding of the work of Christ. He shows at least how one man's death might conceivably bring salvation to mankind, and further why it is reasonable (because consistent with our appreciation of familiar moral territory) to believe it may have happened. That is all I want to claim, and all I think Butler would want to claim for this particular line of discussion. His further evidence is drawn from Scripture, from miracles and prophecies, and we may give these considerations whatever weight we choose. But there is implicit in morality an intelligible pattern directly transferable to what he calls the 'particular dispensation of Providence, carrying on by his Son and Spirit, for the recovery and salvation of mankind' (*A.* 2. 1. 14). Ideally the transfer ought to wait upon a higher point of view, and for normal disputational purposes Butler contents himself with suggesting 'that there may be beings in the universe, whose capacities, and knowledge, and views, may be so extensive, as that the whole Christian dispensation may to them appear natural, i.e. analogous or conformable to God's dealings with other parts of his creation; as natural as the visible known course of things appears to us' (*A.* 1. 1. 23). Everyday moral experience, however, properly grasped, anticipates this perspective. That is the clue which I intend to follow.

What then is morality? Whatever else it may be, it is action, and if it is real moral action it is in some sense or other particular. This is Butler's cardinal insight. It is particular, furthermore, not by meaning less but (somehow) by meaning more. The more particular an action is, indeed, the more morally significant it is; and vice versa. Authentic morality, morality that means something, subsists among particular persons doing particular things in particular circumstances. It is the 'determinate time and manner', the 'particular personal application' (*C.* 19, 21), that distinguish a genuine moral engagement from an abstract and essentially bogus moral stance. Having a particular object built into its dynamic is necessary if morality is not to decline into 'an unquiet disposition to action, progress, pursuit, without end or meaning' (*S.* 13. 5). We find Butler consistently impatient with any purportedly moral approach that savours of remoteness, idle curiosity, abstract generalizing, disconnection or shifting of personal responsibility, broad strategies or policies without particular implementation, of insensitivity to the actual circumstances and the crucial moral challenge of the particular. The particular is the acid test. But expressed in this way the idea is still of course very ambiguous, and we need to try to sharpen its edges by showing how particularity figures throughout moral activity. A good place to start, if only because later features in the analysis will qualify and even apparently dissolve its importance, is with the irreducible moral particularity of individual agents. If morality is decisively a particularizing, it also needs particularizers.

That morality is processed through responsible individual agents seems an obvious enough truth, but it is worth affirming because moralities in practice have ways of accepting it while shunting it to one side, and treating individuals as largely means to, or outcomes of, general states of affairs. But deeds require doers, and it is through particular doers that the point and provenance of moral actions are imported: even those actions that Butler singles out (and we shall return to this theme later) as not primarily 'instances of our love either to ourselves or others; but only instances of our Maker's care and love both of the individual and the species, and proofs that he intended we should be instruments of good to each other, as well as that we should be so to ourselves' (*S.* 1. 7). Each of us is distinct from every other, and this numerical distinctness (which Butler will qualify but not abandon in the further light of our social nature) corresponds to a distinctness of character. It is a determinate, not a notional or an abstract, uniqueness. Further, we are unique both actively and passively: we do things that are uniquely our own action, and things happen to us that are uniquely our own experience, and nobody else's. Butler, for reasons which will emerge, is equally insistent upon both aspects. As to active particularity, this consists in our being not merely characterized by the individual actions through which we exercise and mani-

A God most Particular

fest ourselves, but (more mysteriously and fundamentally) also originative of them. The overt distinctiveness of our behaviour—'the external event, or the thing's being done'—stems from the morally important 'doing of it, or the action' (*A.* 2. 6. 17). Statements about a personal agent are reducible neither to statements about his body nor to statements about his consciousness: both of these are plainly very germane to personal agency, and furnish it with a kind of manifest particularity, public or private, as the case may be, but the particularity of the moral self is, over and above this, an internal particularizing. On this hinges the solemn fact that 'the salvation of every man cannot but depend upon his behaviour, and therefore cannot but depend upon himself; and is necessarily his own concern, in a sense in which it cannot be another's' (*SS* 1. 6); and only marginally less recondite is the strange but familiar phenomenon of those moral failures that relate directly to personal integrity, failures like the internal dislocation experienced by both Balaam and David, a dislocation that is wrong apart even from its impact on others or on the agents themselves (*S.* 7. 10, *passim*).

While asserting, however, that human beings are made for action, and giving this clear priority over their propensity to seek out knowledge, Butler insists on the importance too of the passive particularity of moral agents. In terminology strikingly parallel to that quoted above from the first of his *Six Sermons*, he reminds us that 'from the very constitution of our nature, we cannot but have a greater sensibility to, and be more deeply interested in, what concerns ourselves' (*S.* 8. 7)—where the context is a discussion of the effect of injuries on us. What we feel, what happens to us, is as much marked by particularity in our self as either the actions we perform or their originative source. While strictly distinguishing (in his discussion of personal identity) between a living being and its awareness of itself, he is clear that 'to be endued with consciousness is inseparable from the idea of a person, or intelligent being' (DI 4). Again, while he even goes so far as to remark (in his defence of the possibility of a future life) that 'our gross organized bodies, with which we perceive the objects of sense, and with which we act, are no part of ourselves' (*A.* 1. 1. 9), he can surely only mean by this that a person is not logically limited in his actions to the possibilities of embodiment inherent in this actual collection of material particles: he is not to be identified 'symmetrically' with its sheer passivity (like the inanimateness of mere machines[1]). The self 'animates matter' at any rate, and all actions are done 'by means of some natural passion'.[2] Any other interpretation of Butler's meaning at this point would be inconsistent with the whole drift of his explication of moral action; as we shall see. A moral agent has a unique receptive presence—sentient and affected—as well as a unique originative presence. Butler asserts the complementariness of these two aspects forthrightly but carefully: 'It is not an idea, or abstract notion, or quality, but a being only, which is capable of life and action, of happiness and misery' (DI 9). His metaphysic of personal being as radically active *and* sentient is profoundly pluralistic as well as profoundly relational, and has more affinities with Leibniz (that most Anglican of continental philosophers) than with either Spinoza or Descartes: he is troubled by neither of their characteristic problems—maintaining individual distinctness or genuine interaction, respectively. One final indication that he takes this personal category very seriously indeed is his confident surmise that it will continue beyond this life into the heavenly presence: 'we, our proper self, shall still remain: we shall continue the same creatures we are, with wants to be supplied, and capacities of happiness' (*S.* 14. 10); though an earlier remark warns us not to absolutize the language of distinctness, because the time will come when 'our will is lost and resolved up into his' (*S.* 14. 5). A will to which that can happen is no solidly exclusive particular. But particular in some sense it must be, if morality is authentic.

If we turn next from the agent to his actions we see of course that one simple way of characterizing the particularity of an action is to derive it from the particularity of the agent. But it is more important for our present purpose to see how further aspects of an action's particularity can in turn illuminate what the particularity of the agent amounts to. Actions have their own quality of being particular, and in Butler's analysis there are broadly two frameworks that determine their nature. One of these is the self, the other is the world. But we shall return to these after considering briefly five characteristics that make an

[1] Cf. SP 14.
[2] *A.* 1. 3. 15. Cf. *A.* 1. 1. 9, 11: 'nearly related to and interested in certain systems of matter'.

action 'particular' and that make its being particular an essential ingredient of any proper moral engagement. All five characteristics are embedded in what Butler has to say about morality, and he has something important to say about each, but not systematically. Let me summarize his account by saying that every genuine moral action exhibits particularity in its initial impulse, in its target or objective, in its meaning, in its contributiveness to moral growth, and in its felt immediacy. Let us look at these one by one.

In Butler's view action is experimental in the sense that it arises from particular attractions or repulsions. We are so constructed, and so situated, that every impulse to act is rooted in the feelings of pleasure and pain that God has associated with 'final causes' (*A.* 1. 2. 6) in his providential scheme and that are conveyed and sensed through 'a variety of particular affections, passions, and appetites to particular external objects' (*S.* 11. 5). There may seem to be exceptions to this, when for example what we do arises from some relatively general concern about our well-being, but action proper—the translation of a concern into an actual moral choice—is never disconnectible from particular feelings charged by particular circumstances.[3] Disinterested action, as far as impulse is concerned, is a phantom of the Stoics. Further (and this brings us to the second point), no moral action can be vague in its target: we cannot be indefinite in what we aim to accomplish and still claim to be operating morally. This is an especially dangerous illusion, and Butler emphasizes the importance of seeing ourselves as having to deal with particular duties, of narrowing our objective to something concretely apprehensible, say to 'that part of the universe, that part of mankind, that part of our country, which comes under our immediate notice, acquaintance, and influence, and with which we have to do' (*S.* 12. 3). Piety too needs to be particularized if it is not to 'grow languid even among the better sort of men' (*C.* 10). That is the hallmark of a genuinely moral attitude: not to confine itself to general aims and wishes, but to be set by particular impulses upon particular targets. Preaching to the governors of the London Infirmary Butler says: 'our general disposition to beneficence would not be sufficiently directed, and in

---

[3] Cf. SP 30 with SP 31.

other respects would be very ineffectual, if it were not called forth into action by some or other of those providential circumstances, which form particular relations between the rich and the poor' (*SS* 6. 20). While he sometimes writes as though particular desires were a useful, if regrettable, supplement, given the weakness of rational dispositions,[4] he is clear that their role is inescapable, both for propelling and for specifying actions: without the 'under affections' our actions would be insignificant as well as inert. 'Take away these affections, and you leave self-love absolutely nothing at all to employ itself about; no end or object for it to pursue, excepting only that of avoiding pain' (SP 37).

The first two points represent a kind of externality entering into each action. Circumstances impinge, and occasion and shape what we do. But alongside is the natural tendency of the agent to spell himself out in particular ways, to be refining and implementing his own meanings. The 'affections, passions, and appetites to particular external objects' 'proceed from, or together make up that particular nature according to which man is made' (*S.* 11. 5). The 'occasions' are correlated with our 'own previous bent and bias' (*S.* 1. 10). Butler never separates the two sides. Wanting to do something is already to be plotting a determinate course and letting our character form itself into a meaning specific and particular enough to achieve clarity and effective currency. Even though 'the present world is not our home' (*S.* 6. 13), we can be confident enough in our hedonism to accept that the 'inward frame of man does in a peculiar manner answer to the external condition and circumstances of life, in which he is placed' (*S.* 6. 1). The external objects that activate us, and that we actively choose, are 'objects in which our natural good consists' (*A.* 1. 2. 2). When we say that an action is detailed, it matters little whether we say first that circumstances knocked it into a particular shape or that the agent's erstwhile vague ideal fleshed itself out into a distinctive actuality; so long as we do eventually say both.

Fourthly, because we are 'creatures in a progress of being towards somewhat further' (*S.* 14. 7), an action is not a finished product that is either concluded in the doing or sent out into the world to exercise its impact entirely away from the agent. Being

---

[4] Cf. *S.* 5. 10.

a mixture of internal and external detailing (as we have just seen), it is more like an experimental attempt upon the world by one particular part of it. The agent finds himself in some degree every time he does something: as he acts, something happens to him. That is what it means to be in a 'state of probation', of 'discipline and improvement' (*A.* 1. 5, chapter heading). 'Temptations render our state a more improving state of discipline, than it would be otherwise: as they give occasion for a more attentive exercise of the virtuous principle, which confirms and strengthens it more, than an easier or less attentive exercise of it could' (*A.* 2. 6. 12). In every action I am altered and put at risk, stretching myself into yet another detail of time and space and (as it were) waiting to see what happens: preferably being fortified and clarified rather than weakened or lessened. It is the radical threat that makes us often unwilling to become truly involved in matters, because doing things in particular changes *us*; but not to act at all, or simply to act remotely and abstractly, is to settle for a premature self-characterization—and there is still so much unfinished and undiscovered. Moral growth depends on genuine engagement: it is 'to use and exercise' that 'our nature is formed to yield' (*A.* 1. 5. 4). 'Neither is restraint by any means peculiar to one course of life: but our very nature, exclusive of conscience and our condition, lays us under an absolute necessity of it. We cannot gain any end whatever without being confined to the proper means, which is often the most painful and uneasy confinement' (*S.* 3. 7). This is yet another aspect of the important particularity of moral actions.

The action incorporates, then, two kinds of constraint. There is the initial (twofold) constraint that goes into moving it and shaping it, making it practicable and definite; and there is the constraint it subsequently exercises as it answers back to the agent who generates it, reacting as he acts. Morality is no romantic creation that spontaneously and unhindered imposes our inner meaning on an inert world. It is an accommodation, in which the recalcitrance of the circumstances plays an essential part in the quality of each act taken singly, and in the formation over time of the agent from whom the process of actions stems. Butler may sometimes seem unduly fatalistic about the 'non-negotiable' character of the moral context; (witness his remark about rich and poor that 'this their general intercourse, with the superiority on one hand, and dependence on the other, are in no sort accidental, but arise necessarily from a settled providential disposition of things, for their common good' (*SS* 2. 6.)). But it is not certain that his assessments are any wider of the mark than the indiscriminate optimisms of later political radicals, and his general point can in any case stand.

A fifth and final aspect of the particularity we are trying to elicit from Butler lies in the felt immediacy characteristic of moral actions. In this area Butler is not a 'rationalist' in any of the standard senses of the term. 'Reason alone, whatever any one may wish, is not in reality a sufficient motive of virtue in such a creature as man; but this reason joined with those affections which God has impressed upon his heart' (*S.* 5. 3). We do reason, but taking stock reflectively of our position and the claims that exist on us is insufficient to the latent complexity of things. At best it singles out some limited characteristics and (more dangerous still, morally) it enables us to disconnect ourselves from what is going on. There is no substitute for the unmediated acknowledgement of being simply here and now in an 'infinite scheme' (*A.* 2. 5. 22), the ramifications of which are 'beyond the utmost stretch of our understanding' (*C.* 6); and for the unmediated response to our duty therein, recognized typically 'intuitively' (*S.* 7. 14). Behind this interpretation lies a metaphysical view that the particular is the focus of the infinite, and therefore insusceptible to the necessarily partial analysis of overt rationality; but Butler's concern is more practical. Feeling alone guarantees the occurrence of an intimate encounter between real people (in their unfathomed complexity) and their real environment (in *its* unfathomed complexity). Morality should be first-hand. 'Proof of the existence and presence of any being is quite different from the immediate perception, the consciousness of it' (*S.* 14. 15). This felt immediacy is a mark of any authentic practical knowledge, however comprehensive the object (and the reference in the last sentence is to God), but for us it is especially characteristic of our engagement in the particulars that make up moral life.

Seen in this way, the fivefold quality of particularity inherent in moral actions plainly modifies what we might otherwise have concluded from the brief earlier remarks about the importance of the individual moral agent. There is a creative tension in

Butler's analysis between the distinctness and logical priority of each person, on the one hand, and, on the other, his integral dependence upon the world in which his actions and he himself are formed. Before we go on to examine further the implications of this tension for the two sides, it is worth noting that Butler is careful not to upset the balance by over-indulgence in unidirectional 'causal' language. Of course he does use this kind of language frequently, but he complements it with two other idioms, as if to alert us to the intricate nature of what is going on when actions take place. First, action may often most naturally be seen as a manifestation of what we are, irrespective of whatever consequences might arise. Fixing attention on the revelatory function of an action as a representation of the agent's nature is a centrally moral way of proceeding. 'Acting, conduct, behaviour, abstracted from all regard to what is, in fact and event, the consequence of it, is itself the natural object of the moral discernment' (DII 2). Even when Butler draws aside from abstract considerations of fittingness to the (for him) more congenial discussion of the experienced rough-and-tumble of moral life, he recognizes that there is rightly much more to an action than its causality. So this world is 'a theatre of action, for the manifestation of persons' characters, with respect to a future one: not to be sure to an all-knowing Being, but to his creation of part of it' (*A.* 1. 5. 22). Butler returns to this speculation again[5] and clearly there are theological mysteries into which we need not enter. The point, however, is that in morality an action's significance in a particular set of circumstances is not exhausted by its particular impact upon them. (Notice that Butler uses, from architecture and art, a perfectly acceptable non-causal meaning of the words 'effect' and 'result'.[6]) Secondly, the intention of an action need not always be an intention to effect something in some particular. An action can legitimately be a 'witness': here the agent's concern about the eventual outcome and the immediate outcome, but not about his faithfulness in doing what he ought, is suspended. Butler reminds the Society for the Propagation of the Gospel that when Christ foretold the preaching of the gospel 'what would be the effect, or success of the general preaching of the gospel, is not here mentioned' (*SS*

[5] Cf. *A.* 2. 6. 14.
[6] *A.* 2. 7. 2; cf. ibid. 30.

1. 5). The same distinction is maintained when he discusses how we may perform duties in a non-utilitarian manner, though God (and God alone) determines that their fulfilment shall produce happiness (*S.* 12. 31 n. 22). Positive religious institutions do have a role as particular causal ingredients: they are 'manifestly necessary to keep up and propagate religion amongst mankind' (*A.* 2. 5. 23), and (by the way) are another interesting illustration of the way in which even relatively corporate realities need to be particularized if they are to be morally relevant. This second alternative idiom is less unequivocally non-causal than the first; but being simply a reminder, a 'standing memorial', a 'repository' (*SS.* 1. 7), may be a good way of being active.

Having now opened up our topic by looking at the importance of particular selves in morality, and then at the different shades of particularity in moral actions; and having seen how the fact that actions are essentially particular has implications for the nature of the self and its relationship with its world; we are in a position to revisit the self before moving out again into the world in which it belongs.

The particular personal basis from which particular actions proceed, and which they incarnate, is 'will and character', by which Butler means 'temper, taste, dispositions, practical principles, that whole frame of mind, from whence we act in one manner rather than another' (*A.* 1. 6. 8 n. 8). If Butler intended to offer a rigid twofold or threefold anthropology (say: reason/conscience; general principles of self-love and benevolence; particular appetites), it has to be said—*pace* many of his expositors—that his language disguises the fact well. Since a moral person is not internally heterogeneous in that manner, he can express himself (as he does) with flexibility and imprecision on the subject. The moral struggle, for Butler, is a struggle of the self with itself; not of one distinct part with other parts; and certainly not of one separated factor (say 'conscience' or 'will') imposing its regulation from without. Although he sometimes writes dramatically of the regulative behaviour of conscience, nowhere does he intend to disconnect it from the rest of 'will and character'. If we find him apparently failing to discriminate between 'conscience' and 'reasonable self-love',[7] or between

---

[7] e.g. *S.* 3. 9.

'conscience' and 'benevolence' (said to be 'the sum of virtue' as 'a principle in reasonable creatures' (*S.* 12. 27)), or indeed between either self-love or benevolence and the particular appetites that activate them in real life (saying that 'the very idea of an interested pursuit necessarily presupposes particular passions or appetites; since the very idea of interest or happiness consists in this, that an appetite or affection enjoys its object' (SP 37)); when we find him claiming that 'if by a *sense of interest* is meant a practical regard to what is upon the whole our happiness: this is not only coincident with the principle of virtue or moral rectitude, but is a part of the idea itself' (*A.* 1. 5. 13 n. 16) (and I leave aside consideration of the looseness of his vocabulary); still his 'failure' is more a deliberate refusal to draw misleading lines of division.

There *is* a distinctive moral imperative in the nature of the moral person, just as there is in a civil community, but it is no more despotic in the one case than in the analogous one. Butler was rather proud of the diffusion of legal authority in eighteenth-century England. 'In some other countries the upper part of the world is free, but in Great Britain the whole body of the people is free' (*SS* 5. 5). He begged the Lords: 'Let us transfer, each of us, the equity of this our civil constitution to our whole personal character; and be sure to be as much afraid of subjection to mere arbitrary will and pleasure in ourselves, as to the arbitrary will of others' (*SS* 5. 12). In a sketch of an ideal community, offered in passing to demonstrate the 'happy tendency of virtue', he notes: 'Public determinations would really be the result of the united wisdom of the community' (*A.* 1. 3. 21). The way in which a passion is 'naturally subordinate to the one superior principle' (*S.* 3. 2) must not be confused logically with the way in which a recalcitrant slave is naturally subordinate to his superior despot. The analogy with British political life is supposed to correct, not to perpetuate, that category mistake; for the self is its own conscience, and it is more correct to see vice as a denial not of the 'higher and better part' but of our constitution as a whole (SP 16). Among other characteristics the self possesses a latent form and structure, built up in its engagement with detailed circumstances and in turn endowing those circumstances (and the actions expressed through them) with a specific direction. In a much less dramatic, and more carefully worded, footnote Butler says of the 'higher principle of reflection' that 'the superiority of this principle to all others is the chief respect which forms the constitution':[8] whatever precisely this means, it excludes 'government by intrusion'.

Similarly 'will' is nothing incongruous either. One reason why Butler has no need to determine the abstract question of 'liberty' (*A.* 1. 6) is that it does not matter one way or the other to his descriptive analysis of moral action. It would matter if it were a question of identifying a putatively transcendent item, because the result of such an enquiry would radically affect our understanding of how people act: it would determine what the self consisted of; whereas for Butler we already know that, and the further question is merely what modal status its activity possesses. The question he is happy to leave open is a question about second-order adverbs, not about first-order substantives. The affections and principles of our nature do not require to be handled by something 'extra': they *are* we! Passions have their own dynamism. 'Passion or appetite implies a direct simple tendency towards such and such objects' (*S.* 2. 13)—Leibnizian resonances again.[9] It is natural for reflecting and considering to go on, for this or that particular tendency to be displaced or promoted, for conflicts to be resolved among our many interests, for goals to be pursued that are more comprehensively satisfying than any particular object taken singly; but throughout the regulating, systematizing, deciding, and effecting are internal. Dispositions, clustered and reciprocally ordering themselves in the midst of a detailed and complex world, in response to their implicit rational imperative, issue in particular actions that in turn shape them.

How can this be? and why is Butler so insistent on the role and adequacy of particular motivation? Without it, his descrip-

---

[8] *S.* 3. 2 n. 3. Cf. Hooker: 'the lawful power of making laws to command whole politic societies of men belongeth so properly unto the same entire societies, that for any prince or potentate of what kind soever upon earth to exercise the same of himself, and not either by express commission immediately and personally received from God, or else by authority derived at the first from their consent upon whose persons they impose laws, it is no better than mere tyranny.' (R. Hooker, *Of the Laws of Ecclesiastical Politie* (1593), 1. 10. 8)

[9] Cf. Leibniz: 'there is in things that are possible, or in possibility or essence itself, a certain need for existence, or (if I may so put it) a claim to exist; and, to put it in a word ... essence in itself tends towards existence' (*On the Ultimate Origination of Things* (1697), in *Philosophical Writings*, ed. G. H. R. Parkinson (London, 1973), 137).

tion of action and its implicates would be very different; he would have to preach differently; and he would have had to reconsider the intelligibility of the death of Christ, as his major theological determinant in this matter. We have to consider the world in which the moral process takes place. Moral agents are woven out of, and into, a material world but a world which is also moral and inherently ambiguous. It exhibits final causes under the benevolent and righteous government of God, and God's goodness, according to Butler, is implicit in every aspect of the world (not merely as a prior condition of its existence), though our own very limited perspective prevents our having more than an inkling of what the full import of each circumstance may be, or of what the overall purpose of God may be, or even that there is a unified purpose at all. (Analogy, however, 'suggests and makes it credible that this government must be a scheme, system, or constitution of government, as distinguished from a number of single unconnected acts of distributive justice and goodness' (*A.* 1. 7. 2).) In a moral world there are no bare facts; and in this moral world at least, given its complexity, there are no strictly unequivocal facts either. Events are meanings, doctrine is fact, prophecy is history (*A.* 2. 7. 30); and, like the Scriptures,[10] events can be read—and are seemingly meant to be read—in different ways. 'Nature' has no connotation of value-neutrality for Butler; it is the 'cosmos', the ordered universe with its 'fixed, settled' character,[11] and if it seems bereft of meaning that is because it means so much rather than so little—its basic stratum of complementary perceptions being unfortunately made even more elusive by the disorder associated with sin, a disorder that not only obscures the primary moral intent of things but brings into play a further layer of divine ordinances (in addition to the complicatedly organic creative meaning) to correct or reintegrate matters. It is not obvious what the world means. Butler is optimistic, though. The normal affiliations of pleasure and pain suggest that 'moral government' consists in rendering people 'happy and unhappy, in rewarding and punishing them, as they follow, neglect, or depart from, the moral rule of action interwoven in their nature' (DII 9). The 'intent of nature' (*A.* 1. 3. 15) divulges itself in 'tendencies' that

[10] Cf. *A.* 2. 7. 25.
[11] *A.* 1. 1. 23; cf. *A.* 1. 2. 4.

'are to be considered as intimations, as implicit promises and threatenings, from the Author of nature' (*A.* 1. 3. 38). We can trace the meanings some way, and we have some idea at any rate of why we cannot trace them further: 'since there appears such a subordination and reference of the several parts to each other, as to constitute it properly one administration or government; we cannot have a thorough knowledge of any part, without knowing the whole' (*S.* 15. 6). Particular events embody meaning prior to our launching ourselves upon them (and prior to our being formed by them), and the content of any particular event has ramifications stretching far beyond itself: it may stand for more than it shows. The world is such that moral agents not only must but can emerge and grow in it. This is Butler's version of 'ought implies can'.

We shall return to emergence and growth shortly. What makes action possible is the fundamental consanguinity between who and what the agent is, on the one hand, and what the moral world is, on the other hand. This is why pleasure is not only as important in its way as conscience, but important for broadly the same reason. Conscience is the forward marker, the structural impulse that alerts us to the conditions of ultimate happiness, the happiness designed by our Maker; conscience is our standing reminder that the infrastructure of happiness needs building, often by tactical *dis*engagement (which 'is absolutely necessary to enjoyment' (*S.* 11. 9)). Equally, it 'is manifest that nothing can be of consequence to mankind or any creature, but happiness' (*S.* 12. 28), for 'the good Author of our nature designed us not only necessaries, but likewise enjoyment and satisfaction, in that being he hath graciously given, and in that condition of life he hath placed us in' (*S.* 4. 7). Even

> when we shall have put off this mortal body, when we shall be divested of sensual appetites, and those possessions which are now the means of gratification shall be of no avail; when this restless scene of business and vain pleasures, which now diverts us from ourselves, shall be all over; we ... must have faculties of perception, though not sensitive ones; and pleasure or uneasiness from our perceptions, as now we have. (*S.* 14. 10)

Despite all his preacher's suspicion of contemporary pleasures, Butler cannot relinquish hedonism: the authentic moral faculty, 'whether called conscience, moral reason, moral sense, or divine reason; whether considered as a sentiment of the understanding, or as a perception of the heart; or, which seems the truth, as including both' (DII 2), requires it, because the sacred authority of conscience and the attractions of the external world felt as pleasure are not two different kinds of claim, but one and the same fact experienced under different aspects. We are, essentially, where we find ourselves. Passions, like conscience, are 'implanted in our nature by God' (*S.* 8. 17). The two aspects come closest together in the distinctive pleasure attached to personal integrity, to being consonant with ourselves and with the demands our situation makes upon us: 'Truth, and real good sense, and thorough integrity, carry along with them a peculiar consciousness of their own genuineness' (*S.* 10. 11), but our thoroughgoing dependence underpins their identity across the material and social realm. The consanguinity involved in the dual phenomenon of conscience and pleasure entails that 'to have no restraint from, no regard to others in our behaviour, is the speculative absurdity of considering ourselves as single and independent, as having nothing in our nature which has respect to our fellow-creatures, reduced to action and practice' (*S.* 1. 10).

What is unfortunately lacking in Butler's published work is a detailed account of how this dependence reveals and establishes itself through time: how the agent emerges. To expect anticipations of Hegel might be unfair, but Butler does give some attention to the matter, particularly in his discussion of 'probation' (*A.* 1. 5) and in his sermon on the work of charity schools (*SS* 4). Human beings develop and are developed by the interplay of 'external' (not exactly the right word, given the intimacy of the process) challenges and opportunities and 'internal' capacities. They must perforce *become*: 'mankind is left, by nature, an unformed, unfinished creature; utterly deficient and unqualified, before the acquirement of knowledge, experience, and habits, for that mature state of life, which was the end of his creation, considering him as related only to this world' (*A.* 1. 5. 7), and those deficiencies and capacities extend well beyond this world and its rewards, for there is 'a deeper and more essential want, than any of these things can be the supply of' (*S.* 14. 9). And in practical terms teaching a child to read is as essential to his emergence as a person as giving him food; indeed, given the way in which human nature and human society blend under the ordering of God, it is not a good idea to try to distinguish the two tasks too sharply. Education involves 'endeavouring to put [children] into right dispositions of mind, and right habits of living, in every relation and every capacity' (*SS* 4. 4): not so much doing things to them as bringing them gradually into being as substantial individuals with a part to play in the world. It is not an optional extra. The process will take place anyhow, without our participation (*SS* 4. 1). The full theology of grace necessary to explicate these familiar realities is not supplied by Butler, nor does he supply much of a metaphysics that could make intelligible the elusive identity of natural surroundings and personal centre of action; he is most interested in the existence of the fact, and trusts somehow to his Christian theism to guarantee its significance. His point is that an agent is much more subtle, more porous, more vulnerable, more enduringly inchoate, than simply an absolute starting-point of actions. We have only to examine ordinary actions clearly to see this. A determinate agent exists midway in a scheme of realization that issues in particular actions (and is unreal without them) but rests in a divine moral purpose that characterizes both the particular agent and the world in which he emerges and into which he progressively invests his own contribution.

An individual plays his part the more successfully (taking 'success' in the widest sense indicated by the nature of his conscience and desires), the more he approximates—in his practical understanding of who he is and of what the circumstances facing him really amount to—to that radical character that he and they possess in the fabric of God's purpose. Hence (and here we approach the central, though latent, paradox in Butler's analysis) he will be the more authentically particular, the more comprehensive (and less exclusive) the import of his actions is. There are parts that are 'merely parts', their significance apparently restricted to themselves alone: they owe little and they pay little. Much of our everyday behaviour appears, and even attempts, to be like this; it stems from a 'partial and fond regard to ourselves' (*S.* 10. 2), a 'contracted spirit' (*S.* 11. 1), which is in reality untrue to ourselves and which, if we are not careful, will fix us in a self-designation that is as unnatural as it is immoral. Moral maturation requires us to move beyond this partiality to the inclusiveness of genuine particularity, to recognize that we are not just particularizers but particularized through our place in a world where we have a common interest with others. Compassion and fellow-feeling belong to our nature, so that any action that repudiates them is diminishing ourselves. The imperative of conscience is the imperative to visualize things as they really are (which means seeing them in all their organic interconnectedness) and to act accordingly. But of course our access to the data is severely limited, as Butler never tires of repeating. It is the immediate meaning of a circumstance that strikes us most forcibly. Only when that fails to satisfy the demands of reflection and moral seriousness do we perhaps try to situate it within a wider pattern of meaning and let our practical response be qualified. But laying ourselves open in this way to the meaning within the meaning is being vulnerable. It is letting our imaginations catch up with the truth of our nature, entering personally into more of the implications of being fellow-creatures in God's world, picking up more clues as to who in particular we are meant to be; and (often painfully) embodying them. The *Six Sermons*, which ought to be neither magnified nor neglected, root the deadly seriousness of morality in just this perception of who we are. Negligence in the use of riches, for example, is a betrayal of God's trust and makes the rich 'partakers of other men's sins',[12] while the right use of riches is to 'imitate Almighty God; and cooperate together with him in promoting the happiness of the world ... and, by such exercise of charity, they improve within themselves the temper of it, which is the very temper of heaven' (*SS* 6. 23). It is wrong to interpret this language as merely the rhetoric of a preacher. It is as nearly literally true as any philosophical proposition can be. The perfect part would be a perfect paradigm of the whole, and it would thereby be supremely particular: in contrast, a disconnected part would have ceased to play any really particular part at all.

It is in the light of this that we need to understand Butler's remarks about 'resignation'. This is a key virtue for Butler. Indeed, it is the key to all the others, because it is the essence of moral realism. 'There is a temper of mind made up of, or which follows from all three, fear, hope, love; namely, resignation to the

---

[12] *SS* 2. 10 (cf. 1 Tim. 5: 22).

divine will, which is the general temper belonging to this state; which ought to be the habitual frame of our mind and heart' (*S.* 14. 2). It rests in a general human propensity found quite apart from any overtly religious context. 'We find the principles of it within us; and every one exercises it towards some objects or other; i.e. feels it with regard to some persons, and some circumstances' (*S.* 14. 3). Properly understood, it means neither dull inactivity nor gloomy acceptance of actual events; and it is compatible with the most energetic pursuit of goodness and the most impassioned refusal to believe that the way things appear is always the way they are intended to be. But being resigned does mean not fancying ourselves to be set apart from the natural order: it means recognizing that God is already there, and that our inklings of what has to be done, as well as our capacities to contribute to the doing of it, arise from a providential kinship between ourselves and it, a kinship evidenced in the way conscience marshals its resources out of the particular passions and affections of a human nature that is as sentient as it is prescriptive.

The point we have reached in our presentation of Butler's analysis of morality can be stated briefly as follows. Real moral agents are identified by their concern to be at least particular in relation to the world, to engage in actions that are conditioned by circumstances that in various ways answer to and contribute to those agents' self-articulation. A genuinely moral action incorporates somehow a definiteness of activation, a definiteness of intended reference, a particular focus of meaning, a feedback to the agent himself as part of his self-discovery, and an immediacy in his experience that places it in a different category from that of mere ratiocination. Actions and agents alike are not necessarily reciprocally exclusive: they require a different sort of explanatory concepts from those that might be adequate in understanding brute nature (if there were such a realm). The more particular an action is—the more it succeeds in grappling with what is really going on—the more meaning it has; and the wider the range of ramifications that it embodies. Similarly for agents. Not only *can* an action be particular in this comprehensive way: it *has* to be, for the sake of morality. It is not that, things being as they are, agents are bound to reduce their ideas to particular shapes if they are to have any purchase in the world: the demand is crucial in the moral objective itself. To be moral is to let oneself develop and exercise a personal meaning rich enough to handle each situation with the accuracy and precision of authentic love; approximating to God's own characterization of the facts, and 'taking in' rather than 'shutting out' these factual preconditions.

To the extent that God's relationship with the world is moral too, we might expect it to exhibit similar characteristics. Specifically, we might find it reasonable to understand along these lines the traditionally accepted redemptive event involving God in Jesus. Christianity, in Butler's view, has reinforced belief that this is a moral world under the administration of a moral Governor, but it has also supplied information about another strand in God's government (still 'moral'), that 'extraordinary administration' (*A.* 2. 3. 2) which deals with the results of man's sin by providing a remedy against the ruin that would otherwise ensue from it. The aim of this concurrent activity of God is variously expressed: it is 'for the recovery and salvation of mankind' (*A.* 2. 1. 14), for 'raising them to the perfection and final happiness of their nature' (*A.* 2. 7. 29); in general, it is to correct and stabilize a situation that human behaviour has made abnormal. We can regard it in two ways. The natural way, given a chronological perspective, is to see it as 'additional' (*A.* 2. 3. 5), something put into operation responsively or reactively; and this aspect is important, as we shall see. But, secondly, the redemptive intent is for Butler, as for any Christian theist, as fundamental in God, as germane to his original purpose, as the goodwill evinced in the activity of creation. Everyday analogy suggests something like coalescence between the two, for example in the provision made in nature for the intrinsically harmful tendencies of events to be counteracted by equally intrinsic 'appointments of Providence' (*A.* 2. 5. 5): 'this may be called mercy or compassion in the original constitution of the world; compassion, as distinguished from goodness in general.' A like primary duality of provision may be supposed in the case of God: 'it would be according to the analogy of nature, to hope, that, however ruinous the natural consequences of vice might be, from the general laws of God's government over the universe; yet provision might be made, possibly might have been originally made, for preventing those ruinous consequences from inevitably following' (*A.* 2. 5. 5).

Butler's language is cautious, as well it might be. For us the identity of creative and redemptive love in God (if it is an identity) is obscured by our position in history, but other beings may be able to view the matter more plainly: 'the whole Christian dispensation may to them appear natural, i.e. analogous or conformable to God's dealings with other parts of his creation' (*A.* 1. 1. 23). The reason for not plumping for an interpretation of divine forgiveness as simply responsive and subsequent is that, if we did that, we should be ascribing to God the same weakness with which the exercise of passions is attended in ourselves; and 'God Almighty is, to be sure, unmoved by passion or appetite, unchanged by affection' (*S.* 5. 3). But the lesson to draw from Butler's reservations about divine passions is not that God is not compassionate in some important sense—he clearly is—but that, because compassion is rooted in his primary will, developments neither take him by surprise nor put him on the defensive. They do engage his love in a complex and an intimate manner. The structure or logic of divine compassion (we might say) is comparable with the human form of it, but God's peculiar status gives to his 'responsiveness' an element of control, of supreme versatility, that in large measure will be absent from human beings' assistance to each other; though not altogether absent. God 'gave his Son in the same way of goodness to the world, as he affords particular persons the friendly assistance of their fellow-creatures; when, without it, their temporal ruin would be the certain consequence of their follies: in the same way of goodness, I say; though in a transcendent and infinitely higher degree' (*A.* 2. 5. 10). Butler is wary too of any hint of a theology of 'interpositions', and of the chaos they might imply both in the world and in the wisdom of its Governor.[13] Any redemptive engagement with the world by God must communicate his central meaning and not something adventitious. Even lesser agents such as ourselves will aim to approach this ideal, becoming more mature as our moral responsiveness increases through familiarity with more extensive circumstantial demands.

Neither cancelling the providential connection between sin and punishment, then, nor setting up an exception, God corrects and heals. This is a distinct element in his administration of the

[13] Cf. *A.* 1. 7. 4.

world. How? Partly by 'affording us light and instruction by revelation, additional to what he has afforded us by reason and experience' (*A*. 2. 3. 3); partly by the establishment of the Christian religion as 'manifestly necessary to keep up and propagate religion amongst mankind' (*A*. 2. 5. 23); partly by encouraging repentance for sins. Butler is the last to want to denigrate knowledge and personal practical effort, at least when they combine. But crucial in the redemptive scheme is the fact that Jesus is not just a prophet or the founder and ruler of a Church, but one who 'offered himself a propitiatory sacrifice, and made atonement for the sins of the world' (*A*. 2. 5. 17); so that 'the doctrine of the gospel appears to be, not only that he taught the efficacy of repentance, but rendered it of the efficacy which it is, by what he did and suffered for us' (*A*. 2. 5. 19). Butler has no particular theory about atonement and is content to reproduce biblical texts fairly conservatively—though not passively or literalistically: analysis of his choice of passages suggests strongly a leaning towards an interpretation of atonement that would find Hebrews a central resource, and he warns elsewhere about the dangers in focusing upon the 'forms and representations, and inadequate manners of expression, instead of the real things intended by them: (for signs often can be no more than inadequately expressive of the things signified)' (*A*. 2. 6. 15).

What prevents his attempting to demythologize the New Testament is partly that 'mediation' is a familiar feature of everyday life, and therefore not at all implausible in relation to the work of God. He does not claim that no other mechanism could be employed. Forgiveness might, in principle, be given a generic or 'omni-particular' exercise. (It has to be generic at some level anyway if it is to be secured against the difficulties outlined above.) But if we remember that a particular, properly understood, is not necessarily the contradictory or contrary of a general; and if we look at the facts—experience and revelation, in Butler's terms, rather than abstract reasoning—we may well find ourselves drawn by the discovery that:

> though the efficacy of repentance itself alone, to prevent what mankind had rendered themselves obnoxious to, and recover what they had forfeited, is now insisted upon, in opposition to Christianity: yet, by the general prevalence of propitiatory sacrifices over the heathen

world, this notion, of repentance alone being sufficient to expiate guilt, appears to be contrary to the general sense of mankind. (*A.* 2. 5. 8)

Something had to be done. The mistake was to imagine that the sinners could do it, or that their gods could do it. In fact God has done it. He has processed his redemptive activity in the familiar moral way, through an individual agent whose identity is shaped by history, by the human community, by the cosmos; the meaning of whose life particularizes itself in a reciprocal encounter with external realities; and whose human capacity embraces integrity and vulnerability in one particular focal action that somehow expresses and effects everything that needs to be expressed and effected. The idea is at least intelligible, given God's commitment to the moral way of working; and that a particular action of a particular agent might play this central part in redemption is not impossible, always provided that that particular person were so constituted as to be charged with the *import* to incorporate in what he did.

That one action might be more important than others should by now be a familiar idea: that one agent should be uniquely equipped (but still one of us) is more difficult to grasp. He would have to participate intimately in the divine understanding of things, and engage in them in whatever way the objective of setting universally right what had universally gone wrong requires. What that way is (and therefore what the personal wherewithal needed to tackle the problem is) we have scarcely any idea. We do not even know how far the question is a causal one: 'how far things are considered by the Author of nature, under the single notion of means and ends; so as that it may be said, this is merely an end, and that merely means, in his regard' (*A.* 2. 4. 6). We do know enough about action to recognize that causality can be secondary or covert, and that there may be more to an action than either one specific sort of effectiveness or indeed any transference of causality at all. We may even hazard a guess that causality, in any normal sense, becomes a less appropriate category for describing an action, the more closely the agent is identified with (in the strong sense of being essentially constituted by engagement with) the putative recipient: when I do a kindness for my daughter I may see this as simply causing *x* to happen to her, but it seems equally legitimate to see it instead as a spontaneous expression not just of my character but of our mutual closeness; and the closer we were, the more legitimate this perception would be, whereas the severely causal interpretation actually misses something of the point of the relationship and presupposes a continuing separateness between us which the kindness (if it is warm and genuine) itself transcends. And this is a pale human example merely of the way in which causal may give way to non-causal understanding of the dynamic of moral action.

Butler's language about the person of Christ is strikingly reserved, in contrast to his language about his work. In part this is because the question of who and what Christ is 'in himself' is, from Butler's practical viewpoint, relatively unimportant. Knowing more than that he is the divinely appointed mediator, the 'particular person, in whom all [God's] promises should finally be fulfilled; the Messiah, who should be, in an high and eminent sense, their anointed Prince and Saviour' (*A.* 2. 7. 32), would not be spiritually or morally helpful. Further information would be of a philosophical character, clarifying rather the general question of how a human being can be a decisive embodiment of divine character than the religious question of what my duty to God and man is. Further, Butler is reticent because singling out Christ and discussing his nature in isolation, as it were, from the redemptive action of God would put the emphasis in the wrong place. It would be the same mistake as attempting to describe an action without reference to the agent, or attempting to describe an agent without reference to the community and context that nourish him. Jesus is God's man, and the cognate of his comprehensive particularity is a certain transparency. It is consistent that when Butler traces the process by which the exercise of good dispositions eventuates in a love towards those dispositions themselves, then the transition from 'goodness as become an uniform continued principle of action' to a supposed 'creature perfect according to his created nature', then finally from such a creature supposed 'our proper guardian and governor' to Almighty God who is 'the object of those affections raised to the highest pitch' (*S.* 13. 7–11), he nowhere mentions Christ, and it seems clear that he does not even allude to him. Butler's spirituality is not in the main Christocentric: the person of Christ is not the object of devotion—God is. On the other hand he is not subordinationist either. Guarded though his language is, there is no mistaking his conviction that Jesus Christ is God, God making his definitive act of rectification in a particular embodiment of responsive love that loses nothing significant in the embodying. Christocentric spiritualities may have been apt to concentrate on the particularity of God's presence in this one person in a way that overlooks the whole milieu, natural and supernatural, of his incarnatedness; and that therefore misses much of his integral meaning and impoverishes even the ordinary perception of what (as it were) he was up to. Like every particular presence, Jesus was woven out of realities beyond what he immediately presented. Loving God is enough, provided we adjust ourselves to the fact (as essential to him as any other) that he 'created and invisibly governs the world by Jesus Christ; and by him also will hereafter judge it in righteousness' (*A.* 2. 2. 3), that Christ was 'that divine Person, who was the example of all perfection in human nature' (*S.* 5. 13), and that he was no merely passive instrument in this activity but one who, as well as actively enjoining love upon us by way of command, also enjoined it 'by his example, as having undertaken the work of our salvation out of pure love and good-will to mankind' (*S.* 11. 22). The concept of particularization helps Butler to maintain a judicious balance.

If dependence is radical enough it identifies the agent either with the definitive characterization intended for him in God's purpose (when he is playing his part as he is meant to play it) or (when the agent occupies a uniquely determinative role in the system of things) with God himself. Jesus is supremely dependent. He is therefore supremely free, because all his externalities have been incorporated in the meaning to which he is committed. Butler does not pursue that line, but does emphasize two major symptoms of his dependence: his vulnerability and his death. That the particular agent of redemption should weep with compassion (*S.* 5. 13), and that his redemptive work should focus not upon his birth (about which Butler is quiet) but upon his death, is in neither case surprising. Butler's analysis of compassion scarcely reaches heroic heights or tragic depths, but in his careful and prosaic way he points us in the right direction and gives us sufficient indication of how an action or a series of actions that incorporate suffering and death might be the supreme case of moral affirmation, and might be consistent too with the hedonic presuppositions of moral activation. The 'peculiar calm kind of satisfaction' which accompanies compassion 'proceeds partly from consciousness of a right affection and temper of mind, and partly from a sense of our own freedom from the misery we compassionate' (*S.* 5. 7). One has to be very strong in order to be creatively weak, to engage vulnerably in the world through a relationship that is neither brute assertiveness nor ineffectual surrender but somewhere in between: waiting upon ourselves unfolding, acquiescing in what we are having done through us, wanting to suffer in a definite interest. These are the characteristic qualities of authentic moral endeavour, and the possibilities to which they can extend vary directly with who we are, what resources we possess, what we have it in us to become. If an individual is at odds with himself, partial, abstract, short-term in his apprehension of claims and duties, there is little scope for the vulnerability that grows with the tenacity of accomplishing much without having to be fixedly assertive. If he is simplicity itself—not barren simplicity but the simplicity of inconceivable coherence among infinite details—there is no limit to the power of his sacrificial self-realizing. This is the case with Jesus, Butler believes. Being incomparably significant, he can by dying mediate redemption to the whole world: and (as Butler explains in a footnote, impatiently because the objection is such a manifest red herring) not just to 'such as have the advantage of being made acquainted with it in the present life' (*A.* 2. 5. 10 n. 11). God, as it happens, 'appears to bestow all his gifts with the most promiscuous variety among creatures of the same species' (*A.* 2. 6. 3), but we have no need to avail ourselves of this observation to defend the particularity of the redemptive death of Jesus. Only inauthentic moral events narrow, confine, and exclude. Authentic ones broaden, liberate, and encompass. Hence we are to recognize the long historical process out of which the human Jesus emerges, and which significantly constitutes his identity.[14] Hence too we are to recognize that out of the crystallization of divine compassion represented by the death of Jesus arises the possibility of many further related actions: the focal event clears the ground, reshapes the situation,

---

[14] Cf. *A.* 2. 7 *passim*; esp. 33 ff.

sets it firmly in the light of its complementary characterization, as well as historically bringing into play the further responses it renders appropriate. So kindness may be a way of making amends to our fellow-creatures, not independently but in virtue of the possibilities affirmed by what Jesus did: 'by fervent charity he may even merit forgiveness of men . . . the Christian covenant of pardon always supposed' (*SS.* 6. 2).

The limitations of this essay will be evident enough by now. I have not tried to 'defend the doctrine of the Incarnation'. Nor have I tried to expound Butler's doctrine, because in his published work there is insufficient evidence of what it was; though we may surmise fairly accurately from his antecedents what he would have been saying, had he written a different sort of book. I have drawn rather upon his analysis of moral action to suggest how the idea that God has been active definitively in one person doing one particular thing at one particular time and place might make sense. Moral action which is being authentically moral and not bogus suggests a concept of a God who takes people and places (not 'humanity' and 'the world'!) seriously enough to become intimately engaged with them, and to do this in terms familiar to them from their own struggles to become real moral agents. It suggests an alternative model to the range of contemporary attempts to exhibit God's activity, intentionally or unwittingly, as a case of modern management or bureaucracy: God organizing things for other people to do, making available a commodity that needs marketing, formulating general strategies, providing general oversight; but remaining the while essentially uninvolved. Butler, distinctively English but distinctively orthodox, will have none of it. God is particular: very particular indeed.

8
Butler and Immortality

T. A. ROBERTS

In order to execute his strategy in the *Analogy*, Butler has to establish an analogy between the 'known course of nature' and Christian claims concerning the nature and character of a 'future life'. This strategy would obviously come unstuck if it could be shown that the Christian claim concerning a future life is to be rejected simply because it is false to believe there exists life after death. Not unnaturally, Butler devotes the first chapter of the *Analogy* to establishing the reasonableness of the belief that each person continues to enjoy life after death. The truth, or the high probability of the truth, of this claim is crucial to his whole enterprise.

In developing his arguments in favour of a future life, Butler stresses the importance of arguments based on rational reflection on experience, that is, on the use of reason, or 'abstract reasonings', not in isolation but in relation to the facts or data of experience. The failure to use our rational capacities to 'reflect' on experience is a common failure of mankind generally. The ordinary person is apt to base his ideas unreflectively on his immediate sensations and perceptions and so betrays that reflective power of reason which is a God-given gift to man. Of this reflective power of reason he says it is 'indeed the only faculty we have to judge concerning anything, even revelation itself' (*A.* 2. 3. 1). By reflecting on experience Butler believed we could be convinced of the reasonableness of the belief in the existence of a future life, because the truth of such a belief is highly probable.

With regard to man's rational capacities to acquire truth,

Professor R. F. Atkinson, Exeter University, and Professor R. W. Sharpe, St David's College, Lampeter, offered several useful comments on an earlier draft of this paper, which I gratefully acknowledge.

Locke, it will be recalled, distinguishes between 'truths of reason', 'truths above reason', and assertions which are contrary to or contradict the deliverances of reason. Locke held that the truths of revelation are beyond reason, since their truth cannot be established by the exercise of reason. The propositions of revelation are certainly true, for they are accepted as coming from God, who is the authority for their truth, since God is no deceiver. Locke accepts that reason can establish the truth of the existence of God, but the truth of a proposition such as 'the dead will be raised at the General Resurrection' cannot be established by reason, and so is accepted as a truth of revelation. Butler also accepts the distinction between propositions whose truth can be established by reason and propositions whose truth cannot be established by reason but is revealed. He applies this distinction by holding that the truth of propositions about God, about his government of nature, about his moral government over human beings, can be established by reason reflecting on experience. By analogy with these truths the claim of the Christian religion concerning God's moral government of man's existence in a future life can be shown to have a high degree of probability. A subsidiary proposition of the latter is the claim that by analogy with man's earthly existence, reason can establish with a high degree of probability the truth of the proposition that a future life exists. In brief, the truth of propositions about God's existence and man's relation to him can be established by reason. The realm of revelation for Butler covers those propositions which assert the existence of Christ and the Holy Spirit as the Second and Third Persons of the Trinity, that assert that Christ is the Mediator between man and God—in short propositions which describe the relation between man and Christ and man and the Holy Spirit. The truth of these propositions cannot be established by the exercise of reason reflecting on experience.

What then are the arguments deployed by Butler to show that there is a high probability that a future life exists? Before examining his arguments in detail, one should note two general features about them. First, they are based on what rational reflection on experience will reveal to be general characteristics of man's experience. That is, they do not appeal to a particular kind of experience which a particular individual or group of individuals might have or might have had. A general characteristic of experience is one which all or nearly all men have experienced, or will experience. Thus the experience of being a child, developing into adolescence, and maturing into an adult is a feature or general characteristic of human experience. Similarly the experience of falling in love is a general experience. The experience of falling in love with a particular individual, say the princess of Wales, is not a general but, on the contrary, a particular experience. Similarly the claim of an individual or group of individuals to have had a religious experience, say a vision of God, is a particular not a general experience, for most men do not claim to have had religious experiences. Having religious experience is not a general feature of experience. To say that is not in any way to impugn the validity of such particular experiences. Butler always appeals to general features of experience, and clearly arguments based on such features must, to that extent, be more persuasive than arguments based on appeal to particular experiences. But of course the fact that an argument appeals to general features of experience does not of itself guarantee the validity of such an argument.

The other general point to note is that Butler's approach is quite unmistakably philosophical, rather than theological. This is especially true of part 1 of the *Analogy*. By philosophical one understands not only the intention and aim to produce valid arguments to support vitally important conclusions, but also philosophical in the sense of attempting to consider how one could conceive things to be very different from what they are. Attempting to understand conceptions which are very different from the ones we normally find embedded in our ordinary language and its conceptual structure is one very fruitful way of coming to understand our ordinary conceptions. This attempt is the hallmark of the philosophical approach, of the philosophical method. And there are ever-recurring instances of Butler's use of this method throughout the *Analogy* and particularly in part 1. Although the main topic or subject of Butler's discussions is certain religious claims, his discussions are essentially philosophical, and not theological, in approach. It is, in my opinion, a mistake to think of Butler as primarily a theologian, moral or otherwise. C. D. Broad believes Butler has produced in the *Analogy* a moral theology to rival Kant's.[1] Strictly speaking, his

[1] C. D. Broad, 'Butler as a Theologian', *Hibbert Journal*, 84/21 (1922-3), 637 ff.

discussions fall into the category of theological *ethics* rather than moral *theology*, especially if one holds that 'ethics' is a sub-branch of philosophy, that is conceptual thinking about moral behaviour.

The first argument which Butler deploys to establish the highly probable conclusion that there exists a future life after death is this. Butler wants to counter the objection to a future life which holds that if such a life exists, the mode of one's existence in that life would have to be very different from the mode of one's existence in this life. Butler counters that it seems to be a law of nature that the same individual exists in very different states during his life on earth. Thus his existence as a helpless baby, his existence as a growing child, and finally his existence as a mature adult are each as different as 'two states or degrees of life could be'. Therefore by analogy with the course of nature, it is likely that a person's existence in a future life will be a state very different from anything experienced in this life. That, then, demolishes the objection to the future life based on the consideration that one's future life would be very different from one's earthly existence.

To comment on this argument. By itself it does not prove the existence of life after death. Butler does not believe any one argument can do this. His view is that a series of considerations, one of which is rationally advanced in this first argument, will tend to heighten the probability of the truth of the claim that there exists a future life. Secondly, it is negative, in that it is aimed at removing an objection to, rather than developing a constructive argument for, the existence of life after death. Thirdly, it presupposes the premiss that something existing in very different states at different times remains the 'same person' or 'individual'. Butler acknowledges this and directs attention to his discussion of personal identity in his dissertation 'Of Personal Identity', in which he considers how it is possible for something existing at different times in different states to be the same thing or person. Finally, the structure of the argument is that if an individual lives through states, a, b, and c which are very different from each other, then, if there is a future life, his state in that life d is probably very different from states a, b, and c. So far as it goes this is a perfectly reasonable argument. What Butler fails to notice is that if states a, b, and c are corporeal states of the same individual, then on this argument, if there is a future state *d*, that will also be a corporeal state, even if the conception of 'corporeal' necessary for *d* will be very different from the conception of corporeal by which we say that states *a*, *b*, and *c* are corporeal states of the same individual.

Butler's second argument is that human beings obviously possess certain powers and capacities, such as the capacity to act, the capacity to enjoy pleasure, and the capacity to suffer pain. If we possess these capacities now before death, it is reasonable to assume that we will possess them 'through and after death' (*A*. 1. 1. 3), unless we have good reasons for thinking that death itself destroys these powers. The assumption is so reasonable that we ought to act upon it.

This argument appeals to two premisses. First, if anything exists, it will in all probability continue to exist, 'in all respects as we experience it', unless we have reason to think that its existence will be 'altered'. This assumption lies, for Butler, at the heart of our notion of 'continuance', which in turn lies at the basis of our belief that the world will continue tomorrow as it has done in our past experience. Indeed this assumption lies at the root of our conviction and belief that 'any one substance now existing will continue to exist a moment longer: the self-existent substance excepted' (*A*. 1. 1. 3).

To comment on this first premiss. By the word 'substance', in the expression 'any one substance now existing will continue to exist', it might be taken that Butler meant 'a material or physical object'. But his reference to 'self-existent substance' rules this out, for almost certainly by self-existent substance Butler meant God, and God is not a material object. By 'substance' he must mean 'that which can be individuated', a 'one'. Thus the powers or capacities mentioned in the argument, the power to act, the capacity to feel pleasure and pain, are predicable of 'a substance', the self or consciousness. The force of the assumption appealed to in the argument is that if this 'one' exists now, this fact is a sufficient reason for believing it will exist in the future unless one has overriding reasons for believing its existence will be terminated.

If, maintains Butler, a substance exists, the fact that it exists is sufficient reason for believing it will exist in the future 'in all respects as we (have) experienced it' unless we have reason to believe that its existence will be 'altered'. Now clearly the claim that, if x exists, the fact of its existence is a sufficient reason for thinking it will continue to exist in the future '*in all respects*' (my italics) as we have experienced it, is too strong a claim. A weaker claim that, if x exists, the fact of its existence is a sufficient reason for believing x will continue to exist in most, but not all, the respects we have experienced it, would meet Butler's requirements. As for the qualification, unless we have reason to believe that its existence will be 'altered', Butler should have distinguished, as he does not, between a change and alteration. If the table which is white is painted blue, is that an 'alteration of substance', rather than a 'change of substance'? If the table is broken down and the wood reused to make a stool, does the table 'alter' or does it 'change'? Clearly there is an important distinction here which is relevant to Butler's problem. For if we predicate the capacity to feel pleasure and the power to act of the 'substance' which is Jones's self, and we can predicate of this same substance a certain relation to a particular 'parcel' of flesh and blood which we call Jones's body, then if these same powers and capacities are predicable of Jones's self after the dissolution of his body at death, has the 'substance' which is Jones's self (or mind or consciousness) undergone an existence-alteration or an existence-change?[2]

What do we make of Butler's central assumption that if a 'substance' exists, the fact that it exists is sufficient reason for believing that it will continue to exist in the future unless we have good reason for believing its existence will be terminated? In his comments on this first premiss[3] Broad assumes that by 'substance' Butler means material or physical object. Interpreted in that sense, Butler's premiss is, says Broad, 'no doubt plausible'. Broad continues:

If we leave a chair in our rooms we do expect to find it there when we come back. We do not want any explanation of its still being there; we should only want an explanation if we found that it had vanished. It is,

---

[2] Compare the use of the distinction between alteration and change found in Jonathan Bennett's excellent discussion of 'Substances and Reality' (ch. 3) in his *Kant's Dialectic* (Cambridge, 1974), 56f. There Bennett writes: 'An *alteration* of x is a happening in which x's state changes while x remains in existence. An *existence-change* of x is x's being originated or annihilated.'

[3] Broad, 'Butler as a Theologian', 643.

then, true of material objects that we expect them to go on existing unless there is some positive cause to destroy them. The question is: Is this a general rule which can be applied straightaway to minds, or is it peculiar to material objects? The answer seems to me that it is not a general rule.[4]

Broad points out that it is not a general rule because some things in our experience do not 'continue to be', for example noises or flashes of lightning. Whereas we expect tables and chairs to 'continue to be' because we have constantly found their continued existence to be a fact of our experience, it is equally a fact of our experience that items in our experience have only a transitory and not a relatively permanent existence. There is therefore no general rule of the kind implied by Butler's first premiss.

On Broad's analysis, Butler could offer at least two observations. First, transitory noises or flashes of light are not 'substances' in his sense, and secondly, he does not limit the notion of 'substance' only to material objects. To Butler there undoubtedly exist what we would term 'mental predicates', such as the power to act, the capacity to feel pleasure or pain, and these mental predicates are predicable of a substance which is non-material, non-corporeal. Later Butler proceeds to argue that the relation between a particular non-corporeal substance and a particular parcel of flesh and blood (a human body) is only contingent and not necessary, so that it is logically possible to conceive that this substance continues to exist independently of and apart from any relation to any human body. It is clear that, if we follow Broad, we admit that the existence of a material substance (in the sense of a particular material or physical object or body) gives rise to the general rule that if it exists, then it will continue to exist in the absence of specific reasons why we should believe it will not continue to exist. If, following Butler, we recognize the existence of non-corporeal substances, it is reasonable to assume, on the basis of our experience of the properties of such substances (i.e. the mental powers and capacities already mentioned), that such substances will also continue to exist in the absence of specific reasons why we should believe they will not continue to exist. Butler's answer to Broad would be to insist

[4] Ibid.

that there is a general rule of the kind that Broad specifies, and that this rule applies to both material and non-corporeal 'substances', understanding 'substance' in Butler's sense. The crux of the differences between Butler and Broad would then turn on a wider issue than the question of the existence and application which this general rule specifies. The issue would be whether it is meaningful to talk of the existence of non-corporeal substances independently of and apart from any relation to material substances.

I turn now to consideration of Butler's second premiss. The argument so far is this. We know by experience that mental predicates exist and these are predicable of a non-corporeal substance. If a non-corporeal substance exists, we have every reason to believe it will continue to exist, unless we know of reasons why it will cease to exist. One reason advanced for the future non-existence of non-corporeal substance is that death and the dissolution of the body destroys the existence of non-corporeal substance. The second premiss of Butler's second argument is the outright rejection of this claim.

Butler puts the case like this:

Now, though I think it must be acknowledged, that, prior to the natural and moral proofs of a future life commonly insisted upon, there would arise a general confused suspicion, that in the great shock and alteration which we shall undergo by death, we, i.e. our living powers, might be wholly destroyed: yet even prior to those proofs, there is really no particular distinct ground or reason for this apprehension at all, so far as I can find. If there be, it must arise either from *the reason of the thing*, or from *the analogy of nature*. (*A.* 1. 1. 4; Butler's italics)

Butler thus offers two reasons, in the form of a disjunction, why death cannot be the destruction of non-corporeal substance. First, 'the reason of the thing' does not lead us to believe that this proposition is true, because 'we know not what death is in itself'. We only know the effects of death, namely 'the dissolution of flesh, skin and bones'. These effects are not identical 'with the destruction of a living agent'. As was mentioned above, we predicate certain powers or capacities, such as the capacity to act, of non-corporeal substance, or of 'a living agent', as Butler now puts it. We must distinguish between three things: the actual exercise of such a capacity, the potential exercise of such a capacity, and the basis of the exercise or potential exercise of such a capacity. The phenomenon of sleep allows us to understand the difference between the present exercise of a capacity and the potential exercise of that capacity. During sleep a person's capacities lie dormant and unexercised but they are not destroyed: they lie ready to be used when the person is awake. Finally, says Butler, we do not understand *how* we are able to exercise these capacities: all we know is that the average human being does possess actual or potential capacities of various kinds. Now if we do not understand the relation between the exercise or potential exercise of our capacities, and that in which the capacities are grounded which enables them to be exercised, how can we possibly say that we understand that death is the destruction of these capacities? Butler sums up his argument from 'the reason of the thing' as follows.

Since, then, we know not at all upon what the existence of our living powers depends, this shows further, there can no probability be collected from the reason of the thing, that death will be their destruction: because their existence may depend upon somewhat in no degree affected by death: upon somewhat quite out of the reach of this King of terrors. So that there is nothing more certain, than that *the reason of the thing* shows us no connection between death and the destruction of living agents. (*A* 1. 1. 5; Butler's italics)

In what we may term 'Butler's argument to the reason of the thing' in defence of the premiss that death is not the destruction of living agents, Butler's appeal to 'the reason of the thing', a concept much in use in the first half of the eighteenth century, seems to be based on the following considerations. Butler claims that we do not know what 'death is in itself': all we are aware of is the effects of death. Not to know what death is in itself seems to imply that we do not possess a fully developed concept of death. If we did, our understanding of death would correspond to what the word for the concept, 'death', signifies in reality. Locke, it will be recalled, distinguished between the nominal and real essence of a substance like 'gold'. The nominal essence coincides with the complete definition of 'gold', as that is understood in the light of the latest scientific knowledge at a particular point in time, say 1690 when Locke wrote his *Essay*. But since science may uncover further properties of gold, hitherto unknown, the nominal essence cannot coincide with the real essence of a thing such as gold. Locke implies the human understanding will forever lack a complete knowledge of the real essence of a thing, and this is clearly a limitation on human understanding.

Butler's use of the notion of 'the reason of the thing' appears to resemble the doctrine that substances possess 'real essences'. Are these knowable to man? They are clearly knowable to an infinite intelligence such as God's. We have already noted that what are the objects of knowledge to an infinite intelligence give rise to certain truths, and not to probable truths. Infinite intelligence is not limited, like man, to probability, which for him is the very guide of life. This is because infinite intelligence grasps the essences of things. For Butler, man has not yet grasped the essence of 'death'. Is this a temporary and practical failure, or is it that man in principle can never grasp the essence of death, can never hope to know what 'death is in itself'? Butler seems to be committed to the latter. Is he then in agreement with Locke that man can never know the real, only the nominal, essence of a thing? Butler does want to claim that man does know what some things 'are in themselves'. One of his examples would be virtue. Another is that it is man's essence to seek and enjoy happiness, and that the achievement of this aim is connected with living a life of virtue. Whereas we do not know what the connection is between the powers and capacities of a living agent, and the essence of a living agent in which these capacities reside—if we knew this connection, and if also we knew what death was in itself, we would know whether death was the destruction of living agents—we do know the connection between virtue and happiness, for we know the 'essence' of both.

The notion of real essences is closely tied up with the notion of natural kinds. Butler, in appealing to the 'reason of the thing', in addition to subscribing, it seems, to the doctrine of real essences, may be guilty of the 'essentialist fallacy', that is, of believing that noun-words like 'death' stand for something that has an essence or underlying structure. Whereas many words, e.g. 'water', can plausibly be said to stand for an 'essential something', with its underlying structure, the word 'death' stands for an event, not a thing. As an event, 'death could not have a concealed microstructure; there is nothing we could find about death which would show us that we had been previously mistaken about it in the way we could find out that we had been mistaken about water'.[5] The claim that death is an event, not a thing, clearly undermines Butler's argument to 'the reason of the thing' so that it can hardly get off the ground.

The doctrine of 'the reason of the thing' seems to presuppose the epistemological doctrine that some of our concepts are such that they correspond exactly with that in reality of which they are concepts, so that if we understand the concept fully we understand completely that in reality of which it is a concept. This epistemological doctrine in turn presupposes the metaphysical doctrine that man's reason can produce and understand certain concepts which completely mirror or represent reality because reality is itself essentially intelligible, that is, capable of being understood by man's reason. Such a metaphysical doctrine has its roots in a Platonic metaphysic. Contrast this with Kant's metaphysics, in which he distinguishes between *phenomena* and *noumena*. Noumena for Kant are, not merely in practice, but in principle, unknowable by a being possessing the kind of intellectual capacities which human beings possess. Phenomena in contrast are knowable by human beings. The view of the world which is developed by man's intellectual powers of reasoning and understanding is a view of the world as phenomena: the ultimate reality, noumena, is unknowable, although in some sense, a sense not understood or capable of being understood by us, it lies at the root of phenomena. If noumena are unknowable, we cannot know whether or not reality is intelligible through and through. Though Plato was the philosopher most admired by Kant, there is clearly a great divide between Plato's optimistic view of man's place in the universe—man has the intellectual equipment to understand reality because reality is intelligible and man possesses in reason the key to unlock the intelligibility of the universe—and Kant's more sceptical view that reality in itself is unknowable and will remain unknowable for man. If my analysis of Butler's use of the notion of 'the reason of the thing' is on the right lines, Butler is far more Platonic than Kantian in approach, despite the fact that some have seen in his work close anticipations of Kantian themes.

[5] Here I cite a sentence from Professor Sharpe's written comments to me, which points to a crucial weakness in Butler's argument.

The second reason which Butler appeals to in support of the premiss that 'death is not the destruction of living agents' is that there is no ground in the 'analogy of nature' for thinking to the contrary. Butler's discussion of this point is very brief. He merely asserts, without any elaborate argument, that there is nothing in our knowledge of nature 'to afford us even the slightest presumption, that animals ever lose their living powers: much less, if it were possible, that they lose them by death' (*A*. 1. 1. 5). All that death does is to remove 'the living powers of living agents' from our 'sensible view', that is, from our sense perception. If therefore living agents possessed these powers up to the point we had perception of them, it is probable that they still retain them when these powers are no longer within our perceptual experience. This probability is supported when we consider 'the very great and astonishing changes' which the living agent undergoes in the course of his embodied existence in this life.

Up to this point in his discussion 'of a future life' Butler has appealed to rational considerations of two kinds to substantiate the premiss that 'death is not the destruction of living agents', namely rational considerations based upon 'the reason of the thing', and those based upon 'the whole analogy of nature'. He believes this two-pronged rational approach is conclusive in establishing the validity of his premiss. However he is not content to allow the matter to rest there. He insists on reviewing and countering those 'gross and crude conceptions of things, taking for granted that we are acquainted with what indeed we are wholly ignorant of' (*A*. 1. 1. 7), which persuade some into the error that death is the destruction of living agents. These 'gross and crude conceptions' have their origin in the imagination, a faculty so powerful as often to make 'the voice of reason' difficult to hear, and the imagination flourishes on the basis of 'early and lasting prejudices', by implication irrational. What are these irrational prejudices which must be successfully countered if we are to be rationally persuaded of the premiss that death is not the destruction of living agents? They fall into three main categories.

First, since the effects of death are the dissolution of 'flesh, skin and bones', the destruction of the body is the destruction of the living agent. For this irrational prejudice to be upheld, we must believe that the living agent is 'compounded' as the matter of the body is certainly compounded. This belief presupposes that the destruction of a thing is equivalent to reducing a compound to its constituent parts. In the case of a human material body of flesh and blood, we can 'destroy' it by changing the organized body into its constituent atoms of matter, which are, it might be argued, themselves indestructible. The destruction of the living agent is possible only if the living agent is a compound. But the living agent is not a compound but a simple, single being. To support this latter contention, Butler appeals to one main consideration, stated in two slightly different forms:

1. consciousness is a single and indivisible power, and 'the subject in which it resides must be so too';
2. the consciousness we have of our own existence is indivisible, so that it is a contradiction to suppose one part of it should be here and the other there.

In (1) is Butler drawing attention to the point that the very notion of consciousness implies the unity of consciousness? Thought a cannot occur side by side with thought b in consciousness c unless there is the awareness that both thoughts belong to the one consciousness. This latter might be a necessary condition of self-consciousness but not of consciousness. If an animal, say a dog, has a percept a at t_1 and a different percept b at t_2, is the dog aware that both percepts are his? If not, we might want to predicate 'consciousness' of the dog but not self-consciousness, on the grounds that the dog is clearly 'conscious', differing from a table or dead dog. In that case, if the dog is conscious, what is the force of the claim that his consciousness is 'a single and indivisible power'?

Allowing then that what Butler is referring to in (1) is not consciousness but self-consciousness, which necessarily presupposes the unity of consciousness, does it follow that where we predicate self-consciousness, we also predicate 'a subject in which it resides and which is single and indivisible' as self-consciousness is? Clearly this move is unwarranted. From the fact, if it is a fact, that if we predicate self-consciousness of x, the meaning of 'self-consciousness' implies something single and indivisible, it does not follow that in predicating self-consciousness of x we also predicate something in x in which the self-consciousness resides, which is also itself single and indivisible.

In (2) Butler implies it is a contradiction and therefore it does not make sense to conceive of a consciousness being divided into two parts, one half associated with one body and the other with another. If consciousness of my own existence includes, as it must, my past memories, is it logically inconceivable that there are two minds or consciousnesses experiencing the same set of memories, which are 'mine'? Butler, as I think also Descartes, thought this an impossibility, but is it a logical impossibility, rather than a practical impossibility?

Having established by considerations which he believes are cogent, but which we have questioned, that consciousness is single and indivisible and so the being in which it resides is single and indivisible, Butler by implication establishes that a living agent is 'a single and indivisible being', and therefore is not to be identified with a particular corporeal body, which, being material, is complex not single, and is divisible, not indivisible. Therefore matter or the body is 'not part of ourselves'. The relation between ourselves and a body is therefore external and contingent. If so, it is perfectly possible to conceive of ourselves existing outside and independently of our bodies. Or we can conceive of being conjoined to bodies possessing very different sense organs from those we now possess. The dissolution of our present bodies, and of our present organs, is therefore in no way to be construed as the dissolution of 'the living agent'.

This latter conclusion thus overthrows a second prejudice of the imagination, namely that since death is the destruction of the body it is the destruction of the living agent, since each living agent has had a special 'interest in such matter'. From the fact that we have an 'interest', in the sense of a particularly close relationship, in a particular body or parcel of matter, it does not follow that the destruction of that body is tantamount to the destruction of the living agent. For one thing, the 'parcels of matter' with which we are intimately related undergo considerable changes in the course of time, as when in infancy 'the bulk of their bodies was extremely small, in comparison with what it is in mature age'. Moreover we may lose some of this bulk, and still remain ourselves. Men may lose their limbs or organs of sense such as sight but still remain themselves. Furthermore we know the bodies of animals are 'in considerable flux'. Such considerations teach us 'to distinguish between these living agents ourselves, and large quantities of matter, in which we are very nearly interested'. We have therefore no reason to conclude that what befalls those systems of matter is equivalent to the 'destruction of living agents'. The matter of our bodies has, in accordance with laws of nature, undergone great changes yet we have remained throughout those changes 'the same living agents'. May we not remain the same if by another law of nature, death, we lose the whole of our body? Whereas the changes to the body in life are gradual, and the changes at death are sudden and great, does this in any way suggest that death is the destruction of the living agent? If we have passed undestroyed 'through those many and great revolutions of matter', why should we imagine death to be fatal to us?

Since Butler believes that living agents, and the predicates of living agents, exist independently of material bodies, he can refer, for example, to the power of perception (a predicate of living agents) existing apart from the sense organs, e.g. sight, which are normally associated with them. The power of sight is assisted as much by the use of spectacles as by the eye itself. Therefore neither the eye nor the glasses are to be identified with the power of perception: something apart from the material thing, the eye, or the material thing, the glasses, is the percipient. Both the eye and glasses are merely instruments for the percipient to receive impressions (Butler like Locke uses the term 'ideas') from external material objects, as the Author of nature designed material objects to have this capacity of exciting impressions in the percipient. But the Author of nature can quite as easily devise other means than the use of an eye or glasses whereby the percipient receives impressions of external material objects. In short, sense organs are extrinsic to the percipient and to the power of perception which lodges in the percipient, so that the destruction of the sense organs is in no way equivalent to the destruction of the power of perception which can be predicated of the percipient, the living agent. The experience of dreams, cites Butler, is evidence that the power to receive impressions of external objects is as strong without the instrumentality of sense organs as it is with them.

Butler makes a similar point with regard to the capacity to move. The power and the decision to move do not rest in the limbs. The decision to move can be made even if a man has lost his limbs. His limbs are merely instruments which enable him to execute his decision to move. For this purpose artificial legs, fitted to replace the two lost legs, will do just as well (or nearly as well) as natural limbs. Butler writes,

> Nor is there so much as any appearance of our limbs being endued with a power of moving or directing themselves; though they are adapted, like the several parts of a machine, to be the instruments of motion to each other; and some parts of the same limb to be instruments of motion to other parts of it. (*A.* 1. 1. 13)

From consideration of his observations on the organs of sense perception and the use of our limbs Butler can conclude that both are instruments which we, living agents, make use of in order to perceive and to move. But there is no probability that they are any more than this, and the living agent is not in any more special relation to these parcels of matter than to any other parcel of matter. Therefore there is no probability that the alienation of the living agent from these instruments (sense organs or limbs) or the destruction of these instruments constitutes the destruction of the perceiving and moving agent.

Butler next considers the objection that the above observations concerning sense organs and limbs apply equally to animals, with the implication that animals are immortal. Since we recoil from such a suggestion, the force of the above observations in favour of the view that death is not the destruction of the living agent is much reduced.

With regard to this objection to animal immortality, Butler offers two points in reply. The first is this. Although we do not now actually associate rationality and the capacity to develop morally with brutes, yet they, like us, are capable of great potential development, and there is no logical difficulty in conceiving animals developing a rational and moral nature comparable to that of humans in a future life. As there is great development between infancy and mature adulthood in human beings in the course of this life, so there may be great development between the state animals are in in this life and the state they will achieve in a future life. Clearly in this first objection to animal immortality, Butler assumes that the point of a future life is to afford an opportunity for man, and possibly animals, to develop their rational and moral natures as fully as possible.

Butler's second observation to the objection about animal immortality is to maintain that if animals are immortal, it does not follow that the Author of nature has designed immortality for animals so that they can, like men, develop their rational and moral capacities. Animals may be destined in the plan of God to be immortal even though they are 'not endued with any latent capacities of a rational or moral nature' (*A*. 1. 1. 6). As there is a hierarchy of beings in this present life, the Author of nature may have intended to have a like hierarchy in the future life, and 'the immortality of brutes' would then fit into this scheme of things.

In the light of the above twin observations, Butler dismisses the objections raised with regard to animal immortality to the thesis that death is not the destruction of living agents.

We come finally to the third of the imagination's prejudices which militate against his thesis that death is not the destruction of living agents. The prejudice is that since some mental capacities, i.e. perception, are adversely affected by the effects of death on the body, so all mental capacities are likewise affected. Butler counters this prejudice by insisting that we distinguish between those mental capacities of reason, memory, and affection which he calls 'a state of reflection', and those mental capacities such as perception which belong to 'a state of sensation'. States of sensation 'depend upon our gross body in the manner in which perception by our organs of sense does' (*A*. 1. 1. 17). But states of reflection do not depend on the body, 'after ideas are gained'. Although

> our external organs of sense are necessary for conveying in ideas to our reflecting powers as carriages, and levers, and scaffolds, are in architecture; yet, when these ideas are brought in, we are capable of reflecting in the most intense degree, and of enjoying the greatest pleasure, and feeling the greatest pain, by means of that reflection, without any assistance from our senses; and without any at all, which we know of from that body, which will be dissolved by death. (*A*. 1. 1. 18)

Butler's thought here seems to be that once we have gained a number of impressions or percepts, for which the existence of the body is essential, we can continue in a disembodied state to recall these impressions or percepts ('ideas' for Butler) to mind by the use of memory, to reason about them, and to feel either much pleasure or much pain in relation to them. If this is so, there is 'so little connection' between our bodily powers of sensation and our present powers of reflection that we can conclude that death, which is the destruction of the former, does not even suspend the exercise of the latter nor does it 'interrupt our continuing to exist in the like state of reflection which we do now. For suspension of reason, memory, and the affections which they excite, is no part of the idea of death, nor is implied in our notion of it' (*A.* 1. 1. 19).

Indeed for all we know—'and we do not know what state death naturally leaves us' (*A.* 1. 1. 20)—we may be translated by death into a higher state of reflection than the one we enjoy in this life, as birth introduces us to a total change of the state of life from the one we experienced in the womb. Indeed, when we go out of this world, 'we may pass into new scenes, and a new state of life and action, just as naturally as we came into the present. And this new state may naturally be a social one. And the advantages of it, advantages of every kind, may naturally be bestowed according to some fixed general laws of wisdom, upon every one in proportion to the degrees of his virtue' (*A.* 1. 1. 23). And 'this distribution of advantages, not bestowed by Society as in this world, but by the Author of Nature', may be just as 'natural' as those bestowed by the 'instrumentality of men'. It is a 'shortness of thought scarce credible' to believe that only a system of advantages seen to be so in this world can be termed 'natural', especially if the probability of a future life can be established by reason. But if by 'natural' we mean, *stated, fixed, settled*, 'since what is natural as much requires and presupposes an intelligent agent to render it so' (*A.* 1. 1. 23), then a person's notion of what is 'natural' may be enlarged when he acquires a fuller knowledge of the works of God. And when he has acquired such knowledge he will come to see that the whole Christian dispensation may then appear 'natural', that is, analogous or comfortable to God's dealings with other parts of his creation.

This review of Butler's arguments for immortality will, it is hoped, establish that they are well balanced, cogent, and effective relative to the key philosophical positions which were unchallenged in his day. Those philosophical theologians who believe with Butler that incorporeal substances, notably the Self or spiritual substance, exist independently of corporeal substances or matter, will find much to applaud in Butler's arguments. Those who reject the philosophical argument for the existence of incorporeal substances will think that the basic premiss underlying Butler's approach is mistaken and false.

9

Our Knowledge of Ourselves

ANDERS JEFFNER

It is obvious that many of Butler's main arguments belong to the empiricist tradition as it was further developed by Hume and later refined in modern empiricism. When I dealt with the writings of Butler and Hume some twenty-five years ago, I found Butler's way of connecting to the empiricist tradition particularly interesting as it linked him quite closely to contemporary discussions. But I noted too, of course, that he deviated from empiricism on fundamental points, notably in his metaethics and in his general view of the universe.[1] When I now return to Butler's texts I find these non-empiricist parts of his epistemology (which rest on the heritage from Clarke) to be even more interesting than his empiricism. Here I intend to analyse some of Butler's arguments in 'Of Personal Identity'.[2] I believe that his intuitionist arguments in this brief and lucid essay may have relevance for contemporary discussions that focus on the persistent question of 'the mind's I'.[3]

PERSONAL IDENTITY

Butler's thesis can be rephrased thus: I am certain that there is such a mental fact as my own self and that this self remains constant despite the passing of time. Butler also supposes that other

---

[1] See A. Jeffner, *Butler and Hume on Religion: A Comparative Analysis*, Acta Universitatis Upsaliensis, Studia Doctrinae Christianae Upsaliensia 7 (Stockholm, 1966).

[2] This essay is an addition to his *Analogy*, available in many editions.

[3] A good survey of the discussion of Butler's arguments and an interesting contribution to that discussion are given by Terence Penelhum in his book *Butler* (London, 1985), 129–46. Penelhum comments on many aspects of Butler's essay which I shall leave aside. (I shall put greater stress than Penelhum on the argument which he summarizes on p. 138 as no. 7.)

human beings have the same knowledge about themselves; he calls this the knowledge of personal identity.

NO DEFINITION NECESSARY

Butler introduces the defence of his thesis by taking up an objection to it. Philosophy generally tends to assume that discussion must be preceded by a definition of key terms. But Butler says: 'all attempts to define [personal identity] would but perplex it. Yet there is no difficulty at all in ascertaining the idea' (DI 2).[4] This is very similar to G. E. Moore's argument in his widely known 'A Defence of Common Sense'. Moore discusses the sentence 'The earth has existed for many years past,' noting that some philosophers require an explanation of the ingoing terms before they can say if the expression is true or not. Moore says: 'It seems to me that such a view is as profoundly mistaken as any view can be. Such an expression as "The earth has existed for many years past" is the very type of an unambiguous expression the meaning of which we all understand.'[5] I think both Butler and Moore are correct on this issue and I shall later point out other parallels between their ways of arguing. It was not by chance that Moore selected the motto to his *Principia ethica* from Butler's works. In the following, however, we shall see that Butler is an intuitionist in a sense not shared by Moore.

OUR KNOWLEDGE OF PERSONAL IDENTITY
IS INTUITIVE

As is well known, David Hume's view of personal identity runs contrary to that of Butler, and few parts of Hume's philosophy have been quoted more often than his refutation of a permanent self.[6] The kernel of Hume's argument is simply to apply the basic empiricist norm, namely that we ought not to believe in anything which cannot be demonstrated in the last instance to build

---

[4] Butler was certainly acquainted with the famous definition given by Locke in his *Essay*. See John Locke, *An Essay Concerning Human Understanding* (Oxford, 1894), i. 448. (Some of Butler's arguments are directed against Locke.)

[5] G. E. Moore, 'A Defence of Common Sense', in J. H. Muirhead (ed.), *Contemporary British Philosophy*, ii (London, 1925), 198.

[6] D. Hume, *A Treatise of Human Nature*, ed. L. A. Selby-Bigge (Oxford, 1888), bk. i, s. vi, pp. 251–63.

upon simple sense-impressions. But Butler, like Locke, never accepted this strict empiricism. He meant that we have knowledge of important facts which cannot be traced back to sense-impressions. Among these is personal identity. We know immediately, he says, both the meaning and the fact of personal identity. An immediate knowledge of personal identity seems to be the same kind of cognizance as moral knowledge given through conscience.

Butler's argument for holding a set of truths about reality which cannot be reached empirically is fairly clear. These truths are characterized by the fact that we cannot doubt them without going into absurdities. There are no more reliable facts we can invoke in an attempt to prove or refute these truths. 'It is ridiculous to attempt to prove the truth of those perceptions, whose truth we can not otherwise prove, than by other perceptions of exactly the same kind with them' (DI 11). These perceptions are also embodied in our language in such a way that, if we try to take away words the meaning of which is anchored in intuitive knowledge, language will not 'permit these words to be laid aside' (DI 7). The set of facts we intuitively know belong to the realm of common sense and are reflected in common language.

That faculty which makes it possible for us to reach certain truths is called 'intuition' by Locke and Clarke. Butler sometimes borrows their terms and we will do so here. In analysing thinkers from the dawn of moral sense philosophy, it is not sufficient to distinguish between empirical and rational knowledge and then simply file intuition on the rational side. When it comes to intuitive knowledge in morals, Butler speaks of a faculty of the mind 'whether considered as a sentiment of the understanding, or as a perception of the heart; or, which seems the truth, as including both' (DII 1). In 'Of Personal Identity', he describes this special cognitive ability as 'our natural sense of things' (DI 8). The standard illustrations of intuitive knowledge in Butler's time are often taken from geometry, but I believe these confuse more than they clarify, so we will set them aside for now.

The important points in Butler's claim thus far can be summed up as follows: We understand immediately what personal identity means. The knowledge of personal identity cannot reasonably be doubted without going into absurdities. This knowledge rests on a certain cognitive faculty which is not the same as building on sense-impressions. The concluding sentence demonstrates a fundamental difference between Butler's variety of intuitionism and that of Moore.

CONTEMPORARY INTEREST?

Is Butler's view worthy of consideration three centuries after his birth and in view of the abundance of literature in the field? I believe so, and it can be instructive to spell out the above-mentioned difference between Butler and Hume as it is likewise to spell out the difference between Butler and modern empiricist philosophy. Such a comparison may clarify what an acceptance of Butler's view actually entails. I think the difference between Butler and Hume can be described as a difference in what I will call *belief-norm*. A belief-norm prescribes what kind of argument is a reasonable argument for holding a belief about the real world. Every epistemological theory contains a belief-norm and in this sense theories of knowledge are normative, according to my view. Empiricism is built on a belief-norm that states that the only kind of reasonable argument for a belief about the real world is an argument which ultimately appeals to a sense-impression. When Hume finds that we have no impression of a self, the question is settled as far as he is concerned. His basic belief-norm does not allow him to appeal to other modes of reason. Butler's norm, however, allows us to accept other arguments as reasonable: those appealing to intuition. It is important to notice that such arguments make it possible to add something to empirical knowledge, according to Butler, but intuition cannot replace or refute empirical knowledge. It is true that Butler and his philosophical predecessors as far back as Plato hold that intuitive knowledge has a higher degree of certainty than empirical knowledge, but he never claims that intuition can lead to truths contrary to empirical evidence. The important question now is: Can we give reasonable arguments for our choice of belief-norms? I think we can, but the term 'reasonable' takes on a different meaning, because we must choose among principles that prescribe which arguments we can call reasonable. Let us in arguing for the choice of belief-norms introduce the concept *basic reasonableness*. One argument against a belief-norm that can be said to accommodate basic reasonableness is that the acceptance of said belief-norm opens the door to superstition and fanaticism. This argument seems to lie behind the empiricists' attack on other epistemological standpoints and is sound as far as it goes. But does it refute Butler's position? I cannot see that it does. His intuitive knowledge of the self belongs to the realm of common sense. The risk of being deceived by common sense is not substantially greater than that of being deceived by our sensory faculties. There are perhaps other arguments that accommodate basic reasonableness, but I believe that when they have been taken into consideration we will be left with a real choice between belief-norms all of which have the same basic reasonableness. Perhaps this is one of the unavoidable free choices at which modern existentialists have hinted. However there is one point which perhaps is not completely irrelevant when we consider empiricism. It is very difficult to live consistently as an empiricist. This fact was clearly expressed by Hume himself in the text immediately following his definition of personal identity in the *Treatise*. He writes that he must sometimes set aside his philosophy and apply a common-sense view in real life.[7]

DIFFERENT KINDS OF IDENTITY

A fundamental point of Butler's essay is that personal identity differs from the kind of identity we can ascribe to, for instance, plants. We can say that he asserts a difference between personal identity and corporeal identity. According to Butler, corporeal identity derives from the relation between the particles constituting the material object. The particles themselves can be totally changed during some period of time. The identity of a person is more strict, he argues. He seems to hold the opinion that propositions about personal identity cannot be translated into propositions about relations between particles, nor can they be explained through such relations. Again it can be instructive to compare this viewpoint with that held by Hume. A pivotal point of Hume's essay is that our ideas of personal and corporeal identity are the same and can moreover be explained by the same psychological mechanisms. Hume does not speak of

[7] See esp. ibid. 269.

relations between particles, but the very point of the *Treatise* is to establish the same kind of laws for mental entities that Newton had found for material particles. This is implied in the well-known subtitle of the *Treatise: An Attempt to Introduce the Experimental Method of Reasoning into Moral Subjects*. 'Experimental method' echoes Newtonian argument and 'moral science' is roughly equivalent to the branch we today call the humanities. The difference is in part a consequence of their different epistemological standpoints which we have discussed above. But the difference gains a sharper profile when viewed against ontological claims connected with Butler's theory of intuitive knowledge of personal identity.

ONTOLOGICAL CLAIMS

Butler discusses many arguments that might be brought against his thesis and his own claim grows clearer in the process. One argument is that *personal identity* is equivalent to our *consciousness of personal identity*. Butler's refutation is as follows: It may be true that we cannot distinguish between *personal identity* and our *present consciousness of personal identity*. However, this does not imply that the two are the same. It can be meaningfully asserted that a person who performed a certain act recently is the same person now and at that earlier time, even if the person in question has no memory of his act, and consequently no awareness of being the person who performed the act.

The structure of this Butlerian argument resembles a prominent passage in Moore's *Principia*:

> It is often pointed out that I cannot in any given moment distinguish what is true from what I think so; and this is true. But though I cannot distinguish *what* is true from *what* I think so, I always can distinguish what I mean by saying *that* it is true from what I mean by saying *that* I think so.[8]

According to Moore, the incorrect belief that 'to be true' means 'to be thought in a certain way' plays an important role in Kant's philosophy. To return to Butler, we can now see that his way of thinking is quite different from that of Kant. A particular fact cannot in any way be dependent upon our consciousness of it so

---

[8] G. E. Moore, *Principia ethica* (Cambridge, 1929), 132.

being. Thus far Butler and Moore seem to be in agreement and to differ from the Kantian tradition, but Butler, in contrast to Moore, does not hesitate to make the leap from his analysis of meaning to the sphere of ontology. In his opinion, when we have a consciousness of personal identity which is self-evident and rooted in our intuition, there must be a constant self of which we are aware. It is difficult to find anything impossible or absurd in this though it is, of course, little more than the beginning of a discussion. To gain a bearing on the modern problem of 'mind and matter', it must be supplemented with a theory of the relation between the self and the brain. I have no intention here of entering this enormous field, but simply note that there exist modern forms of dualism which could have compatibility with the Butlerian arguments.

Butler's position in 'Of Personal Identity' runs in part contrary to empiricism, to Kantianism, and to Moore's purism. The purpose of Butler's essay was to eliminate a philosophical obstacle for the Christian belief in a life after death. A modern Christian who desires to retain this same religious belief and think it through is bound either to use Butler's way of arguing or to point out an alternative epistemological standpoint. In my opinion, the meaningful alternatives are few.[9]

---

[9] Penelhum points out an interesting alternative way of thinking in *Butler*, 144 ff., though he does not deal with epistemological questions explicitly. (However, I have difficulties with his concept of 'gap-inclusive corporeality'.)

10
Butler on Conscience and Virtue

BRIAN HEBBLETHWAITE

'Butler exalts conscience, but appears ignorant that a man's conscience may tell him to do the vilest things.' So writes Elizabeth Anscombe in a much discussed paper on 'Modern Moral Philosophy'.[1] This scathing observation about Butler's ethical theory is intended to support a case for locating authority in morals in the divine law over against us rather than in some principle of our own human nature. It is part of Anscombe's argument for holding that without a religious foundation morality loses its obligatory claim and, indeed, should be replaced by sociology. Sociologists, the implication is, are well aware how fallible the psychologically and socially reinforced human mechanism of conscience is. It is a dangerous illusion to exalt conscience. From a religious perspective, it is to put something human and fallible in the place of the divine law. From a non-religious perspective, it is to risk exalting prejudice or some ideologically blinkered judgement or reaction.

In a paper published in the *Journal of the History of Philosophy*,[2] B. Szabados replies to Anscombe's charge by claiming that, had Anscombe considered Butler's Sermons 7 'Upon the Character of Balaam' and 10 'Upon Self-Deceit', instead of concentrating on Sermons 1–3 'Upon Human Nature', she would have realized that Butler himself was perfectly well aware how self-deceit can corrupt conscience. Butler's system is quite capable of recognizing and accounting for the fact that conscience may tell a man to do the vilest things. A corrupt conscience is quite possible. What

[1] G. E. M. Anscombe, 'Modern Moral Philosophy', repr. in *Collected Papers*, iii: *Ethics, Politics and Religion* (Oxford, 1981), 27.
[2] B. Szabados, 'Butler on Corrupt Conscience', *Journal of the History of Philosophy*, 14 (1976), 462–9.

Butler exalts is a conscience free from such corruption. But there is no need to look outside human nature for authority in morals. Equipped with an error theory, such as Butler's psychologically acute understanding of self-deceit, the moralist can avoid the pitfalls unfairly attributed to Butler by Anscombe and retain a naturalistic ethic in which an uncorrupted conscience plays the leading role.

The study of Butler on conscience and virtue that follows is intended to show that neither Anscombe nor Szabados is right. In no way could Butler possibly concede that *conscience* may tell a man to do the vilest things. But Butler's exaltation of conscience is not part of a humanist or purely naturalistic ethic. Butler's ethic, I shall argue, has an essential religious foundation. It is not a divine command theory, but it *is* a form of religious natural law theory, with conscience possessing its supreme authority solely because that is how the Author of nature intended things to be.

Butler certainly exalts conscience. Over and above our various particular passions and our basic long-term principles of benevolence and self-love, 'there is a superior principle of reflection or conscience in every man, which ... passes judgement upon himself' (*S.* 2. 8). Butler is not saying simply that we find ourselves approving of some of our actions and disapproving of others, as David Hume was soon to say. For Butler, dictates of conscience have an inherent and supreme authority. 'Conscience or reflection ... plainly bears upon it marks of authority over all the rest [sc. the other passions and principles of human nature] and claims the absolute direction of them all' (SP 24). This superiority and direction is 'a constituent part of the idea [sc. of conscience] ... and to preside and govern, from the very economy and constitution of man, belongs to it' (*S.* 2. 14). He goes on, in the same paragraph, to insist that this does not mean that conscience is the most powerful principle in man. It is a question of right, not of power. 'Had it strength, as it has right; had it power, as it has manifest authority; it would absolutely govern the world.' But the implication is that conscience does not have such power. Men act against their conscience; but their conscience authoritatively condemns them when they do so, as even Richard III's did at the end of Shakespeare's play.

For Butler, a virtuous life consists in a hierarchically ordered system of propensities and principles, with benevolence (and

Butler on Conscience and Virtue

cool self-love) controlling passion and interest, and with conscience ruling over all. There is a very interesting passage towards the end of 'A Dissertation upon the Nature of Virtue' in which Butler rejects as a 'terrible mistake' the notion that virtue is to be *equated* with benevolence, with acquisition, that is, of a settled disposition always to promote the happiness of others. Certainly we find in the *Fifteen Sermons* such remarks as this: 'it is manifest that the common virtues, and the common vices of mankind, may be traced up to benevolence or the want of it' (*S*. 12. 31). But, in man, benevolence cannot be allowed to override conscience. Our duty is to try to promote the happiness of others 'within the bounds of veracity and justice'. For conscience condemns lying, violence, and injustice, irrespective of any beneficial consequences that such things might have. We get here a categorical rejection of utilitarianism before that theory was explicitly advanced. Butler allows that God may be a utilitarian, but we human beings lack the omniscience which that theory requires if it is to have any plausibility at all: 'were the Author of Nature to propose nothing to himself as an end but the production of happiness, were his moral character merely that of benevolence; yet ours is not so' (DII 8). Our moral character, our human virtue, is rather a matter of benevolence within the framework of conscience. Conscience, not benevolence, has the last word.

It will already be apparent from this account of conscience and its relation to virtue in Butler's thought how impossible it would have been for Butler to concede to Anscombe that 'a man's conscience may tell him to do the vilest things'. Two further aspects of Butler's view of conscience may be cited in support of this contention. In the first place, conscience is clearly, for Butler, a faculty of true discrimination. This is not simply a matter of moral sentiment. Conscience does include felt reaction, but primarily it is a matter of reflection and sovereign judgement, both negative and positive. Conscience convicts a man of wrong motive or action; and it presses the claim of the good. All that Butler says about its authority and its right militates against the possibility of error here.

A mark of this infallibility is the uniformity of conscience. Butler holds that conscience delivers the same judgements the world over. To quote again from the dissertation:

Nor is it at all doubtful in the general what course of action this faculty ... approves and what it disapproves. For, as much as it has been disputed wherein virtue consists, or whatever ground for doubt there may be about particulars; yet, in general, there is in reality an universally acknowledged standard of it. It is that which all ages and all countries have made profession of in public; it is that which ... the primary and fundamental law of all civil constitutions over the face of the earth make it their business and endeavour to enforce the practice of upon mankind: namely, justice, veracity and regard to common good. (DII 1)

So how can Szabados defend Butler against Anscombe by appealing to the former's recognition of the possibility of a corrupt conscience? Careful study of Sermons 7 and 10 will show that Szabados has misinterpreted Butler here. These two sermons are indeed remarkable case-studies, the first of Balaam in the book of Numbers, the second of King David in 2 Samuel 12—the Bathsheba episode. With the most acute psychological penetration, Butler shows how in each of these cases self-deceit makes a good man suppress conscience and, for a time, acquiesce in wickedness with a quiet mind. Now it is perfectly true, as Szabados points out, that, at the end of Sermon 10, Butler speaks of self-deceit as 'this deep and calm source of delusion; which undermines the whole principle of good; darkens that light, that candle of the Lord within, which is to direct our steps; and corrupts conscience, which is the guide of Life' (*S.* 10. 16). It is this passage that gives Szabados the title of his article: 'Butler on Corrupt Conscience'. But, despite Butler's own reference to self-deceit corrupting conscience, his system cannot seriously allow that conscience as such becomes corrupt and, in Anscombe's words, tells a man to do the vilest things. That Butler's rhetoric is, for once, loose and exaggerated here is shown by his mention in this very passage of notions like 'that candle of the Lord', and 'the guide of life'. These could never be characterized as corrupt in themselves. King David may have been corrupted by self-deceit, but his *conscience* was only buried or suppressed till Nathan roused it with his famous parable. It was not David's conscience that told him to steal another man's wife and send her husband to inevitable death at the front. It was desire, buttressed by rationalization and self-deceit. Similarly in Shakespeare's play, King Richard's conscience was belatedly awoken on the eve of Bosworth Field. It was not his conscience that had previously prompted his string of murders.

Butler writes more accurately and strictly in the course of his other study, Sermon 7, 'Upon the Character of Balaam'. There he speaks of 'half-deceit', 'equivocation', 'subterfuges' as infecting Balaam's character; and then adds: 'By these means, conscience may be laid asleep, and [men] may go on in a course of wickedness with less disturbance' (*S.* 7. 10). The key idea, for Butler, in both these sermons, is the possibility, not of a corrupted conscience that itself becomes a source of wickedness, but of a conscience put to sleep or suppressed, so that wickedness may have free rein. There is always the hope and possibility that it can be roused from sleep, as David's was by Nathan and Balaam's by his ass. Not only is this so with fundamentally good characters, temporarily self-deceived as in Butler's two examples, but also with wicked and depraved characters, like Shakespeare's Richard. Or, to take another example, this time from Peter Geach: if a dedicated Nazi gunner, wounded and bleeding to death, stays at his post, machine-gunning a column of refugees rather than seeking medical help,[3] it may be a perverted sense of duty that dictates this action, but it would not on Butler's view be the man's conscience that told him to go on shooting. The Nazi's conscience would have been put pretty thoroughly to sleep by indoctrination in a wicked ideology. But there would always have been the possibility, however remote or faint, of its reawakening—say, through his suddenly seeing a childhood friend among the column of refugees—and of the gunner coming to himself, realizing what he was doing, and repenting in dust and ashes. Conscience as such, then, for Butler, retains its infallibility and authority, even if suppressed and put to sleep. There is always the possibility of its awakening.

But, if we cannot defend Butler against Anscombe along Szabados's path of making Butler concede the point, surely the most plausible move is simply to agree with Anscombe against Butler and say that Butler was quite wrong to exalt conscience as universal, infallible, and supremely authoritative in human nature. Our post-Freudian and sociologically aware generation is bound to be highly suspicious, not only of what Butler says about

[3] P. T. Geach, 'The Moral Law and the Law of God', in *God and the Soul* (London, 1969), 122.

the uniformity and infallibility of conscience, but also about its intrinsic authority. We may be prepared to respect people's conscientious decisions—out of a deeper respect for their rights as autonomous moral agents—but we will often think them wrong for all that. And there are limits to such respect. We do not allow a Jehovah's Witness or a Christian Scientist parent to veto a blood transfusion for an injured child. More broadly, we are all aware of differences of moral judgement amongst the different peoples and cultures of the world, past and present. We will be liable to think of conscience as a product of education and peer group pressure, a process continued in general social conditioning throughout our adult lives. We are familiar with Freud's account of conscience:[4] our primitive drives get repressed under parental and social disapproval and this disapproval gets internalized as what Freud calls the 'superego', a kind of internal censor of socially unacceptable desires and deeds. Admittedly Freud's own account concentrates on and appears most plausible in respect of the negative phenomena of guilt. But a similar sociological account of positive moral discrimination can quite easily be given, as it is by secular ethicists such as J. L. Mackie:[5] our positive moral judgements, expressing that which claims and inspires our commitments and allegiances, are also the product of training and socialization and social interaction.

However, there are certain basic features of the moral life to which these naturalistic, psychological, or sociological accounts fail to do justice. They fail to bring out or account for the *overriding* claims of morality. They fail to explain the way in which our conscience sometimes leads us to stand out against the crowd, against the mores of society. They fail to capture the way in which even a man like Richard III, let alone a man like King David, can be convicted, from within, that what he is doing is an outrage, or the way in which a man like Luther can come to hold that the stand he is taking is a moral necessity. In other words, such reductionist accounts ignore precisely that feature of a man's conscience—its sovereign authority—on which Butler lays such stress in his careful depiction of the key elements in human nature. Such accounts inevitably tend to reduce authority to

[4] See e.g. S. Freud, *Civilisation and Its Discontents* (London, 1930).
[5] J. L. Mackie, *Ethics: Inventing Right and Wrong* (Harmondsworth, 1977).

power in a way which strikes even the empirically minded, introspective, moral philosopher as implausible.

But how can Butler explain this feature on which he has put his finger? In order to answer this question we have to turn our attention to the implicit, and sometimes explicit, theology which undergirds Butler's ethical theory. At the beginning of Sermon 2, Butler observes: 'If the real nature of any creature leads him and is adapted to such and such purposes only or more than to any other; this is a reason to believe the Author of that nature intended it for those purposes.' More specifically, Butler goes on to associate our being God's creatures with our being so constituted that virtue has a prior claim over any particular revelation (*S.* 1. 2). W. R. Matthews, in a footnote to the first of these passages,[6] comments that Butler's formulation of the argument from final causes 'introduces the idea of an intelligent Creator', but goes on to say, 'It may be put without reference to a Designer. Aristotle uses the same idea when he argues that the true function of man is determined by his nature.' However, it is not so easy to bracket out such references to the Author of nature in Butler's text. For the feature of conscience in which we are interested, namely, its presiding authority and claim, is precisely that which cannot be accounted for by purely naturalistic teleological theories such as Aristotle's. Reference to our true nature, or to the true function of some element in it, points inexorably to the idea of our Maker's intention. The authority of conscience is a mark of our nature as God intended it to be. Thus we should take seriously Butler's characterization of conscience, not only as 'moral reason', and 'moral sense' (Butler affirms both aspects), but as 'Divine reason' (DII 1), as 'the guide assigned us by the Author of Nature' (*S.* 3. 5), and as 'that candle of the Lord within' (*S.* 10. 16). Indeed, after bringing out the authority of conscience as its most distinctive characteristic, Butler insists that conscience 'if not forcibly stopped' (e.g. by self-deceit or indoctrination) 'naturally and always goes on to anticipate a higher and more effectual sentence which shall hereafter second and affirm its own' (*S.* 2. 8).

It is interesting to compare this idea of conscience anticipating the divine judgement with Newman's celebrated 'exaltation'

[6] *Butler's Fifteen Sermons and a Dissertation on the Nature of Virtue*, ed. W. R. Matthews (London, 1958).

of conscience in *A Grammar of Assent*.[7] Newman, who was himself greatly influenced by Butler's writings, declares that 'the phenomena of Conscience ... avail to impress the imagination with the picture of a Supreme Governor, a Judge, holy, just, powerful, all-seeing, retributive, and is the creative principle of religion, as the Moral Sense is the principle of ethics'. Butler is less overtly theological than Newman. He does not press this distinction between religion and ethics, still less between conscience and the moral sense. For Butler, conscience is indeed *our* moral sense and *our* moral reason, but precisely as such is it implanted by the Author of our nature and anticipates his final judgement.

Anscombe is able to disparage Butler's view of conscience only because she takes him to be talking about our fallible, purely human, moral sense. But this is to prize the subjective side of conscience apart from its objective foundation in human nature as the Author of nature intended it to be. That is why we have to think in terms of our true nature and its intended structure, if we are to do justice to Butler's ethical thought. That is why Butler's is a theological ethic, even if it is not a divine command theory. That Butler's is a theological version of natural law theory and not a divine command theory will be clear from the foregoing account, not least the reference to the priority of conscience and virtue over any particular revelation. It will be clear, too, why Butler prefaces both Sermons 2 and 3 with the same text—the classical natural law text—from Romans 2: 14: 'For when the Gentiles, which have not the law, do by nature the things contained in the law, these, having not the law, are a law unto themselves.'

So, if we must urge against Szabados that Butler could not allow that conscience may tell a man to do the vilest things, we must urge against Anscombe that Butler has both an explanation and a justification for his exalted view of conscience. Butler's error theory concerning self-deceit, to which Szabados quite properly points, accounts for the phenomena which trouble Anscombe. But neither Anscombe nor Szabados is right to speak, with reference to Butler's thought, of a corrupt *conscience*, which may itself tell a man to do the vilest things.

---

[7] J. H. Newman, *A Grammar of Assent* (London, 1870), ch. 5, s. 1.

This interpretation of Butler on conscience and virtue enables us to dispose of another accusation levelled against Butler's ethics, namely that it commits the naturalistic fallacy.[8] For Butler does not offer his account of conscience and virtue in human nature in purely descriptive, naturalistic, terms. On the contrary, value is built into his account from the very start. We are not given a description of human nature in neutral, value-free, terms, from which evaluative conclusions are then supposedly drawn. The authority of conscience, on Butler's view, is an evaluative principle already built into our nature. There is no way in which, without reduction, a value-neutral description of a human being can be given (such as Desmond Morris attempts, for example[9]). That is why we have to read Butler's depiction of human nature as an account of our true nature. Our true nature is to live virtuously, that is, benevolently, under the rule of conscience. To act in accordance with baser impulses, to put conscience to sleep, to let self-deceit prevail, is to live viciously, against our true nature, however 'natural', in another sense of that word,[10] it may be to do so. And there is no third, neutral, value-free way between a virtuous or a vicious life. So Butler does not commit the naturalistic fallacy. In living virtuously we realize our *true* nature, as we were meant to be.

Alvin Plantinga has recently been exploring the notion of the 'proper functioning' of our cognitive faculties, in an attempt to sketch a theistic epistemology that overcomes certain basic recurring problems with secular, naturalistic, theories of knowledge.[11] It is interesting to ask whether Butler's treatment of our moral faculties can be thought of in a similar way. For Plantinga, a belief has what he calls 'positive epistemic status'—that is, constitutes a justified true belief and therefore knowledge—if and only if the cognitive faculties of the person holding that belief are functioning properly, that is, as God intended them to do, in the environment for which they were designed. This theistic

---

[8] See N. L. Sturgeon, 'Nature and Conscience in Butler's Ethics', *Philosophical Review*, 85 (1976), 316-56, and its refutation by T. Penelhum in his book *Butler* (London, 1985), 61-70.

[9] e.g. D. Morris, *The Naked Ape* (London, 1967).

[10] That other sense of 'natural' is explicitly mentioned by Butler in *S.* 2. 6.

[11] A. Plantinga, 'Justification and Theism', *Faith and Philosophy*, 4/4 (Oct. 1987), 403-26.

epistemology, so Plantinga avers, succeeds in accounting for the possibility of human knowledge in a way secular epistemologies, relying simply on coherence or the responsible sifting of evidence, notoriously fail to do. Could we not say that, in the moral sphere, on Butler's account, a properly functioning conscience always succeeds in convicting us of wrong or prompting us to acknowledge the overriding claims of the good, since that is how the Author of nature designed our moral constitution? In both cases—the grasp of truth and the grasp of obligation—what guarantees success is our God-given nature fulfilling the Creator's intention. A further parallel between the epistemic and the moral cases lies in the common conviction, on a theistic world-view, that there is an intended fit between our faculties and their environment. Indeed, it is a feature of Butler's ethics that the world is so structured that virtue and cool self-love in the long run coincide. If we fulfil our true nature in living virtuously, that is, benevolently under the rule of conscience, we will ourselves achieve true happiness (though that should not, of course, become the *motive* of our action).

But the parallel between properly functioning cognitive faculties and properly functioning moral faculties is not exact. Our cognitive faculties can malfunction—say, through disease or the use of drugs. Certainly our moral judgements can go awry—through self-deceit or indoctrination, as we have seen. But Butler could not allow that conscience as such might lead us astray. In other words, Butler builds proper functioning into his very notion of conscience, in a way that belies the parallel between conscience and our cognitive faculties. In the epistemic sense, the divine guarantee only operates if our faculties are functioning properly; but in the moral case the guarantee is built into the faculty itself. That is why conscience cannot be thought of simply as *our* moral sense or reason. In the moral case, the relevant faculty is endowed with rightness and authority in a way to which there is no parallel in the epistemic sphere. When things go wrong in the moral sphere, it is not a matter of the malfunctioning of a faculty intended to work otherwise. It is rather a matter of the suppression or putting to sleep of a faculty which, if functioning at all, possesses a built-in guarantee.

This is the feature of Butler's moral theory missed by both Anscombe and Szabados in their treatment of Butler on conscience. Whether Butler is right is, of course, another story. But enough has been said to show that Butler's view of conscience stands or falls by its theological foundation.

11
Conscience as Self-Authorizing in Butler's Ethics

STEPHEN DARWALL

There has long been general agreement about the intended meaning of Butler's claim that conscience is supremely authoritative.[1] C. D. Broad nicely articulates this consensus when he writes: 'by saying that conscience has supreme authority Butler means that we regard the pronouncements of conscience, not simply as interesting or uninteresting statements of fact, and not simply as reasons to be balanced against others, but as *conclusive* reasons for or against doing the actions about which it pronounces.'[2] To this it might be added that, according to Butler, we do not simply happen so to regard conscience's pronouncements; we do so *rightly*.

But if the doctrine of conscience's authority is clear enough, how exactly Butler means to ground this idea is far from clear. In fact, there are at least two different, and somewhat conflicting, lines of thought that lead him to this thesis. One is evident on the surface of the text, even if its philosophical power does not match its prominence. This is the idea that conscience provides conclusive reasons because we are designed to be guided by its directives, and that we therefore function properly only when we are so guided.[3] A second line is, I think, more promising,

---

I am indebted to William Frankena and Nicholas White for helpful comments and discussion of this paper.

[1] Butler uses 'conscience' and 'principle of reflection' interchangeably to refer to disinterested, dispassionate reflective approval and disapproval of actions and principles (motives). See e.g. S. 1. 8, 2. 8. He usually reserves these terms for an agent's self-evaluation, although he evidently thinks that this is an instance of an evaluation whose objects are not restricted to self. See e.g. DII 2. I shall adopt the expedient of using 'conscience' to refer to both of these.
[2] C. D. Broad, *Five Types of Ethical Theory* (Totowa, NJ, 1965), 78.
[3] This line admits of both cognitivist and non-cognitivist versions.

but more difficult to tease out and formulate, even though it can convincingly be shown to be an important element in Butler's thought. Put very crudely, it holds that the authority of conscience is a condition of the very possibility of an agent's having reasons to act at all, since only a being who has the capacity for maintaining a self-regulated constitutional order can have reasons to act, and this capacity depends on the agent's taking her conscience to be authoritative. This is a version of a thought that is more familiar in Kant's later formulation that morality obligates from within by virtue of the will's capacity to be a law to itself—that moral agency and autonomy are reciprocals.[4]

In what follows my ultimate aim will be to sketch this second line of thought. I begin in Section I, however, with a discussion of Nicholas Sturgeon's argument that the authority of conscience is actually superfluous in Butler's system. Partly, of course, my aim will be to refute Sturgeon. But Sturgeon's argument also provides a context in which to set out preliminary aspects of the second, 'autonomist' line in Butler: specifically, his suggestion that conscience is self-authorizing in some sense. In Section II, I turn to a consideration of Butler's teleological/functional grounding of conscience's authority. Finally, in Section III, I sketch the autonomist line more fully. When he is thinking this way, I argue, Butler apparently sees the agent's recognition of the authority of conscience as a condition of the existence of the rational moral self. In these moments, conscience is self-authorizing for Butler because it is *self*-authorizing.

I

Surely the most provocative thesis in recent Butler scholarship is Nicholas Sturgeon's claim that the authority of conscience is superfluous.[5] This is a startling claim, to say the least. Commentators have generally regarded the supremacy of conscience as the most distinctive element of Butler's moral philosophy. I agree with this orthodox view, so I must show where I think

[4] Butler was not the only British moralist to take a version of this line. I discuss Shaftesbury's thought in this connection, and give a brief sketch of the larger context of ideas of the period, in 'Obligation and Motive in the British Moralists', in Ellen F. Paul et al. (eds.), *Foundations of Moral and Political Philosophy* (Oxford, 1989), 133–50.

[5] Nicholas L. Sturgeon, 'Nature and Conscience in Butler's Ethics', *Philosophical Review*, 85 (1976), 316–56.

Sturgeon's argument breaks down. But I also think that Sturgeon's analysis succeeds in bringing into relief elements of Butler's view that have been insufficiently appreciated by other commentators.[6] Coming to grips with his argument will not only enable us to see why the authority of conscience is not superfluous; it will help us to get a more adequate view of what Butler sometimes takes the authority of conscience actually to consist in.

In Sermon 2 Butler canvasses three senses of 'nature' in the course of arguing that to disobey conscience is to violate the 'law of our nature' and, therefore, to do what is unnatural 'in the highest and most proper sense' (*S.* 2. 9). Conscience is a principle in the human psyche, so obeying it is natural in one sense. But disobedience is also motivated by 'some principle in man' (*S.* 2. 5). A principle may be called 'natural', secondly, by virtue of its strength. But as any action results from the principle strongest at the time, disobedience will not be unnatural in this sense either (*S.* 2. 6). There is, however, a third sense in which it can be shown that disobeying conscience *is* unnatural, Butler argues. It is possible for an action to be unnatural, not because it 'go[es] against a principle or desire barely, nor ... against that principle or desire which happens for the present to be strongest', but because it contravenes a 'superior principle' (*S.* 2. 11). There is, Butler maintains, a difference between practical principles which, 'not being a difference in strength or degree', is rather 'a difference in *nature* and in *kind*' (*S.* 2. 11). Human nature is a *constitution*—its principles form a constitutional order. An action is thus 'in the strictest and most proper sense unnatural' if it violates a principle that is superior to any by which it is endorsed (*S.* 2. 10). The superior principle, though weaker, none the less has authority; it is the one that should govern.[7] To oppose it is to go contrary to a 'law of our nature'.

Conscience will have supreme authority, therefore, just in case any action contrary to its dictates is thereby made unnatural. As

---

[6] Including recent critics of Sturgeon. See Terence Penelhum, *Butler* (London, 1985), 61–70; and Alan Millar in 'Following Nature', *Philosophical Quarterly*, 38 (1988), 172 n.

[7] Thus, after discussing an illustration of reasonable self-love's superiority to a stronger present appetite, Butler writes: 'if we will act conformably to the economy of man's nature, reasonable self-love must govern' (*S.* 2. 11). And he sums up this whole discussion thus: 'All this is no more than the distinction, which everybody is acquainted with, between *mere power* and *authority*' (*S.* 2. 14).

Sturgeon puts it, 'the supremacy of conscience will be that feature of it which renders unnatural *any* action, however motivated, which conflicts with it'.[8] What creates problems, as he sees it, is that Butler is also committed to what Sturgeon calls the *Full Naturalistic Thesis*: 'that conscience never *favors* or *opposes* any action, except on grounds which include its naturalness or unnaturalness'.[9] If this is so, and if conscience is 'fully transparent' (if, that is 'the *favor* or *opposition* of conscience is never founded on a mistaken estimate of an action's naturalness'[10]), then the only way an action can be contrary to (or in accord with) conscience is by being contrary to (or in accord with) some other superior principle.[11] So, Sturgeon claims, it is only in an uninteresting sense that disobeying conscience is always unnatural. Being contrary to conscience is never what makes disobedience unnatural; disobedience is always unnatural only because it always violates some other superior principle. In Butler's scheme, conscience turns out to be no more than a transparent registrar of the superiority and inferiority of other principles. Sturgeon concludes: 'it makes *no difference whatever to the naturalness or unnaturalness of any action* whether or not conscience is superior to any other principle of action.'[12]

Waiving concerns about transparency, the crucial premiss of this argument is the Full Naturalistic Thesis. Sturgeon acknowledges that Butler never explicitly states that conscience always bases its judgement on grounds of naturalness, but he offers reasons for thinking that Butler is committed to it none the less, which we must consider presently. We should note first, however, that there are passages in which Butler appears explicitly to deny the Full Naturalistic Thesis.[13] The most obvious one occurs right in Sermon 2: 'there is a superior principle of reflection or conscience in every man ... [which] pronounces determinately some actions to be in themselves just, right, good; others to be in themselves evil, wrong, unjust' (*S.* 2. 8).[14] This

---

[8] Sturgeon, 'Nature and Conscience', 319.   [9] Ibid. 328.
[10] Ibid.   [11] Ibid. 344.
[12] Ibid. 347.   [13] Here I follow Penelhum, *Butler*, 62.
[14] In the dissertation, Butler says that the object of conscience is 'actions, comprehending under that name active or practical principles'. And he writes that brutes lack conscience because it does not appear 'that will and design, which constitute the very nature of actions as such, are at all an object of their perception' (DII 2).

certainly seems to say that, at least sometimes, conscience approves or disapproves of actions in themselves and not on the grounds that they are natural or unnatural.[15]

Sturgeon admits that Butler sometimes *says* that conscience judges actions 'in themselves' (e.g. at *S.* 2. 8), but he adds that Butler means in these places to contrast this, not with comparing the action to the nature of the agent (in a judgement of naturalness), but with evaluating actions in light of their consequences.[16] No doubt Butler does have this latter contrast in mind, but he seems to have the former in mind also. For just two sections later, in discussing what he takes to be a clear example of an unnatural action—a man's rushing into certain ruin for the sake of a present gratification—he writes that this 'disproportion arises, not from considering the action singly in *itself*, or in its *consequences*, but from comparison of it with the nature of the agent' (*S.* 2. 10). There seems no reason to suppose, therefore, that when he says in *S.* 2. 8 that conscience assesses certain actions 'in themselves' he means only to contrast this with assessing an act's consequences, and not to contrast it with assessing its naturalness.

The most convincing reason for thinking that Butler must believe that conscience sometimes approves and disapproves of actions (and, perhaps, principles) considered in themselves, and not always on grounds of their naturalness, however, is Butler's whole dialectical strategy in arguing for the authority of conscience in the *Fifteen Sermons*. Commentators frequently note that Butler introduces the *Fifteen Sermons* with a discussion of method:

There are two ways in which the subject of morals may be treated. One begins from inquiring into the abstract relations of things: the other from a matter of fact, namely, what the particular nature of man is, its several parts, their economy or constitution; from whence it proceeds to determine what course of life it is, which is correspondent to this whole nature. (SP 12)

If it is not obvious in the *Fifteen Sermons*, Butler makes it clear in the *Analogy* that he accepts both methods, although, as he says

---

[15] And he may also be taking the same view of some conscientious judgements of principles or principled actions.

[16] Sturgeon, 'Nature and Conscience', 345.

there in announcing his acceptance of the former method, he does not pursue it in that work either.[17] '[I]n this treatise I have omitted a thing of the utmost importance which I believe, the moral fitness and unfitness of actions, prior to all will whatever' (*A*. 2. 8. 11). And he there contrasts these matters of 'abstract principle' or 'abstract truth' with the 'matters of fact' from which we can infer divine moral governance of nature and, therefore, motives to morality and religion. 'And thus,' he concludes, 'the obligations of religion are made out, exclusively of the questions concerning ... moral fitness' (*A*. 2. 8. 11).

A similar contrast is in play in the *Fifteen Sermons*, as the Preface passage makes explicit. Here too he attempts to establish 'our obligations to the practice of virtue' by appealing, not to propositions regarding the 'abstract relations of things', but to 'a matter of fact'. In the *Fifteen Sermons*, however, the relevant facts concern the constitution of the moral agent—the governance of his internal nature rather than the governance of nature as a whole.[18]

These remarks bring out two important points that bear on the Full Naturalistic Thesis and Butler's argument for the authority of conscience. First, Butler evidently accepts the spirit and, perhaps, the letter of Samuel Clarke's doctrine that: 'Some things are in their own nature good and reasonable and fit to be done; such as keeping faith, and performing equitable compacts, and the like.'[19] Since we may suppose Butler must think we have some faculty to apprehend such intrinsic fitnesses (how else would *he* believe in them), and since there is no appropriate

---

[17] Butler says of the first method in the *Fifteen Sermons*: 'The first seems the most direct formal proof, and in some respects the least liable to cavil and dispute' (SP 12). It is worth noting that Butler also says that the sermons 'proceed chiefly in this latter method. The first three wholly.' This suggests that Butler himself thinks, at least, that he makes some use of the first method elsewhere in the *Fifteen Sermons*. Whether or not he does in fact, it is clear enough that his argument that conscience is authoritative is meant to proceed wholly by the second method.

[18] 'Matters of fact' should be read as having scare quotes since Butler's use of this phrase will seem misleading if one has in mind a use familiar from Hume's *Treatise*, bk. III, pt. I, s. I.

[19] Thus, Butler writes: 'Fidelity, honour, strict justice, are themselves approved in the highest degree, abstracted from the consideration of their tendency' (*S*. 12. 31 n.). The passage of Samuel Clarke's is from *A Discourse of Natural Religion*, published in 1706. See D. D. Raphael (ed.), *British Moralists*, v. i (Oxford, 1969), 196. The passage can also be found in J. B. Schneewind (ed.), *Moral Philosophy from Montaigne to Kant: An Anthology* (Cambridge, 1990), v. i, p. 298.

faculty in his moral psychology other than some form of conscience, we may attribute to him the belief that conscience sometimes endorses or opposes certain actions as fit or unfit in themselves.[20]

The second point is that, while Butler accepts that conscience approves certain actions as morally fit in themselves, he none the less thinks there exists a further practical question, one he is anxious to address in the *Fifteen Sermons*, namely, why should an agent do what his conscience approves of, or forbear doing what his conscience opposes? What reason (or rational motive) does an agent have to do so? British moral philosophers of the period frequently raised this question by asking what obligation there is to be moral. Thus Shaftesbury writes at the beginning of book II of his *Inquiry Concerning Virtue or Merit*: 'We have considered [in book I] *what* VIRTUE is and to whom the character belongs. It remains to inquire *what obligation* there is to VIRTUE, or *what reason* to embrace it.'[21] At one point Butler puts his question this way: 'allowing that mankind hath the rule of right within himself, yet it may be asked, "What obligations are we under to attend to and follow it?"' (*S.* 3. 5) That conscience tells us what is intrinsically morally fit and unfit is not a satisfying answer to this question, since it can still be asked: why should an agent forbear doing what is morally unfit?

The claim that conscience is authoritative, therefore, is the claim that we are obligated, in this sense, to follow it—the political metaphor carries through. In following conscience we follow the 'law of our nature' and do what is natural 'in the highest and most proper sense' (*S.* 2. 9). As Butler summarizes his conclusion: 'every man is naturally a law to himself ... every one may find within himself the rule of right, *and obligations to follow it*' (*S.* 2. 4, emphasis added). Evidently, then, he must be assuming it sufficient proof that one should do something (i.e.

---

[20] Butler sometimes uses 'reason' to refer to a capacity to make moral judgements. (See n. 32.) No doubt this use of 'reason' is not meant to refer to what he usually reserves 'conscience' for, namely judgement about the self in particular, and it may be that he thinks that reason apprehends fitnesses and unfitnesses and that he means to distinguish this from any form of conscience. Since I know of no evidence for this theoretical possibility, and since it would not much affect my argument, I shall ignore it.

[21] Raphael, *British Moralists*, v. i, p. 175; Schneewind, *Moral Philosophy*, v. ii, p. 495. For a discussion of the way the concept of obligation was reshaped in this direction in 17th-cent. British thought, see Darwall, 'Obligation and Motive in the British Moralists', 137-45.

that there is conclusive reason or justification for acting) that not doing so would be unnatural or contrary to a law of our nature. But if this is Butler's strategy, he cannot also think that conscience always bases its favour or opposition to actions on an assessment of their naturalness. For then he could not raise the very question he is attempting in the *Fifteen Sermons* to answer: allowing that conscience favours a given action, why none the less should a person so act? What obligation exists to do so? If conscience's favour is itself always made on the grounds of naturalness, no further question of justification can be raised. At least, this is so if, as Butler assumes, establishing that following a principle is natural 'in the strictest and most proper sense' thereby establishes an obligation to follow it.[22]

Despite the facts that Butler explicitly denies the Full Naturalistic Thesis and that he must implicitly deny it in arguing that there is an obligation to follow conscience, he might still be otherwise committed to it. Sturgeon gives several reasons for thinking this is so, the most interesting of which is his contention that Butler actually relies on the Thesis in a crucial argument in Sermon 2 for, ironically, the authority of conscience itself.[23] Before we can consider this, however, we must first note an earlier passage that sets the stage for Sturgeon's interpretation. Butler's first illustration of the superiority of one principle to another, of how acting on one of two conflicting principles can 'manifest a disproportion, between the nature of a

---

[22] Penelhum makes a similar argument in *Butler*, 58–65.

[23] Two others are that Butler says in the dissertation 'Of the Nature of Virtue' that 'our perception of vice and ill-desert arises from, and is a result of, a comparison of actions with the nature and capacities of the agent' (DII 5), and that he says that virtue 'consists in following nature' (SP 13) and that whenever conscience approves or disapproves of an action, it does so on grounds of its virtue or vice (Sturgeon, 'Nature and Conscience', 324–5). Since the dissertation passage explicitly includes 'ill-desert', which obviously brings in 'comparison of actions with the nature and capacities of the agent' by way of assessing potentially excusing conditions, it does not necessarily bear directly on the Full Naturalistic Thesis. (Here see also Penelhum, *Butler*, 68.) And the Preface passage in which Butler says that the *Fifteen Sermons* are 'intended to explain what is meant by the nature of man, when it is said that virtue consists in following, and vice, in deviating from it', occurs just after the section in which he has said that the method he will undertake leads to 'our *obligations* to the practice of virtue' from a consideration of 'what course of life it is, which is correspondent to this our whole nature' (emphasis added). I agree, therefore, with Penelhum that 'Butler's claim that virtue consists in following nature is not intended to help identify what virtue requires, but to help ensure its practice' (*Butler*, 61). It is addressed to the 'obligation' to virtue, to whether there is reason to be virtuous.

man and ... an action' making the action unnatural 'in the strictest and most proper sense', is that of a man who rushes into certain ruin for the sake of a present gratification (*S.* 2. 10). The disproportion makes 'manifest that self-love is in human nature a superior principle to passion' (*S.* 2. 11). Though passion be stronger, self-love should govern. 'Thus,' he concludes, 'without particular consideration of conscience, we may have a clear conception of the *superior nature* of one inward principle to another' (*S.* 2. 11). Sturgeon infers from this that Butler believes that one principle can be superior to another independently of their relations to conscience. Of course, if Butler is to hold the Full Naturalistic Thesis he must believe this. Conscience can make its judgement of something on grounds of naturalness only if the latter is independent of an endorsement by conscience of that very thing. I shall argue below and in Section III that Butler may not actually believe that one principle *can* be superior to another independently of their relations to conscience. If he does not, the Full Naturalistic Thesis cannot possibly be attributed to Butler. But regardless, Sturgeon's reasons do not warrant attributing the Thesis to Butler in any case. To see this, let us accept for the moment that Butler believes what he appears here to assert, namely that self-love is superior to passion independently of their relations to conscience.

Having made (in *S.* 2. 14) the distinction between 'mere power and authority', that is, between a principle's having strength and its being one by which an agent should govern himself, Butler goes on to give two arguments for the supreme authority of conscience. The first involves his claim that the very idea of conscience entails authority: 'you cannot form a notion of this faculty, conscience, without taking in judgment, direction, superintendency' (*S.* 2. 14). Since it does not follow from the fact that conscience claims authority that it has it, Sturgeon remarks that 'Butler needs a second argument, then, and offers one'.[24] The problem, as Sturgeon sees it, is that the one he gives assumes the Full Naturalistic Thesis, and thus undermines its own conclusion.

The argument is a *reductio*. Notice, however, how Butler formulates the premiss to be reduced to absurdity. 'Let us now

[24] Sturgeon, 'Nature and Conscience', 320.

turn this whole matter another way, and suppose there was no such thing at all as this natural supremacy of conscience; that there was no distinction to be made between one inward principle and another, but only that of strength; and see what would be the consequence' (*S.* 2. 16). It is important to realize that Butler here appears to treat the natural supremacy of conscience and the very existence of relations of natural superiority as equivalent; most importantly, that the *reductio* depends on treating the natural superiority of any principle as entailing the supreme authority of conscience. Absurd consequences follow, he argues, from denying that practical principles can differ in 'nature and in kind' and not just in strength. But this can establish conscience's supremacy only if the latter follows from the natural supremacy of any principle. We shall return to this point in Section III below. It means, in effect, that if there are any reasons for an agent to act at all, her conscience must be authoritative.[25]

Butler apparently regards the possibility that there might be no reasons for acting at all—that principles might differ only in strength and not in relative superiority—as what needs to be ruled out in order to demonstrate conscience's authority. To do so, he considers what believing it would constrain us to think of an action of which we would normally disapprove:

[S]uppose a man guilty of parricide ... This action is done in consequence of its principle being for the present strongest: and if there be no difference between inward principles, but only that of strength; the strength being given, you have the whole nature of the man given, so far as it relates to this matter.... Upon comparing the action and the whole nature, there arises no disproportion. (*S.* 2. 17)

He then concludes: 'If there be no difference between inward principles, but only that of strength; we can make no distinction

---

[25] Butler's example in *S.* 2. 10 and 2. 11 of the superiority (in human beings) of self-love to passion, and his remark that 'without particular consideration of conscience, we may have a clear conception of the *superior nature* of one inward principle to another', may seem to contradict this. I will argue below that it need not. See p. 234. Sturgeon writes that Butler 'leaves it unclear which of these two nonequivalent propositions is to be the supposition of the *reductio*' ('Nature and Conscience', 321). He acknowledges that, in order for the argument to be relevant to the authority of conscience, Butler has to think that the latter will follow from the existence of any relations of superiority, but finds it 'ironic that he should believe this', since the argument commits him to an assumption (the Full Naturalistic Thesis) 'which will render superfluous the assignment to conscience of this or any other rank' (p. 321).

between [a parricide and an act of filial duty], considered as the actions of such a creature; but in our coolest hours must approve or disapprove of them equally; than which nothing can be reduced to a greater absurdity' (*S.* 2. 17).

Sturgeon argues that Butler can reasonably think that we are constrained to approve or disapprove these actions equally only if he accepts the Full Naturalistic Thesis—only if, that is, conscience always bases its judgements on grounds having to do with naturalness. Thinking these actions equally natural would then constrain us to 'approve or disapprove them equally'. As Penelhum has pointed out, however, this is not strictly correct. The conclusion that Butler draws here is that we would be constrained to approve or disapprove them equally when considering them '*as the actions of such a creature*'.[26] Even if conscience's judgements of actions as of an agent are never independent of considerations of naturalness, it is consistent with this that conscience also approves and disapproves of actions (and, indeed, principles) considered in themselves. Butler is not committed by the *reductio*, therefore, to the Full Naturalistic Thesis.

Even so, it is an important fact, which Sturgeon is right to stress, that Butler *is* saying here that conscience's judgement of an action, as of an agent of a certain nature, is based on naturalness. Though conscience may disapprove of parricide, as a kind of action, it cannot sustain disapproval of an agent's parricide it believes not to have been unnatural. If we believe such an agent was not in a position to have good and sufficient reason not to kill his parent, Butler thinks, we cannot disapprove of an agent like him doing so. So if we do so, we must think there was such a reason. And since, if there be no difference between principles but relative strength, there will be no such reasons, it follows that if we believe principles differ only in relative strength, we cannot consistently disapprove any agent's parricide. And if the existence of relations of relative superiority between principles entails the authority of conscience, it follows further that we cannot believe that conscience is not supreme and consistently disapprove any agent's parricide. Denying conscience's authority requires one to forbear conscientious judgements of this kind. This consequence, Butler trusts, we will find absurd.

---

[26] Emphasis added. See Penelhum, *Butler*, 67.

Above I said that Butler distinguishes between conscience's approval of an action and there being an obligation to follow this 'rule of right within'; and that his argument that in violating conscience we go counter to a law of our nature and thereby act unnaturally is addressed to the latter. The Full Naturalistic Thesis ignores this distinction. It maintains that the grounds that constitute conscience's authority, namely considerations of natural superiority and inferiority, are the very grounds on which conscience initially approves or disapproves conduct. We have found no good reason to think that Butler believes this, and hence, that his project of establishing the authority of conscience is internally incoherent. At the same time, the present argument suggests that the line between what grounds a judgement of conscience and what grounds conscience's authority, or power to obligate, is not impermeable. Butler assumes in the *reductio* that only if we think that conscience obligates, and that violating it is unnatural, can we disapprove of an agent's doing so.

Viewed this way, judgements of naturalness constrain conscientious judgements of agents' acts; disapproval of an agent's action requires the belief that the action was unnatural. Moreover, Butler's view is evidently not that the latter is simply a necessary ground for conscience's disapproving the agent's act, but also that the judgement that an agent's action is unnatural is itself a judgement of conscience.[27] If this is so, an account of the unnaturalness of violating conscience—of, that is, the obligation to follow conscience—will itself be adequate only if it simultaneously explains a further disapproval of an agent's violating

---

[27] Penelhum is somewhat puzzling on this point. He recognizes that there is no faculty other than conscience to make the 'judgments of practical philosophy' which he rightly thinks to be what judgements of naturalness amount to for Butler. But he appears to think that Butler is simply here 'using the older and more general sense of "conscience" as "inward knowledge or consciousness"'. And he says that 'it may be that Butler does think that an assumption of equality of status between inward principles would disable conscience, and is therefore closer in this passage to committing himself to the Full Naturalistic Thesis than I suggest' (*Butler*, 68). Butler quite clearly says that, were we to believe that there is no distinction in which principles a person should be governed by, we could not approve or disapprove his acts differentially, but this does not involve the Full Naturalistic Thesis. That, if we believe violating conscience not to be unnatural, then we can no longer disapprove of an agent's parricide, does not entail that we cannot initially disapprove of parricide as a kind of act considered in itself and independently of grounds of its naturalness.

conscience, beyond that already involved in (the agent's) conscientious disapproval of an act or principle in itself.

There are several reasons for thinking that this is indeed Butler's view. First, it is simply unclear how an agent's parricide's being unnatural would be a necessary ground for disapproving it unless either judgements of naturalness are made by conscience or conscience judges as a general proposition that no action is to be disapproved that is not unnatural.[28] Second, Butler says in Sermon 2 that his method of establishing an obligation to virtue from 'a review of the nature of man' is 'to be considered as an appeal to each particular person's heart and natural conscience' (*S.* 2. 1).[29] Third, just after he announces in the Preface that his method will be to establish an obligation 'to the practice of virtue' from a 'matter of fact', namely that vice is unnatural, he remarks that he aims here to agree with 'the ancient moralists [who] had some inward feeling or other, which they chose to express in this manner, that ... [virtue] consists in following nature' (SP 13). What could such an 'inward feeling' be for Butler but a judgement of conscience? This theme is repeated several times in the following sections, the doctrine that vice is unnatural being there also called an 'inward perception' and an 'inward conviction' (SP 13. 16).

All of this makes sense on the assumption that Butler understands the judgement that conduct is natural or unnatural (in 'the strictest and most proper sense') to be a judgement of conscience. In addition, there is another very powerful reason for thinking Butler would have to take this view. Like other British moralists of the period, Butler understands the question of whether there is an obligation to virtue to concern the existence of ultimate justification or reason for being virtuous. As Penelhum points out, the question is one asked by those 'who do not deny what virtue requires' but who wonder whether practising virtue is 'what they *should* do'.[30] This, recall, is the question Butler is asking when he queries whether disobeying conscience is unnatural. But there would appear to be no other faculty in Butler's moral psychology from which such a normative judgement can issue but some form

---

[28] In the second instance, an account of unnaturalness would still have to explain why, if that is what unnaturalness is, an agent's act is to be disapproved only if it manifests it.

[29] A caveat is necessary here. See n. 39 below.

[30] Penelhum, *Butler*, 58, emphasis added.

of conscience itself.[31] Self-love, for example, is simply the desire for one's greatest good; it does not make, in addition, any judgement that one *ought* to pursue one's greatest good.[32] There appears to be only one faculty which can make normative judgements: conscience itself.

If this is so, then it would seem that Butler must suppose that conscience is in some sense self-authorizing. But what can this amount to? It is useful to distinguish here between an agent's first-order disapproval, say, of some action, and her (or our) second-order disapproval of her doing what she disapproves as a first-order matter. On the present suggestion, the judgement that disobeying conscience is unnatural would be a second-order disapproval of doing what is the object of a first-order disapproval. But how could any such second-order judgement of conscience establish conscience's authority? How can conscience be genuinely self-*authorizing*? There are, of course, the familiar passages in which Butler says that conscience implicitly claims its own authority: 'as from its very nature manifestly claiming superiority over all others: insomuch that you cannot form a notion of this faculty, conscience, without taking in judgment, direction, superintendency. This is a constituent part of the idea that is, of the faculty itself: and to preside and govern ... belongs to it.' (*S.* 2. 14)[33] But as Sturgeon notes, from the fact that conscience must claim its own authority, it does not follow

---

[31] 'Some form' of conscience, because Butler notoriously uses 'conscience' and 'principle of reflection' to refer to a variety of forms of disinterested, dispassionate, reflective evaluative and normative judgements. (See n. 1 above.) In n. 20 above I discuss the possibility that Butler thinks of what he sometimes calls 'reason' as a faculty distinct from any form of conscience which perceives intrinsic fitnesses and unfitnesses. But even if this were so, this faculty could not make the sort of normative judgement of obligation that Butler's argument requires, since he is abjuring any use of the Clarkean method. (See n. 39 for references for Butler's use of 'reason'.)

[32] Thus in the dissertation Butler distinguishes between self-love and the judgement that a person ought to promote his interest: 'It should seem, that a due concern about our own interest or happiness, and a reasonable endeavour to secure and promote it, which is, I think, very much the meaning of the word *prudence*, in our language; it should seem, that this is virtue, and the contrary behaviour faulty and blamable; since, in the calmest way of reflection, we approve of the first, and condemn the other conduct, both in ourselves and others. This approbation and disapprobation are altogether different from mere desire of our own, or of their happiness, and from sorrow upon missing it. For the object or occasion of this last kind of perception is satisfaction; whereas the object of the first is active behaviour. In one case, what our thoughts fix upon is our condition; in the other, our conduct.' I discuss this passage further on p. 235 below.

[33] See also SP 24, 26, 27; *S.* 2. 8.

that it has it in fact. It is simply unclear how conscience can succeed in being self-authorizing even if it must claim to be so.

II

In Section III I shall argue that Butler actually has a promising line of thought in this general direction. Before I do so, however, we should consider other ideas he has relating to the authority of conscience that are along quite different lines. To this point, I have been presenting Butler's argument that the authority of conscience derives from its being the law of our nature, and, hence, that disobeying it is unnatural, as resting on 'the distinction, which everybody is acquainted with, between *mere power* and *authority*' (*S.* 2. 14). The principles of which we are composed differ not just in 'strength or degree', but also 'in *nature* and in *kind*' (*S.* 2. 11). As we have seen, Butler bases his third sense of 'natural' in Sermon 2, the sense in which he aims to show that disobeying conscience is unnatural, on this distinction (*S.* 2. 9, 10). Going against conscience is unnatural in this sense just in case conscience is in its nature authoritative. So Butler argues in Sermon 2 that the very conception of conscience is of a faculty that claims superiority (*S.* 2. 14), and that denying this claim leads to absurdity (*S.* 2. 17).

The ruling metaphor in this line of thought is that of a *constitutional order*, an order that exists only if relations of authority exist—only if there is a truth about who has the right to govern when the claims of political actors conflict. Likewise, our internal nature forms a constitutional order only if there is a truth about which principles should govern when they conflict. Put in these terms, in arguing that disobeying conscience is unnatural, Butler is maintaining that it is unconstitutional—it '*violates*', as he sometimes says, our internal constitution. '[A]s in civil government the constitution is broken in upon, and violated by power and strength prevailing over authority; so the constitution of man is broken in upon and violated by the lower faculties or principles within prevailing over that which is in its nature supreme over them all'. (*S.* 3. 2)[34] As Butler is thinking of it,

---

[34] See also SP 12, 14; *S.* 2. 10. And note the following passage from Sermon 5 of the *Six Sermons Preached upon Public Occasions*: 'Let us transfer, each of us, the equity of this our civil constitution to our whole personal character; and be sure to be as much afraid of

conscience is unique in that its constitutional role is part of its very concept. It alone, from its very nature, claims authority and superintendency.

At the same time, Butler has another model of human nature which, while he does not distinguish it, is actually quite different from that of a constitutional order, namely a *teleological/functional system*. So viewed, the principles that compose our practical nature can be ordered, but their ordering is not one of relative authority. Nor is the order established by their intrinsic natures. The idea is not that when, say, conscience and an appetite conflict, conscience properly overrides because of its title to govern based on their respective intrinsic natures. Rather it is that the design of the human system is adapted to certain purposes, and that these define an ideal of proper functioning in which conscience overrides appetite when they conflict. On this view of things, while our design and purpose is not in fact such that we would be functioning properly if appetite characteristically overrode conscience, there is nothing in the very nature of conscience and appetite to rule this out. There could be a well-designed system adapted to quite different purposes from those for which our design fits us, one whose make-up included conscience and appetites, but in which these played different functional roles—in which it was not part of the design that conscience, despite its (intrinsic) superintendent pretensions, actually superintend.[35]

'Every work both of nature and of art is a system,' Butler writes in the Preface to the *Fifteen Sermons*. 'And as every particular thing, both natural and artificial, is for some use or purpose out of and beyond itself, one may add, to what has been brought into the idea of a system, its conduciveness to this one or more ends' (SP 14). He then makes his famous analogy between the way a watch is adapted to time-telling and the way our system is adapted to what he here claims to be its distinctive end of virtue. Even if we grant Butler's teleological framework,

---

subjection to mere arbitrary will and pleasure in ourselves, as to the arbitrary will of others. For the tyranny of our own lawless passions is the nearest and most dangerous of all tyrannies' (*SS* 5. 1).

[35] Of course 'superintend' in its occurrence at the end of the sentence must be taken in a functional sense. For convenience I shall continue this use; context should make its meaning clear.

this analogy may seem problematic. We can easily form a notion of the end watches serve without already having some conception of how, internally, they properly function. But is it obvious that this is the case with virtue? Is virtue an independently specifiable 'use or purpose out of and beyond' the well-functioning person to which this functioning is adapted? Or is virtue dependent on what our proper functioning itself is? If there are problems in this direction, however, Butler is in a position to finesse them to some extent, since he also says that our system is adapted to the good or happiness of the agent and others. And these he understands in ways that are independent of any ideal of proper functioning.[36]

Butler calls principles *private* when their proper function in our overall design tends to the good of the agent, and *public* if an analogous relation holds to the good of others (*S.* 1. 4–7). A principle may have a primary function making it public, but with a secondary function to advance the agent's good, or, alternatively, its primary function may be private good and its secondary function public good. Thus, while benevolence is a public principle since its primary function is to promote the happiness of others, Butler argues that it is also part of our design that 'the greatest satisfactions to ourselves depend upon our having benevolence in a due degree'. And because this is so, 'self-love is one chief security of our right behaviour towards society' (*S.* 1. 6).[37] Self-love and benevolence have exactly opposite primary and secondary functions.

Butler first discusses conscience's functional role in Sermon 1. It is evident, he argues, that conscience restrains us from doing harm and leads us to do good to others. In this way its function is the same as any public principle. So why do we need conscience in particular? For one thing, it can second other public principles when appropriate, and take over when these are insufficient to achieve their purpose by themselves:

Thus a parent has the affection of love to his children: this leads him to take care of, to educate, to make due provision for them; the natural

---

[36] Thus, the object of self-love is said to be 'happiness, enjoyment, satisfaction' (*S.* 11. 5). And 'happiness or satisfaction consists only in the enjoyment of those objects, which are by nature suited to our several particular appetites, passions, and affections' (*S.* 11. 9).

[37] As Alan Millar points out, Sermon 11 is not simply rhetorical. Butler is required by his teleology to show the coincidence of virtue and interest. See 'Following Nature', 176.

affection leads to this: but the reflection that it is his proper business, what belongs to him, that it is right and commendable so to do; this added to the affection becomes a much more settled principle, and carries him on through more labour and difficulties for the sake of his children, than he would undergo from that affection alone, if he thought it, and the course of action it led to, either indifferent or criminal. (*S.* 1. 8)[38]

Since in Sermon 1 Butler is concerned to exhibit conscience 'merely as another part in the inward frame of man, pointing out to us in some degree what we are intended for', he takes his discussion of its functional role no further, reserving for Sermon 2 an account of 'the particular place assigned to it by nature' (*S.* 1. 8).

In Section I, I stressed passages from Sermon 2 in which Butler treats the authority of conscience as resting on our *constitutional* nature. This argument, however, is run alongside other arguments for conscience's authority that depend on treating human nature as a teleological/functional order. And, it must be said, these other arguments are, if anything, more prominent. Indeed, Butler begins Sermon 2 by establishing terms for his discussion drawn entirely from the latter framework. 'As speculative truth admits of different kinds of proof, so likewise moral obligations may be shewn by different methods. If the real nature of any creature leads him and is adapted to such and such purposes only, or more than to any other; this is a reason to believe the Author of that nature intended it for those purposes' (*S.* 2. 1). Here, and just after, Butler appears to suppose that it would be a sufficient proof of conscience's authority that it have a controlling function in our actual design. This would make conscience's power to obligate, to provide conclusive reasons for acting, depend entirely on its functional role. Of course, it may well be that the intrinsic nature of conscience fits it for a 'superintendent' role in our overall design. None the less, Butler seems here to be saying, its authority depends directly on the latter and only indirectly on the former.

From Sermon 1 we have that conscience is one of several public principles whose function is to motivate us to do good.

---

[38] Public principles are not of course restricted to forms of benevolence. Nor, Butler is anxious to point out, does conscience approve only of what aims at or produces benefit to others. See e.g. *S.* 12. 31n.; DII 8.

Sermon 2's distinctive dialectical task is to establish that it is not simply one such principle among others, designed to lead us to do good when it 'happen[s] to be stronger than other principles, passions, or appetites', but that we are designed so that 'the whole character be formed upon thought and reflection; that every action be directed by some determinate rule, some other rule than the strength and prevalency of any principle or passion' (*S.* 2. 3). So, Butler now asks, 'What sign is there in our nature (for the inquiry is only about what is to be collected from thence) that this was intended by its Author?' What evidence does our nature provide, that is, that it has a design in which conscience's function *is* to superintend?

Butler points to evidence of two main sorts. One is that conscience is the only faculty that represents itself as superintendent. The other consideration is one Butler mentions briefly in passing, but, brief though it may be, it has several profound implications for Butler's overall view. The passage occurs in *S.* 2. 8, in which Butler begins to explicate the sense of 'nature' in which he takes St Paul to be asserting (in the sermon's topic verse from Romans) that 'the Gentiles *do by* NATURE *the things contained in the law*'. He there quotes from the verse just following: 'which shew the work of the law written in their hearts, their conscience also bearing witness . . .' And then he remarks that 'if there be a distinction to be made between the *works written in their hearts*, and the *witness of conscience*; by the former must be meant the natural disposition to kindness and compassion'. This, Butler continues, is the part of our nature on which he has focused in Sermon 1, 'which with very little reflection and of course leads [a person] to society, and by means of which he naturally acts a just and good part in it, unless other passions or interest lead him astray'. But, he then notes, passions and self-love are 'themselves in a degree equally natural'. And so he concludes: 'since we have no method of seeing the particular degrees in which one or the other is placed in us by nature; it is plain the former, considered merely as natural, good and right as they are, can no more be a law to us than the latter.'

Notice first that Butler says here, perhaps more explicitly than he does at any other point, that neither benevolence nor self-love can be a law to human beings. Some commentators have been tempted by the view that Butler means to accord self-love co-ordinate, or perhaps even superior, authority in relation to conscience, but this passage plainly states that self-love cannot be a law to us.[39] Second, Butler says that we have no way of determining 'the particular degrees in which' various natural principles such as particular passions, self-love, and benevolence are 'placed in us by nature'. Although we can tell well enough that these all have functions in our design, we have no way of telling what their intended role is in any fine-grained way. In particular, he seems to be saying, knowledge of our design does not extend to which principles are to override when they conflict. But if this is so, it follows that when we judge, as Butler believes we rightly do, that an agent's putting himself in mortal danger for the sake of a pressing appetite is 'disproportionate to the nature of man' and, therefore, 'unnatural' we cannot be basing this judgement on any justified belief about the 'particular degrees in which' self-love and appetite 'are placed in us by nature'. This shows that judgements of the superiority of principles other than conscience cannot be based on knowledge of their intended hierarchy.[40]

[39] The usual bases for this claim are the famous 'cool hour' passage at S. 11. 20 and Butler's remark that 'reasonable self-love and conscience are the chief or superior principles in the nature of man: because an action may be suitable to this nature, though all other principles be violated; but becomes unsuitable, if either of those are' (S. 3. 9). Regarding the former, it is worth noting that not only is the passage 'when we sit down in a cool hour, we can neither justify to ourselves this or any other pursuit, till we are convinced that it will be for our happiness, or at least not contrary to it', within the scope of the suppositional 'Let it be allowed'; and not only is the whole discussion preceded by the remark that 'these inquiries, it is hoped, may be favourably attended to: for there shall be all possible concessions made to the favourite passion . . . it shall be treated with the utmost tenderness and concern for its interests' (S. 11. 3); in addition, the sentence just following the 'cool hour' passage shows that Butler rejects the idea that self-interest is ultimately justifying: '*Common reason* and humanity will have some influence upon mankind, whatever becomes of speculations; but, so far as the interests of virtue depend upon the theory of it being secured from open scorn, so far its very being in the world depends upon its appearing to have no contrariety to private interest and self-love' (S. 11. 21; emphasis added). 'Common reason' evidently refers to conscience or the principle of reflection. (This is also supported by other references to 'reason'; see e.g. (S. 5. 3; 12. 9.) Thus Butler is suggesting that while conscience is in fact ultimately justifying, because the 'favourite passion['s] . . . cause is so universally pleaded (S. 11. 3), people are only likely actually to be virtuous if they can be convinced that it does not conflict with self-interest.

[40] Butler gives this as an instance of one principle being superior to another, regardless of the latter's strength; i.e. that the former should govern. As I have remarked, his argument at that point trades on treating our nature as a constitutional system. What the present point would show is that our taking something to have a particular place in our constitutional system is not based on our taking it to have some functional role in our design.

Butler says that neither benevolence nor self-love can be a law to us, but he evidently also means that neither can any fact about their precise role in our design, or that of any other principle (except conscience, as we shall see). We lack access to such truths and cannot, therefore, determine on this basis which principle we should act on when they conflict. There is, then, a design problem for creatures who have the same principles we do (exclusive of conscience) but who are similarly ignorant of the details of their design. Such creatures are unable to follow the instruction: act in accordance with your design—make your design a law to yourself.

Butler immediately notes what he thinks solves this problem: 'But there is a superior principle of reflection or conscience in every man, which distinguishes between the internal principles of his heart, as well as his external actions; which passes judgment upon himself and them' (*S.* 2. 8). By giving us intuitive judgement of which principles we should follow, as well as of which actions we should perform, God has given us a way of regulating ourselves which does not require a knowledge of the precise place of other principles in our design. He gives us a faculty which represents itself as superintendent, so that it can actually function as superintendent. Or, disambiguating 'superintendency', conscience represents itself to us as controlling *de jure*, so that it can control *de facto*. Moreover, we can, he thinks, infer that this is conscience's function, and consequently that we function properly when we follow it rather than other principles when they conflict. Even if the relative functional priority of other principles is not evident to us, the functional priority of conscience is. Butler therefore concludes:

This gives us a further view of the nature of man; shews us what course of life we were made for: not only that our real nature leads us to be influenced in some degree by reflection and conscience; but likewise in what degree we are to be influenced by it, if we will fall in with, and act agreeably to the constitution of our nature: that this faculty was placed in us to be our proper governor: to direct and regulate all under principles, passions, and motives of action. (*S.* 2. 15)

'Proper governor' is neatly ambiguous for Butler's purposes. If it means 'what governs (controls) when we function properly, i.e. as designed' then it follows from the fact that God designed conscience to override that it is our proper governor. But it could also mean 'what has genuine authority', in the sense of title to rule. This is the meaning it must have if our nature is to form a constitutional order, and if disobeying conscience is to be unnatural in the 'strictest and most proper sense'. It is difficult to see, however, how any facts about functional design can establish that. It is precisely this ambiguity, I think, that leads Butler to run his two metaphors together. The more interesting possibility is not that Butler simply confuses the two metaphors, but that he holds that the particular kind of teleological/functional system we are designed to be is one that represents itself as a constitutional order. But in so far as we so represent ourselves, we can hardly take it as a satisfactory argument for conscience's authority that it was designed for this job; nothing follows from that about whether it has genuine title, that is, whether it is 'in nature and kind' superior to all other practical principles. A self-regulating constitutional order will give weight to intention and design only in so far as these are relevant within a constitutional framework. Moreover, if judgements of naturalness are judgements of conscience, then considerations of functional role can be relevant to these only if there is some background normative proposition that makes them so. The bare judgement that conscience is designed to superintend is a judgement, not of conscience, but of the understanding; it is a theoretical finding, and by itself determines no conclusion of the 'practical discerning power', as Butler calls conscience in the dissertation.

Before we return to considering how Butler might be conceiving of conscience as self-authorizing within an internal constitutional order, we should note one further argument he makes along teleological lines. Butler frequently compares the function and purpose of elements of our practical nature to bodily functions; specifically, to that of the eyes. Usually he is concerned just to say that the former are no less obvious than the latter, thereby supporting his conclusion that the purpose of conscience is to superintend (*S.* 2. 1). At one point, however, the terms of the analogy are put in an interestingly different way. 'Now obligations of virtue shewn, and motives to the practice of it enforced, from a review of the nature of man, are to be considered as an appeal to each particular person's heart and natural conscience: as the external senses are appealed to for the proof of things cognizable by them.'[41] By the latter proof, Butler evidently means an inference of the following sort. We have senses in order to sense things and would not need them unless there were things to be sensed. Since God has given us senses for a purpose, there must be 'things cognizable by them'. What would be analogous in the practical case? The most obvious analogy is not one that Butler actually here makes, namely, between the relation between things to be sensed and our senses, on the one hand, and that between the intrinsic rightness or wrongness, or fitness or unfitness of actions, and conscience, on the other. His analogy seems rather to be between the cognitive nature of experience—its presenting itself as something to be believed—and conscience's self-presentation as something to be obeyed. In the former case we can generally rely (in a fallible way) on the testimony of the senses, since God would not have given us these for any reason other than to provide us with reliable beliefs about the external world. Likewise, the argument might go, God would not have given us a faculty that presents itself as something to be obeyed unless it is actually true that it should be obeyed. On this reading, that conscience is designed to superintend is not what makes it authoritative; it is conclusive evidence that it has this authority.

This would leave it an open question how it is that conscience comes actually to have authority. Maybe intrinsic fitnesses or unfitnesses of actions just are, in their nature, conclusive reasons for acting, and conscience is the faculty through which we have access to these facts. God gives us conscience so we can receive these truths. On this view, the existence of reasons for an agent to act and, consequently, of facts about how she should act, will be independent of her conscience. Just as there would still be objects even if we lacked the means to sense them, so there would be facts about how we should act though we lacked any access to them through conscience. So pictured, the authority of conscience would derive from the independent existence of normative practical facts together with the contingent fact that, as God has designed us, conscience is our best access to these.

---

[41] Note that this suggests that the way in which concluding an obligation to virtue 'from a review of the nature of man' involves an 'appeal to conscience' may be no more than the way sense experience is appealed to in the analogous proof of an external world. See n. 27 above.

Butler cannot ultimately accept this picture, I think; at least, it is deeply at odds with other things he says. As we noted in Section I, he treats the existence of a distinction between justificatory weight and motivational strength as equivalent to the authority of conscience in the *reductio* argument at the end of Sermon 2 (*S.* 2. 16). This suggests that a being who lacked conscience could not have genuine reasons for acting—there could be no distinction between the motives she actually acts on and those on which she should act. If this is so, conscience cannot simply be a faculty of access to metaphysically independent normative facts. Moreover, Butler says repeatedly that it is only because we have conscience that we can be a 'law to ourselves', and, furthermore, that 'the faculty which surveys, approves or disapproves the several affections of our mind and actions of our lives, being that by which men *are a law to themselves*, their conformity or disobedience to which law of our nature renders their actions, in the highest and most proper sense, natural or unnatural' (*S.* 2. 9). But to be unnatural 'in the strictest and most proper sense' just *is* to be contrary to weightier reasons—to be contrary to motives on which the agent should act. If what makes an action unnatural in this sense, then, is that it is contrary to conscience, this confirms that Butler thinks that a distinction between 'mere power and authority' cannot be drawn with respect to an agent's motives if she lacks conscience (*S.* 2. 8).

III

These points return us to the line of thought we put aside to explore Butler's natural teleology, namely the idea that conscience is somehow self-authorizing. We must now consider what this might involve. Partly, the thought is that since the question whether conscience should be obeyed is irreducibly normative, it can only be answered by a judgement of conscience of some form. It is crucial to this picture that there be a distinction between the judgement that conscience makes of actions and principles, considered intrinsically, and conscience's judgement of naturalness, that is, of what there is reason for an agent to do. Without this distinction, the Full Naturalistic Thesis looms, and, along with it, the superfluousness of conscience: an action will never be made unnatural, and therefore contrary to a motive that should have governed, by virtue of being contrary to conscience.[42] Suppose, however, that through conscience we do endorse certain actions and principles, considered intrinsically, and oppose others. We can then ask: what should a person do, given the endorsements of her conscience and her nature otherwise considered? As I read him, this is the same as Butler's question: what would it be natural for her to do 'in the strictest and most proper sense'? Now if any question concerning what a person should do is a question of conscience, then this must be one too. But it will be a second-order rather than a first-order question. It will be the question, given an agent's first-order conscientious judgements, how should she act? Suppose that, at this second level, an agent approves her performing acts and acting on principles, which, at the first level, she conscientiously endorses, including when so acting is opposed by other principles, and that she analogously disapproves at this second level of performing acts and acting on principles which she conscientiously opposes at the first level, despite their being favoured by other principles. If this is so, she will be taking her conscience to be authoritative; she will take it that her conscience should govern when it conflicts with other principles.

In arguing that conscience represents itself as superintendent Butler is maintaining, in effect, that an agent with conscience will necessarily judge that he should follow it, at least in so far as he is not self-deceived or his judgement is not corrupted in some other way. To have conscience is to be disposed to acknowledge its authority. But again, we may still wonder what gives conscience this authority. Perhaps we cannot have conscience without some tendency to believe it has authority, but we may still query this very belief; we may ask whether it has the authority it claims and, if so, what it derives from.[43] Even if authoritative

---

[42] On this see Penelhum, *Butler*, 68–9.

[43] Penelhum's reconstruction of Butler's defence of the authority of conscience is puzzling at just this point. He correctly diagnoses the question of conscience's authority as concerning the justification of reasonableness of following conscience. People who raise it 'wonder whether what [conscience] tells them is what they should do' (*Butler*, 58). Ultimately, however, Penelhum thinks Butler is committed to regarding this question as confused, and that the argument 'from nature' reinforces this: 'It amounts, instead, to the claim that every agent is so constituted by providence that, barring special circumstances, he or she will make the judgments that the principle prompts, and *will recognize them to be better reasons for action* than the presence of lower principles or

purport is intrinsic to conscience, without some showing that conscience is itself rationally inescapable, we will lack any convincing argument that conscience's pretensions are realized. Now it seems clear that Butler believes that conscience is rationally inescapable, and not just because being governed by it is our intended function. He apparently believes, as well, that the very having of reasons to act itself requires conscience. But why?

Before we can answer this question we must consider an obstacle to interpreting Butler in this way. Recall that Butler's initial example of the superiority of one principle to another—namely of self-love in comparison with passions and appetites—seems to be independent of the relation of either to conscience. He compares a 'brute creature [who] by any bait [is] allured into a snare, by which he is destroyed' with 'a man [who], foreseeing the same danger of certain ruin, [rushes] into it for the sake of a present gratification'. After remarking that, while both act on their strongest desire, the man, but not the brute, acts unnaturally, he then concludes:

[I]t is manifest that self-love is in human nature a superior principle to passion. This may be contradicted without violating that nature; but the former cannot. So that, if we will act conformably to the economy of man's nature, reasonable self-love must govern. Thus, without particular consideration of conscience, we may have a clear conception of the superior nature of one inward principle to another. (*S.* 2. 11)

This can reasonably be taken, of course, as some evidence against the present interpretation. I doubt, however, that it is strong evidence. And it certainly is not decisive. For one thing, Butler says that self-love is 'in *human* nature a superior principle to passion', and that the action of a 'man' who pursues present passion against self-love is unnatural. One difference between

inclinations with which they conflict. ... It tells someone who questions whether the dictate of a higher principle really is a better reason for acting than the urgings of a lower one, that he is so made by providence that he knows quite well that it *is* a better reason' (p. 59). This does not address the question of what *makes* considerations of conscience conclusive reasons. And to say, as Penelhum does, that 'virtuous action is action done from motives which are implanted in us by providence, and which have a hierarchical relationship' (p. 59), does not help. Whether conscience is superior is precisely what is at issue, and since the relevant hierarchy must be constitutional and not simply functional, it is unclear how any fact about Providence can give conscience supremacy of the right kind.

human beings and 'brute creature[s]' is that we have calm self-love. But that is not the only difference; we also have conscience. And it may be that Butler is thinking that self-love is superior to passion in us because, through conscience, we can favour the former over the latter, but that it would not be in a creature who, lacking conscience, could not. Butler does say that we can appreciate the superiority of self-love in human beings 'without particular consideration of conscience'. But note that he says: 'without *particular* consideration of conscience.' There is, I think, a perfectly good explanation of why he would have said just this if he believed, as I am suggesting he may have, that the natural superiority of any principles at all is equivalent to the authority of conscience.

First-order conscience approves or disapproves not only acts, but also principles (or principled conduct). (see e.g. *S.* 1. 8, 2. 8) And Butler holds that self-love is one of the principles we reflectively approve, at least, when it is properly tempered:

> It should seem, that a due concern about our own interest or happiness, and a reasonable endeavour to secure and promote it, which is, I think, very much the meaning of the word *prudence*, in our language; it should seem, that this is virtue, and the contrary behaviour faulty and blamable; since, in the calmest way of reflection, we approve of the first, and condemn the other conduct, both in ourselves and others. (DII 6)

Butler does say that what we are approving of here is 'conduct', but he appears to mean conduct motivated by a certain principle, namely by 'a due concern for our own interest'. A second example of a principle approved by conscience is, of course, benevolence.[44]

Now in the case where conscience disapproves of an act, and not on the grounds that it manifests a disapprovable principle, but just in itself, there will be no other prominent approved motive not to perform the act other than that it violates conscience. However, in the case where conscience approves of acting on one motive (other than conscience) in preference to another (e.g. self-love in preference to passion) there will be another approved motive for doing so in addition to conscience. In such a case, therefore, there will be some reason to say that

[44] See Sermon 12.

we judge that a human being should defer gratification 'without any particular consideration of conscience', even if we would not, on reflection, disapprove of a being's failure to defer gratification if, lacking conscience, she lacked any way to judge that self-love should override the desire for present pleasure. In the case Butler is discussing, therefore, it may be a background assumption that conscientious judgement provides a (regulating) motive to give preference to self-love over passion, one which, were the agent to lack it, we could not disapprove her action. But while the agent's conscientious motive can be placed in the background of this case, because she has another relevant motive which conscience approves, this would not be true in the case of an act which conscience opposes intrinsically. The only motive for forbearing might be conscience itself. Thus, while the agent's conscience is always relevant, in the latter sort of case it must be given a 'particular consideration' it need not in the former.[45]

What Butler says about his example, therefore, need not be inconsistent with interpreting him as holding that an agent's having conscience is necessary for her to be capable of acting naturally or unnaturally in the 'strictest and most proper sense', or for her principles to manifest relations of superiority or inferiority. Since he explicitly says that conscience is the faculty 'by which men *are a law to themselves*' and that 'their conformity or disobedience to [this] law of our nature renders their actions, in the highest and most proper sense, natural or unnatural', and since his *reductio* argument for the authority of conscience assumes the latter's equivalence with the very existence of a 'distinction ... between one inward principle and another' of relative authority rather than strength, it is not unreasonable to

[45] Another passage that presents a similar problem occurs in the Preface to the *Fifteen Sermons* where Butler criticizes Shaftesbury for holding that the obligation to virtue depends entirely on the virtuous life's being most in our interest, thereby neglecting the obligation provided by conscience. He there concedes to Shaftesbury that '[supposing] a sceptic not convinced of this happy tendency of virtue, or being of a contrary opinion ... leaving out the authority of reflex approbation or disapprobation, such an one would be under an obligation to act viciously; since interest, one's own happiness, is a manifest obligation' (SP 26). Still, the person in question is someone who has conscience. And Butler holds that conscience approves of prudence. Moreover, when he writes 'leaving out the authority of reflex approbation', what he is explicitly excluding is a direct obligation to virtue, when it conflicts with interest. Of course, this requires shoehorning, but any interpretation of Butler does. I claim only to be describing one strand of his thought.

interpret him as holding that the authority of conscience is equivalent to the existence of reasons for acting, and that, were a being to lack conscience, there could be no facts regarding what he should do—no reasons for him to act.

This may still seem a puzzling idea. Even if Butler is bound to think that conscience is the faculty through which we make judgements about what we have reason to do, why should he think that the truth of what conscience judges depends on it in any way? Why does the existence of reasons for an agent to act entail even that an agent *have* conscience, much less that it be authoritative? A key to answering this question, I suggest, is to appreciate the central role that the idea of *autonomy* or *self-regulated constitutional order* has in Butler's thought. What conscience gives an agent is the capacity to guide her life by practical judgement, and this capacity, Butler seems to be saying, is a condition of the very possibility of rational (and moral) agency, and thus, of an agent's having reasons to act.

Butler's preoccupation with autonomy is apparent at the beginning of the Preface of the *Fifteen Sermons*, indeed, in the very first sentence. 'Though it is scarce possible to avoid judging, in some way or other, of almost everything which offers itself to one's thoughts; yet it is certain, that many persons, from different causes, never exercise their judgment, upon what comes before them, in the way of determining whether it be conclusive' (SP 1). By 'judgment', Butler evidently means, not simply judging that something or other is the case, but judging the weight of reasons or justification for some conclusion. Here, of course, he is discussing the exercise of judgement in guiding belief rather than action. But he is also sounding a general theme he will later repeat for the practical case. While we can hardly think at all without judging, judgement is something we can *exercise* more or less, and hence, our beliefs and actions can be guided more or less by its exercise. Many persons, he continues, frequently desire arguments 'for some accidental purpose: but proof as such is what they never want for themselves; for their own satisfaction of mind or conduct in life' (SP 1). What they seek is rationalization, not genuine reasons on which to make their beliefs or conduct conditional.

Butler's rhetorical purpose at this point in the Preface is to work his readers up to the effort he rightly thinks it will take for them to digest the *Fifteen Sermons*. So he tries to convince them that this is nothing they are unable to do, but only, perhaps, something they are not in the habit of doing.

> The great number of books and papers of amusement, which, of one kind or another, daily come into one's way, have in part occasioned, and most perfectly fall in with and humour, this idle way of reading and considering things. By this means, time even in solitude is happily got rid of, without the pain of attention. (SP 3)

> Thus people habituate themselves to let things pass through their minds, as one may speak, rather than to think of them ... Review and attention, and even forming a judgment, becomes fatigue; and to lay anything before them that requires it, is putting them quite out of their way. (SP 4)

He concedes he has no right to demand the attention of his readers, but insists that 'it is also true ... that nothing can be understood without that degree of it, which the very nature of the thing requires'. And, he concludes, 'morals, considered as a science ... plainly require a very peculiar attention. For here ideas never are in themselves determinate, but become so by the train of reasoning and the place they stand in' (SP 6). The general message is unmistakable. Human thought and action can be shaped more or less by the self's own theoretical and practical judgement. At their most heteronomous, people may be habituated simply 'to let things pass through their minds ... rather than to think of them'. However, we can, by 'review and attention', make judgements about what to believe, about which beliefs are best supported by reasons, and thereby make our beliefs subject to reasons we have.

The contrast that concerns Butler in the body of the *Fifteen Sermons* is that between practical heteronomy and autonomy. Here self-governance requires a faculty of *practical judgement*, one by which a person can make a judgement of reasons to act and, through so judging, direct her own actions. And Butler apparently conceives of conscience in just these terms. He refers to it as the 'practical discerning power' (DII 1), and says of it, uniquely, that 'judgment, direction, superintendency' are 'a constituent part of the idea ... of the faculty itself' (*S.* 2. 14). To this principle, he says, 'belongs the adjustment and correction of all other inward movements and affections' (*S.* 2. 1). Conscience is the faculty that makes autonomy possible for us, it is 'that by which men are a law to themselves' (*S.* 2. 4).

Of course, Butler has nothing like Kant's theory of the will as practical reason; he does not think that an agent can on any occasion bring herself to do what she judges she should. Conscientious approval gives the agent some practical leverage on her actions, but only some. On any given occasion, her present habits may overpower the motivational force of her conscientious judgement. But if habit can overpower conscience, it is also something an agent can make use of to realize self-determination. In the *Analogy*, Butler lists 'attention, industry, self-government' as among the traits a person can acquire through practice (*A.* 1. 5. 4).

Why does the capacity for autonomy matter? Recall that Butler concludes the *reductio* of Sermon 2 with the observation that if we cannot judge that the agent has a conclusive reason for forbearing an act of which we disapprove, we cannot disapprove of him for failing to do so. What he is thinking, I believe, is that unless we can suppose that an agent has a way of determining himself by reasons he can have to do what we think he should do—that is, unless he has a way of directing himself by his own judgement that he should so act—we cannot disapprove his failing to do so.[46]

Butler understands the issue of conscience's authority as the question whether violating conscience is unnatural 'in the strictest and most proper sense'. At this point, we do well to recall that if a being's actions cannot accord with or violate its nature *in this sense*, then it acts naturally when it acts on whatever principle happens to be strongest.[47] Conduct which can be natural or unnatural in the 'strictest' sense, therefore, contrasts with conduct which can only be heteronomous, which lacks even the capacity for self-determination. In order for a being's conduct to accord with or violate its constitution, and be natural or unnatural in the strictest sense, the being must be capable of

---

[46] Or unless he could have by a process of self-determining habituation.
[47] Thus Butler remarks of Wollaston that 'a late author of great and deserved reputation says, that to place virtue in following nature, is at best a loose way of talk. And he has reason to say this, if what I think he intends to express, though with great decency, be true, that scarce any other sense can be put upon those words, but acting as any of the several parts, without distinction, of a man's nature happened most to incline him' (SP 13).

autonomy, of being 'a law to itself'. But for this, Butler apparently believes, an agent requires conscience. He must be able to make for himself the distinction between a motive's being strongest and its being one on which an agent like him should act, and be able to determine himself by the latter judgements. In Butler's moral psychology, this is conscience's role. It gives the agent a critical perspective on his own motives through which he can make self-motivating practical judgements.

Thus Butler puts the issue of conscience's authority as whether it is natural 'to let it govern and guide only occasionally in common with [other principles], *as its turn happens to come, from the temper and circumstances one happens to be in*' or whether 'the very constitution of our nature requires, that *we bring* our whole conduct before this superior faculty; wait its determination; [and] enforce upon ourselves its authority' (SP 24, 26; emphasis added). The former alternative would hold true if, as creatures incapable of being a law to ourselves, our conduct could only be heteronomous. If, on the other hand, we can act naturally or unnaturally in the strictest sense, that will be because we can be autonomous, a law to ourselves. And, Butler repeatedly says, it is conscience, and the practical recognition of its authority, that makes autonomy possible for an agent. As he is thinking of it, conscience is not simply a part of our constitution; it is the very root of self-regulated constitutional order. Without it, the agent can draw no contrast between acting on the strongest motives, and acting on the weightiest reasons. Butler thus concludes that 'the whole business of a moral agent' is to 'conform [himself] to it'.

As I have been interpreting him, Butler believes that the authority of conscience is equivalent to the existence of reasons for acting because he believes that a being can have reasons to act (and hence act naturally or unnaturally in the strictest sense) only if he has the capacity for autonomy; and he believes that having conscience and crediting its authority is necessary for that. Only if a being can be a 'law to himself' can he conform to or violate his nature in the 'strictest' sense. Since conscience is 'that by which men are a law to themselves', 'their conformity to or disobedience' to it 'renders their actions, in the highest and most proper sense, natural or unnatural' (*S.* 2. 9).

This is, of course, only the beginning of a line of thought, and it raises as many questions as it answers. Why, for example, is conscience the faculty of practical judgement? And how can conscience be that by which we are a law to ourselves if it consists of responses, 'sentiment[s] of the understanding' or 'perceptions of the understanding', which are simply a given of practical experience, passively received because of the way God has fashioned our psyche? Not only does Butler have no well-worked-out answers to questions such as these, it is unlikely he ever faced them squarely. Since the 'autonomist' line of thought is only one strand in a complex and somewhat tangled skein of thought, this is not entirely surprising. None the less, it is an extremely important strand, one which we cannot well understand much of Butler's moral philosophy without.

12

Butler on Self-Love and Benevolence

R. G. FREY

I do not accept what I shall below refer to as the usual interpretation of Butler on human nature. The moral psychology that I find in *Fifteen Sermons Preached at the Rolls Chapel* (1726) and the later Preface (1729) to that work leans more in the direction of Hobbes than previous commentators on the whole have allowed, a matter I have discussed in my Past Master *Joseph Butler*,[1] but which I hope to deal with at length in *Virtue and Interest*, a work on the moral psychology/philosophy of Shaftesbury, Butler, and Hume that I have under way.

There are (at least) three central difficulties in reaching any settled view of Butler on human nature. These concern the status of benevolence, the relationship between benevolence and self-love, and the relationship between self-love and conscience. In the light of and around these difficulties, three interpretations of Butler on human nature have arisen. The first, and usual, interpretation is also probably the oldest. Virtue consists in acting in accordance with the nature of man, when the parts of that nature and system are in right proportion; these parts are in right proportion when our inward principles exhibit their ordered authority; and these principles exhibit their ordered authority when the particular passions are controlled and regulated by self-love and benevolence and when conscience or the principle of reflection (*S.* 1. 8) controls and regulates self-love and benevolence, as well as the particular passions, and so reigns supreme over the system. Human nature thus appears to have, as it were, three levels: the particular passions; the principles of self-love and benevolence; and conscience. The second interpretation is

---

[1] Oxford, forthcoming.

also a three-level affair, only benevolence is now consigned to the level of the particular passions. The only substantial difference between these first two interpretations concerns the status of benevolence, to which, of course, any claim about its relative authority *vis-à-vis* self-love is tied.

A third, more radical interpretation of the *Fifteen Sermons* is possible. It incorporates a change from the first view with respect to, not merely the status and relative authority of benevolence, but also the relationship between self-love and conscience. On this interpretation, human nature has effectively two levels, with the particular passions and benevolence on one level and self-love and conscience, now reigning jointly over the system, on another. So far as the joint reign of self-love and conscience is concerned, commentators have typically held that there is only a single passage, the 'cool hour' passage (*S.* 11. 20), which supports this more radical interpretation. Certainly, it has had few defenders. Yet, I believe something like this third view is forced upon Butler (as well as Shaftesbury), as he seeks to come to terms with the strength of self-love within us. Given the way I construe Butler's desire to provide actual men, men as they are in this world and not idealized versions of them, with a motive to virtue, it is a mistake to suggest that the 'cool hour' passage is the only textual support there is for this third view of the *Fifteen Sermons*.

Here, I am concerned only with the status (and so relative authority) of benevolence, with the question of whether benevolence is best thought of as a general principle of action or general motive or as a particular passion. I want to suggest that it is best thought of as a particular passion.

For Butler, we have all manner of appetites, affections, and passions. These include hunger, thirst, bodily needs generally, compassion, love, hate, and so on. He normally lumps all these particular passions together because he is anxious to compare and contrast them with self-love (*S.* 1. 7 n. 9; *S.* 11. 5-8) and conscience (SP 14-24; *S.* 2. 12-15). Occasionally, however, there is a remark in passing, as when he suggests that a man can remain good 'though the appetites and passions have not their exact due proportion to each other' (*S.* 3. 2 n. 3), that perhaps indicates that the particular passions are not all on the same level. Again, because he is anxious about the relations of the passions to self-love and conscience, Butler often speaks as if the passions formed a single principle of action. Yet, sometimes, he suggests that several different passions form 'several particular principles' (*S.* 11. 8) in our nature. When passion overwhelms self-love, the principle of our action is said to be passion, whatever the identity of the passion in question; when particular passions are individuated, then it seems that actions which proceed from them have different principles of action or motives.

With regard to the particular passions, Butler makes three important points. First, we have all kinds of such passions or desires, and every one of them, every 'bias, instinct, propension within', is a 'real part of our nature' (*S.* 3. 2). Second, though our passions 'have a tendency to promote both public and private good', as when a desire for esteem leads us to behave in ways that benefit others and is thus satisfied, some passions 'seem most immediately to respect others, or tend to public good' and others seem 'most immediately to respect self, or tend to private good' (*S.* 1. 7). That we have other-regarding passions, such as love, compassion, and desire for friendship, Butler accepts as a matter of course (*S.* 1. 6), and he castigates Hobbes for holding otherwise (e.g. *S.* 1. 6 n. 7). Other-regarding passions are as much a part of our nature as self-regarding ones; we are, in the jargon of Butler's day, as much made for society and to tend the public good as we are for promoting and tending our own good (*S.* 1. 4). Third, our self-regarding and other-regarding passions are not to be identified with self-love and benevolence, respectively. Though Butler maintains this in Sermon 1 (*S.* 1. 7), it is really only in Sermon 11 (though see *S.* 1. 7 n. 9), in his discussion of self-love, that he becomes specific about the difference (*S.* 11. 5-9). Because this difference is important to his refutation of psychological egoism, the claim of difference in Sermon 1 is sometimes confused with that refutation. In fact, the refutation of egoism turns upon the distinction between the object and the possession of a desire, whereas the claim of Sermon 1, in terms of self-love, turns upon the distinction between satisfied desire and self-love.

In Sermon 1, Butler gives this example: 'One man rushes upon certain ruin for the gratification of a present desire: nobody will call the principle of this action self-love' (*S.* 1. 7 n. 9). One cannot equate satisfied desire with self-love; for the (immediate) gratification of a desire is frequently at the expense of self-interest, and we often query whether giving a person what they want is in their interest. We might concede that a desire for heroin was presently a man's strongest desire, concede as well that its satisfaction would bring considerable relief or even pleasure, yet doubt that its satisfaction was in the man's interest. Even if in time we were to conclude that it was, we would not do so by equating satisfaction of desire, or the pleasure satisfied desire may bring, with self-interest. Rather, we would find out more, for example, about the man's goals, plans, hopes, and purposes and how health was related to the fulfilment of some broad array of these.

Self-love is a general desire for one's happiness, and it is 'inseparable from all sensible creatures, who can reflect upon themselves and their own interest or happiness, so as to have that interest an object to their minds' (*S.* 11. 5). Unlike passion, it is a reflective or rational principle (*S.* 11. 5); animals lack it (SP 17–23; *S.* 2. 10). With our interest or happiness before our minds, we can exercise a measure of control over our passions and so try both to avoid being constantly impelled to gratify them at once and to school them in the direction of serving our interest. For passion 'has absolutely no bound nor measure' except what is imposed on it by self-love and conscience (SP 41), and it perpetually runs up against both. As a result, we 'daily, hourly sacrifice the greatest known interest, to fancy, inquisitiveness, love, or hatred, any vacant inclination' (SP 40). Of course, an excess of self-love can lead to vice; in fact, however, men regularly neglect their 'real happiness or interest', when it is 'inconsistent with a present gratification', and thus become 'the authors and instruments of their own misery and ruin' (*S.* 1. 15).

As a reflective principle, self-love restrains and regulates the passions. In this task, it is assisted by conscience. As the *Six Sermons* (1749)[2] at one point makes clear, we cannot 'attain our own personal good, by a *thoughtless* pursuit of every thing which pleases'; rather, the passions 'from their very nature, require to be under the direction of our own judgment [i.e. conscience]' (*SS* 6. 3; italics in original). Butler's emphasis is always upon holding the passions in check, else they usurp the authority of

---

[2] On the whole, these sermons contain comparatively little philosophy and a good deal of moral earnestness of a conservative character.

self-love and conscience and motivate us at the expense of our interest or happiness and judgement.

Self-love aims at 'our happiness, enjoyment, satisfaction' (*S.* 11. 5), and it remains a part of our nature, apparently, throughout life. Certainly, Butler always contrasts it with the particular passions, which come and go (e.g. *S.* 1. 7 n. 9; *S.* 2. 10–11). In the main, the distinction here is between a persistent, general desire for happiness and occurrent, particular desires for this or that particular thing.

(Importantly, Butler never questions the strength of this desire for happiness within us; indeed, he is at pains in Sermons 1–3 and 11 to warn us that the pursuit of our happiness can threaten to leave no room for benevolence and conscience to assert themselves within us. It is no accident, therefore, that Butler repeatedly tries to make his readers believe that there is 'no peculiar contrariety between self-love and benevolence' (*S.* 11. 12) and no 'inconsistency between duty and what is really our present interest, meaning by interest, happiness and satisfaction' (*S.* 3. 8).)

Butler is very clear about the fact that, though self-love aims at happiness, it is not the same thing as happiness. Happiness consists 'in the enjoyment of those objects, which are by nature suited' to our passions; self-love helps us 'to gain or make use of' those objects (*S.* 11. 9). We do not make things suitable to our passions or so as to afford us satisfaction; nature does this. We simply find that we take delight in certain things as a result of their engaging our passions (SP 37), which things self-love then puts us in the way of securing. Without passions, therefore, happiness could not exist:

if self-love wholly engrosses us, and leaves us no room for any other principle, there can be absolutely no such thing at all as happiness, or enjoyment of any kind whatever; since happiness consists in the gratification of particular passions, which supposes the having of them. (*S.* 11. 9)

In other words, the particular passions 'constitute that interest or happiness' (SP 37) at which self-love aims.

Unlike self-love, whose object is 'somewhat internal' (*S.* 11. 5), namely our interest or happiness, the passions have as their objects external things:

particular affections tend towards particular external things: these are their objects; having these is their end: in this consists their gratification: no matter whether it be, or be not, upon the whole, our interest or happiness. (*S.* 11. 8)

There are two points to notice here. First, the particular passions are particular desires for particular objects. One is a desire for food, another for a person's friendship, still another for revenge on one's transgressor; what satisfies these desires is attaining their objects. A desire for a boat is not satisfied through giving the person ice cream; if it were so satisfied, we should in retrospect wonder in what sense it was a desire for a boat. A particular desire is aimed at a particular object, the obtaining of which satisfies the desire. Second, and quite importantly, Butler notices that these features of desires are quite independent of whether the desire, or its satisfaction, is to our interest or happiness. A desire for heroin is aimed at having the drug, and an injection of it satisfies the desire, even if such a desire, or its satisfaction, is not to our interest.

A doctor's desire to cure his patient has as its object the improved well-being of his patient; but, of course, the desire belongs to the doctor. Desires have possessors, those whose desires they are, and if satisfied desires produce happiness or satisfaction, their possessors experience it. Thus, if the patient responds to treatment, the doctor's desire is satisfied, and he may be made happy as a result; but his desire is not aimed at this or any other state of himself, but at his patient's well-being. As Butler remarks, our passions are directed '*towards external things* themselves, distinct from the *pleasure arising from them*' (*S.* 11. 6; italics in original).

Psychological egoism, which involves the claim that our passions are wholly self-regarding, is thus to Butler's mind exposed. Were this view correct, all of our particular passions would have as their object some facet of ourselves. The doctor's desire, however, does not aim at alteration in himself but in another; his desire is *other*-regarding. Sermons 5 and 6 ('Upon Compassion') give numerous instances of such desires, and both there and in Sermon 12 ('Upon Love of Our Neighbour') Butler insists that 'there is nothing strange or unaccountable in our being thus carried out, and affected towards the interests of others' (*S.* 5. 1).

Finally, Butler urges a note of caution over labelling desires 'interested' (*S.* 11. 5). Just as the egoist calls actions done from self-love interested, so he calls actions that flow from the particular passions interested. In so doing, the egoist draws attention to the fact that, if one of our desires is satisfied, the desire-satisfaction is in us; and this risks confusing us. For in so speaking the egoist may lead us to think that, because self-love aims at interest or happiness and is interested because it so aims, the particular passions also aim at interest or happiness and are interested for the same reason. This, as we have seen, Butler denies: self-love is interested because it aims at self; the particular passions, however, aim at 'external objects'. A certain initial plausibility to egoism disappears, once we realize that the desire for orange juice does not aim at self but at orange juice, a fact that is all too easily obscured by the egoist in calling the desire interested.

And so we come to benevolence, about whose status, whether as general principle or particular passion, Butler appears very unclear. At least, there appear to be passages supporting both views. I think, however, that there is a discernible thread to Butler's remarks on benevolence that points to its being a particular passion. (For reasons of convenience only, I group my comments under five headings.)

Limits. Is benevolence the analogue of self-love, an independent and reflective principle that aims at the interest or happiness of others, restrains, and regulates the passions, and enjoys the same natural authority as self-love? Its introduction (*S.* 1. 6) and the claim that the particular passions 'are distinct both from benevolence and self-love' (*S.* 1. 7) seem to start us off on this view. Yet, even there, Butler's examples of benevolence, namely friendship and paternal and filial affections, are of particular passions. And this is a recurring phenomenon: if benevolence really were the analogue of self-love, we should expect it to be a general desire aimed at the interest of happiness of others indiscriminately, of the world at large, of humanity in general; yet, Butler's examples are more limited, typically, confined to family and friends. It can be agreed on all sides that I desire these persons' happiness, but that is not enough to make benevolence other than a particular passion.

Interestingly, too, when Butler comes to discuss benevolence in Sermons 11 and 12, he entitles them 'Upon the Love of Our Neighbour' and not 'Upon the Love of Mankind', and his examples in Sermons 11 and 12 are of the friendship, filial affection variety. What befalls those close to us affects us; we have particular passions devoted to their happiness. Our concern for what befalls others is like the gradually diminishing ripples in a pond, as the extent of our particular passions directed towards others' well-being runs its course.

Moreover, and this is a point noticed earlier by Reginald Jackson,[3] after Sermon 1, benevolence is repeatedly said to be a particular passion, as when Butler speaks of 'ambition, revenge, benevolence, all particular passions whatever' (*S.* 11. 11) or of 'all particular affections whatever, resentment, benevolence, love of arts' (*S.* 11. 13). Indeed, after Sermon 1, benevolence is at times explicitly stated to be subordinate to self-love, as when Butler remarks that 'every particular affection, benevolence among the rest, is subservient to self-love by being the instrument of private enjoyment' (*S.* 11. 19). To be sure, there is a passage in Sermon 11 where benevolence can appear as both general principle and particular passion (*S.* 11. 16). Butler at once, however, goes on to link his discussion there to the pursuit of self-interest, in order to be able to maintain that '*benevolence and the pursuit of public good hath at least as good respect to self-love and the pursuit of private good, as any other particular passions, and their respective pursuits*' (*S.* 11. 16; italics in original).

Now it is widely unnoticed, though not by Jackson, that even the introduction of benevolence in Sermon 1 is qualified in an important respect. There, Butler claims that 'there is a natural principle of *benevolence* in man; which is in some degree to *society*, what *self-love* is to the individual' (*S.* 1. 6; italics in original). I think the phrase 'in some degree' represents an important qualification here: unlike self-love, which is a general desire in all of us for our own happiness, benevolence is not a general desire for the happiness of mankind generally, but particular desires for the interest or happiness of certain other individuals. It is, therefore, 'in some degree' to society what self-love is to the individual.

---

[3] See Reginald Jackson, 'Bishop Butler's Refutation of Psychological Hedonism', *Philosophy*, 18 (1943), 114–39.

Butler often uses these qualifying expressions with regard to benevolence, yet, so far as I am aware, their importance has been overlooked. Not even Jackson tracks them down on an individual basis and divines their import. Let me give another instance, therefore, where I think they play an important role in the discussion of benevolence.

When benevolence is introduced (*S.* 1. 6), Butler gives not only friendship and paternal and filial affection but also compassion as an example. Now we might take compassion to be something felt towards people indiscriminately, but Butler immediately gives as his meaning of compassion 'momentary love', and this seems best understood to be the momentary love of some individual. I show 'momentary love' for the individual in the tragic case before me or in the one that I have read or heard about; I do not show 'momentary love' for all individuals in all tragic cases here and now. Nevertheless, if one follows Butler's discussion of compassion on through Sermon 5, one eventually comes across the claim that men 'naturally compassionate all, in some degree, whom they see in distress: so far as they have any real perception or sense of that distress' (*S.* 5. 2). It is here, in this kind of remark, that I think Butler comes closest to affirming a benevolence towards mankind generally; yet, here, too, the qualifying expression 'in some degree' makes me think that he draws back. Here, I think this phrase draws attention to the fact that I may pity any man of whose plight I am made aware, be he friend or not; but what happens when I am made aware of a particular person's plight is that I pity *him*, that I make the improvement of *his* well-being an object of a particular desire. In other words, what my 'real perception or sense' of a person's distress does is to pick out that individual from others and so place me in something of a relationship to him, wherein his well-being can become the object of a particular desire of mine. Since more or less any individual can be so picked out and in this sense come into something of a relationship to me, I 'in some degree' can 'naturally compassionate' all whose distress impresses itself upon me.

Finally, I think Butler introduces benevolence at the very outset of the *Fifteen Sermons* and in the way he does mainly as a result of the historical context in which he figured. Writing in the aftermath of Hobbes and Mandeville and in the light of

Shaftesbury, it is only natural that Butler should want to nail his colours to Shaftesbury's mast and announce that benevolence is very much a part, and an important part, of our nature. Hobbes is wrong to think that all our passions have facets of self as their object; Mandeville is wrong to think that benevolence is the unintended consequence of the operation of self-love in us; and Shaftesbury is right to think that other-regarding or (what he calls) natural affections are very much a part of our nature (though wrong to think that the parts of our nature are related by strength or force rather than authority). With the importance of benevolence having been stressed, Butler can then probe the status of benevolence *vis-à-vis* self-love. This, in any event, he would certainly have to do, given that all the examples he gives of benevolence upon its introduction involve particular passions.

Significantly, before even this enquiry into the *status* of benevolence gets under way, Butler loses no time in assuring us of the *fact* that benevolence is not incompatible with self-love. In this regard, it must surely be true that the more surprising feature of *Fifteen Sermons* is not the claims made on behalf of benevolence but the prominence given self-love, in making us the sorts of creatures Butler takes us to be. I turn now to one feature of that prominence.

Suitability to nature. At the end of Sermon 3, Butler summarizes his view of human nature in a particularly important regard (*S.* 3. 9), and, if benevolence really were on a par with self-love, we might expect it to figure there. Yet it does not.

When the inward principles of man exhibit their ordered authority, the system of human nature is in harmony and balance. Acts may be suitable or unsuitable, proportionate or disproportionate, to man's nature; when they are proportionate 'to the nature of the agent' they are 'natural', whereas when they are disproportionate they are 'unnatural' (*S.* 3. 9). An act is unnatural or disproportionate, not because it fails to be in accordance with the strongest principle in one at the time (in fact, it may be), but because it involves the usurpation of authority by strength (*S.* 3. 9).

Now this is a very significant passage, because it is integral to Butler's conception of virtue. Virtue consists in acting in accordance with the constitution of man, when the parts of this constitution are in right proportion to each other; the acts in question, natural and proportionate, are right. Vice consists in allowing a lower principle to predominate over a higher one and acting accordingly; the acts in question, unnatural and disproportionate, are wrong (DII 4–5). Wrongness and vice, then, are matters of disproportion, and the disproportion that unnatural acts involves is determined, not by acts' consequences, but 'from *comparison* of it with the nature of the agent' (*S.* 2. 10; italics in original).

In the summary at the end of Sermon 3, the disproportion that wrongness and vice involve is quite clearly stated to arise from 'a difference in nature and kind, altogether distinct from strength, between the inward principles' (*S.* 3. 9). Some principles, Butler assures us, 'are in nature and kind superior to others'. Here, then, is the perfect occasion for Butler to place benevolence alongside self-love and to place conscience above self-love. He does neither:

Reasonable self-love and conscience are the chief or superior principles in the nature of man: because an action may be suitable to this nature, though all other principles are violated; but becomes unsuitable if either of those are. (*S.* 3. 9)

The real significance of this passage lies not in the fact that benevolence is not mentioned nor in the fact that benevolence cannot, therefore, by the very nature of the passage, enjoy the same status and authority as self-love; it lies rather in what is said about suitability. For, quite clearly, an action may violate benevolence and remain suitable to human nature, whereas no action may violate self-love and remain suitable. This seems plainly to mean that, though we have other-regarding passions and so are made for public as well as private life, we cannot violate self-love without being false to our nature. This result is of direct consequence for Butler's ethics, since it partially explains his insistence that benevolence (*S.* 11. 17–19), conscience (*S.* 3. 9), and virtue (*S.* 3. 8) are not opposed to self-love.

To be sure, Butler has said that the principles of self-love and conscience are the *chief* or *superior* principles in man's nature, so it remains open to one to insist that benevolence could still be *a* general principle in man's nature. The whole point to the usual interpretation of Butler on human nature, however, has been to insist upon self-love and benevolence as co-ordinate principles in man, both in status and authority. And I am in the way of arguing that benevolence is best regarded as a particular passion. So, to insist upon regarding benevolence as an independent principle, especially given Butler's examples, requires support in addition to merely pointing to the possibility that the present passage (*S.* 3. 9) may be read to leave open.

If we cannot violate self-love without being false to our nature, then we should certainly expect Butler to claim that benevolence and virtue do not oppose but serve self-love. But why his repeated insistence? The answer, I think, has to do with strength, not authority: men in this world, actual men, are strongly motivated by self-love. It becomes important to show, therefore, that, since there is 'no peculiar rivalship or competition between self-love and benevolence', indeed, since benevolence 'contributes more to private interest, i.e., enjoyment or satisfaction, than any other of the *particular common affections*' (*S.* 11. 19; my italics), actual men are not forced to choose between self-love and benevolence. Perhaps this fact helps in the cause of bringing actual men to be benevolent (and virtuous); its central importance, however, is that it keeps alive in us the possibility of benevolent motivation. For if self-love pulled in a different direction from benevolence, then, given the strength of self-love in actual men and that they cannot violate self-love without being false to their nature, actual men would opt in favour of self-love.

Of course, if actual men were motivated as strongly by the desire for other people's happiness as they are by the desire for their own, then there would be no need to insist upon the fact that benevolence, so to speak, serves self-love. But part of what Butler acknowledges, when he speaks of 'such a creature as man' (SP 26) and, repeatedly, of 'man's condition', is, I think, that there is a considerable discrepancy in strength between the two. Actual men, in other words, though possessed of other-regarding affections which they feel to this or that extent (and, sometimes, to a considerable extent), are nevertheless very powerfully motivated throughout life by the general desire for their own happiness. Thus, self-love and benevolence differ in respect, not only of status and authority, but also of strength. And Butler grasps the point: though he emphasizes authority, not strength, his repeated insistence that benevolence, conscience, and virtue are not contrary to self-love betokens an awareness of how important it is for him to wed these to the strong, motive force of our general, abiding desire for our own happiness. We are, as he is so very aware, much more likely to exhibit concern for others if that concern is unopposed to concern for ourselves.

Butler asserts that self-love and benevolence are nearly 'perfectly coincident' (*S.* 1. 6), but, in truth, he has no more justification for this assertion than did Shaftesbury. True, being benevolent sometimes makes us happy and sometimes serves our own private ends; there are countless instances, however, of where the benevolent act is at the expense of interest or happiness. There is no necessity about the claim of coincidence, and that, or something like it, is what is needed. (Perhaps this coincidence is to be like that which Butler alleges holds between duty and interest, namely, to be a coincidence guaranteed by God (*S.* 3. 8–9). Yet, strictly speaking, this invocation of God's goodness violates the terms under which Butler was to ground morality in human nature and not in religion (*S.* 3. 3–4). For when Butler affirms that 'any plain honest man', 'almost any fair man in almost any circumstance', can tell right from wrong (*S.* 3. 4), there is no implication that only believing Christians or religious people generally are such men as these.)

As for Butler's claim that self-love and conscience are the superior principles in man's nature, many commentators have held that Butler simply cannot mean what he says. Thus, in a footnote to the passage under discussion, Gladstone maintains that 'Butler could hardly mean to predicate of self-love that it was, like conscience, a judicial faculty; or was invested with a like sovereignty.'[4] But why can he not mean what he says? Enamoured of the usual interpretation of Butler on human nature, and convinced that the 'cool hour' passage (*S.* 11. 19) is an aberration, commentators on the whole have either dismissed or de-emphasized passages that link suitability, naturalness, and proportionateness of acts to self-love and, in this sense, place it on a par with conscience.

Love thy neighbour as thyself. I do not think Butler's treatment of this familiar injunction has been sufficiently noticed in connection with his discussion of human nature. Certainly, the relevant

---

[4] *The Works of Joseph Butler, D.C.L.*, ed. W. E. Gladstone, 2 vols. (Oxford, 1896), *S.* 3. 13 n. 1.

passages (*S.* 12. 15–21) bear interesting testimony to how pivotal a notion concern for self is in *Fifteen Sermons*.

It might be thought that the Christian Butler would simply endorse the injunction to love one's neighbour as oneself, but his treatment of it is altogether more original than this. For there is the intriguing question of whether one *can* love another as oneself first to be tackled, before the endorsement of the injunction can make much sense. In this regard, Butler makes two points.

First, we may ask after what is the case. Do actual men in fact love their neighbours to the degree that they love themselves? Typically, of course, they do not. Suppose, however, that they did: Butler proceeds to show that they would still show a partiality to self. That is, even if a person had 'the same settled regard to others, as to himself', even if 'he took their interest into the account in the same degree as his own, so far as an equality of affection would produce it', nevertheless, Butler assures us, 'he would in fact, *and ought to be*, much more taken up and employed about himself, and his own concerns, than about others, and their interests' (*S.* 12. 15; my italics). The reason for this greater attention to self is that, in addition to a general desire for our own happiness, we have a whole series of 'affections, appetites, and passions' that are necessarily 'peculiar to ourselves' (*S.* 12. 15). Thus, while some of our particular passions[5] may be felt in common, others are not, and we all recognize that we have desires or wants with regard to ourselves that we do not have with regard to others. Butler, concludes, therefore, that even assuming equal love for ourselves and others, 'regards to ourselves would be more prevalent than attention to the concerns of others' (*S.* 12. 16).

This seems a quite plausible, factual claim; what attracts notice is that Butler seeks to buttress it with the *moral* claim that I drew attention to above, namely, that we *ought* to show greater regard to ourselves (*S.* 12. 16). His reason is that 'we are in a peculiar manner ... intrusted with ourselves', with the result that 'care of our own interests, as well as of our conduct, particu-

---

[5] I here, as earlier, lump affections, appetites, and passions together under the heading of particular passions, and I treat them as desires. It is clear that a paper solely on these would have to draw distinctions among them, and beyond the very general level of distinguishing desires from needs.

larly belongs to us' (*S.* 12. 17). Use of the word 'intrusted' here doubtless calls to mind the idea that we are 'intrusted' so by the Almighty; presumably, then, if any claim of morality is present at all, it would be held to stem from an obligation to look after ourselves under which God has laid us. A non-religious person has no reason to accept a moral claim on this basis (and I have earlier remarked upon the injection of religious considerations into Butler's attempt to ground morality in human nature).

But one does not have to be religious here, to see that, in addition to self-love, or the general desire for our own happiness, prudence exerts itself within us in most intimate fashion to tend our interests, and to a degree that benevolence on the whole does not exert itself within us to tend the interests of others. This concedes that we have no moral obligation to look after our interests but acknowledges the fact that we do so look after them, and to an extent and degree that we on the whole do not look after the interests of others. Though prudence is distinct from self-love, it reinforces or supplements it; benevolence neither plays exactly the same role as prudence nor matches its strength, and it typically falls very far short of the strength of self-love. In this way, though we have benevolent passions and so are made for society, self-love and prudence go together to lead us to show greater 'regards to ourselves'. The best that can be said, therefore, is that we must love others as ourselves 'so far as this is possible' (*S.* 12. 19), and this in turn makes plain that the supposition that a person has 'the same settled regard to others, as to himself' is just that.

Second, why cannot one urge that actual men, though they do not love others as themselves, ought to do so? If the preceding remarks are correct, however, this suggestion will not do, since it would demand an impossibility of us, namely that we exhibit, as it were, more than our nature would allow us to exhibit. Obligation cannot outstrip nature, or, in Butler's terms, 'moral obligations can extend no further than to natural possibilities' (*S.* 12. 18). Here, also, his underlying point is straightforward:

we have a perception of our interests, like consciousness of our own existence, which we always carry about with us; and which, in its continuation, kind, and degree, seems impossible to be felt in respect of the interests of others. (*S.* 12. 18)

Clearly, it cannot be demanded that we feel and exhibit a like regard to others as to ourselves, if our 'affections, appetites, and passions' are arrayed in such a way as not to permit this.

This point about impossibility matters: it supplements the view that self-love, but not benevolence, is a chief or superior principle in man's nature. As we saw earlier, our acts cannot remain suitable, natural, and proportionate if they violate the principle of self-love. We now know, in addition, that our acts cannot be faulted for failing to show the same degree of regard for others as for self, and this means that our acts cannot fail to be suitable, natural, and proportionate because they fail to show equal regard for others.

Where are we left? We must show some regard for at least some others; we must do the best we can to love these others as we love ourselves; we must love them to an equal degree to ourselves 'so far as this is possible'. We shall not all manage to love the same number of others or to love them to the same degree; in fact, all that can be said is that it is up to each of us to settle upon the exact proportion of regards for others and regards to self that we shall take to be the due or right proportion. This represents, I think, a weakening of any demand benevolence might be thought to exert upon us, since we may settle in our own cases what its due proportion is to be with regard to self-love. We cannot pursue self-love and interest to the degree that it becomes mere vanity and selfishness, but we equally cannot be held to some standard level of benevolence that will count as the level that must be felt and exhibited in order for our nature to be in harmony and right proportion. *We* set that level. Butler writes:

Both our nature and condition require, that each particular man should make particular provision for himself: and the inquiry, what proportion benevolence should have to self-love, when brought down to practice, will be, what is a competent care and provision for ourselves. And how certain soever it be, that each man must determine this for himself; and how ridiculous soever it would be, for any to attempt to determine it for another; yet it is to be observed, that the proportion is real; and that a competent provision has a bound; and that it cannot be all which we can possibly get and keep within our grasp, without legal injustice. (*S.* 12. 14)

A 'competent provision' for ourselves has a 'real' bound and cannot be allowed to degenerate into greed (which is always a danger with us); but what counts as a 'competent provision' for the interests of others is, in practice, vis-à-vis self-love, up to each of us to set for ourselves. Given a good faith effort to fix the bound or proportion well short of selfishness, yet given the strength of self-love and prudence within us, it seems exceedingly probable that we shall fix the bound very favourably for ourselves. As a result, it is not merely the case that acts can violate benevolence and remain suitable, natural, and proportionate to our nature; it is also the case that the level of benevolence that must be felt and exhibited (in our acts) on our parts, in order that our nature be in right proportion, is up to each of us to fix for ourselves. The latter result supplements the former and shows how concern for others is a variable in our natures in a way that concern for self never is, something which Butler accepts.

Interest or happiness, direct and indirect. I think we can best understand some middle passages in Sermon 12 ('Upon the Love of Our Neighbour') in the light of some distinctions it seems necessary to draw between self-love and benevolence. (In part of what follows, I draw upon some work by J. O. Urmson,[6] though I make no attempt to reproduce his concerns or arguments.)

First, do actual men have a general desire aimed at the happiness of others *indiscriminately* or humanity *in general*? It seems not, when these others are strangers; when they are family and friends, it seems more plausible to regard actual men as having particular desires, varying in strength from person to person and from occasion to occasion, aimed at some facet of the well-being or relief of misery of certain particular individuals. Whereas actual men do not seem to have a general desire aimed at the happiness of humanity in general, self-love, on the other hand, is an independent principle precisely because it is a general desire throughout life aimed at one's own happiness. Importantly, as I indicated earlier, compassion forms no exception to these remarks.

Second, do actual men have a general desire aimed at the

---

[6] See J. O. Urmson, 'The Goals of Action', in J. Kim and A. I. Goldman (eds.), *Values and Morals* (Dordrecht, 1978), 131-42.

happiness of others indiscriminately or humanity in general? Here, there are two points to notice, the second of which, as Urmson stresses, involves an important asymmetry between self-love and benevolence.

To begin with, we can distinguish a desire to relieve a person's misery from a desire for that person's happiness. One may give a beggar £5 without concerning oneself at all with the beggar's happiness; one simply desires to relieve his present want. Because there is no contradiction involved in desiring an improvement in a person's circumstances but not desiring that person's happiness, compassion or pity, sympathy or fellow-feeling seem unlikely to ground a claim that actual men have a general desire aimed at the happiness of others.

Moreover, if interest or happiness really does consist 'in the gratification of certain affections, appetites, passions' (*S.* 11. 16), then a general desire for others' happiness would amount to a general desire aimed at the satisfaction of (some of) their particular passions. As Urmson indicates, however, when one gives the beggar £5, there typically is no desire that some of his particular desires be satisfied; one simply wants to mitigate his circumstances, which, as a matter of fact, he himself may or may not desire to see improved. Again, suppose the £5 enables the beggar to satisfy a desire to see a certain film and so perhaps to experience happiness: in giving the money to him, one does not desire that this desire of his be satisfied. It is true that the money enables the beggar to be happy, but one does not desire the satisfaction of the particular passion that brings this about. One can, in other words, make the beggar happy without desiring the satisfaction of some of his particular passions.

There is, then, as Urmson notes, a marked asymmetry between self-love and benevolence: I cannot desire my own happiness without seeking the satisfaction of some of my particular passions, but I can readily desire an improvement in another's situation without seeking the satisfaction of some of their particular passions. With respect to happiness, self-love and benevolence operate quite differently, and this should not be true, if benevolence really were the full analogue of self-love and so a general desire aimed at the happiness of others (in general).

Third, do *actual* men have a general desire aimed at the happiness of others indiscriminately or humanity in general?

Here, the contrast is with men as idealized abstractions, and Butler almost uniformly throughout *Fifteen Sermons*, when he notes the 'condition' or 'present circumstances' or 'present state' of men, alludes to just how important it is to show actual men that this or that course of action is not in opposition to the pursuit of their own happiness. We have already noticed this with respect to benevolence (and virtue) in Sermon 11, where he is emphatic about it (*S.* 11. 19). In the middle sections of Sermon 12 (*S.* 12. 20–4), he returns to something of a version of this theme. His aim now is to show that the happiness of others can be fostered and increased through making oneself into a particular sort of person. Exactly what sort of person is an interesting affair.

The 'general temper of mind' of one who loves his neighbour is set forth by Butler in a profound tone:

this meekness, and in some degree easiness of temper, readiness to forego our right for the sake of peace as well as in the way of compassion, freedom from mistrust, and disposition to believe well of our neighbour, this general temper, I say, accompanies, and is plainly the effect of love and good-will. (*S.* 12. 21)

This benevolent temper of mind 'extends to every different relation and circumstance in human life' (*S.* 12. 22), and Butler clearly is at great pains to recommend it to us. It makes us 'better, more to be desired, as to all the respect and relations we can stand in to each other' (*S.* 12. 22); it prevents 'our giving just cause of offence, and our taking it without cause' (*S.* 12. 24); and it will lead us in the case of real injury to make every allowance and, 'without any attempts at retaliation', to consult only our 'own and other men's security for the future, against injustice and wrong' (*S.* 12. 24).

There can be no doubt, then, that Butler would have us cultivate this temper of mind within ourselves. In the case of actual men, however, what incentive to do so will he give them? Neither here nor elsewhere does he appeal to love of benevolence (or virtue) in itself; always he appeals to interest or happiness. A benevolent man, says Butler, is 'disposed to make use of all external advantages in such a manner as shall contribute to the good of others, as well as to his own satisfaction' (*S.* 12. 22). What counts as his own satisfaction is illuminating:

He will be easy and kind to his dependants, compassionate to the poor and distressed, friendly to all with whom he has to do. This includes the good neighbour, parent, master, magistrate: and such a behaviour would plainly make dependence, inferiority, and even servitude, easy. (*S.* 12. 22)

To be sure, we are once again given examples of particular passions, this time linked to particular roles we can occupy; but the central point here is that Butler has included under the heading of one's own satisfaction precisely the benefits that flow from making oneself into a person of charitable temperament. In a word, the charitable person on this view, in serving others, serves himself, and when Butler says of such a person that he is a 'common blessing to the place he lives in: happiness grows under his influence' (*S.* 12. 22), it is important to realize that this increase is to be found not only in (some) others but also himself. Thus, actual men have a good, self-regarding reason for cultivating a charitable temper of mind in themselves.

Notice, however, what is not said: the charitable person is not said to have the happiness of others as the aim of his desires, else he is not charitable; it is just that others can possibly achieve happiness through his dealing compassionately with them. The aim of the magistrate in dealing compassionately with the poor wretch before him is not to make the man happy; it is to administer justice tempered with mercy. The aim of the parent in disciplining a child kindly and humanely is not to make the child happy but to improve its conduct. And the aim of the master in regimenting and recompensing his work-force is simply to get through the work-load as carefully and expeditiously as possible. In other words, others may possibly be made happy as the result of our compassionate dealings with them, even though we do not deliberately seek to make them happy; but we have a good, self-regarding reason for cultivating a charitable temper of mind in ourselves, whether others are made happy or not.

It is, I hope, therefore, clear that, when Butler appeals for 'humanity' and 'common good-will' towards 'fellow-creatures' (*S.* 12. 23), what he is calling for is making ourselves into caring people, people who 'naturally compassionate all' of whose distress they are made aware. We have a good reason to develop such a temperament in ourselves, which shows itself in our kindly behaviour towards those who fall within our notice. Goodwill towards others will restrain the 'spirit of party' (*S.* 12. 23), a partiality for one's group or kind; it will restrain an excessive partiality for self which degenerates into selfishness and vice; and it will make us happy. It is striking, I think, that Butler's appeals for goodwill, humanity, fellow-feeling, etc. are infused with exactly that tinge of concern for interest and happiness that would have us avoid vice and the lure of intense particular passions in favour of a 'real' self-love. It is not only the 'cool hour' passage that is in this vein.

Benevolence as the sum of virtue. We come, finally, to the concluding passages of Sermon 12 (*S.* 12. 25-33), in which Butler considers, and affirms, the claim that benevolence includes within it all virtue or is the sum of virtue. I think a proper understanding of this claim lies in understanding how the relevant passages follow on from those in the previous section.

In the present passages, Butler writes of benevolence, not as a 'blind propension', but as a 'principle in reasonable creatures' (*S.* 12. 27). His point, however, is not that benevolence is a principle in the sense of a general motive, but that it is a principle in the sense that it is the sort of thing that reason can direct. It is not something blind or without direction, not something haphazardly felt, for this or that creature, indiscriminately. In claiming that benevolence is a principle in this sense, Butler is claiming nothing more than that reason can guide it, and in claiming this he means to assert that reason will tell us that several affairs of others should concern us. Among these he includes 'the care of some persons, suppose children and families', whose care 'is particularly committed to our charge by Nature and Providence', and those in certain 'circumstances, suppose friendship or former obligations', which circumstances 'require that we do good to some, preferably to others' (*S.* 12. 27). (Once again, the examples are of particular passions.) What reason does is to tell us to pay 'particular regard to these relations and circumstances' (*S.* 12. 27); it then assists our charitable temperament in helping us to discharge the care and obligations in question. But these are directed towards particular persons, not the world at large; we do all that is *demanded* of us, though it would be nice if our benevolence or charity were quite extensive, if we attempt to 'do good to all with whom we have to do, in the degree and manner which the different relations we stand in them require' (*S.* 12. 28).

I think this notion of a relation in which we stand to others is an important one in the discussion of benevolence. We stand in certain rather specific relations to some others, and reason assists benevolence in attending to these; we might also be thought by some, however, to stand in the relation of fellow-human to all other human beings and so to have some feeling of benevolence for them as well. And when Butler speaks of 'the end of benevolence, the greatest public good' (*S.* 12. 27), it might be held that it is the latter view that he has in mind. As we saw earlier, however, in the cases of these indiscriminate others, we are to compassionate all, *to the extent that we can*, when and if we become aware of their plight, and in these concluding passages of Sermon 12 Butler soon makes it clear that we are to think of the respects in which we stand to others, not in some general vein, but rather in the particular vein—e.g. neighbour, parent, master, magistrate—that we noticed in the last section.

Society, Butler writes, consists of 'various parts, to which we stand in different respects and relations', and a 'just benevolence' would lead us 'to have due regard to each of these, and behave as the respective relations require' (*S.* 12. 29). He then follows this up with the claim that the lack of a just benevolence, or the lack of it to a 'due degree', can lead to a 'general neglect of the duties we owe towards our friends, our families, and our country' (*S.* 12. 30). Here, 'our country' is to be understood as a person or group of persons and so operates as 'our friends', as connoting a group of individual persons to whom we stand in some, more or less definite relation, which relation holds among all the individuals taken to comprise the group. Here, too, then, we are given examples of particular passions. The point is that, whether by feeling or reason or both, we show benevolence towards some others to varying degrees; when others stand in some distinct relation to ourselves, we have, and have good reason to have, particular passions that exhibit themselves in the kindly, humane, and compassionate treatment of them.

As for everyone else, for all those, if one insists, that stand in the relation of fellow-human to one, one must do the best one can to encompass them under the reign of that gentle temper of mind that it is to our interest to cultivate in ourselves. How far we succeed, what will count as the due or right proportion of regard for others, is up to each of us to determine in our own case. To the extent that benevolence were to demand a considerable regard, let alone a like regard, for all other persons indiscriminately, to that extent it would somewhat undermine Butler's emphasis throughout *Fifteen Sermons* on family, friends, and 'the welfare of those who depend upon' us (*S.* 12. 30) as the benchmark of people who actually do stand in a definite relation to us and so exert demands upon us. We must always, of course, treat charitably those who come before us, and, if we can ease their lot, so be it; but little more is *demanded* of us in their case, since they stand in no distinct relation to us.

With regard to the extent of benevolence, it would be well to recall that Butler had no illusions about the miseries of slavery; yet he in print (*SS* 1. 8), and Berkeley in practice, show a good eighteenth-century respect for the institution. Slaves must be taught the gospel and ought not to be regarded as cattle, but they may be treated 'with the very utmost rigour'. The only sense of benevolence overtly on display in this passage is that of charity, though how exactly one is to treat slaves charitably while at the same time using them 'with the very utmost rigour' remains unclear. Certainly, the happiness of slaves, or aborigines (*SS* 1. 9), is never in the picture. Interestingly, Butler claims that we owe aborigines charity in a 'much stricter' sense because of 'neighbourhood, and our having gotten possessions in their country' (*SS* 1. 9). At once, he goes on to particularize the matter: 'incidental circumstances of this kind appropriate all the general obligations of charity to particular persons; and make such and such instances of it the duty of one man rather than another' (*SS* 1. 9). Put differently, we have come to stand to some aborigines in a certain relation, as, indeed, we have to some slaves; we must treat them all with charity, but we must treat those that fall specifically under our notice and tutelage with at least this much. For, at least in the case of the aborigines, the fact that I displaced these people from their land leaves them in a distinct relation to myself, wherein their present plight is traced to my door.

Lastly, a word about Butler's claim that the 'common virtues' of mankind 'may be traced up to benevolence' is necessary, since here he says that 'benevolence seems in the strictest sense to include in it all that is good and worthy' (*S.* 12. 32). It is clear what Butler means: we think well of those who show pity and compassion, well of those who exhibit fellow-feeling and sympathy, well of those whose actions betray a definite limit to acquisitiveness, selfishness, and greed. This much is agreed, in an abstract or idealized fashion; the question is whether it is reasonable and practicable to demand that actual men measure up to this idealized version of themselves. Certainly, they must try, try to attain some due proportion in the parts of their nature; yet, how far must they succeed? The answer remains unclear in Butler, and I have tried to show that there is no correct answer, only the answer that each of us decides upon in our own case, so far as a due proportion between self-love and benevolence is concerned. Even when he is praising the benevolent man, Butler never loses sight of the caveat over benevolence that is always required in the cases of actual men. Thus, while it may be true that 'benevolence seems in the strictest sense to include in it all that is good and worthy', this is true only if we leave 'out the particular nature of creatures, and the particular circumstances in which they are placed' (*S.* 12. 32). But these are things we cannot leave out and discuss actual men; we can think about idealized versions of them and, with respect to these, think that benevolence may indeed include all that is good and worthy. Actual men, however, are the products of their nature and their circumstances; the former includes the fact that self-love and prudence are powerful forces within them, the latter the fact that appeals to their own happiness best motivate them. It is with men as they are in the world as it is that benevolence or regard for others must cope and is effectively reduced to exhibiting what charity we think we can.

I have suggested that self-love and benevolence are not on an equal level and that benevolence is best thought of as a particular passion. It remains an important part of the nature of actual men, so far as it is construed as a concern for some others that can vary in degree from person to person; but it is not a part of their nature that readily motivates them, in the absence of some appeal to their interest or happiness, and it is a part that motivates scarcely at all, when the others in question are among the undifferentiated mass of humanity in general. This is not a version of psychological egoism, obviously, since we do have other-regarding passions that cannot be reduced to some facet of self-love; neither is it a position, however, in which benevolent motivation exists in actual men simply out of a love of (all) others. We may come to want to be benevolent for its own sake; but, if anything is clear in Butler, it is that he never assumes that we *will* come to want this. As a result, he never neglects to give us an interested reason to pursue benevolence. The position, then, is one concerned with motivation and the effective prospect of motivating actual men to be benevolent, in the face of prudence and of their powerful desire for their own happiness.

That we desire, and desire powerfully, our own happiness, that 'nothing can be of consequence to mankind or any creature, but happiness' (*S.* 12. 28), is never in doubt in *Fifteen Sermons*. That we require assurance that benevolence will not be at the expense of this powerful desire, that, indeed, we require an interested motive to benevolence, is equally never in doubt. It is hard as a result not to see self-love and benevolence in quite different lights.

13
Butler on Benevolence

DAVID MCNAUGHTON

Butler believes that the elements of the human mind are hierarchically ordered. While it is universally agreed that he places the particular appetites, passions, and affections[1] at the bottom of the heap there is much dispute about the number and ranking of the superior principles. In particular, there has been a protracted debate about the position of benevolence in the hierarchy. Is benevolence a third superior principle, to be included with self-love and conscience, or is it merely a particular affection, with no more claim to authority than any other? If it is a superior principle, should it be ranked on a par with self-love or just below it?

Of the two (relatively) undisputed superior principles, it is with self-love that benevolence is most naturally compared. Both are affections concerned with the promotion of well-being or happiness. While particular affections are always classified by Butler as inferior, the superior principle of self-love is contrasted with them as general. So the question of whether benevolence is a superior principle has naturally resolved itself, in the literature, into the question of whether benevolence is best seen as a particular affection, like curiosity, ambition, or resentment, or whether it is sufficiently similar to self-love to be ranked with the latter as a general principle. The evidence is mixed. There are only a few occasions in the *Fifteen Sermons* on which Butler actually calls benevolence a general principle; he

---

The works of Butler I discuss in this paper are his *Fifteen Sermons Preached at the Rolls Chapel* and his dissertation 'Of the Nature of Virtue'; the latter was originally published as an appendix to his *Analogy of Religion*.

[1] Butler does not make clear distinctions between these three terms and I shall use them more or less interchangeably, except where the context demands a distinction.

more commonly classifies it with the particular affections.[2] Nor does he offer one consistent account of the relative status of benevolence and self-love. In some passages he treats them as if they were co-ordinate principles; in others, benevolence is included with the other affections and contrasted with self-love. There is, however, a body of critical opinion, most recently joined by Terence Penelhum in his excellent book on Butler, which favours the view that benevolence, in Butler's considered opinion, is both a general and a superior principle.[3]

Two aspects of this debate merit critical scrutiny. The first, which I have already mentioned, is the prominence given in the search for similarities and differences between the two principles to the issue of generality. As I hope to show, there are a number of ways in which a principle may be said to be general. Failure to distinguish them carefully has confused the commentators and, perhaps, even Butler himself. Indeed, as one might expect in such a long-running debate, it will emerge that each side has got hold of an important truth. The second is the assumption, on the part of those who claim that benevolence is a superior principle, that their task is complete once they have shown that benevolence is similar to self-love in several important respects. Their claim goes through only if it is by virtue of those features which it shares with benevolence that self-love is a superior principle.

---

[2] Butler uses the term 'general' to describe human benevolence (or goodwill, which I take to be a synonymous term) at *S.* 5. 2, *S.* 6. 2, and *S.* 12. 11. In addition, he says that 'general benevolence is the great law of the whole moral creation' (*S.* 8. 1). The most complete inventory of passages relevant to the debate can be found in G. K. Riddle, 'The Place of Benevolence in Butler's Ethics', *Philosophical Quarterly*, 9 (1959), 356-62.

[3] Among those who incline, with more or less conviction, to the view that Butler holds benevolence to be a general principle are: C. D. Broad, *Five Types of Ethical Theory* (London, 1930), ch. 3; A. E. Taylor, 'Some Features of Butler's Ethics', in his *Philosophical Studies* (London, 1934); S. A. Grave, 'The Foundation of Butler's Ethics', *Australasian Journal of Philosophy*, 30 (1952), 73-89; T. A. Roberts, *The Concept of Benevolence* (London, 1973), ch. 2; T. Penelhum, *Butler* (London, 1985). Among those of a contrary opinion are H. Sidgwick, *Outlines of the History of Ethics* (London, 1967), 191-201; R. Jackson, 'Bishop Butler's Refutation of Psychological Hedonism', *Philosophy*, 18 (1943), 114-39; T. H. McPherson, 'The Development of Bishop Butler's Ethics', part I, *Philosophy*, 23 (1948), 317-31; part II, *Philosophy*, 24 (1949), 3-22; A. Duncan-Jones, *Butler's Moral Philosophy* (Harmondsworth, 1952); T. A. Roberts, in his introduction to his edition of *Butler's Fifteen Sermons* (London, 1970). Riddle, in 'Benevolence in Butler's Ethics', and D. D. Raphael, 'Bishop Butler's View of Conscience', *Philosophy*, 24 (1949), 219-38, take the view that Butler offers a dual account of benevolence and thus, in different places, adopts both positions. As far as I can ascertain, those who think that benevolence is a particular principle agree that it is of inferior status, and those who think it a general principle also think that it is superior. It is this equivalence that I wish to question in s. II of my essay.

Accordingly, in the first part of this essay I shall examine the ways in which self-love and benevolence can be seen as similar, paying special attention to the issue of generality. In the second, I discuss what bearing the conclusions of the first part have on the status of benevolence in Butler's hierarchy.

I

Does Butler hold that benevolence, like self-love, is a general principle? C. D. Broad is in no doubt. 'I have assumed throughout that [Butler] regards benevolence as a general principle which impels us to maximize the happiness of humanity without regard to persons, just as he certainly regards self-love as a general principle leading us to maximize our own happiness.'[4] Sometimes, Broad admits, Butler lapses from grace and talks as if benevolence were just a particular affection. Thus, in the first sermon, he gives as examples of benevolence (at *S.* 1. 6) 'particular impulses which aim at the benefit of some particular person, e.g. paternal and filial affection'.[5] On Broad's construal, benevolence is a general principle because it is general with respect to persons.[6]

As an interpretation of Butler this suffers from two difficulties. First, although Butler sometimes speaks as if benevolence embraced all mankind, he denies that this is so when he explicitly considers the question in Sermon 12. The universe, mankind, our country, are all rejected by Butler as objects too vast, general, or remote to be the concern of the ordinary person.

[T]he Scripture ... has with the utmost possible propriety put the principle of virtue upon the love of our neighbour; which is that part of the universe, that part of mankind, that part of our country, which comes under our immediate notice, acquaintance, and influence, and with which we have to do. (*S.* 12. 3)

Although Broad's statement is false as it stands, it could easily be amended along these lines; this would still leave us with a contrast between concern for the welfare of a particular person and

---
[4] Broad, *Five Types*, 71.
[5] Ibid. 71-2.
[6] In at least two of the places in which he calls benevolence or goodwill general, namely *S.* 5. 2 and *S.* 6. 2, he appears to be using the term in this sense.

a more general benevolence which extends to all those with whom we have to do.

The second difficulty is that, on this account, benevolence is not general in the same way as self-love, but only in an analogous respect. This is brought out when we reflect that, in the sense in which benevolence is general, self-love is particular; for the latter affection aims at the benefit of one particular person—its owner. Indeed, for all that we have seen so far, filial and parental affection might be general in the sense in which self-love is general. Before we resort to Broad's solution, it seems worth enquiring whether self-love and benevolence might not be general in the same respect. We need, therefore, to get clearer about the way in which, in Butler's view, self-love is a general affection.

Butler distinguishes self-love from the particular affections at *S.* 11. 5:

> Every man hath a general desire of his own happiness; and likewise a variety of particular affections, passions, and appetites to particular external objects. The former proceeds from, or is self-love; and seems inseparable from all sensible creatures, who can reflect upon themselves and their own interest or happiness, so as to have that interest an object in their minds; what is to be said of the latter is, that they proceed from, or together make up that particular nature, according to which man is made. The object the former pursues is somewhat internal, our own happiness, enjoyment, satisfaction; whether we have, or have not, a distinct particular perception what it is, or wherein it consists: the objects of the latter are this or that particular external thing, which the affections tend towards and of which it hath always a particular idea or perception. The principle we call self-love never seeks anything external for the sake of the thing, but only as a means of happiness or good: particular affections rest in the external things themselves.

What we are offered in this passage is in fact a double contrast between those affections whose objects are both particular and external, and self-love, whose object is both general and internal. But the second contrast, as many commentators have pointed out, is unsustainable. If we interpret Butler, as it seems we must, as meaning that the object of an affection is internal where it is a state of the owner of the affection, and external where it is not, then his claim that self-love is alone in taking an internal object is clearly false.[7] Many appetites and affections typically involve desires that their owner be in a certain state. Butler's failure to see this point is due, at least in part, to his inadequate analysis of the object of an affection. The object of desire for Butler is substantial rather than propositional; what an agent desires is a thing or kind of thing. Thus the object of hunger, on his account, is food, which does seem suitably characterized as an 'external object'. This account of the object of hunger, as Broad points out, is insufficiently specific.[8] The object of a butcher going to market is food, but he need not be hungry. What a hungry person desires is that he eat food, that is that he be in a certain state. Hunger is thus correctly characterized as having an internal and not an external object.

Putting aside the distinction between internal and external, and amending Butler's account of an object of affection accordingly, what contrast is Butler here drawing between the particular and the general? An affection is particular if its object is. Each particular appetite, passion or affection, he suggests, is attracted (or repelled) by some specific (kind of) state of affairs which it seeks to realize (or avoid). Thus the object of compassion is that the distressed be relieved, the object of fear is that I avoid danger, and so on. In what sense is self-love a general affection? One would expect, by analogy, that it is general because its object, one's own happiness, is general. Butler's account of happiness is that it 'consists only in the enjoyment of those objects which are by nature suited to our several particular appetites, passions and affections' (*S.* 11. 9). There seem, however, to be two ways in which, on this account of happiness, it might be said to be the general object of

---

[7] Jackson, in 'Butler's Refutation', examines, and rejects, two other interpretations. His first suggestion is that '[t]o be external is, perhaps, no more than to be distinct from every manifestation of the affection and especially from what Butler calls "the pleasure arising from its gratification"' (p. 128). The difficulty with this account is that the object of self-love is not the pleasure arising from its own gratification, but the pleasure arising from the gratification of the particular affections. The object of *every* affection is external in this sense. His second suggestion is that by 'external' Butler meant 'distinct from the pleasure of the owner of the affection' (pp. 136-7). If self-love is, as Butler thinks, the only affection whose object is the pleasure of the owner, then self-love will be the only affection that has an internal object. Jackson rightly describes this as 'a monstrously arbitrary definition' (p. 137). It seems more likely that Butler's meaning is the one I discuss in the text, and that he overlooked its flaws for the reason given.

[8] Broad, *Five Types*, 67-9.

self-love. Firstly, self-love is a second-order affection, whose object is the enjoyment of their objects by (first-order) affections *in general*, rather than the enjoyment of its object by some affection in particular. Secondly, my happiness *in general*, as a goal, is to be contrasted with the more specific aims given by the particular affections. What determine the specific content of my happiness in general are my particular passions, with whose satisfaction self-love is concerned. Normally when we are motivated by self-love there will, of course, be some specific affection(s) which we in fact wish to satisfy. But a concern for my own happiness can motivate me even when it has been given no specific content, as when I 'go through some laborious work upon promise of a great reward, without any distinct knowledge what the reward will be' (*S.* 1. 7 n.).

Can benevolence be general in either of these ways? On the second account it seems that it can. For, just as self-love aims at its owner's happiness in general, rather than at some more specific good for him, so there may be a benevolent concern with the happiness in general of some other, rather than with some specific good of hers. Both affections would be general because their object, happiness, is general and requires further specification. Just as the content of my self-interested concern for my own happiness will be determined by my particular affections, so the content of my benevolent concern for your happiness will be determined by your particular affections. We might illustrate the similarity between the two affections in this regard by pointing out that Butler's case of the person labouring for a great reward can be adapted to fit benevolence. A person can be motivated to work simply by the thought that some other person, a friend perhaps, will be given a great and unspecified reward. We should note that, on this account, benevolence is general whether it is concerned with the good of all those with whom we have to do or, as filial and parental affection are, only with the good of some particular persons.

On the first account, however, benevolence is a particular affection. On this construal, we are not to think of happiness as in itself a general (because unspecific) object, no matter whose happiness is in question. Happiness is, rather, a general object only from the point of view of its possessor. What makes *A*'s happiness a general object for *A* is that *A*'s self-love has as its object the enjoyment of their objects by his affections in general. Every other object of A's affections is particular. From the standpoint of A, B's happiness is thus not a general object for A. It is a particular object for A in that it is the object of one of A's affections. To put the contrast in a slightly different way, A's benevolence is not a second-order desire, but a first-order desire that someone else be happy, and is itself one of the particular affections with which A's self-love concerns itself.[9]

I have extracted two contrasts between particular and general from this passage, on only the second of which benevolence comes out as a general principle. It seems likely, however, that Butler saw himself as drawing only one. It is perhaps worth enquiring which of them Butler primarily had in mind in this passage. I think it is clear that it must be the first. His famous refutations, in Sermon 11, of psychological egoism and hedonism depend on his explicitly contrasting self-love, as general, with the love of our neighbour (here equated with benevolence), which is classified as one of the particular affections. In this passage he is setting up that contrast, so that any interpretation of his remarks which allowed benevolence to rank as general must be ruled out. Self-love is general in both senses. Perhaps Butler thought that only an affection which was general in the first and primary sense could be general in the second. That would explain his mistaken belief that every particular affection, including benevolence, has 'a particular idea or perception of its object', if by that he meant that a particular affection cannot be concerned with someone's good in general, without further specification.[10]

It seems then that those who claim that Butler's official account of the distinction between particular and general commits him to the view that benevolence is a particular affection are in the right.[11] But we have also discovered a sense, whether or not it is Butler's, in which benevolence can be thought of as a

---

[9] I am greatly indebted, in this paragraph, to Jackson's illuminating discussion in 'Butler's Refutation', 127-8.

[10] We find confirmation of this view when we recall that my desire for your happiness would clearly be a desire for an external object.

[11] I do not mean to imply that all those who hold that benevolence is particular have done so for this reason. Some hold that view because they do not think Butler believed that there was such a thing as a benevolent concern for people in general as distinct from concerns for particular people.

general affection in the same way that self-love is, because it has as its object the happiness in general of some person(s).

Those who argue that Butler did think of benevolence as a general principle concede, however, that he sometimes describes it in ways that make it sound more like a particular affection. So we might ask whether there are other-regarding affections which are particular, in our second sense, and whether Butler ever equates them with benevolence. There seem to be two ways in which a benevolent impulse might fail to qualify as general. General benevolence is concerned, firstly, with all aspects of another's good or happiness rather than some one particular aspect of it and, secondly, with his long-term rather than his short-term good. It seems perfectly possible, however, to be motivated by a particular benevolent impulse which is directed only at one aspect of someone's good, or only at his short-term good. When Butler introduces benevolence in the *Fifteen Sermons* he seems to allow that such particular benevolent impulses can properly be identified with benevolence itself.

And if there be in mankind any disposition to friendship; if there be any such thing as compassion, for compassion is momentary love; if there be any such thing as the paternal or filial affections; if there be any affection in human nature, the object and end of which is the good of another; this is itself benevolence, or the love of another. Be it ever so short, be it in ever so low a degree, or ever so unhappily confined; it proves the assertion, and points out what we were designed for, as really as though it were in a higher degree and more extensive. (*S.* 1. 6)

Here Butler enumerates various ways in which benevolence as it is found in humans can fall short of the ideal. It can be directed only towards some people, and not towards all of those with whom we have to do. This is a distinction which we have already come across in discussing Broad. It can be weaker than it should be, a point we will consider later. Butler also allows, however, that benevolence may be short-lived or momentary. It is, of course, possible to have a fleeting concern for someone's long-term good, but it seems consistent with the tenor of this passage to suppose that Butler would have allowed that a passing concern with someone's immediate good constituted benevolence. Moreover, compassion, as Butler shows in a later discussion, is only concerned with another's good under a particular aspect, that of preventing and relieving distress. In the later passage he contrasts it with general goodwill or benevolence, from which it is claimed to be distinct.

The social nature of man, and general good-will to his species, equally prevent him from doing evil, incline him to relieve the distressed, and to promote the positive happiness of his fellow-creatures: but compassion only restrains him from the first, and carries him to the second; it hath nothing to do with the third. (*S.* 6. 2)[12]

There seems, then, to be good reason to agree with Penelhum's claim that, in the passage from *S.* 1. 6, Butler is using benevolence as 'a generic term covering all other-regarding affections',[13] and also with his claim that there are later passages where he distinguishes particular benevolent impulses from benevolence itself.

Before considering other parallels between benevolence and self-love to which commentators have drawn our attention, it will be useful to sum up our discussion of generality. There are three ways in which benevolence, on Butler's considered account, might be said to be general.

1. It is concerned with the good or happiness in general of the person(s) towards whom it is directed, and not just with some aspects of it;

2. it is concerned with their happiness over a whole life, and not just with their happiness at a particular time;

3. it is concerned not just with the happiness of some particular person(s), but with the happiness of all those with whom one has to do.

Self-love is also general in the first and second senses but cannot, of course, be general in the third. Self-love, however, is a general affection in a sense in which no other affection, including benevolence, can be: it is a desire that our first-order desires in general should be satisfied. It is of this last sense that Butler is usually thinking when he calls self-love a general principle; when he calls benevolence general he seems to have the third sense primarily in view.

---

[12] See also *S.* 5. 2: '[W]e plainly consider compassion itself as an original, distinct, particular affection in human nature; whereas to rejoice in the good of others, is only a consequence of the general affection of love and good-will to them.'

[13] Penelhum, *Butler*, 32.

The other parallels between benevolence and self-love, which largely stem from similarities already discussed, can be dealt with more briefly. First, both are rational, reflective principles in that benevolence 'requires the capacity to distinguish, in others, the difference between short-term satisfactions and long-term good that self-love requires us to distinguish in ourselves'.[14] That is, reason is required, not only to calculate how best to achieve the goal given by the affection (which is true to some degree of all affections), but also to determine what constitutes the unspecific goal of happiness in any particular case. Second, benevolence and self-love are principles which assess our other affections, and decide which of them should be gratified and which frustrated in order to maximize our chances of achieving their respective goals. They thus generate second-order desires to act on certain first-order desires and not on others.[15] Third, while both are capable of motivating us on their own, they can face stiff competition from insistent particular desires which pull us in a contrary direction. Fortunately, they can both be aided by what Butler sometimes calls 'under affections'; particular desires which normally, but not always, impel us to the same goal as the general affection. In an important passage, to which Penelhum draws our attention, Butler explicitly makes this claim of benevolence.

Is it possible any can in earnest think, that a public spirit, i.e. a settled and reasonable principle of benevolence, is so prevalent and strong in the species, as that we may venture to throw off the under affections, which are its assistants, carry it forward and mark out particular courses for it; family, friends, neighbourhood, the distressed, our country? (*S.* 5. 10)

Each general affection will have its own set of particular under affections and passions which Penelhum, following Butler in *S.* 1. 6–7, divides into two types. Firstly, there are appetites, affections, and passions which, though they do not have as their

---

[14] Ibid. 34.

[15] This is not to say that benevolence is itself a second-order affection or desire in the way that self-love is. The object of A's self-love is the enjoyment of their objects by her own affections in general. The object of A's benevolence is the happiness of, say, B; that is the enjoyment by B of the objects of B's affections. To secure that end, however, A will have to inhibit herself from acting on any of her desires that are incompatible with it and encourage herself to act on desires likely to promote it.

intended object the good of either oneself or another, yet tend to promote either private or public good, and are implanted in us by Providence for that purpose. Hunger, Butler tells us in a footnote to *S.* 1. 7, is a private passion, desire of esteem a public one.

Secondly, there are some affections which, though particular, have as their goal some good for others, and other affections which, though particular, have as their goal some good for oneself. We have already met the former; they are the particular benevolent impulses with which, in *S.* 1. 6, Butler appears to identify benevolence. Butler, as far as I know, does not give examples of particular affections which have as their aim some aspect of one's own good, but it seems plausible that there might be some. Concern for one's own health is a concern for one's own good, but it is not a concern for one's good as a whole, and may indeed on occasion be incompatible with it, as the exaggerated anxiety of the valetudinarian reveals. These particular affections are, Penelhum suggests,[16] specifications or particularizations of the relevant general affection. Thus the particular other-regarding under affections stand in the same relation to benevolence as the particular self-regarding under affections do to self-love.

Penelhum tries to complete the parallel by pointing out that, at least in normal cases, each general affection will reinforce its own under affections because they further the same end as it does. This is true, so far as it goes, but it ignores an important disanalogy. The gratification of many of my private passions, or my self-regarding affections, will not have any noticeable effect on the public good. The general principle of benevolence will not, therefore, reinforce those impulses. Self-love, however, has an interest in the gratification of all my desires *per se*, including my other-regarding affections, for the gratification of any is part of my happiness.[17]

These similarities between benevolence and self-love, though not complete, are striking. The case for seeing these two affections as on a par with each other, in the respects we have looked

---

[16] Penelhum, *Butler*, 34.

[17] Of course, the satisfaction of one may lead to the frustration of many, or even to my certain ruin, and then self-love will oppose it. But that does not alter the fact that self-love has a direct interest in its gratification, though it has a stronger interest in its frustration. These points are made with force and clarity by Broad, *Five Types*, 73-4.

at, is well made out. But does it follow that benevolence, like self-love, is a superior principle?

II

Butler's account of superiority rests, as is well known, on a difference between the felt strength and the authority of a principle of action. If there were no superior principles then we should be acting according to our natures in following the strongest impulse. A superior principle, however, has an authority which is independent of its felt strength, so that the question of whether we should act on its edicts is settled by appeal to its authority. That authority is a rational one; the verdicts of a superior principle provide better reason to act than the promptings of an inferior one. To act on an inferior principle in defiance of a superior one is, in Butler's terms, to act contrary to our nature.

Do the admitted similarities between benevolence and self-love provide reasons to support the claim that Butler thought of benevolence as a superior principle or, at least, that he 'would have accepted it as the most appropriate development of his insistence that there is a natural principle of benevolence in us'?[18] That will depend on whether the superiority of self-love is connected with its possession of those features which it shares with benevolence. No one, so far as I know, makes a case for saying that there is such a connection, or even sees that a case needs to be made. I shall argue that there is no connection.

At the end of Section I, I outlined three important respects in which benevolence and self-love are similar. Each might be thought to have a connection to superiority. The first respect is rationality. Benevolence, as well as self-love, is a rational principle; must it not therefore have the rational authority to which that status entitles it? To argue thus would be, I believe, to confuse two quite different ways in which a principle can be rational: roughly, the distinction between reason as a guide to help us achieve a given end, and reason as directive, determining what our ends should be. Benevolence and self-love are motives which only a rational being can have. Firstly because, once we have

[18] Penelhum, *Butler*, 61.

determined what someone's long-term happiness consists in, we need to use reason instrumentally to enable us to choose the best route to realize it. Secondly, and more interestingly, we need to use reason to discover what constitutes a particular person's happiness. As we have seen, this will involve finding out what he desires. Since it is highly unlikely that all his desires can be satisfied, we also need to use skill and judgement to calculate how they can best be harmonized in one coherent and satisfying life. (In separating out these two elements I do not mean to imply that they can, in practice, be considered in isolation from each other.) This account of the calculative rationality of the two general affections is quite silent, however, about the rational authority of the verdicts of those principles, about what weight should be given to their deliverances in deciding what we have best reason to do. It is undeniable that benevolence is a rational principle in that its exercise requires calculative rationality. It is a controversial thesis, which by no means follows from that claim, that it is what we might call a principle of reason, a principle whose dictates are authoritative, in Butler's sense. Self-love is indeed a rational principle which is also a principle of reason, but we must not suppose that the one entails the other.[19]

Moreover, if all that is required for an affection to be a principle of reason is that it requires rational reflection to recognize its object, then affections other than benevolence, ones clearly regarded by Butler as particular and inferior, will have to be elevated in the hierarchy. Ambition, for example, leads us to aspire to success; but just what constitutes success in some field of endeavour or, even more strikingly, in one's life as a whole, is a matter that will require reflection of a sort similar to that needed to determine what one's happiness is. Settled and deliberate (as distinct from hasty and sudden) resentment is another affection

[19] Penelhum appears to slide from one sense of reason to the other when he writes that Butler's language suggests that 'conscience is the only reflective principle, the only faculty by which we "reflect upon our own nature" and on the motives and actions *proper* to it. While he often talks in this way, it is clear that self-love, and, if the preceding section is sound, benevolence also, require reflection upon our motives and actions, and cannot function without it, since each necessarily involves a consciousness of my own nature, or that of others, and its needs' (*Butler*, 35; my emphasis). The first sentence, as the word 'proper' indicates, is about what ends we ought to have. The second sentence simply reminds us that we cannot exercise self-love or benevolence unless we are capable of the calculative use of reason, and has nothing to do with the authority of those principles.

which, on Butler's account in Sermon 8, requires reason to discern its object, though for different reasons. '[I]t is not natural, but moral evil; it is not suffering, but injury, which raises that anger or resentment' which is a feeling of indignation against, and a desire for the punishment of, the perpetrator (*S.* 8. 7). Only a rational being, indeed only one capable of moral reflection, could discern the proper object of settled resentment, but that does not make resentment a superior principle.

I have argued that the fact that benevolence is a rational general principle is independent of the question of whether it is a superior principle. Did Butler, however, see these questions as independent? (It is, perhaps, easier to separate them with Kantian hindsight.) Or did he think that a rational principle is, by its very nature, also a superior principle? There is one passage which might suggest the latter answer. At SP 24 he says that 'a disapprobation of reflection [is] in itself a principle manifestly superior to a mere propension'. By a 'disapprobation of reflection', in this context, Butler means, however, a judgement of conscience. His normal practice is to identify reflection with conscience, and approbation and disapprobation is the characteristic form its judgement takes. So the remark cannot be extended to cover rational principles such as benevolence which, in an everyday sense, might be said to involve reflection.

There is a striking passage which strongly suggests that Butler did make the distinction on which I have insisted. Towards the end of Sermon 12, Butler is considering whether benevolence is the whole of virtue; first he seeks to clarify what might be meant by such a claim.

[W]hen benevolence is said to be the sum of virtue, it is not spoken of as a blind propension, but as a principle in reasonable creatures, and so to be directed by their reason: for reason and reflection comes into our notion of a moral agent. And that will lead us to consider distant consequences, as well as the immediate tendency of an action: it will teach us that the care of some persons, suppose children and families, is particularly committed to our charge ... *Reason, considered merely as subservient to benevolence, as assisting to produce the greatest good*, will teach us to have particular regard to those relations and circumstances; because it is plainly for the good of the world that they should be regarded. ... All these things must come into consideration, *were it only to determine which way of acting is likely to produce the greatest good*. Thus, upon supposition that it were in the strictest sense true, without limitation, that benevolence includes in it all virtues; yet *reason must come in as its guide and director, in order to attain its own end*, the end of benevolence, the greatest public good (*S.* 12. 27; my emphasis).

When Butler speaks of reason 'considered merely as subservient to benevolence' he is implicitly contrasting reason in its instrumental sense with reason in some other sense. While he does not say what that other sense is, the natural assumption is that it is the directive use of reason which determines what our ends should be. For it is directive reason, presumably in the form of conscience, that will decide whether benevolence is the whole of virtue; that is, whether we ought to make the maximization of happiness our sole moral end. So he here views these two uses of reason as distinct and separable. Benevolence is only described as being 'reasonable' in the first sense.

I want to go further and suggest that the contrast Butler has in mind in this passage is that between a principle that is reasonable in the sense that it brings in reason as its 'guide and director', and a principle that is reasonable in the sense that it is identical with reason itself. I have already pointed out that Butler usually identifies conscience with reflection. I take reflection to be (a form of) reason, so that he is claiming that conscience, as a superior principle, is (a form of) reason. Now self-love, as an affection, cannot perhaps be wholly identified with reason. Nevertheless, since self-love is a superior principle, and not simply one that uses reason calculatively, we might expect to find that it is sometimes identified with reason. Here is a passage where this seems to be so. At the end of *S.* 11. 5, from part of which I have already quoted at length, he contrasts self-love 'which belongs to man as a reasonable creature reflecting upon his own interest or happiness' with the particular affections which, 'though quite distinct from reason, are as much a part of human nature'. If we take Butler literally then, by implication, self-love is not distinct from reason; it *is* reason.[20] Note that all the other affections, including love of our neighbour or benevolence, are here described as distinct from reason.

I turn now to the second respect in which benevolence resembles self-love. In the pursuit of its goal, benevolence will

---

[20] I shall be returning to this theme later. I do not mean to imply that this is the only way this passage can be read, only that it is a natural way to read it.

encourage action on some desires and prohibit action on others. Is this evidence that it is a superior principle? No, for the pursuit of any goal may involve the formation of second-order desires of this kind. Ambition, to use an earlier example, may lead one to suppress some desires and encourage others. What makes a principle superior is not that it determines which passions and affections should be acted on and which suppressed if it is to achieve its goal, but that it has authority to determine what our goals should be. That benevolence has the one function is no evidence that it has the other.

The third respect in which self-love and benevolence resemble each other involves their relationship to their own under affections. Butler holds that, in humans, the superior principles are often motivationally weak. Each superior principle has its under affections which provide motivational support for it and we would be foolish to try to do without them.[21] When Butler talks, in the passage at *S.* 5. 10 which I have already quoted, in similar terms of the weakness of the 'settled and reasonable principle of benevolence' and its need for support from the under affections, is this not evidence that he is thinking of benevolence as a superior principle? For only a superior principle, we might think, can be weaker than it ought to be, and thus need assistance from under affections to exert its proper influence. The passage need not, however, be read in this way, for it is false that it is only superior principles which can be weaker than they ought to be. Each principle has its own due proportion to every other, a proportion determined by conscience.[22] So conscience may determine that benevolence should have a greater proportional weight in our lives than its native

---

[21] See e.g. *S.* 5. 3, where Butler insists that '[r]eason alone, whatever anyone may wish, is not in reality a sufficient motive of virtue in such a creature as man' and that it is only when 'those affections which God has impressed upon his heart . . . are allowed scope to exercise themselves, but under strict government and direction of reason . . . [that] we act suitably to our nature'.

[22] '[T]he several appetites, passions, and particular affections, have different respects amongst themselves. They are restraints upon, and are in a proportion to each other. This proportion is just and perfect, when all those under principles are perfectly coincident with conscience, so far as their nature permits, and in all cases under its absolute and entire direction. The least excess or defeat, the least alteration of the due proportions amongst themselves, or of their coincidence with conscience, though not proceeding into action, is some degree of disorder in the moral constitution' (*S.* 3. 2 n.). See also *S.* 5. 3, part of which was quoted in the previous note.

strength might suggest, without benevolence itself being a superior principle.

All that has been shown so far is that the reasons which are typically offered for thinking that Butler held, or should have held, that benevolence is a superior principle are not good ones. It remains possible that Butler did, on independent grounds, think that it is a superior principle. The direct textual evidence, however, tells against that claim. Butler nowhere calls benevolence a superior principle; on only one occasion does he claim that acting contrary to benevolence would be violating our natures, and the passage is not decisive.[23] At the end of the third sermon he quite explicitly states that reasonable self-love and conscience are the superior principles in our nature, and that 'an action may be suitable to this nature, though all other principles be violated; but becomes unsuitable if either of these are' (*S.* 3. 9). The deliberate omission of benevolence is surely significant.

I have been arguing, not only that Butler did not classify benevolence as a superior principle, but that the similarities between it and self-love so far adduced give no reason why he should have done. That still leaves open the possibility that there might be good reason for him to elevate benevolence in the hierarchy. A major difficulty in dealing with this question is that Butler does not give much guidance as to what it is about a principle that fits it for its superior role. Certainly, his two candidates have a respectable pedigree; the claims of both self-love and virtue to be the voice of reason have not lacked advocates.

---

[23] In *S.* 1. 15 Butler says that a person's nature can be considered in two respects; as it leads him to attain his own greatest happiness and, in his social capacity, as it leads him to 'right behaviour in society'. 'Men follow or obey their nature in both these capacities and respects to a certain degree, but not entirely: their actions do not come up to the whole of what their nature leads them to in either of these capacities or respects: and they often violate their nature in both. *I.e.* as they neglect the duties they owe to their fellow-creatures, to which their nature leads them; and are injurious, to which their nature is abhorrent.' Grave, in 'The Foundation of Butler's Ethics', 75, takes this passage to be decisive in favour of the superiority of benevolence, but it does not seem to me to be so, for the following reasons. Firstly, at the end of the first sermon, Butler has not yet put forward his distinction between inferior and superior principles, and so has not given the notion of violating our natures the precise meaning it acquires in the second sermon. Secondly, putting that to one side, to act contrary to benevolence would, in the present context, be to act viciously, and thus to act contrary to nature in violating our conscience—as, indeed, Butler's use of the word 'duties' suggests. So it is not clear whether it is as opposing benevolence or as opposing conscience that vice is here said to be a violation of our nature.

The former represents private interest and the latter public; two points of view which seem to have a special claim to our allegiance. This suggests, however, that there is no reason to introduce benevolence as an independent principle of reason on the side of public good. Butler does not so much argue that conscience and self-love are superior as remind us that we already believe that their edicts have rational authority. Whether, as Penelhum suggests,[24] our intuitions would support the claim that benevolence has authority, independently of the verdict of conscience, seems to me doubtful.[25]

Those who hold benevolence to be a superior principle have, of course, to say something about its relation to the other two superior principles. I want, finally, to see if and how benevolence might fit in, were the case for its inclusion as a superior principle to be accepted. That discussion will take us into another disputed area of Butlerian exegesis—the relation between conscience and self-love. In the course of it, we shall find an additional reason for thinking that Butler rejects any claim that benevolence is a superior principle.

The existence of two acknowledged superior principles, representing the points of view of duty and interest, raises the question of which takes precedence in the case of a conflict. Butler himself is at great pains to maintain that there can be no real conflict between the two. 'Duty and interest are perfectly coincident; for the most part in this world, but entirely and in every instance if we take in the future, and the whole' (*S.* 3. 9). Nevertheless, he does broach the topic on occasion and there is general agreement that his considered opinion, despite some notorious passages in Sermon 11, is that conscience is supreme. Were there a conflict, self-love would have to give way. This position can, however, be understood in two ways, and which one we adopt will affect our picture of how benevolence might fit in if it were added to the existing two. On one interpretation, there is a hierarchical ordering within superior principles, with conscience at the top. Two superior principles are hierarchically

---

[24] Penelhum, *Butler*, 60.

[25] Our intuitions strongly support the view that some benevolent actions are supererogatory and not obligatory. If the dictates of benevolence provide better reasons, by their very nature, than those that arise from other desires of ours, there is a danger that there will be no place for supererogation.

ranked if the verdict of the first provides, because of the kinds of consideration it takes into account, a weightier reason to act than the verdict of the second. Where the verdicts of two superior principles conflict the verdict of the higher overrides that of the lower. On this picture, no irresolvable conflicts will arise from adding further superior principles to the hierarchy, provided that each is given an appropriate ranking. It is this interpretation that Penelhum adopts, and it allows him to suggest, largely on the strength of Butler's remarks in Sermon 12, that Butler would probably place benevolence in third place behind self-love.[26]

The difficulty with this interpretation is that, even where Butler most insists on the supremacy of conscience, he refrains from drawing the conclusion which that interpretation requires, namely that moral requirements, by their very nature, provide weightier reasons for acting than prudential ones. The most striking instance occurs at SP 24-8. Having roundly declared, in SP 24, that conscience 'claims the absolute direction' of all other principles, Butler argues, in SP 26, for the superiority of his position to Shaftesbury's. Since Shaftesbury takes it that the only obligation we are under is one of self-interest, his defence of virtue consists in showing that 'virtue is naturally the interest or happiness, and vice the misery, of such a creature as man, placed in the circumstances which we are in this world'. While endorsing Shaftesbury's claim, Butler presses two difficulties. First, while duty and interest generally coincide in this life, there may be 'particular exceptions'.[27] What reason have we to be virtuous in such a case? Second, what reason for being virtuous could we offer to the person who is sceptical of Shaftesbury's claim? Not only can Shaftesbury's system provide no reason to be virtuous in such cases, but it tells us to act contrary to the requirements of morality, where self-interest demands it, because pursuit of self-interest is our only obligation. If we now add to the picture the obligation, for which Butler has argued, which springs from the authority of conscience, then there is a reason for taking the virtuous course.

---

[26] On the hierarchy, see Penelhum, *Butler*, 59. On the ranking of benevolence, see pp. 35, 61.

[27] Butler allows that there are exceptions to the coincidence of duty and interest if we restrict our consideration, as here, to this life.

Does this addition provide an answer to the question of what someone should do in such circumstances, all things considered? Butler considers the objection that the obligations on each side simply cancel each other out. His reply is that 'the obligation on the side of interest does not really remain' (SP 26). What is his reason for this claim?

If the first interpretation were correct we would expect it to be that moral requirements override prudential ones. But in fact he rests his claim on another difference between the two obligations. Judgements of self-interest always involve complex calculations about consequences and are thus liable to error; prudential obligations 'can at the utmost appear no more than probable'. We may be mistaken in our belief about what is in our best interest, particularly when we take into account the possibility of a future life. The judgements of conscience, by contrast, are not calculative in this way.[28] Conscience 'pronounces determinately some actions to be *in themselves* just, right, good; others to be in themselves evil, wrong, unjust' (*S.* 2. 8; my emphasis). It judges an action right or wrong, in other words, because of the kind of action it is, rather than because of its consequences. Even where consideration of consequences is necessary for the exercise of a particular virtue, as in the case of benevolence, it is the intention to produce good consequences that is alone the concern of conscience.[29] It follows that judgements of conscience are not subject to the kind of uncertainty to which judgements of self-interest are prone. In a case of apparent conflict 'the certain obligation would entirely supersede and destroy the uncertain one' (SP 26).

Given his (controversial) account of the judgements of conscience, Butler is entitled to this argument. The puzzle is why, if the first interpretation is correct, he does not also just come straight out and say that, were the two to conflict, the demands of duty are superior to those of self-interest. Since he is here writing to clarify his views, rather than addressing a sermon to a particular audience with special concerns, there seems no reason for him not to add this claim, if he believes it. His silence is

---

[28] The case of conscience shows that it is not a necessary condition of a principle's being superior that it involves the employment of calculative reason. I have been arguing, in the second part of this essay, that it is not a sufficient condition either.

[29] A point he emphasizes at DII 2.

evidence that he does not believe it.[30] This suggests an alternative interpretation of the relation between the two superior principles. On this view, Butler regards duty and self-interest as independent sources of rational obligation. As such, each has an equal claim on us; neither overrides the other and there is no higher authority than reason itself to which we can appeal. Thus the recognition either that an action is against our interest, or that it is morally forbidden, equally lays upon us a requirement to refrain from performing that action; an obligation which, as rational beings, we must fulfil.[31] If practical reason is not to be fractured, and at odds with itself, the requirements of interest and virtue must be identical. This, by the providential arrangement of God, they are. Any conflict, as we have seen, must be apparent, not real, the result of a misunderstanding of our interest. The supremacy of conscience over self-love lies, not in the one kind of reason being superior in nature to the other, but in the immediacy and consequent certainty of the judgements of conscience. I have not space to consider the question at length, but I incline to the view that this second interpretation fits Butler's text as a whole rather better than the first.[32]

On this second understanding of the nature of a superior principle, could benevolence find a place as a third principle of reason, alongside self-love and conscience? If benevolence were another voice of reason, then, to avoid practical reason being fractured, it would have to deliver its verdicts from a distinctive third point of view, and yet those verdicts would have always to coincide with those of self-love and conscience.

Whether benevolence can meet these conditions depends on the relation between it and virtue. In his earlier writing, Butler appears sympathetic to the idea that benevolence might be the whole of virtue. If that were the case then the first condition could not be met, for the voice of benevolence would not be

---

[30] An argument that an author does not believe a thesis simply because he does not assert it is comparatively weak. But it is greatly strengthened if an alternative thesis can be found which coheres with everything he holds. This is what I attempt to do in what follows.

[31] I have already drawn attention to the passage at *S.* 3. 9 which strongly supports this interpretation.

[32] An interpretation along these lines is suggested, perhaps not surprisingly, by Sidgwick, *History of Ethics*, 196-8. I have already hinted at it in my earlier suggestion that a principle of reason is, in effect, reason itself.

distinct from that of conscience. The two would be trivially coincident, because their viewpoints would be identical. Later, in a footnote to *S.* 12. 31 (presumably added after the sermon was delivered) and even more forcefully in DII 8, Butler unequivocally rejects this equation. There are certain duties, summed up under the general titles of justice and veracity, which are incumbent on us quite independently of any tendency our actions may have to increase the general well-being. Conscience must thus oppose benevolence where acting benevolently would be in breach of such a duty. It is tempting to argue that, in this case, the second condition could not be met. For, it seems, the course that would maximize happiness will sometimes be different from that which conscience decrees. In which case, including benevolence as a third superior principle would lead to a fracture in the voice of reason, a possibility which I think Butler would find intolerable.

Butler does, however, consider a possibility that would enable the proponent of the claims of benevolence to evade the second horn of this dilemma. Suppose, he says, that God 'were to propose nothing to Himself as an end but the production of happiness', then his only reason for

> giving us the ... approbation of benevolence to some persons rather than others, and disapprobation of falsehood, unprovoked violence, and injustice, must be, that He foresaw this constitution of our nature would produce more happiness, than forming us with a temper of mere general benevolence. (DII 8)

If this supposition were true,[33] then there would be a theological guarantee that in following conscience we would, in fact, be acting in a way that would maximize happiness, as well as self-interest.[34] Butler could then, if he wished, include benevolence as a superior principle and argue, as in the case of self-love, that any

---

[33] Grave, in 'Foundation of Butler's Ethics', 85-6, argues, rather plausibly, that it is false on Butler's own premisses, that God is a utilitarian, for God's motives in rewarding virtue and punishing vice are primarily retributive. If Grave is right, then there seems no reason to believe that God will maximize the happiness of his creatures, since that is no more what reason demands in his case than in ours.

[34] The matter is rather more complex than I have represented it here. On this supposition, it is true that, in following our conscience, we would be producing more happiness than we could produce by adopting any other pattern of motivation. But it would not be true that each particular action of ours would maximize happiness, for our 'constitution' would sometimes lead us to choose non-optimific acts.

conflict between it and conscience must be apparent and not real. Benevolence, on this account, must give way to conscience, not because it is inferior to it, but because it is a calculative principle, and thus its judgements are less immediate and certain than those of conscience.[35]

So, even on my understanding of the nature of superiority, Butler could have found a place for benevolence as a superior principle. That he is not in fact inclined, in this passage, to take this line is pretty obvious.[36] The theological claim that would guarantee the coincidence of duty and the greatest general happiness is only put forward as a supposition. Moreover the obligation to virtue is here taken to override the claims of benevolence in a way that is inconsistent (on the understanding of superiority I advocate, though not on the more traditional interpretation favoured by Penelhum) with the latter's claim to superior status. That Butler did think of benevolence as a superior principle, I deny; that he should have thought of it as superior, I dispute; that he could have included it as a superior principle without inconsistency, I allow.

Butler has a very simple hierarchical system, in which there are just two classes of principle, superior and inferior. I have argued that benevolence belongs in the latter camp, but Butler's classification scarcely seems to do justice to the undoubted similarities between it and self-love. The solution, I believe, would have been for Butler to complicate his classificatory scheme, to allow a distinction between rational and non-rational inferior principles. Both Butler and his commentators are sometimes inclined to speak as if all particular principles are unreflective and impulsive, the sorts of appetites, affections and passions which an animal could possess. What I have tried to show is that some of the particular affections essentially involve the use of reason. Nothing in Butler's system should prevent him acknowledging this, or admitting that benevolence is as clear an example of a rational principle as is self-love. To be inferior, in Butler's sense, is not to be a non-rational impulse.

[35] Butler does make this last point about benevolence at *S.* 12. 27.
[36] Grave, 'Foundation of Butler's Ethics', 77, claims that the view in the previous paragraph does represent Butler's position. But he rests his claim on the premiss that Butler thinks of God as a utilitarian, a premiss which he himself later undermines. (See n. 33.)

14
Butler on God and Human Nature

ALAN MILLAR

I

The whole of Butler's *Fifteen Sermons* is 'an attempt of shewing men to themselves, of shewing them what course of life and behaviour their real nature points out and would lead them to' (*S.* 2. 1). In carrying through this project Butler seeks to clarify and defend the claim that virtue consists in following our nature and vice in deviating from it (SP 13). The enterprise raises a number of questions. Obviously, there is the problem of how to interpret this claim. How must we conceive of our nature if we are to make sense of either following or deviating from it? In what sense is the life of virtue natural and the life of vice unnatural? And assuming that these notions are intelligible how far are they plausible? Other questions arise from the fact that the *Fifteen Sermons* are the work of a moralist with the very definite aim of encouraging people to the practice of virtue. It is not clear how a review of our nature of the sort envisaged is supposed to achieve this. It is on this matter that Butler may be thought to be morally suspect. Why, for instance, is he so keen to insist that public and private good coincide? Is it (as *S.* 11. 21 might suggest) because he thinks that we will not take steps to promote public good unless we are assured that doing so will be beneficial to ourselves?

These problems take us to the heart of the methodology of the *Fifteen Sermons* but they will receive adequate treatment only if due regard is paid to the details of Butler's moral psychology. In this essay I shall draw upon Butler's discussions of such topics as compassion, resentment, and love of our neighbour, for it is in connection with these that the methodology developed in the first three sermons can be seen at work. One of my aims is to show how central to Butler's thought is the teleological theology which permeates the *Fifteen Sermons*. But I shall also be concerned to explore the possibility of embedding some of Butler's key ideas in a non-theological view of the world.[1]

II

One point is fairly clear though it has been given surprisingly little attention in Butler scholarship. On Butler's view, the behaviours to which our nature points and leads us are behaviours for which we are adapted. We follow our nature when we live in ways for which we are adapted. Butler's treatment of specific aspects of our nature provides good indication of what these claims mean, though he nowhere provides an explicit analysis of the concept of adaptation.

'Compassion', Butler writes, 'is a call, a demand of nature, to relieve the unhappy; as hunger is a natural call for food' (*S.* 6. 6). Part of what is implied here is that human beings by and large are capable of experiencing compassion and when they do they are motivated (have at least some inclination) to relieve the unhappy. But this in itself does not capture the idea that our nature points to and leads us to relieve the unhappy. It is equally true that human beings by and large are capable of experiencing jealousy and that when they do they are motivated to harm those of whom they are jealous, yet Butler certainly does not think that we are adapted to harming others. However, there is an asymmetry between the two cases. In Butler's framework the fact that we have a capacity to experience compassion is to be explained by the fact that having such a capacity results in our being motivated in appropriate circumstances to relieve the unhappy. The full explanation draws on Butler's theology, and in particular on assumptions about the purposes of God. God intends that we relieve the unhappy. To this end he fashions us with the capacity for compassion so that we will relieve the unhappy. The explanation then is teleological. A feature of our

[1] This essay further develops a line of interpretation set out in Alan Millar, 'Following Nature', *Philosophical Quarterly*, 38 (1988), 165-85. References to, and dicussion of, recent and not so recent Butler scholarship may be found in that work. I am grateful to Andrew Brennan, Antony Duff, and Murray Macbeath for useful comments on earlier drafts of the present essay and especially for helping me to correct mistakes in the treatment of evolutionary theory.

make-up is to be explained in terms of the ends which it subserves. There is no mystery as to how a feature can be explained in such a way since God makes things in the way he does in order that they may serve his purposes. The asymmetry with the case of jealousy derives from the fact that although the capacity for jealousy often results in our harming others we are not endowed with that capacity *in order* that we should harm others.

Implicit in Butler's thought is the following thesis: A characteristic c of a thing x is adapted for ϕ-ing if and only if (1) c is conducive to ϕ-ing, and (2) x's having c is explained in terms of the fact that c is conducive to ϕ-ing. This could be called *the core concept of adaptation*. The core concept is really a concept-schema. It requires filling out by means of an explanatory framework which shows how it is that a thing's having a certain characteristic is explained by the fact that having such a characteristic is conducive to the performance of some task. In the case of human artifacts the framework is supplied by human intentions and productive activity. Thus the sharpness of a knife is adapted for cutting (is an adaptation for cutting) in that the knife has been designed and made so that it can cut well. The explanation for the knife's sharpness is in terms of an end to which sharpness is conducive. There is no mystery about how this can be so for the end in question figures in the explanation only to the extent that it is something for which the knife was intended. When Butler uses the concept of adaptation in his discussions of human nature the relevant explanatory framework is his theology. Suppose we have a characteristic which is adapted for ϕ-ing. In that case our having the characteristic is to be explained in terms of the fact that God has by design made us so as to be conducive to ϕ-ing. In fact on Butler's view of our nature a human characteristic is adapted for ϕ-ing if and only if it has been designed by God for ϕ-ing.

Considered both individually and collectively we have many traits which lead us to vice rather than to virtue and these may be as constant features of our characters as morally commendable traits. Butler has to make plausible sense of the notion that despite the fact that we manifestly have such traits they are not built into our nature. This is where the concept of adaptation comes in, for it enables him to distinguish traits which are natural from those which are not. Vice is not natural in the special sense which Butler requires, because the characteristics which make up our motivational system are not adapted to vicious behaviour. But Butler makes a much stronger claim about vice. He regards vice as a deviation from our nature. This idea is not captured by the claim that vicious traits are not adaptations. The problem is that not all stable human characteristics need be conceived as being built into human nature by God's design. Characteristics which are not thus built in would not be adaptations in the required special sense. Even so, they might be morally neutral and as such need not be in any way at odds with the ends for which we were designed. To do justice to the idea that vice is a deviation from our nature we need the idea that vice is maladaptive or, in other words, that vice renders us unsuitable for living in the ways for which we were adapted.

Part of Butler's programme is to show that traits which might seem to be at odds with virtue admit of an explanation which is consistent with our being designed for virtue and not for vice. Consider Butler's discussion of resentment in Sermon 8. There he distinguishes between sudden resentment or anger, and settled resentment. The primary function of anger is 'to resist and defeat, sudden force, violence, and opposition, considered merely as such, and without regard to the fault or demerit of him who is the author of them' (*S.* 8. 6). Though it may serve to prevent or remedy injury, in the sense of wrongdoing, associated with sudden force its function is self-defence rather than 'the administration of justice' (*S.* 8. 6). Settled resentment, on the other hand, concerns injury, again in the sense of wrong-doing, rather than physical harm. '[T]o prevent and to remedy such injury, and the miseries arising from it, is the end for which the passion was implanted in man' (*S.* 8. 8). So both the capacity for anger and the capacity for resentment have a proper function which is in no way vicious. Only when these capacities are abused do they lead to vice. A person may be unusually prone to sudden resentment and cause much harm as a result. But such a person is not adapted to causing harm because not prone to such resentment in order that he may cause harm. His harmful traits are actually contrary to his nature in that they are at odds with living the kind of life for which he was designed. The capacity for settled resentment may similarly be abused as, for instance, 'when we fall into that extravagant and monstrous kind of resentment, towards one who has innocently been the occasion of evil to us' (*S.* 8. 11). The passion was intended for the prevention and remedy of injury, but in this case there is no injury.

Evidently the concept of adaptation also has a role in theodicy. On Butler's account the fact that we have well-entrenched vicious traits does not impugn the goodness or power of God. Such traits are deviations. They are not features which are built into our make-up by design. Butler has to hand an explanation of how we come to have such traits. They are not due to faulty workmanship on God's part but rather to our freedom. Butler does not explore this theme in the body of the *Fifteen Sermons* but in the Preface he writes: 'A machine is inanimate and passive: but we are agents. Our constitution is put in our own power. We are charged with it; and therefore are accountable for any disorder or violation of it' (SP 14). Whether such a view will yield an adequate theodicy is not our present concern. The point which I am most concerned to press is that the notion of adaptation bears a heavy load in making plausible sense of the idea that virtue consists in following our nature and vice in deviating from our nature.

The formulation of the core concept of adaptation which I gave earlier dealt with particular characteristics or traits. Butler does tacitly employ such a notion but he often speaks of our nature as a whole as being adapted to virtue. This is worth noting. The mere fact that we have traits which are adapted for virtue is in itself compatible with our having traits which are adapted for vice. But if our nature as a whole is adapted for virtue it follows from that alone that vice is maladaptive.

Butler thinks of our nature as a whole as forming a 'system, economy, or constitution'.

[I]t is an one or a whole, made up of several parts; but yet, that the several parts even considered as a whole do not complete the idea, unless in the notion of a whole you include the relations and respects which those parts have to each other. Every work both of nature and of art is a system: and as every particular thing, both natural and artificial, is for some use or purpose out of and beyond itself, one may add, to what has been already brought into the idea of a system, its conduciveness to this one or more ends. (SP 14)

Applying this general idea to ourselves, 'it will as fully appear, that this our nature, *i.e.* constitution, is adapted to virtue, as from the idea of a watch it appears, that its nature, *i.e.* constitution or system, is adapted to measure time' (SP 14). It follows that a proper account of our nature so far as concerns behaviour must go beyond a mere listing of the features which are by design conducive to virtue. It must show that the basic elements (parts) of our nature co-operate with one another in leading us to virtue. In Sermon 8 there is a striking passage where Butler speaks of the relation between compassion and indignation, the settled resentment at wrongdoing.

> Since ... it is necessary for the very subsistence of the world, that injury, injustice, and cruelty should be punished; and since compassion, which is so natural to mankind, would render that execution of justice exceedingly difficult and uneasy; indignation against vice and wickedness is, and may be allowed to be, a balance to that weakness of pity, and also to anything else which would prevent the necessary methods of severity. (*S.* 8. 13)

Here the emphasis is on indignation balancing compassion, but the underlying principle allows for the possibility of compassion balancing indignation. The point is that the proper functioning of either indignation or compassion will maintain an appropriate balance between them. Only if the right balance is maintained will these elements of our constitution, and thus our constitution as a whole, serve virtue.

Butler's celebrated claim that conscience is supreme must be viewed in the light of the central importance he gives to the idea that our nature taken as a whole is adapted to virtue. Conscience is that 'principle in man, by which he approves or disapproves his heart, temper and actions' (*S.* 1. 8). It is a basic element of our nature which is adapted for virtue in that its function is precisely to reflect on, judge, and ultimately adjust our behaviour and attitudes so that we live virtuously and not viciously. Its supremacy consists in the fact that our nature taken as a whole is adapted to following its dictates. The explanation for the fact that our nature comprises the elements that it does, including conscience, standing in the relations to one another that they do, lies in the fact that the system as whole conduces to our following the dictates of conscience.

For Butler the supremacy of conscience illustrates the idea that our nature is a system of constitution, in the sense explained earlier. The governing role of conscience in relation to the principles of benevolence and self-love, and our various appetites, passions, and affections, is partially constitutive of the particular system which our nature comprises. Note, however, that for Butler, saying that virtue is natural does not simply mean that virtue is in line with what conscience demands. It means rather that the system which comprises our nature is adapted to virtue. Moreover, the very idea that conscience is naturally supreme is to be explained in terms of the fact that the system as a whole is adapted to following its dictates.[2]

In this section I have sought to clarify the sense in which for Butler virtue is natural. But there is a real problem about how we are supposed to tell that a trait is natural. This problem is acute in the area of moral psychology which is Butler's main concern.

III

We have seen that within Butler's theological framework a trait is adapted for some end if and only if it was designed for that end by God. This thesis does not settle the question whether judgements about adaptation should be based on judgements about design or vice versa. Clearly the thesis could be used in conjunction with specific assumptions about the purpose for which a thing was designed to yield conclusions about the end for which it was adapted, or, in other words, its proper and natural function. The methodology here could be described as top-down, that is to say, from assumptions about God's design to conclusions about what is natural. Butler seems to endorse this approach when he writes that '[t]he due and proper use of any natural faculty or power, is to be judged of by the end and design for which it was given us' (*S.* 4. 7). But the *Fifteen Sermons* also contain indications of a bottom-up strategy whereby judgements about God's design are to be based on judgements about proper function. For example, at the beginning of Sermon 2 he writes, 'If

---

[2] I stress this point because it is sometimes thought that the supremacy of conscience accounts for the naturalness of virtue and the unnaturalness of vice. See Nicholas Sturgeon, 'Nature and Conscience in Butler's Ethics', *Philosophical Review*, 85 (1976), 316–56. Discussion of this point may be found in Millar, 'Following Nature', s. iv.

the real nature of any creature leads him and is adapted to such and such purposes only, or more than to any other; this is a reason to believe the Author of that nature intended it for those purposes' (*S.* 2. 1). A clear presupposition of this passage is that we can have reason to think that the nature of a creature is adapted to some end without relying on the assumption that it was intended for that end.

There are problems for both approaches. The top-down approach must rely on detailed assumptions about God's design, but these are simply not available antecedent to judgements about how things are adapted. The bottom-up approach leads to a somewhat similar problem. We have characteristics which are vicious or lead to vice as well as characteristics which are virtuous or lead to virtue. How are we to tell which of these characteristics are adaptations? Granted that the presence in our nature of those which are adaptations is to be explained in terms of the ends to which they conduce, it remains an open question how we are to determine which characteristics are to be explained in this way.

Fortunately the text of the *Fifteen Sermons* makes it fairly clear how Butler actually proceeds. Notwithstanding Sermon 4. 7, he does not adopt the top-down strategy, starting from detailed assumptions about design and deriving judgements about adaptation from these. But nor does he adopt a simple bottom-up strategy. For considerations of design do underpin his claims about adaptation. What he does is examine our nature in the light of highly general assumptions about design. Among these assumptions are the following: God is good and has made us so that we may be good. He must therefore have ensured that there is a 'correspondence between the natural and moral world' (*S.* 6. 1) for otherwise we could not be expected to live in accordance with the moral requirements to which reason and revelation show us to be subject. God also, more generally, provides for the circumstances in which we are placed and although he has not arranged things in this world for our satisfaction none the less '[t]here is a kind provision made even against our frailties' (*S.* 6. 5).

These assumptions are not about this or that feature of our make-up but they place significant constraints on what our nature must be like. When Butler discriminates among our characteristics and treats some as adaptations he does so in the light of these assumptions conjoined with observations about the kinds of behaviour to which these characteristics are conducive.

The significance of these remarks may be illustrated once again by drawing on Butler's treatment of resentment and in particular the following passage already quoted in part:

The natural object or occasion of settled resentment ... being injury, as distinct from pain or loss; it is easy to see, that to prevent and to remedy such injury, and the miseries arising from it, is the end for which the passion was implanted in man. It is to be considered as a weapon, put into our hands by nature, against injury, injustice, and cruelty. (*S.* 8. 8)

Let us for the sake of argument grant Butler what is in effect a terminological claim, namely that the proper object of resentment is injury. Even so, it is consistent with this claim that the capacity for resentment results from a capacity for anger at actions done to us which we strongly dislike. Perhaps this more general capacity is adapted to defending us against the perpetrators of such actions without regard to the moral quality of the actions. This possibility cannot be ruled out merely by a conceptual analysis of resentment showing that an emotion or attitude is properly called resentment only if aimed at wrongs done to one. In Butler's thought it is ruled out by theological assumptions. God would not have given us a capacity for settled and deliberate anger directed willy-nilly at things done to us which we strongly dislike, for it may be that some such actions are entirely appropriate from a moral point of view. Had we been given such a capacity the moral and natural orders would be out of step. We would have been designed to resist actions to which morally we ought to submit. Essentially similar considerations favour Butler's own view that the capacity for resentment is adapted for resisting and remedying injury. It is no objection to this reading that Butler takes sudden anger to be directed willy-nilly at sudden violence, for everyone has a right to resist sudden violence.

The point I wish to stress is that Butler does not have to assume as a premiss that resentment is designed to enable us to resist and remedy injury. All he needs are highly general assumptions about God's intentions which flow from an understanding of the divine attributes. Combined with observations about resentment as we actually find it in human beings, these assumptions serve to support his own view of the ends for which that passion is adapted and thus expressly designed.

These considerations show how Butler would deal with a phenomenon like sexual lust. It might be argued that men have a capacity for sexual lust aimed indiscriminately at attractive women and that this capacity is adapted towards their having intercourse with as many women as possible. Butler would rule out this hypothesis as being inconsistent with the harmony between the natural and moral order and he would explain lust as inordinate sexual desire, that is to say sexual desire which transgresses its natural stint and bound.

IV

The methodology, outlined in the previous section, for arriving at judgements as to what is natural relies on assumptions as to what is good or bad from a moral point of view. This is clear in relation to the example of lust. The argument here would be that since it is morally wrong to have sexual intercourse with as many women as possible it cannot be that God has designed and thus adapted the nature of men for that purpose. Clearly then the methodology demands that we have some prior grasp of what is morally required of us.

But now two interpretative problems arise. We noted in the first section that the review of our nature presented in the *Fifteen Sermons* is meant to encourage people to the practice of virtue. Any adequate interpretation of Butler must provide some account of how this aim is supposed to be achieved. It must therefore explain how the fact that virtue consists in following our nature and vice in departing from it may serve as an encouragement to virtue. This first problem is about the motivation to virtue. The second problem concerns the content of virtue. Butler does appear to think that the review of our nature not only encourages us to the practice of virtue but shows us what virtue requires of us. Thus in Sermon 2 he speaks of the 'inward frame of man' as a 'guide to morals' and he explicitly supposes that in showing human beings to themselves we show them the 'obligations of virtue' (*S.* 2. 1).

So far as the motivational problem is concerned the crucial consideration is that the moral and natural worlds are in harmony with one another. The upshot is that, despite suggestions by philosophers such as Hobbes to the contrary, morality as Butler conceives it is feasible for such creatures as we are. Butler's insistence that we have in us a principle of benevolence leading us to public good, as well as a principle of self-love leading us to private good, must be viewed in this light. It is meant to convince us that we have the resources for living as we are morally required to live. The same may be said of the natural supremacy of conscience. The review of our nature is supposed to make it clear not just that we have in us a faculty, conscience, whereby we approve and disapprove of our temper, heart, and actions, but also that we are adapted to following its dictates and indeed to regarding these dictates as having supreme authority over us. Aspects of our nature which might be thought to be at odds with virtue, such as our capacity for resentment and even self-love, are shown to have a proper role when kept within their proper bounds.

Suppose it is granted that the doctrine of the harmony of the moral and natural worlds serves to encourage us to the practice of virtue, still it might be wondered, especially in view of our previous discussion, how this illuminates the sense in which a review of our nature can encourage us to the practice of virtue. There is indeed a prima-facie difficulty at this point for the line of interpretation I have been pursuing. In the previous section it was suggested that Butler assumes on theological grounds that the moral and natural worlds are in harmony. This assumption when combined with detailed facts about our psychology and circumstances yields judgements about the course of life for which we are adapted. The difficulty which seems to arise is simply that the assumption of harmony is already in place when the review of our nature is conducted. It is not established by the review. So it might seem that we still lack an explanation of the role of the review in encouraging us to virtue.

The appropriate response is, I think, fairly straightforward. Although Butler deploys the assumption of harmony in conducting his review of our nature his investigation of the details of our psychology and circumstances is meant to confirm the assumption and spell out its implications in concrete terms. So, for instance, we do not have to take it on trust that our nature leads us towards love of our neighbour. We are enabled to appreciate how this can be so.

There remains the problem concerning the content of virtue.[3] How can a review of our nature help us to see what is morally required of us? As we have seen, Butler's whole approach in the *Fifteen Sermons* assumes a certain conception of virtue. He is primarily concerned to show that, despite suggestions to the contrary, we are indeed adapted to living virtuously. But he takes for granted that we all know in broad outline what it is to live virtuously. A remark in his later dissertation 'Of the Nature of Virtue' spells this out.

Nor is it at all doubtful in the general, what course of action this faculty, or practical discerning power within us, approves, and what it disapproves. For, as much as it has been disputed wherein virtue consists, or whatever ground for doubt there may be about particulars; yet, in general, there is in reality an universally acknowledged standard of it. It is that, which all ages and all countries have made profession of in public: it is that, which every man you meet puts on the show of: it is that, which the primary and fundamental laws of all civil constitutions over the face of the earth make it their business and endeavour to enforce the practice of upon mankind: namely, justice, veracity, and regard to common good. (DII 1)

The problem, then is just this: If we all have a faculty informed by this 'universally acknowledged standard', how can an investigation of our nature shed light on what is morally required of us?

The passage just quoted from the dissertation provides a clue. Butler thinks that we have a grasp of certain highly general constraints upon our conduct having to do with justice, veracity, and regard to common good. These constraints are, he thinks, universally acknowledged. But there is room for doubt and dispute about what in detail they require of us. This is where the review of our nature comes to our aid. The underlying principle is, once again, the harmony of the moral and natural worlds. What is required of us in detail must be such as could reasonably be expected of us given our nature and circumstances.

[3] It now seems to me that Millar, 'Following Nature', underplays the problem of content. The ensuing discussion in this section is meant to remedy this defect.

This general approach is quite explicit in Sermon 12 where Butler considers the proper scope of benevolence. This is to be determined by 'attending to the nature of it, and to the nature and circumstances of mankind in this world' (*S.* 12. 2). It is not at issue, at this point, that we ought to be benevolent and that we are by nature motivated to benevolent action. The question is, 'To whom are we required to be benevolent?' God loves the whole universe but that is not possible for limited creatures such as we are. Even love of country is more than can be expected of the generality of humankind. So Butler writes:

There plainly is wanting a less general and nearer object of benevolence for the bulk of men, than that of their country. Therefore the Scripture, not being a book of theory and speculation, but a plain rule of life for mankind, has with the utmost possible propriety put the principle of virtue upon the love of our neighbour; which is that part of the universe, that part of mankind, that part of our country, which comes under our immediate notice, acquaintance, and influence, and with which we have to do. (*S.* 12. 3)

Thus the highly general requirement of 'regard to common good' is meant to be made more specific by consideration of our nature and circumstances. Butler uses essentially the same strategy in reflecting upon the proportion which love of our neighbour and self-love should bear to one another (*S.* 12. 13). Whether such a strategy can be effective is a further question to which we shall return in Section VI.

In a rather obscure remark in the Preface to the *Fifteen Sermons* Butler identifies 'two ways in which the subject of morals may be treated'.

One begins from enquiring into the abstract relations of things: the other from a matter of fact, namely, what the particular nature of man is ... from whence it proceeds to determine what course of life it is, which is correspondent to this whole nature. In the former method the conclusion is expressed thus, that vice is contrary to the nature and reason of things: in the latter, that it is a violation or breaking in upon our own nature. Thus they both lead us to the same thing, our obligations to the practice of virtue; and thus they exceedingly strengthen and enforce each other. (SP 12)

The first method mentioned by Butler appears to be that adopted by Samuel Clarke. Moral truths are regarded as being akin to mathematical truths and capable of being known a priori. Butler does not deny that such an approach is legitimate but he prefers to adopt the second empirical method. It might seem puzzling that Butler should think that the very same truths which reason can discern a priori can be arrived at via a consideration of our nature. If the interpretation I have been developing is correct the solution of the puzzle is this: Butler does not suppose that we can read off moral truths from our nature. In enquiring into our nature he takes certain highly general moral truths for granted. But he also assumes that the natural and moral worlds are in harmony, and that means that human beings are so constituted that they can feasibly satisfy moral requirements. Moreover, where the precise nature of these requirements is in doubt an investigation of our nature can be of help. For it may disclose the kinds of life to which our nature and circumstances lead us and the kinds of life for which we are not suited. From this we can make inferences about the kind of life which we ought to and may lead. There is no illegitimate transition here from non-moral judgements, about our nature and circumstances, to moral judgements. The transition is mediated by highly general moral assumptions and by the theologically grounded principle of the harmony of the natural and moral worlds.

V

As we saw earlier, Butler is not primarily concerned to tell us how we ought morally to live. He assumes that on fundamentals we shall agree on that. What he is concerned to urge is that, barring pathological cases, each of us is attuned to living morally. It follows that morality is not a circumscription of our liberties which wars against the drift of our motivational principles. Nor is it something which commends itself only to our reason conceived as something abstracted from our actual system of motivation. Nor, again, is morality to be understood primarily as a system of socially inculcated principles, though this is not to say that education has no role in the development of moral awareness or moral dispositions. On Butler's view we are literally made for virtue, and this is true of human beings generally however culturally different they may be.

Butler's emphasis on the substantial unity of human nature

contrasts sharply with the individualism which characterizes more recent thought. The kind of individualism I have in mind is not a worked-out theory, but a group of themes. First, human beings are conceived as centres of desire. This means that in our dealings with one another the most salient fact with which we have to reckon is that we each have desires which together with our beliefs explain our behaviour. Secondly, the range of possible desires is taken to be in effect limitless, since virtually anything can be an object of desire and there is endless scope for diversity between people in respect of what they desire. Thirdly, it is held that the only ethical contraints on what may be desired flow from the effects of these desires on others. Fourthly, there is the idea that a person flourishes when his or her most central desires are satisfied. Since there can be enormous variations between people in respect of their central desires there may be enormous differences in respect of what makes for their well-being. There is therefore no prospect of an account of human well-being which is both generally applicable and substantial in the sense of going beyond the bare idea of the satisfaction of central desires.

These themes are reflected in contemporary moral theory. Utilitarianism can seem attractive from an individualist perspective because although it makes the maximization of happiness the test of right conduct, it may allow that what makes for happiness may vary radically from person to person depending on their diverse desires. Contractualist theories focus on the reconciliation of competing interests among individuals in society. The project of moral theory for the contractualist is essentially to identify principles which people with conflicting interests and limited sympathies who have to live together could not reasonably reject. Part of the motivation for the approach is to address the problem posed by the fact that, since the requirements of morality circumscribe our opportunities for desire satisfaction, we may well wonder what reason there is to be moral. But that problem only looms large when people are conceived as in the individualist perspective. Anyone may sometimes find that the requirements of morality conflict with their inclinations. But only from the individualist perspective does that automatically become a problem for morality rather than for one's inclinations.

Butler's position could not be more different from the individualism which I have described. For Butler '[e]very one of our passions and affections hath its natural stint and bound' (*S.* 11. 9). If this is so then some of our desires (and emotions) may be unnatural in Butler's special sense. In other words they may render us unsuitable for leading the course of life for which we are adapted. There are two reasons why we should care about this. One is simply that our well-being is tied not to the satisfaction of our central desires, whatever they may happen to be, but rather to the proper functioning of the 'system, economy, or constitution' which makes up our nature. Maladaptive desires are inimical to well-being. The second reason is that <u>the course of life for which we are adapted is the life of virtue</u>. The natural stint and bound of our passions and affections coincides with the requirements of morality and we have reason to submit to these requirements.

Those who find that individualism underplays the substantial unity of human nature and who find congenial the idea that virtue is natural and vice unnatural may well be attracted to Butler's views. It is of some interest to consider how far his position on ethics and human nature is tied to his theology.

VI

Throughout the previous discussion I have stressed the role of Butler's theology in his treatment of ethics and human nature. On Butler's view it is thanks to God that what is natural for human beings is good from a moral point of view. Leaving aside theological considerations there is nothing inevitable about the harmony of the moral and natural orders. Butler could perfectly well admit that all or some of us might have been endowed with a nature which conduced to vice rather than virtue. If God had designed some people to be domineering and brutal then the behaviour which flowed from these characteristics would be natural for such people. This point serves to underline the fact that for Butler the claim that a mode of behaviour is natural does not entail that it is virtuous. Butler needs substantial theological assumptions to warrant taking the fact that a mode of behaviour is natural as a reason for thinking it to be virtuous. As I observed towards the end of Section IV, this very fact enables Butler to avoid the charge that he makes illegitimate inferences from non-moral claims about what is natural to claims about what is morally required or permitted.

With these points in mind it is of some interest to consider whether the idea that virtue is natural and vice unnatural makes plausible sense within an explanatory framework which does not incorporate Butler's theological assumptions.

If the supposition that virtue is natural and vice unnatural is to make sense in a non-theological framework then a concept of adaptation which is suitably akin to that which is implicit in Butler's thought must have a role in such a framework. The core concept of adaptation has it that a trait of x is adapted for ϕ-ing if and only if (1) the trait is conducive to ϕ-ing, (2) x's having that trait is explainable in terms of the fact that it is conducive to ϕ-ing. These conditions are independent of theological notions. In Butler's thought theology bears on adaptation only in so far as it supplies a form of explanation which lends substance to condition (2). If a non-theological explanatory framework could fill this role then it would provide an alternative filling out of the core concept of adaptation. Darwinian evolutionary theory seems to fit the bill.[4]

According to the theory adaptations may be conceived as traits which have evolved through natural selection. Elliott Sober provides a more precise formulation: 'if a trait is an adaptation for performing a particular task, then it must have evolved because there was selection for the trait, where the trait's selective advantage was due to its helping perform the task.'[5] This is broadly in line with what I have been calling the core concept of adaptation. An adaptation must be conducive to performing some task and the organism's having the trait must be explained in terms of the fact that having such a trait is conducive to performing the task. But the form of explanation makes no literal use of the notion of intelligent design. The idea is rather that now or at some time in the past the ability of organisms of the relevant type to perform the relevant task must have been advantageous to these organisms

[4] I raised the question of whether Butler's project could be transferred to an evolutionary framework in Millar, 'Following Nature'. The points emphasized in this section are rather different from those discussed in the earlier paper.
[5] Elliott Sober, *The Nature of Selection* (Cambridge, Mass., 1984), 196.

in the strictly biological sense which means that their chances of surviving to reproduce were increased.

There is no doubt that evolutionary theory can make sense of a concept of adaptation which is structurally akin to that which is implicit in Butler's thought in so far as it incorporates the core concept of adaptation. What about the idea that we are adapted to virtue and that vice is maladaptive? Well, if we are adapted to virtue in the evolutionary sense then obviously (1) the cluster of traits which conduces to our being virtuous must be or have been biologically advantageous and (2) any traits which conduce to vice must be maladaptive. Both (1) and (2) are highly problematic.

Benevolence is not the whole of virtue, as Butler himself observed (DII 8), but it is a large part of virtue. There has been much discussion among evolutionary theorists and particularly among sociobiologists, about whether benevolence as we ordinarily conceive it could be a trait of organisms which have evolved through natural selection. Some theorists have delivered a negative answer and drawn the conclusion that benevolence is an illusion. The problem is that according to classical Darwinian theory natural selection would favour 'organisms that are best at facilitating their own survival and reproductive success'.[6] Benevolence seems to be of no help in this respect and in so far as it incurs a cost to the agent would be positively disadvantageous. The problem is discussed by sociobiologists in terms of altruism, defined as behaviour which benefits others and which incurs or may incur a cost to the agent. One possible explanation for the evolution of dispositions to altruistic behaviour is in terms of 'reciprocal altruism'. Essentially the idea is that altruistic behaviour would be biologically advantageous if it resulted in others reciprocating. Another line of thought uses the notion of kin selection. Although altruistic behaviour may incur a cost to the agent, if directed at kin it could raise the chance of the agent's genes being passed on, since kin who are helped may have their chances of surviving to reproduce increased. So even if the agent's fitness is lowered the average fitness of organisms genetically akin to the agent may be increased.

[6] Ibid. 216.

It has been noted by many writers that altruism in the sense which figures in these explanatory accounts is a far cry from altruism in the usual sense, which implies that the agent cares about the recipients of his or her altruistic behaviour and would be prepared to help others whether or not it was of any advantage. One response to this is simply to deny that genuine altruism exists. But there is another response more favourable to the prospects of an evolutionary account of morality. Michael Ruse summarizes the position:

[I]n the face of our general inclination to serve ourselves, because it is biologically advantageous to us to help and cooperate, morality . . . has evolved to guide and stiffen our will. We are moved by genuine, non-metaphorical altruism. To get 'altruism' [in the biological sense], we humans are altruistic.[7]

The thought is that altruism in the familiar sense leads to behaviour which is altruistic in the biological sense. Ruse further suggests that altruism in the familiar sense has evolved because the behaviour to which it leads is altruistic in the biological sense. Of course, this account needs filling out. In particular it needs an account of why it is that evolution was not content with altruism in the biological sense. Ruse is aware of this and addresses the point.

Logically, there is no demand by Darwinism that we be moral. 'Altruism' could have been effected, as with the ants, by firm genetic control. But then we would have had to waste the virtues of our brain power, and the flexibility which it gives us. Conversely, 'altruism' could have been effected by purely rational, consciously self-directed decisions. But this would have required massive brain power to calculate probabilities and the like. And pure rationality might not have been sufficiently rapid for real life. . . . Thus selection has taken a middle-road option, setting within us epigenetic rules that will incline us towards actions that are (unbeknownst to us) 'altruistic' in the biological sense.[8]

On this view altruism turns out to be an efficient way of promoting 'altruism'.

It is outside the scope of this essay to assess the line of thought which Ruse offers. What I want to stress is that if

[7] Michael Ruse, *Taking Darwin Seriously* (Oxford, 1986), 222.
[8] Ibid. 221.

successful Ruse's proposal would go some way to showing that altruism or, if you prefer, benevolence could be an adaptation. But even if this should turn out to be so we are still a long way from Butler's central claims: that we are adapted to virtue and that vice is maladaptive. Suppose it to be established that we have many adaptive traits which suit us for virtue, it would not follow that vice is maladaptive. To arrive at this conclusion it would need to be shown that vice is prejudicial to biological fitness, and there is no reason to think that this is so. The world being the way it is one might well suppose that at least a modest amount of vice could be positively beneficial. Another obvious problem is that, as we have noted already, benevolence is not the whole of virtue. It might be possible to provide an evolutionary explanation of other traits which figure in our motivational system and bear on morality, but that would not be a routine task and goes beyond what writers like Ruse explicitly argue for.

For the sake of argument, however, let us suppose that there is available within the framework of evolutionary theory an account of our nature which makes it plausible that we are adapted to virtue and that vice is maladaptive. It is a further question whether and how this would contribute to our detailed moral thinking in the way required for Butler's project. The problem I have in mind here is best approached via a problem which arises for Butler himself.[9]

As we saw in Section IV, Butler wants a review of human nature not only to encourage us to the practice of virtue but also to illuminate the content of virtue. He thinks, for example, that attention to our nature and circumstances will make it clear that the requirement to love our neighbour bears on those who come 'under our immediate notice, acquaintance, and influence, and with which we have to do' (*S.* 12. 3). The trouble is that, even granted this limitation, there are many possible accounts of the scope of benevolence reflecting different weightings to the demands of family, friends, fellow-citizens, and foreigners, not to mention non-human animals. It remains unclear how a review of our nature could favour any one account over others. It needs to be borne in mind that claims about what we are adapted to are highly theoretical. They cannot simply be read off from facts

[9] My formulation of difficulties for both Butler and the evolutionary theorist who tries to take over Butler's project owes much to points raised by Antony Duff.

about our psychology. Suppose that most people have a strong disinclination to have much regard to the interests of, say, non-human animals. That would not settle the question of whether or not such a trait is an adaptation, and it is difficult to see how within Butler's framework that question could be settled. An individual perplexed by the morality of eating flesh can expect little help from considerations about what is natural.

Within Butler's framework the fact that a trait is an adaptation would provide a reason for thinking that we should follow where that trait leads. The problem just noted arises because of the difficulty in determining what traits are adaptations. There is a related but distinct problem for an evolutionary theorist seeking to provide an evolutionary basis for Butler's project. Granted that genuine altruism of limited scope is an adaptation explicable in terms of kin altruism or reciprocal altruism, how can that fact help to resolve moral perplexities about the proper scope of benevolence? The problem here is not about whether a certain trait is an adaptation but about the moral significance of adaptations. Butler's theological assumptions will sanction the move from 'x is an adaptation' to 'We should follow where x leads', but the evolutionary theorist has no assumptions which can plausibly fill the same role. Such a theorist may argue that, nevertheless, facts about our nature have an important bearing on morality, since an acceptable morality must be one which human beings could feasibly live by. So even if a review of our nature will not help us on matters of detail as much as Butler hoped, it may inform us about the sorts of morality which would be unrealistic and to that extent would be in keeping with Butler's aims. At this point, though, we run up against a very fundamental issue. Why should we not seek through education and other means to counteract the effects of our nature? Given a conflict between what seem laudable ideals and the actual bent of our nature, why should the ideals always lose out?

In a discussion of the scope of benevolence Ruse argues that the love commandment conflicts with the implications of modern evolutionary thought if it is interpreted as applying indifferently to all human beings.[10] Part of the problem has to do with the feasibility of obeying the commandment on this strong

---

[10] See 'Evolutionary Theory and Christian Ethics', in Michael Ruse, *The Darwinian Paradigm* (London, 1989).

interpretation, given the way in which evolution has fashioned us. The similarity to Butler's view is striking, but the point in itself is hardly decisive. Even granted that an acceptable morality should be one which human beings are capable of following and that evolution has inclined us to favour kin and those who might reciprocate our help, we may yet be able, and have reason, to extend the scope of our benevolent concerns. There is, however, another line of thought which Ruse deploys. He notes that some Christians might argue that the difficulty of obeying the unrestricted love commandment is not to the point if it really is the case that we are obliged to do so. He counters this response by arguing that it mistakenly takes moral requirements to be objective in the sense of holding independently of human nature or facts about human desires or needs. 'Morality', he writes, 'is just an aid to survival and reproduction.'[11] From this he infers that the objectivity with which moral claims seem to be endowed is an illusion. The issue here is large and difficult. The point I wish to make is relatively modest. Suppose that with Ruse we reject the view that moral requirements hold in virtue of non-natural moral facts, such as facts about God's commands. It does not follow that reflection on moral matters is empty or futile. Reflection may lead us to extend the range of our concerns. For example, we may find that there is no morally relevant difference between a class of people whose interests we routinely take into account and a class of people to whose interests we are indifferent. The power of such reflection is real enough. Through it one might overcome indifference to slaves or to people of a different colour. Its legitimacy or otherwise is determined by the structure of the concepts which it involves and its harmony with our moral experience, our sense of what matters. Such reflection may transform present inclinations even if these inclinations are explained by evolution.[12]

VII

The idea that what is natural is good has a certain currency in the context of recent popular preoccupation with the place of

---
[11] Ibid. 268.
[12] The expansion of moral concern through reason is a theme of Peter Singer, *The Expanding Circle* (Oxford, 1981).

human beings in the wider natural world. Sometimes this idea simply articulates admiration or love of nature in general. Sometimes, I suspect, it reflects a metaphysical vision to the effect that there is a kind of harmony between the natural world as a whole and the requirements of some ideal moral stance. Butler serves well to illustrate how such a vision might be worked out, but he also brings to light difficulties which stand in the way of bringing considerations about human nature to bear on claims about the content of virtue. I have sought to show that the attempt to develop the view that virtue is natural and vice unnatural in terms of what I called the core concept of adaptation requires a framework which will supply a relevant form of explanation. I have also hinted at some of the problems involved in the attempt to carry over Butler's aims into the framework of modern evolutionary theory.

Index

action, moral 141-2, 143-52, 154-5, 158, 160, 164, 168
Acton, John Emerich Edward Dalberg, first baron 76, 82, 94
adaptation, concept of 295-7, 299-302, 309-10, 312-13, 315
affections, *see* passions
agnosticism 101, 106, 109, 112
altruism 310-12
analogy 7, 13, 18, 25, 26, 27, 34, 122-3, 127, 129-30, 155, 161, 170, 172, 180, 230
Anscombe, G. E. M. 197, 198, 199, 204, 206
apologetic 97, 98, 106, 115, 122, 131, 136, 139
appetites, *see* passions
Aquinas, St Thomas 15, 97
Aristotle 66, 82, 203
Armstrong, Richard 75
Arnold, Matthew 20, 74, 91
Atkey, Antony 10, 14, 17
atonement
 see also Christ, work of 7, 163
authority 49
autonomy 237, 238-40

Bacon, Francis 77
Bagehot, Walter 71, 74
Balguy, John 10, 13
Barnard, Lord 53
Barnes, Albert 63, 67
Barrington, Shute, bishop 43
Barrow, Isaac, bishop 30-1, 37
Barth, Karl 110
belief-norm 192-3
benevolence 225, 227-9, 243-4, 249-54, 258, 261, 263-6, 269-70, 274, 275-7, 286, 289, 299, 303, 305, 310, 312, 313
 and conscience 153, 198, 199, 290
 and self-love 243, 249, 250, 252-3, 254-5, 259-60, 266-7, 269, 271-2, 278, 279-85, 287, 291
 see also altruism
Bell, J. Hyslop 76
Benson, Martin, bishop 38, 42, 45, 46, 47, 55, 59, 60
Berkeley, George, bishop 94, 265
Bernard, J. H., archbishop 82, 93-4, 130
biblical criticism 19, 20, 108, 114
Blackburne, Francis, archdeacon 55n.
Blackburne, Lancelot, archbishop 1
Bradley, F. H. 85
Bristol, city and diocese 39-45
Broad, C. D. 171, 174-6, 209, 271, 272, 276
Brown, David 115
Browne, Peter, bishop 94
Brumfitt, J. H. 12
Bultmann, Rudolf 19
Butler, Joseph, nephew of JB 60

Calderwood, Henry 78
Caroline, Queen 1, 37
Chandler, Edward, bishop 52, 55
Chapman, Thomas 53
charity schools 51, 57, 157
Christ:
 person of 165-6
 work of 19-20, 108-9, 133, 142, 143, 155, 161, 163, 166-7
 see also atonement; Incarnation
Chubb, Thomas 44
Church, R. W. 65
Clarke, Samuel 10, 73, 130, 189, 191, 214, 305
Coleridge, S. T. 65, 74, 90
Collins, Anthony 9
compassion 251, 259, 294, 298

conscience 71, 82, 133, 152, 153,
    156, 157, 159, 197-8, 199-200,
    201-7, 268, 284-6, 288, 298-9
  authority of 209-37, 239-41, 287
  and autonomy 238-40
  and benevolence 153, 198, 199,
    290
  and self-love 152-3, 243-6, 253,
    255, 289, 290
  and virtue 198, 199, 205
consciousness 181-2
contractualist theory 307
Courtney, W. L. 85

Dale, R. W. 74
Darwin, Charles 78
death 176-86
deism and deists 7, 9-10, 15, 18, 19,
    20, 22, 24, 27, 31-2, 34, 35, 91,
    98, 99-103, 106, 109, 112-13,
    129, 131
Descartes, René 117, 146
Dolben, Sir John 54
Durham, diocese 52-5, 57-8

Eagar, Alexander 77
egoism, psychological 245, 248, 266-
    7, 275
empiricism 189, 191, 192-3
Enlightenment 9
epistemology 117-18, 121, 179, 205-
    6
evil 87-8, 136
evolutionary theory 8, 27, 79-80,
    309-10, 312, 315
experience 170-1

Farrer, Austin 113
Flint, Robert 78
Forster, Nathaniel 38, 54, 59, 60
Freud, Sigmund 202
Full Naturalistic Thesis 212, 214,
    216, 217, 219-20, 232
future life, *see* immortality

Geach, Peter 201
Gibbon, Edward 49

Gladstone, William Ewart 21, 63, 64,
    65, 66, 74-6, 91, 94, 255
Gooch, Sir Thomas, bishop 37, 40
Gore, Charles, bishop 84, 89, 90
governance, divine 130, 155
grace 12, 158
Green, T. H. 81, 84-5, 86, 89, 90

Hamilton, Sir William 69, 70
Hammond, Edward, archdeacon 40
Hampden, R. D., bishop 65, 66
happiness 247, 256, 259-62, 273-5
harmony 303-4, 306, 315
hedonism 148, 156-7, 275
Hegel, G. W. F. 75, 82, 85, 157
Hennell, Sara 71, 74, 76
Herring, Thomas, archbishop 46
Hick, John 137
hiddenness of God 29-33, 35, 137,
    139
Hilton, Boyd 65, 66
historical knowledge 108, 110
Hoadly, Benjamin, bishop 46
Hobbes, Thomas 243, 245, 251, 252,
    303
Holland, H. Scott 84, 89, 90, 91-2
hospitals 44, 51-2, 57-8
House of Lords 39, 45-7, 59, 153
Hume, David 7, 82, 84, 107, 108,
    115, 130-1, 189, 190, 192, 193,
    198, 243
Huxley, Thomas 77, 78, 80

idealism 85
identity:
  corporeal 193
  personal 172-3, 182-4, 189-91,
    193-5
ignorance 76-7, 117, 119, 122, 128-
    9, 131, 135-6, 139
imagination 180, 182, 185
immortality 78, 169-70, 172, 176,
    180, 186
  and animals 184-5
Incarnation, doctrine of 113, 142,
    168
individualism 307
intuitionism 189-93

Index

Jackson, Reginald 250
James, William 86, 100, 104
Jowett, Benjamin 65, 67, 83
justice of God 13-14

Kant, Immanuel 9, 18, 69, 75, 82, 83, 84, 85, 110, 115, 171, 179, 194, 239
Keble, John 68
Kingsley, Charles 77
Knight, David 78

Law, William 8, 10
Lee, James Prince, bishop 93
Leibniz, G. W. 146
Lessing, G. E. 1, 10, 18, 22-3
liberty 49, 154
Liddon, H. P. 89
Lightfoot, Joseph Barber, bishop 65
Locke, John 16, 82, 97, 108, 117, 120-4, 127, 131, 135, 177-8, 183, 191
Lotze, Hermann 85

Mackie, J. L. 103-5, 108, 109, 202
Mandeville, Bernard de 251, 252
Mansel, H. L. 65, 68, 69, 70, 71, 72, 73, 74, 77, 94
Marston, H. J. R. 94
Martineau, James 71, 73, 80, 81, 83, 84, 85
materialism 103
Matthews, W. R. 203
Maurice, F. D. 65, 69, 72, 73, 83, 84, 89
Methodism 8, 44, 55
Micheletti, Mario 30
Mill, John Stuart 69, 70, 74, 80, 82, 86
miracle 18, 20, 27, 108, 143
Moore, G. E. 190, 192, 194, 195
Mossner, E. C. 27, 64

naturalistic fallacy 205
natural law 142, 198, 204
nature, human 205, 223-4, 226, 243-4, 252, 293-8, 300, 302-4, 306, 308, 312-13

Newcastle, Thomas Pelham-Holles, first duke of 53
Newman, John Henry, cardinal 8, 18, 68, 69, 70, 71, 73, 82, 89, 90, 100, 104, 203-4
Newton, Sir Isaac 31, 194

Oakeley, Frederick 67
obligation, moral 215-16, 221, 257
Ogden, Schubert 19
Origen 18, 92
original sin 11-12
Oxford, university of:
  and JB's reputation 64-70, 82-3, 89, 96

Paley, William, archdeacon 67
parity argument 128
particularity 144-5, 158-9, 160-1, 166, 168
Pascal, Blaise 2, 29-35, 118, 124, 125-7, 132, 133, 135, 137
Pascal's Wager 29, 125-7
passions, particular 153, 154, 157, 234, 243-50, 260, 262, 264, 266, 269-70, 272-3, 278-9, 299
Pattison, Mark 67, 83, 96
Penelhum, Terence 29-30, 219, 221, 270, 277, 278-9, 281n., 291
perception 183, 185
Plantinga, Alvin 205-6
Plato 65, 82, 93, 179, 192
Potter, John, archbishop 37, 39
Powell, Baden 72
probability 18, 19-20, 29, 72, 73, 78, 82, 99, 101, 120, 122-8, 132, 170, 172
probation, intellectual 102, 105, 136-8, 157
prophecy 18, 20, 35, 108, 143
providence 12, 49, 118-19, 137, 147
prudence 257, 259, 266
Pusey, E. B. 69

Rahner, Karl 14, 27
Rashdall, Hastings 80, 83, 84, 85-9
reason 8-11, 15-18, 21, 22-4, 27, 99-103, 110, 150, 169-70, 263, 280-3

resentment 296-7, 298, 301-2, 303
resignation 159-60
revelation 16, 17, 18, 22-3, 27, 33, 71, 111-12, 114, 133, 137, 170
Romanes, George 79
Romanticism 8, 9
Rousseau, Jean-Jacques 9, 49
Ruse, Michael 311-12, 313-14
Russell, Bertrand 95, 100, 101

SPG 47-8, 151
scepticism 14, 118, 132
Schleiermacher, F. D. E. 9
scientific knowledge 77-9, 109, 110
scripture, authority of 111
Secker, Thomas, archbishop 37, 38, 40, 42, 45, 46, 47, 53, 59, 60, 61
self-consciousness 181, 194-5
self-deceit 197-8, 200, 204
self-love 152-3, 198-9, 217, 222, 225, 227-9, 234-5, 246, 249, 254, 257, 258-9, 263, 269-70, 273-4, 275, 277, 286, 290, 299, 303, 304
  and benevolence 243, 249, 250, 252-3, 254-5, 259-60, 266-7, 269, 271-2, 278, 279-85, 287, 291
  and conscience 152-3, 243-6, 253, 255, 289, 290
Schneewind, J. B. 66, 84
sensation 185-6
Shaftesbury, Antony Ashley Cooper, third earl of 215, 236n., 243, 244, 252, 255, 287
Shakespeare, William 198, 200, 201
Sharp, Thomas, archdeacon 55, 57
Sidgwick, Henry 66, 80, 81, 85, 88
sincerity 14
slavery 50, 265
sleep 177
Smith, Goldwin 72
sociobiology 310
Spinoza, Baruch 146
Spooner, W. A. 60, 61, 87
Stanley, A. P. 67
Steere, E. 45
Stephen, Sir Leslie 8, 69, 74, 91

Stoicism 147
  and deism 32
Sturgeon, Nicholas 210-13, 216-17, 219, 222
substances 173-8, 186-7
superior principle 269-70, 280, 284-6
Sutherland, Stewart 106-7
Szabados, B. 197, 198, 200, 201, 204, 206

Talbot, Charles, first baron Talbot of Hensol 37
Talbot, Edward, bishop 70
Taylor, A. E. 83, 84, 86, 87, 95
theodicy 297
Tillich, Paul 19
Tillotson, John, archbishop 15
Tindal, Matthew 10, 13, 14, 17, 20-1
Toland, John 10, 15, 17
toleration, religious 22
trinity, doctrine of 17, 133
Troeltsch, Ernst 24-5, 26
Tucker, Josiah 43-4
Tyndall, John 78-9

Urmson, J. O. 259-60
utilitarianism 199, 307

vice 253, 293, 295-7, 300, 302, 308-10, 312, 315
virtue 100, 134, 136-7, 178, 199, 205, 225, 243, 252-3, 263, 287, 293, 295-300, 302, 304, 308-10, 312, 315
Voltaire, Françoise-Marie Arouet de 1, 10, 11, 12, 13, 21, 22

Walpole, Sir Robert, first earl of Orford 41
Waterland, Daniel 10
Watts, Isaac 8
Wesley, John 8, 40, 43, 44, 55, 56
Westcott, Brooke Foss, bishop 65, 81, 92-3
Whewell, William 82, 93
Whitefield, George 40, 44

KEEP *the* MEN
ALIVE